MARKETING
A BRIEF INTRODUCTION

MARKETING
A BRIEF INTRODUCTION

DAVID STOKES

WENDY LOMAX

Australia • Brazil • Canada • Mexico • Singapore • Spain • United Kingdom • United States

THOMSON

Marketing, A Brief Introduction
David Stokes and Wendy Lomax

Publishing Director John Yates	**Publisher** Jennifer Pegg	**Development Editor** Leandra Paoli
Content Project Editor Alison Walters	**Manufacturing Manager** Helen Mason	**Senior Marketing Manager** Angela Lewis
Typesetter ICC Macmillan Inc., India	**Production Controller** Maeve Healy	**Cover Design** Fink Creative, UK
Text Design Design Deluxe, Bath, UK	**Printer** C & C Offset Printing	

British Library Cataloguing-in-Publication Data
A catalogue record for this book is available from the British Library

Brief contents

Contents

About the authors

DAVID STOKES

Dr David Stokes is Enterprise Director at Kingston University. Educated at Oriel College, Oxford and the City University Business School, he has had wide experience of marketing in both the private and public sectors in a career involved in the management of both large and small enterprises. The subject of his PhD thesis was the development of marketing practices in public sector primary schools during the 1990s. As well as teaching marketing at a popular business school, he is actively engaged in developing marketing strategies for a number of medium-sized companies. A member of the Academy of Marketing's special interest group in marketing and entrepreneurship, he is also author of *Small Business Management and Entrepreneurship* published by Thomson Learning.

WENDY LOMAX

Professor Wendy Lomax is Professor of Marketing at Kingston Business School. She took a first degree in Management Science at UMIST, and followed it with ten years in the private sector at blue chip companies such as Ford Motor Company, United Biscuits and GlaxoSmithKline. Her doctorate was at London Business School, examining the longitudinal effects of cannibalisation on line extensions. She teaches marketing at undergraduate and postgraduate levels, specialising in new product development and branding. Her wide publication record covers papers on word-of-mouth marketing, branding and, most recently, charities' marketing. As Senior Examiner on the Professional Postgraduate Diploma of the Chartered Institute in Marketing, she has published a text on Analysis and Evaluation with Butterworth Heinemann.

Acknowledgements

Dedicated to our line extensions

Andrea, Bryony, Kim and Kit; Kate, Oliver, Alice and Sophie.

LIST OF REVIEWERS

- Bill Barlow, University of Abertay
- Elaine Collinson, University of Strathclyde
- Frances Ekwulugo, University of Westminster
- Jillian Farquhar, Oxford Brookes University Business School
- Niki Hynes, University of Strathclyde
- Mark Lloyd, Richmond upon Thames College

Preface

THE PURPOSE OF THIS BOOK

The purpose of this book is to provide a course of study which engages the reader in both the practice and the theory of marketing. It aims to enable the reader to discover marketing principles through both their own experiences and their reflections on what happens around them, supported by information on the main theories of the subject.

As an introductory text, it can be used in the classroom by students following full- or part-time business and management courses at university or college. It is also suited to those studying at home as part of a distance learning programme or for their own interest and self-development. The material in the book has been developed from the teaching of, and feedback from, marketing components in a large variety of undergraduate and postgraduate courses, as well as workshops and seminars for practising managers.

NOT ANOTHER MARKETING BOOK!

There are many publications that cover the same theoretical ground as this book. *Marketing: A Brief Introduction* aims to fill a need by being different in three main ways:

- The reader is encouraged to learn actively from a series of short case studies before theories of marketing are presented. In this way, practical examples aim to stimulate the reader's comprehension, rather than rely on a passive absorption of information.
- The book applies established marketing principles to a wide variety of contexts. The text draws on cases and examples from entrepreneurial and small business contexts, the non-profit as well as the private sector, and from services and business-to-business markets as well as the traditional areas of consumer marketing.
- Principles of marketing are presented concisely, recognising that many readers wish to gain an overview of the subject as quickly as possible, before studying particular aspects in more detail, or because their academic specialisation lies in other fields.

APPROACH

The book is structured around an active learning approach. Although a considerable amount of information is presented in the text, the aim is to impart skills and knowledge by engaging the reader in interesting activities and exercises which build on existing experiences and understanding. Marketing is ideally suited to this approach because we experience and witness it consciously or unknowingly most days of our lives. The primary focus of marketing is on customers and their needs, and we are all customers with needs. Therefore we can draw on our own experiences as consumers in a wide range of contexts to develop and check our understanding of marketing theory and see how it is applied in practice. We can use our experiences as a shopper to develop a better understanding of retail marketing. We can reflect on our own use of education and health services to better understand the marketing of services in the public sector.

We are all exposed to advertising and packaging messages and can think of those that influence us and those that have less impact. If we have access to the Internet, we can make our own judgements on the implications of this latest development on marketing. Marketing activities are going on around us all the time from market surveys in the high street to mail shots received at home, and they all offer an opportunity to learn about marketing.

HOW TO USE THIS BOOK

This book can be used as a workbook with the facilitation of a teacher or lecturer in the classroom, as the basis of unsupervised work at home, or as a mixture of both.

In whatever manner it is used, the case studies, questions and activities are the basis for the learning process. It is recommended that the book is used in the following way:

- First read the short case study at the beginning of each chapter. The cases describe a particular scenario and ask you to draw conclusions about marketing principles from it.

- Attempt the questions at the end of this case. If necessary, use the '*see*' references to sections in the chapter to complete the activities, but first try to develop answers independently. If you can discover marketing principles for yourself by observing them in practice, you are more likely to fully understand and appreciate the theory.

- Read through the chapter and the examples.

- Reflect on your understanding of the text through the 'Checkpoint' exercises, which relate theory to personal experience.

- Attempt the activities at the end of the chapter, including the final case study. These activities are designed to develop and confirm your understanding of theory by personal experimentation and practice. Although it may be tempting to move on to the next chapter, it is important to attempt the ongoing exercise 'Developing a marketing plan' at the end of each chapter so that skills can be built incrementally.

ACTION LEARNING

In summary, to get the most out of this book follow an action learning cycle:

Practise – Reflection – Theory – Experimentation

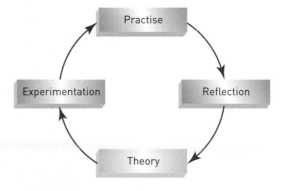

- *Practise* marketing as an outside observer – for example, by considering first the case study at the beginning of each chapter, which describes an aspect of marketing in action

- *Reflect* on what this reveals about marketing through the activities at the end of the case study

- *Theorise* about the principles of marketing as described in the main text and the examples given of marketing in practise

- *Experiment* through your own personal experiences in the checkpoints and exercises in each chapter

- *Practise* what you have learned through the ongoing exercise of developing a marketing plan

Walk through tour

Chapter 7

PRODUCTS: CHARACTERISTICS AND STRATEGIES

Learning Objectives appear at the start of each chapter and are designed to help you monitor your progress and understanding

In-depth Case Studies at the beginning and end of each chapter introduce and reinforce marketing principles and theories . Each case is accompanied by questions to help you test your understanding of the issues

For Example boxes are provided throughout each chapter and provide practical examples of marketing principles and theories

Marketing Mistakes is an important feature which highlights that not all marketing campaigns are successful as shown by real world examples

Checkpoint exercises are provided throughout each chapter and encourage you to link theories of marketing with your own personal experiences

Entrepreneurial Marketing boxes illustrate how marketing principles are applied in an entrepreneurial context

Developing a Marketing Plan appears at the end of each chapter and allows you to practise what you have learned by developing your own marketing plan

About the website

Visit the *Marketing: A Brief Introduction* companion website at **www.thomsonlearning.co.uk/stokes_lomax** to find valuable teaching and learning material including:

FOR STUDENTS

- Links to relevant websites related to chapter material
- Multiple choice questions to test your understanding
- Examples of possible examination questions (with suggested outline answers) so that you can confirm your understanding of the chapter topics

FOR LECTURERS

- An Instructors' Manual including teaching material built around the textbook content
- Additional case study notes
- PowerPoint™ slides to accompany each chapter of the book

FURTHER RESOURCES

- ExamView® – This testbank and test generator provides a large amount of different types of questions, allowing lecturers to create online, paper and local area network (LAN) tests. This CD-based product is available only from your Thomson sales representative.

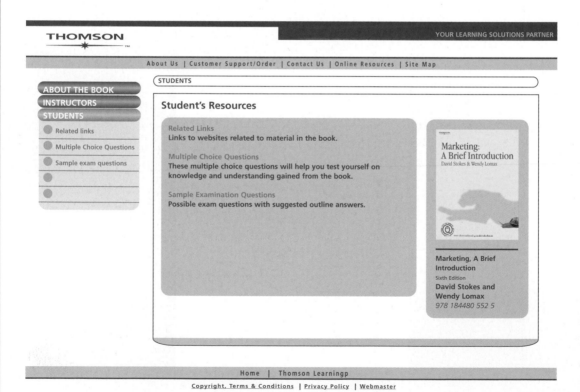

Part 1

MARKETING PRINCIPLES AND ANALYSIS

Chapter 1

WHAT IS MARKETING?

LEARNING OBJECTIVES

By the end of this chapter the reader will be able to:

- Define 'marketing' as a strategic and tactical approach to business
- Understand the principles underpinning the 'marketing concept'
- Appreciate the historical evolution of marketing
- Examine the effectiveness of marketing principles in different contexts, especially in smaller, entrepreneurial enterprises and services
- Assess the social effects of marketing

INTRODUCTION

Marketing is an elusive term. It describes both a management strategy focusing on customer satisfaction, and a series of functions such as advertising, product development, selling and market research. This chapter introduces the concept of marketing by exploring basic marketing principles and comparing them to alternative approaches. It looks at the development of marketing, its adoption by various sectors of our economy and the impact of the Internet. It considers how marketing practices in smaller entrepreneurial firms differ from classical marketing theory. It concludes by examining some of the concerns expressed about the effectiveness of some marketing strategies and their potential social effects.

1.1 MARKETING PRINCIPLES

1.1.1 Traditional marketing theory

If you asked people to give an instant definition of the word 'marketing', their responses would vary. Some would associate it with 'advertising', 'selling' or 'research'; others with 'making profits' or 'finding out what people want'. A few might have less favourable descriptions, seeing it as

CASE STUDY

....

METROPOL ZOO

Case studies such as this, at the beginning of each chapter, are designed to help you 'discover marketing' by giving you the opportunity to observe and consider principles in practice through a specific scenario, before reading about them in the more generalised context of the sections which follow. Read the case study then consider the issues that it raises as you read the rest of the chapter.

Metropol Zoo had reached a crisis point in its long history as one of the world's leading zoological gardens. Despite a growth in the number of people making visits to other attractions, the city-centre zoo had seen a steady decline in the number of its visitors in recent years. In 1991, the zoo attracted over one million of the estimated fifteen million visitors to the city through its gates; fifteen years later, this had fallen to under 800,000 of twenty million city tourists.

Traditional attractions such as the Metropol Museum had revamped their image with innovative, interactive exhibits whilst new, purpose-built, themed attractions added to the visitor's choice. Competition for the 'family day out' had intensified with the development of many exciting adventure parks within an hour's travel time of the city. The image of the zoo was tainted by environmental concerns stimulated by animal rights activists who continued to protest about the captivity and exploitation of wild animals. Falling attendance had coincided with a reduction in the amount of public funds available to the zoo as both central and local governments had reduced their grants and subsidies.

A new strategy was needed to deal with the deteriorating financial position that now threatened the very existence of the zoo. Some out-of-town zoological gardens had successfully developed fun parks alongside their animal enclosures, but Metropol Zoo's position in the heart of an already overcrowded city ruled out this option. Now a radical new proposal had been put forward for consideration by the directors of the zoo. This used virtual-reality technology to create exciting wildlife scenes and adventures within the space limitations. The removal of the stock of large caged animals would make room for a series of simulators and interactive exhibits. These showed animals in their natural environment in ways which the zoo could not normally re-create, and even more importantly, put the visitor in the role of participator and not just observer. Virtual-reality expeditions simulated not only animal habitats but also exciting experiences such as white water rafting or ballooning as the visitor explored the great outdoors. Computer games allowed participants to choose survival strategies in a variety of hostile environments from deserts to jungles whilst lion attacks could be experienced from the perspective of the herd of deer.

The proposals had split the directors of Metropol Zoo into two opposing camps. One group, led by the finance director, Alnur Rhajiv, argued that the changes would transform the commercial viability of the zoo because they met customer needs more closely. The opposing lobby, led by the director of conservation, Jane Chan, claimed they would be selling out to short-term market forces when the public would support the long-term conservation work of the zoo if it was properly publicised.

I hope my presentation has illustrated some of the excitement as well as educational value which our latest equipment can now offer to your visitors. For this is certainly what customers want in a world where fantasy adventures are increasingly dominating the entertainment market whether in books, films, television programmes, computer games or simulated events.

Izabella Jollop, the salesperson from Visionary, a company marketing virtual-reality equipment, sat down at the end of her presentation to the directors of Metropol Zoo. Despite their divided opinions on the proposals, the directors were all clearly impressed by the capabilities of computerised graphics and sensory effects. It was the chairman, Sir Ralph Noon, who spoke first: 'Your technology is very impressive – congratulations. But our expertise lies in conservation not computerisation. Zoological gardens have always been a sanctuary for the natural world, an escape from the latest developments of society. These new products do not seem to play to our strengths at all.'

Izabella was quick to respond: 'No, but they complement them. You have the knowledge and understanding of the animal kingdom. These machines can help you demonstrate it to people who are confined to concrete jungles for 90 per cent of their lives. With these new technologies we can go on safari for the day and experience other worlds without leaving our own. It's what the customer needs – a convenient and inexpensive way of experiencing nature.'

Jane could contain her disagreement no longer: 'But it's not the real thing at all. People are not experiencing nature through your products. They are experiencing another man-made imitation of it. And imitations are not what people want any more. We have moved away from artificial ingredients and additives in many of our products – in food and body care products, for example – and we are increasingly demanding natural products and ingredients. It's the same with animals. Our customer surveys tell us that over 60 per cent of people still want to see the big cats and elephants for real before they disappear altogether.'

Alnur sighed: 'Yes, but people never know what they want until it is presented to them. This marketing idea of asking people what they need just doesn't work in practice. If you had asked a Victorian what they wanted to travel around in during the day and entertain them at home in the evening, they would not have mentioned a car or a television set. Very few people know the possibilities of the technology we have just seen. So what's the point in trying to find out what people want when they don't know what is possible?'

The chairman re-entered the fray on a favourite theme: 'If you are saying that we should ignore public opinion which we believe is ill informed, I would agree with you. That's exactly why we haven't given in to pressures from these so-called environmentalists who claim to stand for animal rights. Without us, some of these animals wouldn't have an existence at all.'

Alnur had heard this argument before and answered with his usual response: 'But opinion, however ill informed, is on their side. Look at our falling gate receipts as the proof. We have no choice but to adapt to the times. This new technology is not going to disappear. I visited one American national park where you can watch wildlife films on giant wrap-around screens at the entrance.'

Jane had to respond to this: 'And how long is this particular fad going to last? Just because computer graphics and a few gimmicks have awakened people's imaginations, it doesn't mean we have to jump on this particular bandwagon. We are being asked to change our entire policy on breeding and keeping animals in captivity. This is not something we can turn off and on like a tap just because fashions in entertainment shift temporarily. We are a public service, not a product that can be sold like a Hollywood movie. I am sure we can put forward our case as conservationists, not exploiters of animals, and attract our visitors back again with some positive publicity.'

Izabella listened unmoved as the debate intensified around her. She knew that, whatever they decided, the customer was always right.

QUESTIONS

1 Give the directors your advice on their future marketing strategy. Which approach best represents the marketing concept of identifying and satisfying customer needs? *See sections 1.1 and 1.2*

2 There are alternative approaches, or 'business orientations', to customer orientation. What alternative orientations are illustrated here? *See section 1.3*

3 Do you think Jane Chan is right in saying that marketing a zoo is not the same as selling a Hollywood movie? What are the similarities and what are the differences? *See section 1.4*

4 What criticisms of the marketing concept are illustrated in this case? How would you answer them? *See section 1.5*

5 The directors are considering new attractions made possible by advances in technology. In what ways could other technological developments, such as the Internet, help? *See section 1.5*

6 Zoos are playing a more important role in conservation work by breeding endangered species in captivity. For example, the birth of the 325-pound baby elephant, shown right, was hailed as a brave new hope for an endangered species when he was born at a prestigious North American zoo. How can marketing help to develop more understanding of this part of the work of zoos?

© ISTOCKPHOTO.COM/HEIKO POTTHOFF

Marketing is useful in many contexts, including attractions such as zoos

'getting people to buy something they don't really want'. Marketing can be all these things – except, hopefully, the last. Even business owners are confused by the term, often differentiating between 'sales' and 'marketing' as separate activities.

The reason for this diversity of meaning is that marketing is both a management philosophy and a function in an organisation. As a philosophy, it insists that an organisation is focused on the needs of customers. As a function, it includes activities which affect customers such as pricing, advertising, selling and market research.

Traditionally, marketing theories involve four elements: the overall philosophy or *market orientation* of the business, *the market intelligence* or information-gathering used to underpin this orientation and inform activities, *the strategy* used in relation to customers in the marketplace and *the marketing methods* used to win and keep customers.

■ *Market orientation*: The key assumption of marketing theory is that the customer should be central to everything an organisation does. The concept of market or customer orientation requires that a detailed understanding of customer needs should precede and inform the marketing of products and services. This applies to the development of new products and services as well as the management of existing businesses and products.

This is sometimes referred to as the 'marketing concept' which, if adopted, means that an organisation sees the customer as central to everything it does. All activities are driven by what the customer needs. It is based upon the premise that no company or institution can exist for very long without customers. A business does not survive unless someone regularly purchases what it has to offer. Even a non-profit organisation, such as a public service or a charity, cannot justify its existence without its equivalent of 'customers': a college needs students, a hospital exists to help patients and a charity needs donors. Accepting that organisations cannot exist without customers, the marketing concept gives them the key role in determining strategy. Customers are consulted on what their needs really are, and products or services developed to meet those needs. (See section 1.2 for a fuller analysis of the marketing concept.)

■ *Market intelligence*: To focus on the needs of the customer, an organisation requires market intelligence in order to understand what those needs are. This includes formal research and information-gathering activities in all areas that could influence the future of the organisation including:

— the internal environment of the stakeholders, resources and culture of the organisation

— the micro-environment of customers, competitors, suppliers and distributors

— the macro-environment of social, technological, economic and political influences

(Various aspects of understanding the marketplace are considered in Chapters 2, 3, 4 and 5.)

■ *Marketing strategy*: Marketing strategy defines how an organisation competes in the marketplace through the three stages of market segmentation, targeting and positioning. First, the marketplace is divided through research and analysis into market segments – groups of customers who have different needs. Second, one (or more) of these segments is chosen as the most appropriate target for marketing effort. Third, a product or service is offered to this target market that is positioned appropriately to appeal to the target customers. (See Chapter 6 for more on marketing strategy.)

■ *Marketing methods*: Marketing methods implement the strategy through a combination of activities and techniques that are designed to make the product or service sell to the target customer. These include product/service enhancement, pricing, selection of distribution channels and advertising. Such activities are referred to as elements in the 'marketing mix', commonly summarised as the four 'Ps' of product, pricing, promotion and place, or extended to seven 'Ps' in services marketing theory by the addition of physical evidence, people and process. (See Chapters 7–11 for more on the elements of the marketing mix.)

In summary, traditional marketing starts with the orientation of the enterprise around customer needs. In order to ensure this, formalised gathering of market intelligence underpins all aspects. A process of segmentation, targeting and positioning is used to develop a marketing strategy that meets customer needs. This strategy is implemented through the elements of the marketing mix. This has been condensed into a definition of marketing by the UK Chartered Institute of Marketing as: 'the management process responsible for identifying, anticipating and satisfying customer requirements profitably'.

FOR EXAMPLE

Marks and Spencer became one of the UK's most successful retailers by continually adapting to changes in customer needs, but ran into trouble when it ignored this basic principle. The original concept of meeting the need for a wide range of products offering exceptional value for money was developed in the late nineteenth century by Michael Marks, who sold a range of low-priced goods on market stalls with the advertising slogan 'Don't ask the price, it's a penny'.

His son Simon Marks and partner Israel Sieff continued the same theme of value for money when they took over the business in 1915 but they developed new ways of fulfilling it. The low overheads of the market stall were exchanged for the buying advantages of bulk purchases as they rapidly expanded into a large company of many stores. Perceiving that their customers' main requirement at that time was for a wider range of affordable clothing, M&S adopted a price limit of five shillings per item in the late 1920s. However Simon Marks recognised that customer needs were never static when, in the 1930s, he described successful retailing as involving 'constant alertness and study of the changing habits, desires and tastes of the consumer'.

By the 1960s, Marks and Spencer had used this understanding to shift their appeal away from a reliance on low price to an additional in-sistence on offering only goods of the highest quality. They implemented this policy through rigorous quality control methods and demon-strated their faith in what they sold by offering immediate refunds or exchanges for any faulty items. As other retailers began to deliver equiva-

Advertising the opening of the Marble Arch store, London, 1930

lent levels of quality, in 1993 the new chairman Sir Richard Greenbury stated a need for improved service levels to complement their quality and value for money philosophy: 'Providing friendly and efficient service for an increasingly discerning and demanding customer is a top priority'. The numbers and knowledge of shop floor staff were increased to implement this latest interpretation of customer needs.

Expansion into overseas markets and internal power struggles over who was to run the com-pany distracted directors from the marketplace. The company began to lose touch with key cus-tomer groups. By the late 1990s, M&S's mainstream customers, women over 35 years old, expected fashion as well as value for money and quality. The company's own brand, St Michael, began to lose its appeal as newer, designer labels became widely available. As sales growth slowed and profits dropped, the board announced its intentions to 'refocus the company towards the customers'.

They set up a 'Customer Insight Unit' to understand the shopping habits and demographics of their customers. In 2000, the new chairman, Luc Vandervelde overturned M&S's traditional policy of selling only under the St Michael trademark and introduced sub-brands of new ranges such as the Limited Collection, Salon Rose lingerie and Count on Us reduced-fat foods, reflecting the company's perceptions of how consumer needs had changed. Their website offered the option of ordering products directly over the Internet. Further evidence of the new emphasis on fashion was the appointment of high profile designers to key posts. In 2001, they subcontracted not only the manufacture but also the design of 'per una', a new range of women's clothes to George Davies, the founder of the Next chain of stores. After decades of not advertising, the company also decided to start doing so. The new competitive environment meant they had little choice.

Consumers' verdicts on these changes were uncertain, and by 2005 the business was still underperforming its competitors on the High Street. This prompted a takeover bid and another management change as Stuart Rose took over from Luc Vandervelde as the chief executive. Despite lower profits and declining clothing sales in 2005, the company beat off the unwanted bid, and set about returning the business to its 'core values of Quality, Value,

WWW.MANDSLIBRARY.CO.UK

Per Una illustrates a new emphasis on fashion for Marks & Spencer

Service, Innovation and Trust' (Annual Report, 2005/6). This list has grown from the quality and value propositions of the early M&S years, illustrating how far consumer demands have developed in response to the greatly increased choice of products on offer.

By 2006, the actions taken to refresh merchandise and refurbish stores had resulted in a return to growth of both sales and profits. However, the future still looks difficult as customers are not totally convinced that such a traditional retailer can adapt sufficiently to their needs in the current marketplace.

M&S's past success story and recent need for drastic action illustrate both the benefits of focusing on customer needs and the dangers of complacency in interpreting them.

1.2 THREE PRINCIPLES OF THE MARKETING CONCEPT

Three ideas are fundamental to the marketing concept:

■ Customer orientation

■ Organisational integration

■ Mutually beneficial exchange

1.2.1 Customer orientation

If an organisation focuses itself first and foremost on the needs of customers then it is *customer-orientated*. There are alternative orientations that companies can adopt, as we will explore later. Customer-orientated organisations centre their strategies and activities on the needs of the marketplace as expressed by actual and potential customers. Such companies strive not just for more sales but *customer satisfaction* in all that they do. They want 'customers who come back and products that don't'.

FIGURE 1.1
The process of customer satisfaction

There are usually several stages to achieving this aim:

- *Finding out what customers want or anticipating what they will want.* This is normally done by regular communications with consumers in the marketplace by a variety of means ranging from formal market research to informal conversations and contacts.

- *Fulfilling the perceived needs of customers.* The identification of customer requirements is followed by the mobilisation of resources to fulfil those needs. The perceived needs of the marketplace are translated into products or services.

- *Monitoring progress towards satisfying customers.* By encouraging a continual flow of reactions from the marketplace, organisations can check the extent to which they are satisfying customers.

- *Improving customer satisfaction.* Customer orientation implies a continuous effort to improve existing levels of satisfaction and the flexibility to change in line with shifts in customer needs.

These stages represent a management process that continuously identifies customers' needs, translates them into products, evaluates satisfaction with those products and improves them as necessary. It is this evolutionary aspect of marketing which has led companies like Marks and Spencer to shift their interpretation of customer needs over the years and pay the price if they fail to do so. Figure 1.1 illustrates this process of customer satisfaction.

ENTREPRENEURIAL MARKETING

Two customer-orientated entrepreneurs decided to open a restaurant. They found there was a need for a fast-food style restaurant (there were none in their local area, despite the popularity of such restaurants in other geographic markets with a similar population profile). They bought premises, equipment and supplies and opened a restaurant.

Customer response was monitored by talking to customers and placing a suggestion box in the restaurant. After three months the partners reviewed the situation.

They found that customers wanted quicker service times and more vegetarian and light options. In reaction to comments made, they improved the standards of customer service in the restaurant and modified their menu. They evaluated satisfaction with these changes and made further modifications as necessary. As marketing entrepreneurs, they had learned the principle of adapting their plans according to the changing needs of their customers.

1.2.2 Long-term customer relationships

Customer orientation usually implies establishing and maintaining long-term customer relationships. One-off sales from a large number of buyers are usually less beneficial than developing the loyalty of a smaller group of customers over a period of time. The advantages of keeping customers so satisfied that they remain loyal include:

- It costs more to attract new customers than to retain existing ones

- A satisfied customer recruits new ones by making recommendations to their friends and acquaintances

- A satisfied customer is less likely to shop around when considering a repeat purchase

- Customers are more likely to buy other products or services from a company they have already bought from

CHECKPOINT

From your own personal experiences as a customer, think of an organisation that you consider to be 'customer-orientated'.
    Think also of one that is not.
    What led you to these conclusions?
    What were the essential differences in the way you were treated in each case?

1.2.3 Organisational integration

Marketing is an overall business philosophy, a way of doing things as well as a set of management techniques, so it has to permeate the entire organisation. Everyone in the organisation has to understand the marketing concept if it is to be a guiding principle behind all activities. The marketing department cannot implement the concept of customer satisfaction alone. Each employee has to be a part-time marketer. Marketing has to be integrated into all levels and all functions of an organisation. It runs from the chief executive to the receptionist; from the sales department to service delivery or production areas.

The reason for this is straightforward. Everybody in an organisation can affect the level of satisfaction a customer receives. This applies most obviously to anyone in the organisation who communicates directly with customers, such as receptionists, salespeople, credit controllers, and delivery staff. It also applies to those who are less visible but who nevertheless have an impact on customer satisfaction. This could be because their efforts can be judged directly by customers (for example, those involved in production or maintenance) or because their work has an impact on how effectively others in the organisation can serve customers (for example, personnel and accounts staff).

In Figure 1.2 this principle is illustrated for a company organised along departmental lines. Some departments do not have the customer as a natural focus for their day-to-day activities, because they have little direct communication with the marketplace. Nevertheless, they are an integral part of customer satisfaction, like a spoke in a wheel revolving around the hub of customer needs. If they fail to function in line with customer needs, they can have the effect of a broken spoke, causing the wheel to buckle and not run true.

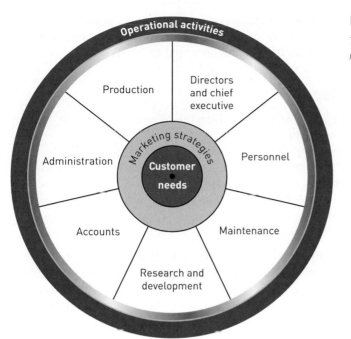

FIGURE 1.2

*The organisational
marketing 'wheel'*

FOR EXAMPLE

The entrepreneurs who set up a restaurant found that customer satisfaction came from a combination of factors including the service of the waiting staff, the quality and variety of food prepared by the kitchen staff, and perceptions of the environment as influenced by the cleaning and maintenance staff. If there were problems behind the scenes then customers were likely to feel the impact without necessarily understanding the cause.

For example, one regular customer was irritated because their favourite menu item was not available and complained to the waiter. She was not aware that the problem was caused by a bookkeeper who overlooked some payments to suppliers who in turn refused to deliver some vital ingredients. It was not just the entrepreneurs who established the restaurant who needed to be customer orientated. It was everyone.

New information and communication technologies are influencing the development of marketing in many ways, as we will discuss later. One of the less obvious ways is through improvements to internal communication within an organisation. Employees now have instant access to each other and customer information via email and intranets (internally linked computer systems). Customer enquiries and contacts can be handled efficiently through computerised systems providing instant access to relevant information.

Internal communications are easier to manage in small companies where employees can meet on a daily basis. The challenge comes when the company grows. As there are more and more employees, the company will need to formalise its internal communications. Suddenly meeting over coffee is not enough and the company needs to think about newsletters and intranets to make sure that all employees understand what the company is trying to achieve.

1.2.4 Mutually profitable exchange

The marketing concept cannot be a one-sided process in which the customer is the only winner. The organisation that serves the customer has to gain too.

It seems only logical to ask customers what they want and then provide it for them. However this 'customer is king' approach has to be balanced to make sure that the king does not turn into a tyrant. Customer needs cannot be met at any price. An organisation has needs too, varying from the need to suitably reward its employees and shareholders to requirements to reinvest in new products or equipment and to conform to the law of the land. These place two main types of constraints on an organisation's ability to deliver what customers want.

■ *External constraints* can limit an organisation's power to serve its customers. For example, we all want goods at lower prices but inflation or high rates of interest may force businesses to continue to raise prices to survive. Public services may be unable to meet all the demands of their users because of financial or political constraints. Society may justifiably impose constraints on how far organisations can go to satisfy individual customers (for example, restrictions on buying alcoholic drinks for certain age groups).

■ *Internal constraints* also influence an organisation's ability to meet customer preferences. The aims and objectives of a business may preclude it from certain markets. The strengths and weaknesses of an organisation indicate which customers the organisation is capable of satisfying and those that it is not. Successful companies, in fact, tend to target their activities towards what they know they are good at, avoiding markets where they have less to offer.

FOR EXAMPLE

....

As we have seen, Marks and Spencer have always believed that their strengths lie in retailing. From the beginning they avoided any direct involvement in manufacturing, even though this was a function which vitally affected their customers' levels of satisfaction. Their philosophy has been to influence how items are made rather than manufacture them for themselves, leaving the actual production to specialised organisations.

In this way, marketing acts as a link between suppliers and consumers. A supplier has certain abilities and potential to provide goods and services; consumers have certain desires and needs. Marketing is the process that brings the two together by matching the capability of a company or organisation with the needs of customers.

The result is an *exchange* that should benefit both parties. In the commercial world this means:

■ The company receives payment and some profit to meet future customer needs

■ Customers receive benefits that satisfy their wants

This represents a balancing act between the needs of the customer and the goals of an organisation, as represented in Figure 1.3.

Customer satisfaction   Organisational goals   FIGURE 1.3

The balancing act

CHECKPOINT

You are the owner of a vineyard producing mainly sweet dessert wines. Over the last decade the demand for your wines has declined as consumers' tastes have changed. As it will take at least five years to grow new productive vines, you now have to make some decisions on your marketing approach.

How will you match your particular strengths to consumer demand to ensure a 'mutually profitable exchange'?

ENTREPRENEURIAL MARKETING

The aims of the entrepreneurs who set up the restaurant were to make money and enjoy the task of running their business. Customers were happy and came back for more. However, although the restaurant satisfactorily filled a need, it did not meet the objectives of the entrepreneurs. Its location in a small town meant that the number of potential customers was relatively small. Recession in the economy and high local unemployment caused a drop in custom that could not be countered by service improvements and marketing tactics. As the business began to lose money, most of the pleasure for the owners was replaced by worry. With their personal goals no longer being met, the entrepreneurs decided to close the business and turn away even their satisfied customers. Customer satisfaction and organisational goals were not in balance.

1.3 ALTERNATIVE ORIENTATIONS

Organisations are not always marketing orientated – in other words, they may not always focus primarily on the needs of the customer. There are other ways of approaching business which may be appropriate in certain circumstances. These are:

- **Production orientation**: Emphasises efficiency of production before consumer choice

- **Product orientation**: Emphasises quality of product or possibilities of technology

- **Service orientation**: Emphasises the specialist nature (and sometimes the jargon) of the particular service on offer

- **Sales orientation**: Emphasises the techniques of marketing, particularly selling techniques, rather than the overall philosophy

1.3.1 Production orientation

Production orientation assumes that markets need products to be made available in large quantities at the lowest possible price. Producers should therefore standardise products as much as possible in order to increase production and benefit from the economies of scale made possible by higher throughput.

This is useful if demand for a product is greater than supply. Availability through increased production then becomes the first priority. This was the case for many goods in Europe immediately after the Second World War and in the former communist eastern bloc countries such as Poland and Czechoslovakia, where shortages were common. It can also be beneficial when the costs of manufacturing and distributing a product put it beyond most pockets.

In this case the rationale of the business owner might run as shown in Figure 1.4.

This was the logic behind many aspects of commerce in the nineteenth and twentieth centuries. For example, new automated looms reduced the price of cloth and made more of it available to wider markets, but standardisation of production meant that fewer types of weave and colour were produced than had been made previously by small-scale craft workers. Automobile usage began as an expensive hobby for the rich because of the high costs of producing each car individually. Henry Ford (amongst others) changed all that by concentrating on less choice and the higher production efficiencies of standardised products. This philosophy, epitomised by Ford's famous comment that customers could have any colour providing it was black, made sure that the car rapidly became available to more and more people.

FIGURE 1.4

Rationale of the production-orientated business owner

This philosophy has also been the justification for the creation of large monopolies. If production or the provision of services is concentrated, then economies of scale will operate to produce lower prices. In many markets it can now be seen that competition provides even greater stimulus to lower prices with the added benefit of greater consumer choice and influence. However, there have been many examples where concentration of resources has initially favoured consumers. For example, the introduction of a uniform postal system in Britain in 1840 meant that for the first time a letter could be sent anywhere in the country for the standard price of one penny. Previously postal services had been fragmented and much more expensive with the receiver of a letter paying the charge calculated on a per-mile basis.

Production orientation may have originally made possible the widespread availability of some products and services, but increasingly customers now demand products that are tailored to their individual needs.

1.3.2 Product orientation

'Product-orientated' organisations focus their efforts primarily on producing better products of higher quality and with more features. It is assumed that customers always want improvements to the specification and features of the products they buy before other considerations.

In this case, the rationale of the business owner might run as shown in Figure 1.5.

Organisations based on a philosophy of product orientation devote their energies to continuous improvements to existing products or the design of the 'ultimate' advanced product. Such organisations are sometimes successful because there is sufficient demand for their product developments.

However, there can be problems in this approach:

■ Product improvements may be desirable but not at the expense of other ingredients in the marketing mix, such as pricing or reliability. Better performance may increase prices beyond the level that many customers are prepared to pay. Concorde was a technological breakthrough in passenger flying. Unfortunately the operating costs made it a service which only a very few could afford and the social costs of noise pollution to the environment restricted it to a small number of routes.

FIGURE 1.5

Rationale of the product-orientated business owner

FOR EXAMPLE

The history of the British motor car industry contains many examples of vehicles with higher specifications than their rivals, but which were outsold in world markets because the increased performance was at the expense of reliability. In the 1970s, the Triumph Stag's design and specification were heralded as breakthroughs for high performance saloons. Unfortunately its unreliability, compared to cars like BMW with adequate but less advanced engineering, made it less popular. BMW went on to become market leader in the performance saloon category, whilst Triumph has disappeared.

■ Immediate demand for new products or features is not guaranteed just because they become technologically possible.

FOR EXAMPLE

Many advanced features have been incorporated into DVD players, such as the facility to programme recording requirements up to a year in advance. However, research has shown that consumers rarely use these functions and do not know how to carry out many of the operations of which their equipment is capable. In response to the problems of this product-led development, some manufacturers have introduced products that are simpler to use, including all-in-one television/recorders.

■ Focus on improving one particular way of doing things may blind a producer to possible substitute products which may fulfil the same need in a different way. Organisations can develop 'tunnel vision' by assuming customers need developments to existing products when really they need a better way of performing the same job, regardless of the product.

FOR EXAMPLE

Typewriters were the standard way of reproducing one-off documents such as letters on paper. Many large companies including IBM and Remington continuously invested in developments to give their customers better products, such as the introduction of electric typewriters and later the 'golfball' typing head. Their efforts were concentrated on improving the typewriter and they overlooked a better way of achieving the same end. Newcomers to the market transformed 'typewriting' into 'word processing', particularly after the introduction of personal computers.

Whilst product improvements may seem desirable, they are not always the best method of meeting customer needs.

FIGURE 1.6

Rationale of the service-orientated business owner

1.3.3 Service orientation

The products of some organisations may not be physical, but intangible services that may involve specialised knowledge or skills. The delivery of some services involves a very specialised understanding of disciplines such as accountancy, law and medicine, or of trades such as carpentry, plumbing and typesetting. As professions are based on a high degree of specialisation it follows that those outside of the profession have less knowledge and depend on those within the profession to specify and deliver the appropriate service. This can lead to misinterpretations of demand by the professionals, whose in-depth knowledge may blind them to what is really required.

In this case, the rationale of the business owner might run as shown in Figure 1.6.

Whilst in most instances, professionals identify correctly the type of service a particular customer requires, in some cases they may be blinded to real needs by their specialist knowledge. This orientation around the service may, for example, lead accountants to produce complex and detailed reports full of accurate information that unfortunately is meaningless to managers who are meant to be guided by them.

FOR EXAMPLE

Lawyers produce legal agreements which may seem faultless to fellow lawyers but which are incomprehensible to those who have to implement them. One company had an agreement (or licence) to manufacture another company's patented product. The solicitors who drafted it understood the terms of the agreement very well. Unfortunately the managers responsible for implementing the production process could not fully understand the agreement and frequently did not abide by the terms. This was uncovered by the auditors of the licensor and the company was liable for heavy fines.

Another problem with legal services is that they can often be 'distress' purchases – that is, a purchase that the client is forced into rather than chooses to make, such as divorce or criminal proceedings. An added complication is that the clients have no opportunity to try out alternative lawyers so that they will never know whether they achieved the best outcome or not, since they only get one chance.

Monopolies may encourage services to focus inwardly rather than outwardly towards the customer. In the public sector, services such as education and the health service are delivered to customers, who may have little choice in what they receive. Whilst the professionals who deliver such services may believe they always act in the best interests of their users, customers can have other views, which tend to be suppressed in deference to the specialist knowledge of the professional. As a result, opportunities to improve services may be missed because of the lack of proper consultation between deliverers and users. Recognition of this problem has lead to attempts to address it through the creation of artificial markets, for example, within the public sector, and practical efforts such as the appointment of more parents as school governors and the surveying of patients' satisfaction in hospitals.

1.3.4 Sales orientation

Some organisations concentrate on selling and promoting, using some of the techniques of marketing, without adopting the overall philosophy of responding to real customer needs. The focus of sales-orientated companies is on how to sell their existing products or services, rather than on finding out what they should offer in order to meet customer requirements more closely. The sales concept assumes that the existing products or services of the organisation meet most customer needs and that sales or promotional techniques are all that is required to increase acceptance and demand.

In this case, the rationale of the business owner might run as shown in Figure 1.7.

Problems in this approach include:

■ The product or service on offer may not meet customer needs. The producer has misread the marketplace and is now selling something that is out of step with demand.

FIGURE 1.7 *Rationale of the sales-orientated business owner*

FOR EXAMPLE

This approach is not limited to physical products. It can often be seen at work in politics, for example when a political party decides what it thinks is best and then attributes widespread opposition to 'presentation' problems. This in turn justifies the use of sophisticated public relations exercises attempting to 'sell' the policies to an unwilling public. Both Conservative and Labour governments in the UK have run into problems using such tactics to sell unpopular taxation changes. In the early 1990s, Margaret Thatcher's government introduced the now notorious 'poll tax'. Opposition was put down to a lack of understanding that would disappear when the benefits of the new tax over the old system of rates were felt in practice. The answer was an intensive campaign to sell the new system that was only finally scrapped when it became obvious that this approach was not working. Tony Blair's government had similar problems in 2000 when mounting discontent over increases in the price of fuel culminated in a blockade of petrol depots. Although the disruptions were officially put down to the activities of a vocal minority, the government recognised more widespread discontent by reducing duties on some fuels.

- The real usefulness of a product is well below the expectations (or claims) of the organisation selling it. The limited acceptance of the product or service only encourages the seller to convince wider markets of the 'necessity' of their offering. This is a particular problem when the sale is of a 'one-off' product (one that is unlikely to be repurchased). As the seller does not depend on repeat purchases, they can be less concerned with how their product lives up to the claims made for it, and spend more time finding the next sale.

FOR EXAMPLE

Sellers of one-off products (e.g. time-share holiday apartments) can be particularly tempted into using high-pressure sales techniques to overcome what they believe to be 'natural' resistance but which in reality represents a more fundamental objection to purchasing. This has led to government intervention to insist that contracts for the purchase of certain goods and services such as insurance policies contain clauses enabling customers to cancel their agreement within a certain period of time.

- When individuals or organisations do not have access to the most suitable products they adopt a sales orientation to sell what they have available.

  Sales people may be tempted to pose as 'consultants' offering 'solutions' to fit customer needs when, in reality, they have only one product or range to sell. Organisations are sometimes forced to adopt this position because superior products or services are not available to them.

FOR EXAMPLE

The Xerox Corporation of America and their UK partners Rank Xerox, successfully excluded other companies from selling plain paper office copiers for many years because of their protective patents. Competitors were forced to sell copiers using coated paper, often overcoming resistance to this inferior product by using hard sell techniques. These companies acknowledged the inferiority of what they were selling by switching to plain paper copiers as soon as the Xerox patents expired.

Whilst a sales orientation may overcome short-term problems caused by surplus or obsolete stocks it does not provide long-term solutions to customer needs. It therefore tips the balance towards meeting organisational objectives at the expense of the customer.

1.3.5 A summary of the marketing concept and alternative orientations

The marketing concept, orientated around customers, and alternative orientations that organisations can adopt, are summarised in Table 1.1

It is important to note that an organisation's aims do not necessarily change with its orientation. These are alternative strategies for achieving the same objectives. The growing popularity of the marketing concept has come about because it works. More and more successful companies have adopted a marketing orientation, particularly as competition has increased. Large and small organisations in diverse sectors including the not-for-profit and public sectors are also recognising the benefits of this approach.

TABLE 1.1 *Alternative orientations*

ORIENTATION	FOCUS	METHODS	AIMS
PRODUCTION	Production efficiency	Higher volumes and lower costs through standardisation and centralisation	
PRODUCT	Product improvement	Customer benefits through advanced products and features	
SERVICE	Service delivery	Develop specialist skills and knowledge	**Increased profits (private sector) Improved provision of services (public sector)**
SALES	Sales volume	Use promotional techniques to sell more existing products and services	
MARKETING	Market needs	Fulfil customer needs, aligned to own strengths for mutually profitable exchange	

MARKETING MISTAKES

PETS.COM

Sometimes we learn more from what goes wrong rather than from what is done well. Good practice is often more easy to understand by considering what does not work, and understanding the problems and issues rather than analysis of success.

For this reason, one of the most interesting periods in the development of marketing strategy was during the so-called 'dot.com bubble' from 1997–2001 when there was much speculative investment in new Internet companies. Many had unsound business models and overlooked basic marketing realities such as attracting a customer base large enough to justify optimistic expansion plans and make profits

One of these was Pets.com, set up to sell pet accessories and supplies over the Internet. It launched in August 1998, went public on NASDAQ (a major US stock exchange) in 2000 and into liquidation only nine months later. The market concept was in fact sound, as witnessed by the existence of several pet suppliers on the Internet today (e.g. Petsmart.com). The mistake was to assume that the market would be large enough to support an extensive marketing campaign and a substantial infrastructure of systems and warehousing dedicated only to an Internet business. In order to at-

tract customers to the website, Pets.com rolled out an expensive advertising campaign using TV, print, radio and a Pets.com magazine. One advertisement alone at the Super Bowl cost the company over one million US dollars. The company also made significant investments in business processes and infrastructure, including warehousing. As a result, the business needed a very large critical mass of customers that would spend the necessary $300 million for the company to break even. But the take-up of Internet shopping was much slower than this. The management of the company made the simple mistake of taking customer demand for granted – they assumed that the majority of pet owners would want the convenience of Internet shopping and adopt this method very quickly. Pet owners proved to be much more conservative and resistant to change in their shopping habits, and the percentage who shopped on the Internet was too low for a company with large overheads such as Pets.com to survive.

There was one marketing success story in this failure: the unnamed Pets.com dog, a basic sock puppet with buttons for eyes, a stick microphone and a watch around its neck. It became an advertising icon with media appearances and even a court case.

1.4 THE DEVELOPMENT OF MARKETING

1.4.1 The need for marketing strategies

The concept of marketing is as old as commerce itself. Exchanges of goods and services between different members of society were made easier by the development of the marketplace – literally a place where people could meet and trade their surpluses for items they needed. As the numbers of transactions increased, merchants arrived to simplify the exchange process by providing a centralised buying and selling point. They provided a service that helped those with a surplus – something to sell – trade with those who had a shortage – a need to buy.

These merchants, whether they operated in the ancient bazaars of the Middle East, the medieval cities of the Mediterranean or the shops of Victorian England, based their trade on understanding what the buyers in the marketplace wanted and knowing where to get it at the right price. To fulfil their role in society, they had to be 'customer orientated'.

Why do modern organisations need marketing strategies and specialist managers to implement this basic principle, which earlier traders instinctively understood?

- Companies and other organisations have become more remote from their customers because of their size. Economies of scale made possible by the industrial revolution meant that businesses became bigger. As organisations grew they developed layers of management to run them. This removed key decision-makers at the top of the management structure from direct contact with the marketplace and the customer. The merchant's intuitive understanding of demand, arising from regular customer contact, could not be gained from a remote boardroom. Marketing has developed techniques such as market research to overcome this deficiency.

- The complexity of modern business may distract attention from the customer. Modern managers work in an environment subject to a complicated mixture of forces and influences. Employees, suppliers, government, financial institutions, unions, competitors, potential competitors, not to mention bosses, all compete with the customer for management time and attention. The customer is often forgotten in the urgency of dealing with immediate problems.

- Systems and policies can create inflexible organisations unable to respond quickly to changes in customer needs. Organisations need policies and systems to deal with their increasingly complex environment. Efficient work needs order, not chaos, around it. Unfortunately order can also create inflexibility. Established ways of doing things are often difficult to change. However, customer preferences are constantly changing and require adaptable organisations to keep up with them.

- Many more products and services are now possible than are needed. The development of technology and information has created endless possibilities for new products and services. Translating these possibilities into products with a viable demand is an increasingly difficult task. As there is a surplus of invention, modern marketing techniques are needed to predict and support the winners in the marketplace.

These influences represent forces that increase the chances of customer needs being ignored or misread. The increased number of potential products and services that can be made available to customers has increased the possibility of customers making errors in those choices. The development of large organisations working in complex environments has increased the chances of customers being disregarded or misunderstood by those aiming to serve them. The discipline of marketing has developed in order to counter those influences which lessen the chances of correctly interpreting customer preferences.

1.4.2 The historical development of marketing

Although marketing can be said to have originated with the development of surpluses within an economic system and therefore with the beginnings of trade itself, it has only developed into a formalised management concept in relatively modern times. The adoption of the concept has been gradual, its influence not being felt equally in all parts of our economy, and some sectors embraced its principles before others.

Since the 1950s the sequence of adopting marketing principles in many countries has followed the pattern outlined below:

FIGURE 1.8 *Adopting marketing principles*

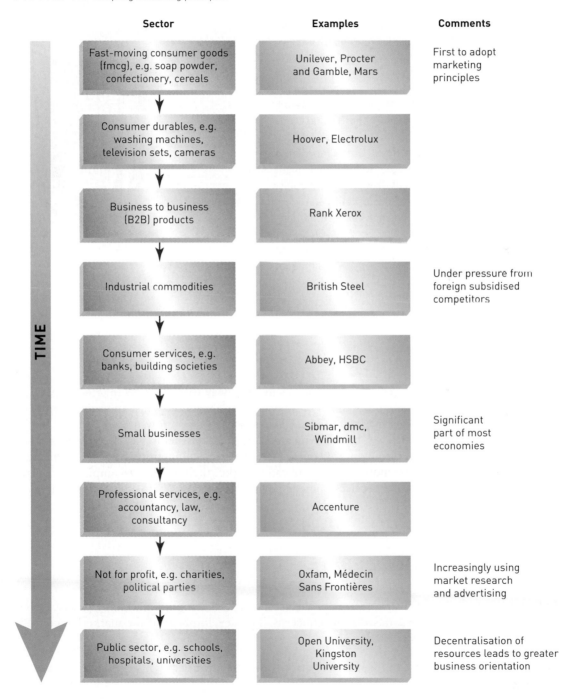

Sector	Examples	Comments
Fast-moving consumer goods (fmcg), e.g. soap powder, confectionery, cereals	Unilever, Procter and Gamble, Mars	First to adopt marketing principles
Consumer durables, e.g. washing machines, television sets, cameras	Hoover, Electrolux	
Business to business (B2B) products	Rank Xerox	
Industrial commodities	British Steel	Under pressure from foreign subsidised competitors
Consumer services, e.g. banks, building societies	Abbey, HSBC	
Small businesses	Sibmar, dmc, Windmill	Significant part of most economies
Professional services, e.g. accountancy, law, consultancy	Accenture	
Not for profit, e.g. charities, political parties	Oxfam, Médecin Sans Frontières	Increasingly using market research and advertising
Public sector, e.g. schools, hospitals, universities	Open University, Kingston University	Decentralisation of resources leads to greater business orientation

TIME

FOR EXAMPLE

Shell is one of the most recognised brands in the world, promoted by a mass of advertising since the company was formed in 1897. It began in Victorian times with a merchant trader called Marcus Samuel who bought and sold everything from rice to sea-shells. When Marcus Samuel died, his two sons, Marcus Junior and Sam, took over the family business and branched out into transporting illuminating oil to the Far East. The venture prospered, and in 1897 the 'Shell' Transport and Trading Company was formed. Then, in 1907, Shell entered an historic alliance with the Royal Dutch Petroleum Company which became the Royal Dutch/Shell Group (now simply the Shell Group) of Companies. Shell recognised the value of marketing early on. Although many of its campaigns focused on consumers, with slogans such as 'Go Well, Go Shell', they also recognised the value of marketing to businesses, as this poster from 1979 aimed at farmers illustrates.

Shell targeted farmers with a specific oil designed especially for them

Over the last half-century or so, marketing has moved away from its roots in large companies selling fast-moving consumer goods. Small businesses increasingly recognise the benefits of marketing in their struggle to survive and prosper. Political parties are now presented to us in the same manner as the products we buy. Towns and cities market themselves to attract tourists, industry and events such as the Olympic Games. The increasing competition for jobs has brought marketing to the level of the individual as applicants market their services to employers. Entrepreneurs can market goods and services immediately and inexpensively to an international audience via the Internet.

1.5 THE MARKETING DEBATE

In this way, managers in diverse sectors of the economy have adopted marketing practices, but the spread of marketing has raised some concerns. The development of the marketing concept has generated debate in two key areas:

■ Are traditional marketing principles still effective in the newer contexts in which they are being applied?

■ In particular, are the principles of marketing as practised by entrepreneurs different to the traditional marketing concepts?

■ Are there potentially harmful, social effects in marketing activities, especially when applied to sensitive areas such as education and health?

1.5.1 Is marketing effective in all contexts?

Management critics have raised important questions about the development of marketing:

■ *Does the concept apply in all market conditions?* Is it appropriate to use the marketing concept in all markets – for example, in industries where technology is changing so rapidly that customers cannot keep sufficiently up to date to express informed preferences? New products such as personal computers were not developed because market research indicated a strong need but because innovators made them possible. In other markets, the specialist is always going to be better informed than their customers; how far should accountants, solicitors and teachers go in meeting their customers' requirements if they believe they are misinformed or misguided, for example?

FOR EXAMPLE

In some markets customer preferences can change rapidly, but the lead time for new product development is much longer. Consumer preferences for wine have shown many fluctuations in recent years as the predominance of the traditional European growers has been challenged by newer tastes from California, Australia and South America. Unfortunately for established vineyard owners who may wish to respond to the competition with new products of their own, a new vine can take five years from planting to producing a drinkable crop. In that time consumer tastes may have moved on again. How can suppliers meet customer needs in these circumstances?

■ *Does customer orientation discourage longer-term investment and originality?* Market research among potential consumers is unlikely to have come up with many of the key modern inventions (e.g. DVDs, MP3 players and the Internet) because they were unimaginable before they were invented. Research and development based only on customer preferences is likely to be risk-free and lead to modifications to existing products rather than radically different concepts. Most people are more able to visualise improvements to products with which they are familiar than to visualise totally new ones. Breakthrough concepts and products are the province of the dreamer or innovator who is prepared to step into the unknown. Marketing on the Internet has been driven largely by new companies, not established ones. The leading dot.com consumer marketing companies, Google, eBay and Amazon, are new ventures.

Concerns such as these imply criticism for a market-orientated, rather than a customer-orientated, approach. As we have seen, the marketing concept recognises that the strengths and needs of an organisation, as well as the requirements of customers, have to be taken into account. A traditional vineyard may have to rely on its long-established reputation for quality rather than make changes to accommodate every new whim of the market. Managers may be tempted to ignore organisational expertise and needs in an effort to meet short-term customer requirements at all costs. The marketing philosophy looks for solutions that will be of long-term benefit to the consumer. This includes encouraging innovations that are too advanced for most consumers to visualise but still meet a known need. However it is true that existing organisations do become over-focused on the way things are, rather than on the way things could be. It is sometimes left to visionary entrepreneurs to create the innovations that meet customer needs more closely than existing products and services. Manufacturers of traditional vacuum cleaners refused to accept James Dyson's concept of the bag-less machine. He had to prove that his new product met customer needs more closely, by successfully selling his breakthrough product himself.

■ *Does traditional marketing place too much emphasis on the transactions of buying and selling products rather than building relationships with existing and potential customers?* Modern marketing had its origins in fast-moving consumer goods where the emphasis was on moving tangible products rapidly through the distribution chain to targeted, yet anonymous, groups of consumers. The shift in our economy towards services, rather than manufactured products, means that longer-term relationships between sellers and buyers have become more significant than the actual moment in which a transaction takes place. The marketing of consumer services tends to rely more on the building of goodwill between the parties involved than the promotion of specific products. In industrial, or business-to-business markets, the building of long-term relationships through personal contacts is often more important than taking a specific order. Hairdressers, accountants and directors of advertising agencies often take their clients with them if they change company because the relationship is more important than the organisation. Several influential marketing commentators have criticised traditional 'transactional marketing' and expressed a need for a different type of 'relationship marketing'. One of them summed up this emphasis as follows:

> Marketing can be seen as relationship management: creating, developing and maintaining a network in which the firm thrives. A new approach to marketing stresses the building of relationships rather than the promotion of products (Gummesson, 1987).

The concept of 'customer relationship management' (CRM) adopts this relationship focus in order to provide products and services tailor-made to individual preferences. Electronic commerce can provide organisations with a wealth of data on individual customers through computerised transactions, loyalty schemes and tracking devices on the Internet. This information can be used to customise products and services more closely to customers' specific needs. For example, buyers can specify the exact configuration and features of the computer they require and order it directly from manufacturers such as Dell Computers, who assemble made-to-order PCs.

1.5.2 Can marketing principles guide entrepreneurs who react to an instinctive rather than a formalised understanding of the marketplace?

Individual entrepreneurs often start with an idea, and then try to find a market for it. Opportunities are often prompted by instinctive feelings about the market derived from personal experiences, or the knowledge that something can be done in a different way. Their innovations tend to flow from inventions that find a home in the marketplace, rather than careful research into customer needs that is then translated into new products. Entrepreneurs tend to do it the other way round to the principles of traditional marketing, investigating customer reaction after the development of the product or service.

FOR EXAMPLE

James Dyson was not just the designer of the revolutionary vacuum cleaner that bears his name. One of his earlier inventions that claimed to have 'improved on the wheel' was stimulated by his own personal experiences as a builder. Whilst renovating an old farmhouse, he became annoyed by the problems he perceived with a conventional builder's wheelbarrow: it had a narrow wheel and thin tubular legs that were unstable for heavy loads and sank into soft ground, and it had a metal body with sharp edges that could damage buildings and did not carry cement efficiently. As an entrepreneurial designer, he set about improving on what seemed to him a primitive product that had scarcely improved from the wooden barrows made centuries earlier. The result was the 'Ballbarrow', with a ball instead of a wheel and a round, softer container made from plastic with fatter feet.

Unfortunately the building trade did not share his enthusiasm to replace their traditional barrow for his new model and 'many of the advantages were simply not perceived by the builder as advantages at all. Research amongst builders may have predicted this reaction before the product was developed. Dyson's product did eventually succeed in the marketplace. It found a different type of customer – gardeners – who did perceive the advantages of the Ballbarrow as real benefits over the conventional wheelbarrow.

The Ballbarrow was appreciated by gardeners, rather than the original target market of builders

Entrepreneurs like Dyson have a zeal for developing new concepts and products, demonstrating an orientation towards innovation rather than a slavish acceptance of what customers say they want. This is not necessarily based on a disregard for customer preferences. Rather it is accepting that sometimes customers do not know what they need because they do not know what is possible. Market research into new products or services always has this issue to overcome: how can existing customers specify new product developments when they have neither the vision nor the technological competence necessary to understand what is possible? They will tend to be guided by what is already available and base their judgement of new ideas on what already exists.

Market research among potential consumers is unlikely to have come up with many of the breakthrough inventions in telecommunications that have shaped our modern world because they were unimaginable before they were invented. Research and development based only on customer preferences is likely to lead to modifications to existing products rather than radically different concepts. Most people are more able to visualise improvements to products with which they are familiar than to visualise totally new ones. For this reason, many key innovations come from outside of, rather than from within, an existing industry. Marketing on the Internet has been driven largely by new companies, not established ones. The leading dot.com consumer marketing companies, such as eBay and Amazon, have not been developed by the existing retail giants. Existing organisations do become over-focused on the way things are, rather than on the way things could be.

According to Theodore Levitt, an early management guru, innovation is 'unnatural' because it means letting go of what has been mastered and trying out the unknown. Inertia is a more natural state, as James Dyson discovered when he tried to licence his revolutionary Dual Cyclone bag-less vacuum cleaner to the existing industry leaders such as Hoover and Electrolux, all of whom turned down the concept. He had to prove that his new product met customer needs more closely than the standard industry product by successfully manufacturing and selling his breakthrough product himself.

The entrepreneurial approach is to formulate ideas or opportunities intuitively and then look for market acceptance, rather than adopting the market-oriented approach of analysing the market systematically for unfulfilled customer needs. Successful entrepreneurs are more opportunistic in that they have a propensity to act once they see a potential opportunity, and immediately evaluate the attractiveness of this based on past experience and industry criteria rather than formalised research. It would seem that entrepreneurs prefer to pursue innovations first and seek market acceptance second, rather than follow a more structured investigation into customer needs that could either miss the real market or the competitive time frame.

1.5.3 What are the social effects of marketing?

Marketing has been seen as symptomatic of some of the problems in a modern capitalist society. It has been accused of:

- Encouraging consumption at the expense of the environment
- Stimulating individual desires and greed and disregarding the need to be of service to others
- Brainwashing gullible consumers into buying products and services that they do not really need or want
- Facilitating the sale of shoddy or otherwise undesirable goods
- Inflating prices because of excessive expenditure on advertising and promotion
- Encouraging competition at the expense of the common good

These concerns have been partly responsible for the emergence of consumerist and environmental movements attempting to prevent the exploitation of both people and the planet.

The supporters of marketing point out that it has led to a number of benefits to society:

- It has provided a wider choice of affordable goods
- It promotes efficiencies and lower prices through economies of scale and competition in the marketplace
- It effectively communicates what is on offer from suppliers
- It develops the notion of serving others through the concept of serving customers

---

CHECKPOINT

As a minister in the government, you have been asked to introduce legislation which curbs some of the excesses of organisations which seek to over-exploit consumers through sophisticated marketing techniques whilst retaining the benefits which marketing can give to society.

What do you suggest?

FIGURE 1.9 *The balancing act of societal marketing*

Possibilities for new products and services → Wide range of rapidly changing choices → Organisational and environmental complexity → Launch of new products and services

Customer preferences

© ISTOCKPHOTO.COM

1.5.4 *Societal marketing*

The criticism remains that, by following the notion of consumer sovereignty, marketing can disregard the wider needs of society. Marketing may bring together suppliers and customers whose needs are both met but sometimes at the expense of other members of society. For example, oil companies have met customer requirements for a range of energy products but at the expense of environmental damage, even to those societies who have not directly benefited from the cheap, accessible energy sources.

For this reason, the concept of 'societal marketing' places a third element into the balance between supplier and customer needs – the longer-term needs of society. The concepts of conventional marketing have been expanded to include these three elements:

■ Customers' short-term wants and long-term needs

■ Organisational needs in the long-term as well as the short-term

■ Societies' interests and welfare throughout the world

Although there are still many pressures and temptations to make short-term profits from short-term consumer requirements, there is evidence that organisations are increasingly developing strategies which include longer-term considerations of the needs of their customers and the welfare of society in general.

The development of the concept of 'relationship marketing' emphasises long-term relationships in the business environment aimed at developing goodwill even at the expense of short-term transactions that acquire customers.

FOR EXAMPLE

The Body Shop, one of the UK's most innovative retailers, based its customer appeal on a concern for the environment. Its body care products are developed from 'natural' substances, packaged in environmentally friendly, recyclable containers. Employees are encouraged to take time off for voluntary service in the community. Founder Anita Roddick used company resources to support endangered societies in South America and research into sustainable business activities. As well as the usual Annual Report to shareholders, the Body Shop reported on its non-commercial achievements in a 'Values Report', which judged its performance against social and environmental criteria. Since its first shop opened in Brighton in 1976, the company has heavily influenced the development of the body care market by appealing not only to customers' cosmetic needs but also their social needs to express concerns for the environment. This was explicitly recognised in 2006 by L'Oréal, part of the cosmetics establishment, when it acquired the company.

1.6 SUMMARY

■ Traditional marketing starts with the orientation of the enterprise around customer needs. In order to ensure this, formalised gathering of market intelligence underpins all aspects. A process of segmentation, targeting and positioning is used to develop a marketing strategy that meets customer needs. This strategy is implemented through the elements of the marketing mix.

■ As a management philosophy, the marketing concept represents a strategy involving three basic propositions:

— customer orientation: the primary focus of the organisation is on the needs of the customer

— organisational integration: everyone in the organisation accepts and implements a customer orientation: it is not just the responsibility of the marketing department

— mutually beneficial exchange: there has to be a balance between the needs of the customer and the strengths of an organisation so that it too can have its needs met

■ Alternative orientations which can be adopted include:

— production orientation: focusing on the efficiency of supply

— product orientation: stressing the highest possible product specification and quality

— service orientation: emphasising the expertise of the service deliverer

— sales orientation: using sales techniques to sell what is available

■ Although the basic principles of marketing are as old as trade itself, it has developed rapidly as a body of knowledge since the 1950s, with successive industry types and economic sectors adopting a more customer-orientated approach.

■ The Internet has created new opportunities for marketing and enabled organisations to become more accessible to individual customers; the most rapid development of Internet applications has been in business-to-business, rather than business-to-consumer, markets.

■ Traditional marketing principles have been challenged for several reasons:

— the seeming lack of effectiveness of marketing strategies in some market conditions or circumstances

— entrepreneurs' abilities to successfully develop new businesses based on individual intuition rather than formalised assessment of market needs

— the potentially detrimental effects on society, which has led to the notion of 'societal marketing', which puts the welfare of society into the balance alongside customer and organisational needs

1.7 ACTIVITIES

BUSTING DIVA

Danièle's Hromek's business Danièle Hromek followed what might be considered an entrepreneurial route to starting her business, Busting Diva. She simply followed her instincts – in her case stylistic ones. Style had been a driving force for Danièle from the time when, as a three year old, she demanded that her socks were changed because they didn't match. This childhood interest turned into an adult passion and Danièle has been involved in design all her working life. She has worked as a freelance photo editor for websites and women's magazines. She's completed courses in interior styling, fashion styling and personal shopping as well as magazine editorial and website design. Gaining her experience globally, Danièle has lived in London, Paris, Barcelona, Sydney and Vancouver.

This passion for style and (she claims) her realisation that she is completely unemployable led her to start Busting Diva. She believed that there were many people who wanted to dress well and look stylish but just did not have the time to devote to it. Without formally researching the marketplace, she began to offer styling advice and shopping services. By making services available outside of normal working hours and during weekends, she was able to attract busy people who did not have time to shop for themselves and who wanted advice on how to look their best. She offered styling, shopping and lifestyle services in fashion, beauty and interiors with a direct personal service at home or in the workplace.

Launched in 2000, her business was successful in offering these services direct to customers. At first, she won new clients from personal recommendations but more recently she has undertaken more formal marketing activities. She has focused particularly on public relations (PR), backed by an informative website. From interviews for TV, radio and magazines, she has had sufficient media coverage to attract attention. For those interested to find out more, the Busting Diva website (www.bustingdiva.com) gives details of all their services in an interesting way, including some case studies and a feedback link. Feedback has proved

Busting Diva capitalised on the value of style to its target consumers

useful in giving them a clearer picture of how to improve what they do and new directions to follow.

Theo Müller's business Recently Busting Diva teamed up with yoghurt specialist Müller for its marketing campaign entitled 'Add Some Colour to Your Life'. This was designed to promote awareness of the Müllerlight range and encourage customers to try some of its new varieties. The origins of Müller food products stem from Ludwig Müller, who established a small Bavarian village dairy in 1896. It was not until 1970 when his grandson Theo Müller took over that the family business started on the road to becoming an international brand. Theo believed that the regional popularity of his dairy's products could be translated into a national success if he improved the recipes and promoted the brand name with much more marketing support. The dairy introduced innovative products, including the 'split pot' format that contained both sauces and dairy products in the same container. It worked, and the company expanded rapidly into an international business with sales of £625 million, employing 2,400 people.

To promote new health-orientated products, Müller was looking for a partner to add value to their campaign with complementary services that helped women make the most of themselves. Although a small company, Busting Diva met this need. Visitors to Müllerlight stands in shopping areas were able not only to sample the new products but also to receive advice on which colour tones were most complementary to their individual characteristics through a colour consultation.

The successful promotion with Müller has raised an important strategic issue for Danièle. Should she focus her marketing strategy to attract more corporate accounts such as Müller, or concentrate on her original customer base of individual clients?

QUESTIONS

1   In what ways is Busting Diva a market-oriented business? What needs is it fulfilling? Has it shown signs of not being market oriented?

2   What potential differences in marketing between large consumer goods corporates like Müller and small businesses like Busting Diva are illustrated by this case?

3   Busting Diva's campaign with Müllerlight illustrates aspects of the debate over the social impact of marketing. What potential positive and negative social impacts might possibly arise from marketing campaigns such as this?

4   What advice would you give to Danièle about the direction of her marketing strategy?

DEVELOPING A MARKETING PLAN

At the end of each chapter, you will find activities like this one under the heading of 'Developing a marketing plan'. These are designed to build into a marketing plan around a product or service of your choice. A fuller overview is given in the preface.

Where are we now?

The first step is to choose a subject for your marketing plan. This should be a product or service that you can find out about in terms of its potential market and customers, and make recommendations about its marketing strategy and tactics. Bear in mind the following points when making your decision:

■ Choose a product or service that interests you. You are much more likely to be motivated to do the required research and analysis about something that you personally find interesting. If you have an interest in the topic you could have a head start in understanding the market as you may yourself be a customer or potential customer. Consider products related to your hobbies or sports, special interests, where you live, your family background, and where you work or study.

■ Your product or service can exist now, or it can be a fictional new development provided this does not stray beyond the realms of what is currently possible (a spinning wheel that converts corn into gold will not do!).

■ It will probably be more manageable to choose a particular product or service rather than a generic range of products or an industry, for example a specific car rather than 'saloon cars' or the 'motor car industry'. A study that is limited in scope but represents a detailed evaluation of the marketing possibilities of one product or service is more beneficial than broad generalisations about a wider area.

■ Your choice does not have to be in the private business sector. It can be in the non-profit sector such as a charity or club. It can be a public service such as a course of studies, a library, a hospital (or related medical service) or local leisure facilities.

■ You will need access to information about your chosen topic, so make sure it is freely available. Avoid areas where there could be security problems (for example, military developments or 'sensitive' business areas because of competitive intelligence).

1.8 FURTHER READING AND REFERENCES

Customer orientation

Greenley, G.E. (1995), 'Market Orientation and Company Performance, Empirical Evidence from UK Companies', *British Journal of Management*, No. 12, pages 1–13.

Harris, L.C. (2002), "Developing Market Orientation: An Exploration of Differences in Management Approaches', *Journal of Marketing Management*, Vol. 18, pages 603–632 (available on EBSCO).

Jaworski, B. and Kohli, A.K. (1993), 'Market Orientation: Antecedents and Consequences,' *Journal of Marketing*, Vol. 7, pages 53–70.

Kohli, A. and Jaworski, B. (1990), 'Market Orientation: The Construct, Research Propositions and Managerial Implications', *Journal of Marketing*, April, Vol. 54, No. 2, pages 1–18.

Narver, J. and Slater S. (1990), 'The Effects of Marketing Orientation on Business Profitability,' *Journal of Marketing*, Vol. 54, pages 20–35 (available on ABI INFORM).

Relationship marketing

Fournier, S., Dobscha, S. and Mick, D.G. (2001), 'Preventing the Premature Death of Relationship Marketing', *Harvard Business Review*, October, Vol. 76, No. 1, pages 42–51.

Gronroos, C. (1994), 'From Marketing Mix to Relationship Marketing: Towards a Paradigm Shift in Marketing', *Management Decision*, Vol. 32, No. 2, pages 4–20.

Gummesson, E. (1987), 'The New Marketing – Developing Long-Term Interactive Relationships', *Long Range Planning*, Vol. 20, No. 4, pages 10–20.

Rigby, D.K. and Leddingham, D. (2004), 'CRM Done Right', *Harvard Business Review*, November, Vol. 82, No. 1, pages 118–129.

Rigby, D.K., Reichheld, F.F. and Schefter, P. (2002), 'Avoid the Four Perils of CRM', *Harvard Business Review*, February, Vol. 80, No. 2, pages 101–109.

Entrepreneurial marketing

Stokes, D. and Wilson, N. (2006), *Small Business Management and Entrepreneurship*, 5th edition (Thomson Learning), Chapter 12.

Internet development

Chaffey, D., Mayer, R., Johnston, K. and Ellis-Chadwick, F. (2003), *Internet Marketing*, 2nd edition (Pearson Education), Chapter 1.

Chaston, I. (2001), *E-Marketing Strategy* (McGraw Hill), Chapter 1.

Keynote Report (2000), *Internet Usage in Business*, 4th edition (Keynote Ltd).

Chapter 2

THE MARKETING CONTEXT

LEARNING OBJECTIVES

By the end of this chapter the reader will be able to:

- Understand a classification of the significant influences on marketing decisions
- Assess the effects of internal influences
- Assess the effects of influences in the immediate context of the organisation
- Assess the effects in the more general context of the organisation
- Appreciate what managers can do to understand and change these influences

INTRODUCTION

This chapter looks at the internal and external influences on marketing decisions. Business managers cannot directly control the environment in which their organisations operate, but factors such as economic and competitive conditions have a crucial influence on marketing decisions. A continuous appraisal of this environment is therefore an important part of the marketing process. This chapter categorises the types of environmental forces facing marketing management and gives some examples of their effects. It examines the internal aspects of an organisation that affect marketing strategies, the external environmental factors (competitive, social and economic contexts) and the role of marketing management in relation to these forces.

2.1 THE MARKETING ENVIRONMENT

The ability of an organisation to satisfy the needs of its customers is conditioned by the environment in which it operates. This environment can be classified into three parts:

- *The internal environment* such as the objectives, stakeholders, resources, culture and structure of the organisation, which determine the scope and conduct of its marketing activities

CASE STUDY

··

ROBOTS AND REFORM IN THE HEALTH MARKET

Max Polonski settled into his airline seat, pulling out the papers he needed to read on his flight from New York to London. He was the owner of the Robotic Research Corporation of America and was on his way to a series of meetings to test the viability of launching their latest product, 'Georgie', in the UK and the rest of Europe. Following its launch two years earlier, Georgie had become an instant hit in America where each product had produced savings of up to $100,000 a year in hospitals. Georgie was a robot capable of delivering up to 350 lbs (160 kg) of materials to predetermined destinations, or cleaning and polishing floors. In American hospitals, Georgie was loaded in a central materials management department with goods from X-rays to toilet rolls and programmed for delivery destinations. Using its memory map, it calculated the route and set off around the long corridors typical of large hospitals. Sensors guided it round any obstacles whilst it calculated the deviation to ensure it returned to its route. A centralised controller watched progress and in the event of problems, Georgie could use pre-recorded messages such as 'I am lost. Please report my position to the operator.' to ask for help from passers-by. Georgie could also clean the floors it travelled over as the flick of a switch changed it from 'carry' to 'clean' mode and activated its brushes and polishers. Georgie was a very efficient worker, available seven days a week and twenty-three hours a day (the other hour was for recharging its batteries and undergoing any necessary maintenance). It could do the work of three human workers, allowing more resources to be devoted to patient care.

Max had decided the time was right to launch Georgie into the UK as a springboard into European markets. On the plane, he looked first through his briefing notes on the healthcare market in the UK.

File note: UK Healthcare Market

Market: 75 per cent of UK healthcare is provided by the public sector through the National Health Service. Expenditure on the NHS since its inception in 1948 has quadrupled after taking account of inflation. Actual expenditure has risen from £400 million in 1949 to £57 billion in 2003/4. The private sector currently has a 25 per cent share of healthcare expenditure and is becoming increasingly important especially in the care of the elderly.

Demand for healthcare is growing at the same time as the costs of its provision are escalating. The UK population is ageing as life expectancy has increased to over 75 years for males and to over 80 years for females. Increasing numbers of elderly persons in the population has already caused short-term funding problems. The shrinking of young age groups combined with increasing older age bands has longer-term funding implications. Technological advances in surgical techniques and drug treatments have increased the costs of some healthcare and mean more illnesses can be treated. Cost-cutting measures include an increase in day surgery for minor operations.

A further major problem is serious staff shortages. The NHS is the largest single employer in Europe, with around one million employees. Expansion of healthcare services, relatively low pay for medical and support staff, and full employment in the national economy have led to chronic shortages in the NHS. The government has attempted to improve the position with advertising and other initiatives to recruit and retain staff, but the problem is not likely to be solved easily.

Industry structure: The NHS was been repeatedly re-organised by successive governments in line with themes for changes in other public services. The separation of the role of purchaser from the role of provider – a split of management responsibility between those who specify the quality of a service and those who provide it – created markets or at least 'quasi-markets' in healthcare.

'Purchasers' are the Primary Care Trusts (PCTs) responsible for deciding what services are required in their area, arranging and paying for contracts with providers of the services, and setting and monitoring quality standards. Doctors' practices also control budgets to purchase healthcare for their patients. 'Providers' include hospitals, community health services, and family health services.

The Patients' Charter of 1991 laid down expectations of the health service, specifying standards in such areas as waiting lists, complaints and information. The Labour government has attempted to tackle problems with extra funds targeted at specific objectives, such as the reduction of waiting lists.

The private sector is still very dependent on private medical insurance for its income. However it is playing an increasing, complementary role alongside the NHS. Some NHS patients are now treated in private hospitals and some NHS hospitals provide private healthcare facilities. The government's private finance initiative has tried to introduce external funding into the NHS and encourage partnerships with private healthcare organisations.

Max considered how his business would cope with supplying this fast-changing sector. Their long-term objectives were clear: 'to be the most recommended international supplier of robotic products to the healthcare market'. But so far their customers had been confined largely to private sector hospitals in North America. His company was young, as were most of its managers. It was still relatively small, employing only forty-five people, although it was growing very rapidly, driven on by the innovative ideas and enthusiasm of a youthful team led by Max – who had just celebrated his twenty-ninth birthday. Their international strategy was to use Georgie as the spearhead for penetrating the European market. Max's visit was to evaluate not only the potential market for the product, the level of competition and other likely barriers to its acceptance, but also the logistics of selling, supplying and servicing a complex technological product at a distance.

METRALABS GMBH, DIVISION ROBOTICS, GERMANY

Georgie was successful in the US, but now faces a different challenge in the UK

To help him with this evaluation, Max had arranged to meet a number of healthcare managers. His first appointment was with Ruth Steinberg, who was the newly appointed director of marketing at Queens Hospital Trust. Ruth had informed Max that she needed to introduce innovations that not only produced efficiencies, but also produced good publicity for the hospital that needed to market itself to patients and to healthcare purchasers alike. As Max looked forward to their meeting, he recalled her words on the telephone:

'The aims of marketing here are the same as any other organisation – more satisfied customers. But the environment is very different to, say, marketing consumer goods. Healthcare is an emotive subject, as it is so often a matter of life and death.'

QUESTIONS

1 What types of internal influences on marketing decisions face Max Polonski? What illustrations of these does this case provide? *See section 2.1 and 2.2*

2 What are the main influences in the external environment which face Max and the Robotic Research Corporation in marketing their products in the UK healthcare market? What illustrations of these does this case provide? *See sections 2.3 and 2.4*

3 What internal and external factors are particularly important for Ruth Steinberg to consider in marketing Queens Hospital? How would you advise her to manage them? *See sections 2.2 to 2.6*

FIGURE 2.1

*The environment of
the marketing
process*

■ *The external, micro-environment* of competitors, customers, suppliers and intermediaries,
which have a direct influence on marketing decisions

■ *The external, macro-environment* of social, technological, economic and political forces,
which have a more indirect influence on marketing strategies

These environmental forces are the 'sea' in which an organisation either swims or sinks in its efforts to meet customer needs through its marketing decisions. Figure 2.1 illustrates this environment, in which marketing decisions are made.

We will explore each of these influences in more detail, illustrated by some examples.

2.2 THE INTERNAL ENVIRONMENT

Some forces are outside of the marketing management function but remain within the internal
environment of the organisation. These can be summarised under the following headings, which
are discussed below:

■ Objectives

■ Stakeholders

■ Culture and structure

■ Resources

2.2.1 Objectives of the organisation

Marketing decisions are made in the context of a specific organisation and its objectives. One organisation may want to grow as quickly as possible, whilst another may not wish to grow at all.

These overall objectives are clearly a major influence on marketing plans and decisions and an understanding of corporate objectives is a necessary first stage in the marketing planning process (see Chapter 12).

One basic difference between the objectives of different types of organisation is the role of *profit*:

■ *In the private sector*, the profit objective is usually taken for granted and marketing is often seen as a means of maximising the profits of a business.

■ *In the non-profit sector*, there are a variety of organisations, including social enterprises and clubs, that have objectives other than profit. Social enterprises are businesses with social aims and objectives whose surpluses are reinvested to meet those aims, rather than being driven by the aim of maximising profits for shareholders. Social enterprises tackle a wide range of social and environmental issues and operate in all parts of the economy using business solutions to achieve public good. This does not necessarily mean that such enterprises behave differently to private sector organisations. Many are very business-like in the way in which they are run – indeed some exist to promote aspects of the private sector, such as the Confederation of British Industry (CBI). An example of smaller social enterprise is Striding Out, a pioneering support network for young people with enterprising ambitions. (See the case study on page 40.)

■ *In the public sector*, where organisations are controlled by the government, the role of profit is also replaced by other objectives. A state hospital, for example, does not have the objective of maximising profits but of providing high-quality patient care.

2.2.2 The marketing environment in the public and non-profit sector

Historically, marketing did not play a significant role in the management functions of public services and the non-profit sector. As we saw in Chapter 1 (section 1.4.2), it has been increasingly adopted in recent years, spurred on by the increased competition and changes to funding methods. However, the environment of these non-profit organisations still influences their ability to fully adopt marketing principles.

There are several factors that potentially inhibit the marketing of public services:

■ Public sector organisations operate in restricted market conditions. Some are effectively monopoly suppliers (e.g. social services). Most exist in heavily regulated markets, subject to ongoing direction from one or more source (e.g. the educational 'product' of a UK school is prescribed by the National Curriculum).

■ Objectives may be multiple and contradictory (e.g. cut costs and improve services simultaneously). This is often because more than one group of people can lay claim to being the 'customer' of a public service. It may be difficult to regard the users of a service as 'customers' (e.g. inmates of a prison), or it may be inappropriate to consider their expressed needs in the same way as traditional consumers (e.g. the desire of school pupils for longer playtime and less homework, or for students to have less assessment).

■ Public services are accountable to a wide audience and ongoing public scrutiny because they are intended for the general good. All activities can be scrutinised by the public in a way that does not exist in the commercial world, especially for smaller enterprises such as private family businesses. For example, UK schools have governing bodies of typically twelve to fifteen governors, in contrast to equivalent-sized private sector enterprises that are generally controlled by one or two owner-managers.

■ Specific consumer groups are not targeted because services are generally available to all, so there is less specialisation than in the private sector (e.g. most state schools admit both boys and girls of all abilities, whilst private schools are selective in their admissions).

FOR EXAMPLE

A town library provides services funded by ratepayers and controlled by local government. It has constraints in line with those listed above:

■ It is a monopoly supplier of free book loans for many of its customers. Many people do not have access to other libraries for the publications they require and they therefore have no choice of supplier for this service.

■ It has contradictory objectives. One objective is to provide a loan facility to as many people as possible, and a measure used to monitor the success of the library is the number of users taking out books. Another objective, set by the controlling council, is to keep costs to a minimum, restricting expenditure to a tightly defined budget. The more books a library has, the more its services are used, and the more it is judged to be meeting the first objective. The second objective, however, demands restrictions on book purchases and therefore limits the use of the library.

■ It has less freedom to determine its own destiny. There are considerable constraints on management initiatives to improve services as all major decisions not only go through an internal hierarchy but are also subject to the scrutiny of an elected body – in this case, the county council. The county council only meets five times a year and any items for consideration first have to pass through a complex structure of subcommittees. As decisions can therefore involve many stages and take a long time, the library is sometimes very slow to respond to changes in customer needs.

■ Customers are not targeted and often have imprecise or conflicting needs. As its services are available to the general public, the library does not target one group in particular. Rather, it has to accommodate as best it can the needs of many different customer types, sometimes with unclear or even conflicting needs. For example, the heaviest users of the library are children, who are stimulated by exciting environments, and senior citizens, who prefer peace and quiet.

FOR EXAMPLE

The US has twice the percentage of adults engaged in early stage entrepreneurial ventures as the UK – about 12 per cent in the USA compared to 6 per cent in the UK (GEM, 2006). The British government believes that the US's relatively greater economic resilience and prosperity can be attributed in part to this higher propensity towards entrepreneurship. A key area of difference is amongst young people who are much more likely to start a business in the US than in the UK.

One person who is trying to do something about this is Heather Wilkinson, who has created a social enterprise aimed at supporting young people who want to start a new venture. She comes from a family of entrepreneurs, and started her first business, Just Blush, at the age of twenty-four. As a trained make-up artist, she provides services for weddings, events, fashion shows and parties.

In June 2005 Heather left a full-time job to set up Striding Out, a social enterprise that offers coaching and networking to connect young entrepreneurs aged eighteen to thirty, to the support they need for the different stages of their business journey. The enterprise aims to open doors to new opportunities, and provide budding entrepreneurs with the personal and professional skills they need, as shown in Figure 2.2.

FIGURE 2.2 *Creating a sustainable business*

CHECKPOINT

Do you think the marketing of Heather Wilkinson's social enterprise Striding Out would be different to marketing a small, private-sector business? If so, in what ways? For example, what would be the advantages and disadvantages in attracting young people to join a social enterprise such as this compared to a private business?

2.2.3 Stakeholders

Every organisation has stakeholders – groups of people or individuals who are affected directly or indirectly by the performance of the organisation. They may have a direct stake in its fortunes as employees or shareholders, or they may be external stakeholders such as suppliers or

FIGURE 2.3 *Examples of conflicting expectations of marketing decisions among stakeholders*

Stakeholders	Conflicting expectations of marketing decisions
LARGE COMPANY Institutional shareholders (e.g. pension schemes, investment trusts) Private shareholders Non-executive directors Senior managers Junior managers Employees Unions	Senior managers and institutional shareholders may wish to invest in longer-term marketing strategies involving corporate advertising. Junior managers and some private shareholders may prefer more visible, shorter-term results from marketing campaigns to gain promotion or maximise capital gain.
SMALL COMPANY Owner-manager Partners Managers Employees Investors	The owner-manager may desire the independence and personal control of a relatively static business and only undertake marketing activities if existing sales are threatened. Other partners and managers advocate proactive marketing campaigns to generate more sales growth.
PUBLIC SERVICE (A LIBRARY) Local taxpayers Councillors Officers Employees	Councillors, responding to the need to keep down the local taxes of their voters whilst improving services, expect more efficient use of the same level of resources. Officers interpret this into a marketing strategy which promotes greater use of the existing library facilities and book stock by extending the opening hours and shortening the loan period of popular books. Employees object to working the increased number of unsocial hours and users dislike the pressure to return books quicker.

customers. These stakeholder groups often have different expectations of the organisation; for example, employees expect good pay and job security, whilst shareholders expect a high return on their investments. Sometimes these expectations are in conflict and compromise objectives are needed to satisfy the interested parties. Marketing decisions not only have to conform to corporate objectives, but must also take into account possible conflicts of emphasis among stakeholder groups.

Figure 2.3 shows some examples of internal stakeholder groups for different types of organisations and potentially contentious areas that may have an impact on marketing decisions.

2.2.4 Resources of the organisation

The resources available to an organisation form another important influence on marketing. Small and large firms exhibit differences in their approaches to marketing, and small firms have become an important factor in the development of marketing practice.

Smaller firms

During the last fifty years, smaller businesses have played an increasingly significant role in the national economies of Europe and the United States. In the UK, the total business population increased from 2.4 million firms in 1980 to 4.4 million in 2005. This growth came from smaller businesses employing fewer than fifty people and particularly micro firms of fewer than ten employees. The vast majority of all businesses (99 per cent) now employ fewer than fifty people. These firms account for approximately 50 per cent of total employment, and 40 per cent of total sales turnover.

After significant growth during the 1980s, the business population stabilised in the 1990s but has recently begun growing again. Again, much of the growth in the number of businesses has been provided by very small businesses, especially single-person organisations – enterprises with no employees other than the owner. Nearly 75 per cent of all enterprises in the UK are of this type and they employ about 16 per cent of the working population (see Figures 2.4 and 2.5).

This pattern of growing business populations, fuelled by increasing numbers of small firms, is common around the world. Of the 20 million-plus enterprises in Europe, 93 per cent now employ fewer than ten people. In Australia, 98 per cent of the 2.2 million businesses are small (fewer than fifty employees). New Zealand has nearly 300,000 firms, of which 97 per cent are small.

The owners of these small businesses often have a paradoxical attitude to marketing because of their relative shortage of resources. On the one hand, they may dismiss marketing campaigns as something that only larger companies can afford. On the other hand, the same

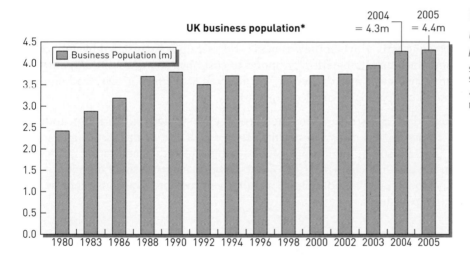

FIGURE 2.4

UK business population

SMALL BUSINESS SERVICE, 2005.

*GREAT BRITAIN AND NORTHERN IRELAND

FIGURE 2.5 *Profile of the UK business population, 2000–2005*

Percentages

SIZE	NUMBER OF BUSINESSES			EMPLOYMENT		
(Number of employees)	2000	2004	2005	2000	2004	2005
None	**70**	**73**	**72.8**	14	16	**15.7**
1–9	25	23	**22.7**	17	17	**16.7**
10–49	4	4	**3.7**	13	14	**14.4**
50–249	0.6	0.6	**0.6**	11	12	**11.9**
250+	0.2	0.2	**0.2**	45	42	**41.3**

owner-managers adopt market-oriented practices because the small size of the business allows them to stay close to the customer and adapt rapidly to new needs. One of the advantages which small firms have demonstrated over larger companies is their ability to respond flexibly to shifts in customer demand.

The resources of small firms do not usually run to specialist marketing departments. Responsibility for marketing is often taken by the owner-manager, who may have little knowledge or experience of specialised aspects. This environment tends to give marketing in the small firm a distinctive style with a number of characteristics:

- *Lack of formalised planning of marketing strategies*: marketing in small firms tends to be ad hoc, often in reaction to competitive activity.

- *Restricted in scope*: small firms are unable to incur the same pro-rata level of marketing expenditure as larger companies. Fixed costs (such as salaries or rent) tend to account for a higher proportion of sales revenue than in larger companies, leaving the small firm less to spend on marketing activities.

- *Simplistic and haphazard*: small businesses rely more on random, basic marketing efforts than sophisticated, integrated campaigns.

- *Evolutionary*: marketing practices in new ventures tend to evolve with the business. An initial phase of marketing activity when the business is first set up is superseded by a more reactive approach in which marketing efforts respond to customer enquiries or competitive threats. More positive marketing approaches may be adopted as the firm grows, leading to the planned, integrated campaigns of larger companies.

Whilst small firms may adopt a customer-orientated strategy to survive and thrive in today's competitive markets, resources and other constraints restrict their use of the tactics and techniques of marketing. These resource limitations often combine to create marketing strategies that are dependent on the personal characteristics of the owner-manager, a small number of existing customers and personal recommendations to acquire new customers, as illustrated by the following case of a start-up business.

ENTREPRENEURIAL MARKETING

Carolyn Foster set up DuckEgg with the aim of providing a website design and management service to developing businesses. She knew from experience that owners of fast-growing firms wanted a rapid service at low cost. By doing most of the work herself and keeping overheads down, she was able to offer both. Although she had been trained in computer graphics, her experience of marketing was limited to designing promotional material. Her first customers came from personal contacts rather than any planned campaign, but the customer base increased gradually as existing clients recommended others. One customer in particular was expanding very quickly and took up more and more of her time as their Internet applications grew. They demanded personal attention to their problems, and soon she was spending half of her time on their business. Eventually, their continued expansion meant they could employ their own full-time webmaster, and Carolyn's business lost over half of its turnover. However, she had learned much about marketing in these early business dealings and she invested more resources in a marketing campaign aimed at building a wider base of customers.

Larger firms

Marketing tends to become a specialist function as companies grow. In larger companies, a marketing department is given the responsibility of carrying out the various processes of researching, planning, implementing and controlling marketing programmes. The environment of such a department includes other functional areas of the organisation, such as production, finance and human resources.

Because large companies have the resources to employ specialists, marketing programmes tend to be professionally conceived and executed. However, there are potential problems in this particular marketing environment:

- *Marketing managers become remote from the customer.* Changes in customer needs can be overlooked as each marketing specialist concerns themselves only with their part of the jigsaw without seeing the overall picture.

- *Other departments leave marketing to the specialists*, forgetting that it is not just a business function but a concept that has to involve everyone.

- *Marketing planning is done in isolation* by the marketing group with insufficient integration into the work of other departments.

2.2.5 Culture and structure of the organisation

Culture

Marketing decisions are taken within the context of the internal culture of an organisation. This culture consists of the underlying values, attitudes and assumptions that an organisation adopts. It influences the way in which an organisation considers new ideas and options, how it reacts to events around it and how it structures itself. In many organisations, cultural factors work subtly; in others, the culture is such a powerful force that it resembles an ideology. For example, the Body Shop has advocated specific values relating to the environment, animal rights and traditional communities with a missionary vigour and operational style that has been described as 'management by infection'.

Structure

The distribution of responsibility and authority within an organisation is an important part of its culture. The organisational structures that result influence all decision-making including marketing. Some typical structures include:

- *The entrepreneurial organisation*: the owner-manager or small group of entrepreneurs retain centralised control over all-important decisions, including marketing

- *The professionalised organisation*: decision-making is delegated to specialists, usually organised into functional departments such as finance, production and marketing

- *The divisionalised organisation*: operating divisions take the day-to-day decisions relating to their designated products or services, within a policy framework laid down by head office

- *The holding organisation*: operating units, often in very diverse areas of business, are encouraged to act almost like independent organisations under the umbrella of a holding company

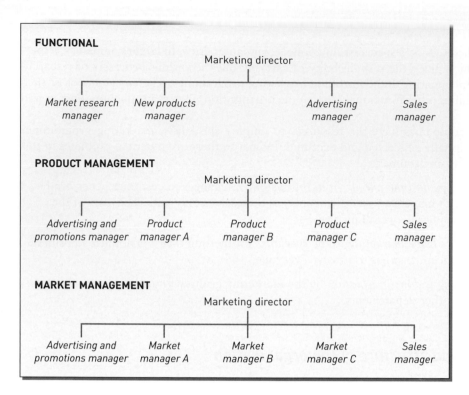

FIGURE 2.6

Some options for organising marketing

The structure of the marketing function reflects the overall culture and structure of the organisation. In an 'entrepreneurial' organisation, the owner-managers may make all the important marketing decisions, calling in outside specialists such as advertising agencies when needed. In a 'professionalised' organisation, a specialised marketing department may control all the day-to-day marketing decisions. This can be organised in a number of ways. Some of the options for various types of organisations are illustrated in Figure 2.6.

■ *Functional specialists*, for example a market research manager, an advertising manager, a new products manager and a sales manager, all report to the marketing director. A common organisational form reflecting the specialist nature of some marketing tasks, this structure becomes less appropriate as an organisation grows and becomes involved in more markets and more products.

■ *Product managers* have individual responsibility for the marketing of products or brands supported sometimes by specialists such as an advertising and promotions manager. This structure is typical of companies marketing branded consumer products, for example, soft drinks and cereal producers.

■ *Market managers* have responsibilities divided according to customer groups and markets rather than products. Service companies are often organised this way; for example, banks and financial institutions appoint separate managers responsible for marketing to businesses and domestic users.

These influences on marketing decisions that are primarily internal to the organisation are summarised below in Figure 2.7.

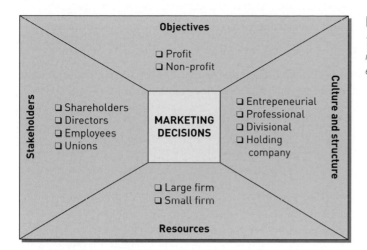

FIGURE 2.7

The internal marketing environment

CHECKPOINT

Consider the educational establishment at which you are studying or one with which you are familiar (e.g. a former school or college).

Assume that you have been asked to advise them on developing a marketing strategy. Analyse the *internal* environmental factors which would influence your recommendations.

2.3 THE MICRO-ENVIRONMENT

Marketing decisions may be directly affected by a number of external forces in the immediate market environment of the organisation, or 'micro-environment'. These include the following categories, as discussed below:

- Suppliers
- Intermediaries
- Customers
- Competitors

2.3.1 Suppliers

The ability of an organisation to acquire the resources it needs to meet its own customers' requirements crucially affects its chances of success. Other businesses, organisations or individuals are the suppliers of these resources. The resources needed vary widely and include:

- Equipment, raw materials, components and supplies bought from other companies
- Premises and associated services such as telephones, heating and cleaning supplied by landlords and other companies

■ Specialised services such as training and advertising offered by agencies and institutions

■ Financial resources and services supplied by banks, investors and credit card companies

Relationships with suppliers may be overlooked because priority is given to dealing with customers, but the ability of an organisation to meet their customers' needs may rely heavily on suppliers.

FOR EXAMPLE

Jaguar Cars was a loss-making subsidiary of British Leyland when John Egan took over as managing director in 1980. A key problem was Jaguar's poor reputation for reliability, particularly in the crucial export market of the USA. An analysis of customer complaints found that faulty components from suppliers were to blame for 60 per cent of key failures. Egan decided to involve the suppliers in improving quality to a much higher standard. He renegotiated purchasing contracts to include penalty clauses for fault levels above an agreed level. He invited suppliers to join internal groups, monitoring quality levels so they understood the problems more fully. By 1984 sales had increased in all major markets, especially the USA, and Jaguar finally shrugged off its unreliable image. Its present owners, Ford, have been able to build on this earlier marketing success, hinging on the support of its suppliers.

Theories of relationship marketing reinforce the importance of suppliers and other 'markets', as well as customers (see Chapter 3). Managers today recognise the importance of building partnerships with important suppliers in order to serve the common interests of their organisations. Successful buyers no longer depend on playing power games with suppliers (such as deliberately keeping visiting salespeople waiting). Instead they make use of advances in information and communications technology to make their relationships with suppliers more effective:

■ *Electronic Data Interchange (EDI)* allows customers and suppliers to handle transactions electronically. Orders and invoices can be sent via computers, avoiding the need to re-key data into accounting and stock control systems. Many businesses now trade with their supply chain in this way and many larger organisations make it a condition of doing business with them.

■ *'E-procurement'* – buying goods and services for business through the Internet – is also growing rapidly. Manufacturers offer products through electronic catalogues and websites. Larger companies have set up their own 'electronic marketplaces'. For example, the WorldWide Retail Exchange consists of over 100,000 companies supplying goods and services to about twenty major retail chains such as Boots, Marks & Spencer, and Tesco in the UK, Casino in France, and K-Mart and JC Penney in the United States. The advantage for the purchasing retailer is that they can ensure a competitive marketplace of approved suppliers, whilst the suppliers achieve exposure to the largest potential customers.

2.3.2 Intermediaries

Organisations do not always deal directly with the consumer of their product or service (more of this in Chapter 3). Intermediaries help in the processes of selling and physically delivering products to customers. These include:

■ *Sales agents*, who represent a number of different organisations in the marketplace by promoting and selling their products and services

■ *Wholesalers*, who provide easier access to retailing outlets, which can be fragmented numerically and geographically

■ *Retailers*, who provide access to consumer markets by locating themselves in convenient shopping areas

These intermediaries play an important marketing role in penetrating the market for a particular product, and any changes to the way in which they operate can be crucial.

FOR EXAMPLE

Smiths Crisps were the household name for crisps in the 1950s and '60s. Famous for their little blue salt packets, Smiths products sold extensively through many small outlets such as grocers and public houses. By the 1970s distribution of food products was changing rapidly with the growth of multiple retailers and supermarkets. The popularity of out-of-town superstores in the 1980s reinforced the concentration of retailing into fewer, much larger outlets. At first Smiths did not change fast enough to cope with this rapidly changing environment. The short shelf life of their crisps was designed for distribution through localised outlets such as the corner shop and pubs and instant or rapid consumption once purchased. The new supermarket chains needed longer-life food products in larger sizes suitable for more leisurely, family consumption. Competitors such as Golden Wonder crisps, ready salted in family-sized, longer-life plastic packs, took an increasing share of a rapidly growing market. By the 1980s, Smiths failure to respond to changes in the distribution environment had reduced its share to 14 per cent of a market it once dominated. Smiths responded with new marketing strategies more suited to the changed needs of the intermediaries in the marketplace, improving Smiths position in the snacks market. Interestingly, these strategies included a nostalgic appeal to previous consumption habits by re-launching the blue salt packet.

Smiths Crisps lost out to the stronger brand of Walkers

IMAGE COURTESY OF THE ADVERTISING ARCHIVES

Golden Wonder was in turn knocked off the market leader pedestal by Walkers, who launched an iconic marketing campaign featuring Gary Lineker and other football players. Smiths became part of Walkers (owned by PepsiCo) and took all the famous Smiths brand names as its own, with the exception of Smiths Salt 'n' Shake, a brand that was developed from the original concept of the salt twist. Apart from Salt 'n' Shake, little is left of Smiths, although an older generation still recognises the many snacks developed by the company that are now sold under different names.

2.3.3 *Customers*

If intermediaries come between an organisation and the final consumer or end user of the product, then these intermediaries may themselves become the customer who buys the product. In the example above, Smiths sells its crisps to its direct customers in the snack trade such as the supermarkets and other retailers rather than the consumer. Marketing strategies can target the end user, thereby aiming to 'pull' the product through the trade. Alternatively products can be 'pushed' into the distribution trade in the expectation that they will be sold on to the consumer. (The changing role of customers in a supply chain is examined more fully in Chapter 3.)

2.3.4 *Competitors*

Organisations usually have to compete with other organisations for customers. The success or failure of private sector businesses has depended for some time on their ability to satisfy customer needs better than competitors. In many markets, competition comes not only from *direct rivals* but also *substitutes* that perform the same task in a different way or compete for the same slice of disposable income. For example, a restaurant competes not only with other local restaurants, but also with other methods of eating conveniently (such as take-aways and ready-made meals) and other places of social contact (such as public houses and coffee bars).

Markets have become increasingly competitive in areas that traditionally were not considered subject to competitive forces. The environment of some industries, such as gas, electricity and telecommunications, was made more competitive by the removal of state control and monopoly status of suppliers. Public services such as education and the health service have entered a more competitive arena by the introduction of many changes to the way they are structured and operate.

FOR EXAMPLE

State schools at primary and secondary level faced little competition until the education reforms introduced during the 1980s and 1990s came into effect. Parents and children had very little say in their choice of school unless they joined the small minority (approximately 7 per cent) of pupils paying fees for education in private schools. The Education Reform Act of 1988 introduced many changes, aimed at making educational provision more competitive, on the assumption that this would improve its quality. The introduction of two key concepts in particular has made the school environment more competitive:

■ The idea of 'parental choice' gives parents the right to send their children to whichever state school they choose providing it has enough space to take them. Parents can become active customers in the sense that they can exercise some choice based on what different schools have to offer.

■ Schools are allocated money mainly on the basis of the numbers of pupils attending a particular school. The more pupils a school admits, the more funds it receives. Moreover, a school has considerable freedom over how it uses the money allocated to it. Headteachers can decide whether to spend additional funds on more staff, new books, computers or other facilities. Schools have a real incentive to attract as many pupils as possible by competing with neighbouring schools. Not only do they receive more money by doing so, they can spend it according to their own local priorities.

Some schools have adapted to these changes in the educational environment very rapidly, adopting marketing strategies to increase pupil numbers and hence the resources available to their school. Others are more reluctant to fully embrace what they consider to be unnecessary commercial practices. Whatever the rights and wrongs of the moral argument, the management of schools has changed fundamentally.

The role of competitive forces is considered more fully in Chapter 4.

These influences on marketing decisions that are largely in the micro-environment of the organisation are summarised in Figure 2.8.

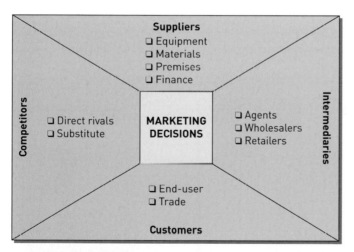

FIGURE 2.8

The micro-environment

CHECKPOINT

Consider the educational establishment at which you are studying or one with which you are familiar (e.g. a former school or college).

Assume that you have been asked to advise them on developing a marketing strategy. Analyse the *micro-environmental* factors that would influence your recommendations.

2.4 THE MACRO-ENVIRONMENT

The marketing environment also includes forces that have a more general impact on organisations. These are sometimes summarised by the acronym 'STEP' or 'PEST', representing the following influences:

- Sociocultural
- Technological
- Economic
- Political

2.4.1 Sociocultural environment

Social and cultural forces condition how individuals translate their needs into the specific products and services they want. If marketing is to play its full role in matching product benefits to customer needs, then an understanding of the social and cultural environment is essential. This environment can be subdivided into demographic and cultural aspects:

- *The demographic structure* of a society describes its human population in terms of size, location, age, ethnic origin, occupation, sex and other statistical measures

FOR EXAMPLE

The UK population is growing again and now approaching 60 million. It is also ageing, with 16 per cent of the population now aged 65 or over.

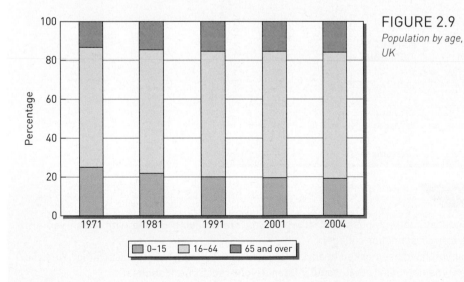

FIGURE 2.9
Population by age, UK

FIGURE 2.10 *Population by gender and age, mid-2004*

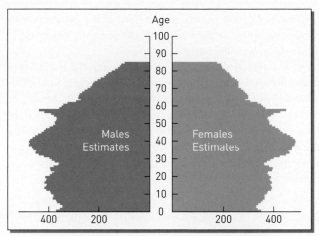

Population (thousands)   Population (thousands)

In mid-2004 the UK was home to 59.8 million people, of which 50.1 million lived in England. The average age was 38.6 years, an increase on 1971 when it was 34.1 years. Approximately one in five people in the UK were aged under 16 and one in six people were aged 65 or over.

The UK has a growing population. It grew by 280,600 people in the year to mid-2004, and the average growth per year has been 0.4 per cent since mid-2001. The UK population increased by 7.0 per cent since 1971, from 55.9 million. Growth has been faster in more recent years. Between mid-1991 and mid-2003 the population grew by an annual rate of 0.3 per cent.

The UK has an ageing population. This is the result of declines both in fertility rates and in the mortality rate. This has led to a declining proportion of the population aged under 16 and an increasing proportion aged 65 and over.

In every year since 1901, with the exception of 1976, there have been more births than deaths in the UK and the population has grown due to natural change. Until the mid-1990s, this natural increase was the main driver of population growth. Since the late 1990s, although there has still been natural increase, net international migration into the UK from abroad has been an increasingly important factor in population change.

■ *The culture* of a society is made up of a complex mixture of many beliefs, values, customs, habits, laws and understandings that are learned from parents and other members of society. Some or these cultural influences (e.g. observing traditions such as birthdays and religious festivals) are deeply ingrained and take many years to evolve. Others are more fickle, presenting constant marketing challenges because of their impact on the buying habits of society (e.g. our rediscovered concern for the natural environment with increased emphasis on 'green' issues).

Marketing management constantly needs up-to-date information in both demographic structure and culture as changes can present threats to current strategies or offer opportunities for new ones.

MARKETING, 19 JULY 2006, PAGE 33.

FOR EXAMPLE

Consumers are becoming increasingly conscious of the nutritional content of the products they eat and buy. Pressure from consumer and government groups has encouraged companies to put salt, sugar and fat content as well as intake-level warnings on packaging.

The lack of a single overarching system is a problem, but it leaves brands with the flexibility to develop their own. For Sunny D this provided an opportunity for the brand's new owners, Sunny Delight Beverages Company. The brand, although successful, had been dogged with criticisms of its added sugar, artificial colourings and preservatives. The launch in June 2006 of a new healthier recipe allowed the new owners to make a virtue of the more positive nutritional information. The new design was developed after consulting with parents.

The result was a design in which annotations and comments about the ingredients are a key element. Sunny D became the first soft drink to include guideline daily amount (GDA) information on the pack front.

Sunny D responded to criticism with a new healthier recipe

SUNNY D IMAGES, TEXT AND LOGO ARE USED WITH PERMISSION FROM THE SUNNY DELIGHT BEVERAGES COMPANY

2.4.2 Technological environment

Advances in technology affect the marketing environment in a number of ways:

■ *The creation of new opportunities for products and services* is the most obvious impact of technological change. Advances in information and communications technology have generated large numbers of new products. Each successful new product presents opportunities for additions and refinements to add to the proliferation. More powerful, smaller computers, advanced mobile phones and digital television have spun off different products as new applications of the technology emerge.

MARKETING MISTAKES

The Kellogg Company is the world's largest producer of cereals. From its inception in the early twentieth century, it became one of the leading exponents of marketing fast-moving consumer products. The Kellogg's brand, controlled from the headquarters in Battle Creek, Michigan, USA, is recognised globally. But even such a global name could not overcome local culture and social habits.

During the 1990s, competition intensified in Kellogg's core American and European markets, whilst market growth stagnated. Kellogg's marketing managers looked therefore to other markets for sales growth. The second largest population in the world resides in India and rapid economic growth was fuelling consumer spending. In 1994, Kellogg's launched Corn Flakes into the subconti-

nent with an expensive marketing campaign. At first, sales were encouraging, but soon peaked. This did not deter Kellogg's from launching other brands such as Frosties and Honey Crunch.

Despite extensive marketing activities, the cereal products failed to make headway in the Indian market. The problem was not the Kellogg's brand but the concept of eating cereals for breakfast. This was not common practice in India, where a bowl of vegetables is the preferred first meal. Kellogg's early sales success was due to experimentation with this different way to start the day, but repeat purchases were rare. Even the marketing power of Kellogg's could not change traditional eating habits.

© PETER YATES/CORBIS

Kellogg's failed to take account of cultural differences in India

FOR EXAMPLE

Computer games have developed into a large, international market for companies such as Nintendo in the United States. Their success has created marketing opportunities for the development of new products. British brothers Richard and David Darling invented 'Game Genie', a device for making computer games more or less difficult for the player. Nintendo were concerned at the effective upgrading of their products with no benefit to themselves and sued on the grounds of copyright infringement. Game Genie survived such legal action, and sales of this complementary device alone were over £100 million per annum.

■ *Technological advances can also change the distribution of existing products and services.* For example, the way in which we obtain cash to spend has evolved from bank counters to dispensing machines. Digital products such as music and print can be downloaded via the Internet. Groceries, holidays, pensions and a whole range of other products can now be ordered from a computer or telephone at home and delivered direct to the consumer.

■ *Our consumption patterns and lifestyles evolve* as a result of technological changes. There have been many recent examples. Developments in transportation systems have changed our purchasing habits as the spread of car ownership enabled convenient shopping further from home, culminating in the need for one-stop, out-of-town shopping centres. New technology in the kitchen, from microwaves to mixers, has reduced meal preparation times, allowing our eating habits to fit in with busy lifestyles and creating the need for a whole new range of food products.

■ *Marketing techniques have changed* as a result of technological possibilities. New ways of gathering information have had a particularly significant impact on consumer marketing.

FOR EXAMPLE

Electronic point of sale (EPOS) data capture allows major retailers to analyse sales, control stocks and evaluate marketing programmes at hitherto unknown levels of speed and accuracy. The laser reading of barcodes on product labels at checkouts provides fast and detailed information about what is sold and when – information that can then be used to improve the turnover and efficiencies of the store. It is used to control and re-order stock and provide statistics that can monitor the sales of individual products by the minute.

A marketing tool developed from this technology targets customers with discount coupons based on what they have just purchased. Computerised equipment at the checkout scans customers' purchases and promotes other products by giving them discount vouchers for items they have not bought. This can be used by competitors to tempt customers away from the brand they have just purchased the next time they shop. For example, if a customer's purchases include a tin of Campbell's soup, they may be given a discount voucher to buy Heinz next time. It can also be used to promote categories of product that the customer has not purchased. If a store wishes to promote, say, its delicatessen lines, then vouchers are given to anyone without delicatessen items in their basket.

2.4.3 Economic environment

The economic environment affects how much we have to spend and how we are likely to spend it. Therefore, it plays a significant role in determining the likely demand for products and services. Marketing is influenced by local, national and international economic factors.

■ *The local economy* of a region is important, particularly when exceptional circumstances create significant variations to national trends. High levels of unemployment created by the decline of the dominant local industry may depress demand for luxury goods in that area, for example.

■ *National economic factors* such as interest rates, exchange rates, unemployment levels and rates of inflation have obvious implications on products and services in the marketplace. Marketing planning involves making assumptions about these key statistics and evaluating the impact of any likely changes. As Britain's post-war economy has been dominated by 'boom or bust' cycles, successful organisations have had to demonstrate the flexibility to respond quickly to changed economic climates.

■ *International economic developments* have longer-term significance, and are sometimes more difficult to evaluate. Changing growth rates in other national economies affect exports and imports, which in turn influence national and local economies.

There can be wide variations even in countries which are geographically quite close. If we take Central and Eastern Europe as an example we can see that the average monthly income varies significantly, even when the countries are bordering. The average monthly income in Bulgaria is £106, in the Czech Republic it is £424, in Croatia it is £530 and in Slovenia £742.

FOR EXAMPLE

....

The Chinese economic area, including China, Taiwan, Korea and Hong Kong, has become a fourth power to rival North America, Japan and Europe in the world economic hierarchy. This economic area has expanded counter-cyclically to the rest, averaging annual growth rates of between 7 and 8 per cent in times when the more established economies were showing much lower or negative growth rates. China itself has been exporting at record levels, helped by a plentiful supply of cheap skilled labour. For western economies, this presents a threat and an opportunity: the threat of a further erosion of the manufacturing base, particularly in labour-intensive industries, and the opportunity of a fast-growing export market for specialised goods and services which are not available in China.

2.4.4 Political environment

The political environment of laws, regulations and interventions by central and local government, political agencies and pressure groups is an increasing influence on the marketing of any organisation. Recent legislation has had two main aims:

■ *To protect the consumer*: there are many UK and EC regulations designed to protect the consumer from being harmed by products or misled by suppliers. Products and services, and the environment in which they are sold, have to conform to health and safety standards. Customers are entitled to accurate information about what they are buying and to take back anything that does not do what is claimed. In some circumstances, customers have a legal right to change their minds; after signing a contract for insurance cover or a time-share apartment, for example, customers have an enforced 'cooling-off' period of thirty days in which to reconsider their decision away from any pressure created by the sales environment.

■ *To ensure full and fair competition*: organisations are also protected from each other. Legislation regulates competition in the private sector in order to prevent one or more suppliers dominating a particular market against the interests of customers. The EU is particularly concerned to see that companies in different member states compete on equal terms, free from artificial subsidies which may distort competition in favour of the less efficient. However the position is different in other markets.

India, for example, is currently maintaining many restrictions on direct foreign investment, preventing overseas retailers from establishing full operations there. This appears to be designed to give the fledgling Indian-organised retail sector time to mature. Organised retailing accounts for only 3 per cent of the overall market in the country, but is growing fast, boosted by the same demographic shifts seen in the west. India's government is keen to protect that emergent spending power from foreign firms until the domestic players have developed sufficiently to compete.

In the UK, public sector services have been forced to become more open to competitive forces. Some services, such as the maintenance of public places and buildings by local authorities, hospitals, schools and other government institutions are subject to compulsory competitive tendering which ensures that a number of competing bids are taken into account before contracts to supply a service are awarded.

These political pressures to increase the power of the customer over the supplier affect all aspects of marketing, from the design and pricing of a product to how it is promoted and distributed.

FOR EXAMPLE

The marketing of beer came under UK government scrutiny when the Monopolies and Mergers Commission investigated the big breweries. Their report, published in 1989, described the supply of beer in Britain as a complex monopoly. Six large brewers including well-known names such as Bass, Whitbread and Courage controlled many of the outlets for their products: 87 per cent of all public houses were either owned by breweries or 'tied' to them in a way that restricted sales to their products only. According to the Commission, the big breweries had used this stranglehold on the distribution system to keep out smaller competitors and increase prices unjustifiably. As a result of the report, brewers that owned more than 2,000 pubs were forced to free half of those above this minimum level from any tie to the brewery and allow them to become 'free houses'. Pubs that remained tied to a brewery were forced to sell at least one cask-conditioned beer ('real ale') from an independent brewery. This political intervention changed the scope of marketing activities in the industry. The UK beer market has been static for some time, and demand has shifted away from traditional dark British beers to lagers and premium ales such as the best-selling brands Stella Artois, Guinness and Caffrey's. This change in the market coupled with the pressures of regulation caused the major UK breweries to rethink their strategies. Bass and Whitbread intensified their efforts to diversify whilst selling off their brewing interests. Scottish and Newcastle, now the largest UK brewer, expanded outside of the UK by acquisitions such as Kronenbourg.

Which external environmental factors will be particularly influential in shaping your chosen career in the next five years?

2.5 MANAGING IN THE ENVIRONMENT

2.5.1 Scanning the environment

All of these factors, from industry-specific influences to general economic trends, form an environment that affects marketing decisions. Information about this environment is therefore a crucial input into the marketing process. The accelerating pace of technological change makes it harder to keep up, whilst the increased competitiveness of markets means that it is even more essential to do so.

Some organisations systematically analyse their environment to formally assess the possible impact of trends and external events. Environmental scanning techniques can help this analysis. QUEST (an acronym for 'Quick Environmental Scanning Technique') is one technique that allows managers of an organisation to pool their views on the future in a systematic way.

Other managers keep in touch with their environment in less formal ways. Successful entrepreneurs often develop informal networks to keep them in touch with what is happening around them. Some seem to have an instinctive understanding of developments in their environment. Alan Sugar, the founder of Amstrad, described one of the reasons for his success as an 'inbuilt aptitude for scenting the way the wind is blowing'. Research studies among a number of entrepreneurs suggest that those who succeed work hard at developing contacts to give them as much feedback from their environment as possible.

Whatever way it is gained, making judgements about the likely trends and events in the environment is a key part of the marketing process. This is not always easy to get right. Management over-reactions to external factors are as frequent as not doing enough.

2.5.2 Changing the environment

Marketing management cannot directly control these factors in the macro-, micro- and internal environment. For this reason they are sometimes referred to as the 'uncontrollable' elements in the mix of possible marketing decisions.

This does not mean that marketing management always accepts passively what is happening around it. The relationship between marketing and external forces is an interactive one and there are times when marketing influences its environment. Some instances of this include:

- *Influencing the internal environment* within an organisation. We described one of the key principles of the marketing concept as organisational integration, which means that the entire organisation has to adopt a customer-orientated strategy, not just the marketing department (Chapter 1, section 1.2.3). Managers may need to monitor decision-making within other departments of an organisation and influence them towards a customer-based approach.

- *Managing the micro-environment.* Organisations may try to actively manage aspects of their immediate micro-environment such as their relationships with suppliers and intermediaries.

MARKETING MISTAKES

Western economies slowed down in the late 1980s, affecting a number of key sectors. The aircraft industry looked as though it would be particularly affected by downturns in travel and tourism. The leading aircraft maker, Boeing, acted swiftly by cutting out many of its suppliers and reducing its workforce drastically. When orders picked up again, the company could not cope with the increased demand. Its competitor, European Airbus, gained from Boeing's inability to produce enough jumbo jets.

The 1990s provided a decade of unprecedented economic growth. Many organisations flourished in this stable, predictable climate. By 2000/2001, growth slowed – quickly in the United States and more slowly in Europe. Managers were faced with a situation of uncertainty that many had not faced before. Mistakes were again made by over-hasty reactions to the changing environment. For example, Marks and Spencer decided to close down its French stores in 2001, but found it had acted too swiftly without proper consultation with the French unions. Public relations and sales were worsened by the resulting court case.

We have already seen how Jaguar set about regulating their suppliers through contractual arrangements (see section 2.3.1.)

■ *Modifying the external environment.* In some instances, organisations use marketing techniques to modify the external forces that particularly affect them. Organisations 'market' their viewpoints on certain issues through direct representations and lobby groups to try and influence decision-makers at local, national and international levels.

FOR EXAMPLE

The large breweries made strong representations to the government and members of parliament following the report of the Monopolies and Mergers Commission on the supply of beer (see section 2.5.4). This pressure forced the government to modify the Commission's initial proposals, which recommended more sweeping reforms including the forced sale by the breweries of many of their pubs.

Whether they are actively managed in this way or simply monitored for their possible effects, environmental influences are an important initial input into the marketing decision-making process.

CHECKPOINT

Think of an entrepreneur who has rapidly developed a business (such as Alan Sugar of Amstrad, Anita Roddick of Body Shop or Richard Branson of Virgin). What environmental factors have helped the development of their business? Which internal and external factors may threaten them or provide them with opportunities in the future?

2.6 SUMMARY

- An understanding of the context within which an organisation operates and the environmental influences around it are an essential part of the marketing decision-making process. Three types of environmental factors have important effects on the marketing process: the internal environment, the micro-environment and the macro-environment.

- The internal environment of organisational factors are:
  - objectives: profit is a common objective in the private sector, although some smaller businesses prefer independence to growth; the public sector, for example, has other, sometimes conflicting, objectives such as the provision of a high-quality service whilst meeting spending targets
  - stakeholders: many groups from shareholders to employees with a vested interest in an organisation may place different emphasis on marketing strategies
  - resources: large and small firms differ in the way they approach marketing because of differences in their human and financial resources
  - culture and structure: the internal culture, made up of organisational values, beliefs, and assumptions, influences the marketing decisions an organisation makes and how it structures itself for decision-making

- The micro-environment of external forces specific to an organisation include:
  - suppliers, who influence the resources available
  - intermediaries, who come between a business and the final consumer
  - customers in the trade or end users
  - competitors trying to satisfy the same customer

- The macro-environment of forces having a more general impact include:
  - Sociocultural changes to the structure and attitudes of society
  - Technological advances in what is possible
  - Economic factors at local, national and international level
  - Political and legal constraints

- Managing marketing in this environment involves:
  - scanning it to understand what is happening and likely trends
  - influencing it when this is possible and appropriate

2.7 ACTIVITIES

CASE STUDY

DMC plc

DMC's environmental analysis allowed them to capitalise on trends in the photocopier market

Jon Hill swivelled back in his chair and thought.

He and his fellow directors had built up DMC plc from scratch. They sold mainly photocopiers, printers and MFPs (multifunctional products, such as combined fax/printer/copiers) from leading manufacturers such as Canon, Panasonic, Samsung and Sharp. Their growth came from a commitment to high service levels and an aggressive buying policy. The business was now split into two divisions – Direct Sales and Distribution – to serve the needs of end users and trade customers respectively. This meant that in some instances DMC ended up competing directly with its own suppliers and customers.

Started in January 1991 with three staff, DMC grew within the year to a turnover of just over £200,000. By 2006, the business had reached a turnover of more than £12 million and a staff of seventy-five employed in offices in Croydon, Manchester and Shrewsbury.

But even this impressive growth was not enough for Jon. He was shrewd enough to realise that their growth could not continue in the increasing competitive environment without a more structured approach to their business. Whilst they were very good at selling they were unstructured in their approach to marketing. Jon had convinced his fellow directors to take on a marketing manager, Shrey Brahambhatt. Since they had never had a marketing manager before, the directors had no preconceptions.

Shrey had arranged a board meeting to present his initial findings. Although Jon had persuaded his fellow directors to take Shrey on, he wanted Shrey to prove his worth. He was not one to suffer fools gladly, and had no interest in analysis for its own sake.

He looked up at the door opened and Shrey walked in with his laptop ready to begin his presentation.

Shrey started with an outline of what he wanted to cover: 'Good morning all. I'd like to take half an hour of your time to describe my findings on the macro-environment in which DMC operates. The macro-environment is the factors we cannot alter but that we must adapt to. The structure I will use is that of a PEST analysis.'

One of the directors, who had an MBA, interrupted. 'I thought it was STEP or PESTLE. How is that different?'

Shrey agreed. 'Yes, those are very similar frameworks and all lead to the same point. The important thing is not so much the order that you cover the factors in as the outcome of them. I am using PEST but you could use any of them.'

He moved on to discuss the political factors affecting DMC's current and future business. As he explained, critical to DMC was a number of new EU measures, such as the EU directive RoHS (Restriction of Hazardous Substances) (2002/95/EC) which came into effect on 1 July, 2006. Under this directive, manufacturers of all applicable electrical and electronic products (including photocopiers) are prohibited from using six hazardous materials in their products in the EU market and must conform to RoHS compliance standards. Also another EU directive, WEEE (Waste from Electrical and Electronic Equipment) (2002/96/EC) mandates the treatment, recovery and recycling of electric and electronic equipment (90 per cent of which ends up in landfill). All applicable products in the EU market after 13 August, 2006 must pass WEEE compliance and carry the 'Wheelie Bin' sticker.

Jon was frustrated. This was going to be all analysis with no action. 'What does that mean to us?' he snapped.

Shrey explained. 'I was going to come on to that. You'll see on the next slide that next to each factor I've summarised the implications of each for DMC. So here next to RoHS you can see that the likely implication is increased cost for manufacturers (R&D, quality control, etc.). They are very likely to pass on this additional cost to dealers, distributors and retailers and hence may affect DMC's margins. We will also be required to provide compliance declarations to customers if they ask. For WEEE, the implications are very similar. Squeeze on margins and need to demonstrate compliance.'

Shrey covered other legislation and then moved onto to an issue that would affect their promotional activity. 'Under the Privacy and Electronic Communication (EC Directive) Regulations 2003, organisations in the UK are able to register their telephone numbers and facsimiles to Corporate Telephone Preference Service (CTPS) and Fax Preference Service (FPS), respectively, to avoid receiving unsolicited sales and marketing calls and faxes. Direct marketing companies such as DMC are obliged to screen data as frequently as is necessary to ensure that nobody protected by Regulations is contacted. This regulation also allows individuals to opt out of receiving any form of electronic communication'. As Shrey pointed out, since its launch in early 2005 more than 40,000 organisations in the UK have registered with CTPS.

The Direct Marketing Association (DMA) expects 10,000 new registrations every year.

Jon looked concerned. Telesales, especially cold calling, was a primary source of business development for DMC. 'What does that mean for us?' he asked.

Shrey responded. 'I don't think we have much choice but to comply. It will cost an extra £50 a month and hassle for screening data. But non-compliance with this will incur a £5,000 fine.'

Jon agreed. He was beginning to see the value of the analysis for the business and how it could be used.

Shrey moved on. As far as he could see, the UK economy was fairly strong on most indicators, which favoured DMC because as long as business was prospering, the demand for office equipment would remain buoyant. Projections were also good with forecasts of average annual GDP growth: 2.5 per cent (2006–10); inflation and unemployment set to remain below 3 and 5 per cent, respectively (2006–10) and no major swings in interest rates were expected in near future.

So with economics out of the way he moved onto the social and cultural issues that might impact on DMC's future.

He reported on the non-appearance of the much-predicted paperless society. 'Despite the increase in electronic communication, the output of printed documents continues to soar. Although organisations are reducing the percentage of documents that take the form of paper, the sheer volume of information is increasing at a faster rate, meaning that more pages are being printed or copied. In addition, there is still a tendency to back up electronic information with paper and to print out emails. While a large percentage of this paper is produced from printers, the output from copiers and other devices is also increasing. Within the home, the growing use of the Internet, email and digital photography continues to feed the rise in paper output. This is all good news for us.'

Another factor Shrey pointed out was that organisations are increasingly convinced of the value of colour in documents: 'Colour helps to get information noticed and can make it quicker and easier to comprehend data. One study reports a 75 per cent increase in message retention. Growth in the use of the Internet, and its reliance on colour, means more downloading of data and a need to print out some of this information in colour. However, common perception of colour equipment is that it is expensive to buy and maintain. Overall, though, this should have a positive effect on DMC's balance sheet as colour equipment generates higher service revenue, as well as initial margin.'

Shrey highlighted another important trend. Visual appeal of office equipment had become important and colour, size and shape were no longer regarded as frivolous considerations.

'One of our major suppliers is planning to launch the first stylish photocopier in early 2008 and other manufacturers are likely to follow. Wireless copiers/printers are also in the pipeline. This offers us upgrade opportunities as we can add value by recommending equipments that enhance the decor of customers' offices.'

Shrey was coming to the end of his presentation.

'And finally, perhaps the most exciting aspect of the macro-environment for us is technology. It offers both opportunities and threats. A simple opportunity, for example, is to adopt VoIP (Voice over Internet Protocol), which allows us to make voice calls (telephone) and video calls (desktop video-conferencing) using the Internet as a transmission method. SMEs, especially those like us who engage in telemarketing, are likely to get the most from VoIP as all calls to other VoIP users are free and other calls are cheaper than traditional telephony. We make over 15,000 telephone calls a month, so it makes sense to implement VoIP and reduce cost.'

Shrey was in full flow, enthused by the potential that technology offered his company. He went on to illustrate that it was not just about cost reduction.

'According to a recent survey conducted on behalf of *The Economist*, knowledge management offers the greatest potential for productivity gains than any other activity in organisations worldwide. The same survey projects a major shift in IT expenditure towards knowledge management, which historically has been focused on financial management and reporting. However, it also suggests that improving the productivity of knowledge workers (research and development, marketing, finance and IT) through technology, training and organisational change has become a major boardroom challenge.

DMC can leverage this opportunity by providing bespoke document management solutions to customers. The real value to customers will not be the hardware and software but the implementation, training and management of post-implementation change.'

The suggestion was greeted by animated discussion. The company was used to selling hardware and servicing the machines. This would be a huge shift.

Shrey moved on. 'Our market is changing and we have to move with it. We have to look for ways to add value. The products are changing rapidly. From being able to only print and copy, machines are becoming core communication devices. For example, we don't just have fax: we have iFax, scan to email, scan to network and so on. Machines are also becoming less dependent on external hardware such as the PC to perform day-to-day functions. Customers can print documents straight away by inserting their USB stick. They can scan and email documents directly from the machine, store and retrieve information directly from the equipment. Machines are becoming more and more convenient and user-friendly. Now customers can control the cost of printing and copying as equipment provides information such as usage rate, user, and remaining life of consumables on their PCs.'

Shrey paused. 'Here is our opportunity. The pace of change has left customers baffled for two reasons: first, customers are unable to decide on the equipment that is best suited to their needs; second, and more important, they are unaware of the other crucial benefits, or hidden needs, that these machines can bring into their business. Here, DMC have an opportunity to educate, guide and provide "bespoke solutions" based on customers' needs and help them reduce cost and increase efficiency.'

Shrey looked at his audience. The presentation was certainly not what they had been expecting.

Jon spoke first. 'I think we need some time to think about this.'

QUESTIONS

1 Provide a summary chart of Shrey's findings. Are there any implications he has missed?

2 Are there any other factors you would have included in a PEST analysis of this market? Has Shrey missed anything?

3 How would you structure a PowerPoint (or other) presentation of an environmental analysis?

4 What would you do in Jon's position?

5 What could be the impact of the Internet on a business like this?

DEVELOPING A MARKETING PLAN

AN INTERNAL AUDIT

Carry out an internal review or 'audit' of the organisation or product of your choice. This should enable you to summarise its strengths and weaknesses in relation to any future marketing activities. In particular consider the objectives, resources, culture and structure of the organisation or enterprise that will implement the marketing plan. Identify basic information such as product range, sales or income, past marketing objectives, methods and success rates, where they exist. (See also Chapter 12 for a summary of areas to be covered.)

2.8 FURTHER READING AND REFERENCES

Public sector marketing

Sargeant, A. (2005), *Marketing Management for Nonprofit Organizations* (Oxford University Press), Chapter 3.

Entrepreneurial marketing

GEM (2006), *Global Entrepreneurship Monitor Report 2005*, London Business School.
Stokes, D. (2006), 'Marketing in Small Firms', in Carter S. and Jones-Evans D. (eds), *Enterprise and Small Business Development* (FT/Prentice Hall).

Impact of the internet

Chaffey, D., Mayer, R., Johnston, K. and Ellis-Chadwick, F. (2003), *Internet Marketing*, 2nd edition (Pearson Education), Chapter 4.

Chapter **3**

CUSTOMERS AND COMPETITORS

LEARNING OBJECTIVES

By the end of this chapter the reader will be able to:

■ Understand the difference between market 'needs' and 'wants'
■ Differentiate between the features and benefits of a product or service
■ Analyse the structure of a market as a complex chain of buyers and suppliers
■ Assess the significance of markets other than the direct buyers of a product or service
■ Evaluate the competitive forces at work in a particular industry or market

INTRODUCTION

The theme of 'customers' and their 'needs' is of such significance in the study of marketing that this chapter looks at the meaning of these words more closely. It seeks to define customer 'needs' compared to 'wants' and examines some of the different types of customers. It looks at how customers are grouped into markets with different needs that are reflected in differing perceptions of the benefits of buying a particular item. Markets are not restricted to direct consumers of what an organisation produces. Other groups influence the marketing environment, including distributors, employees and suppliers and these all have to be considered in a marketing strategy. The competitive forces at play in any given market also require careful analysis as these indicate the power you have in the marketplace.

3.1 NEEDS, WANTS AND DEMANDS

We have described marketing as an exchange process that matches the capabilities of suppliers with the needs of customers. If sufficient people *want* a product or service then the role of marketing is to match this *demand* with the supply of a product which meets this *need*. Notice

CASE STUDY

··

KITWELL JEANS

Dominique Saldo was working on a marketing strategy report to the directors of her company, Kitwell Ltd. She had recently been appointed as marketing manager of this clothing manufacturer and wanted to make an impact with her first presentation to the board. The problem was that the way forward was far from clear in her mind.

Kitwell was a long-established producer of work clothing and men's and boys' jeans. Originally a manufacturer of workwear garments, the company had turned to making jeans in the 1950s. This had almost certainly saved the company from the fate of many other manufacturers in the post-war years who found themselves unable to compete with cheaper production of textiles and clothing, principally in the Far East. The clothing industry had become increasingly polarised into a small number of large companies able to generate sufficient economies of scale to survive and a large, fragmented group of smaller manufacturers relying on their rapid, flexible response to demand from specialised markets.

Fortunately for Kitwell, they concentrated on what was to become the most profitable product sector of the clothing market – jeans. The metamorphosis of jeans from the utilitarian working garment of the early century to a symbol of youthful rebellion in the 1950s and 60s continued into the next century as they became a highly branded fashion garment. Jeans are still an essential item in any young person's wardrobe. Consumers buy sixty million pairs per annum in the UK, representing sales of over £1 billion at retail prices. Approximately £10 million of advertising supports well-known brand names that control an estimated 85 per cent of total sales. The brand differentiation of otherwise similar products has allowed prices to become relatively high and manufacturer's margins remain good compared to other sectors of the clothing market.

Kitwell had prospered by developing good relationships with the key outlets for jeans – the multiple chains and specialist jeans retailers. Instead of competing with the top brand names, Kitwell had concentrated on producing own-label garments for the multiples and one-off special products and sale offers for the specialist retailers. They sold direct to the larger retail chains and through wholesale warehouses and cash-and-carry outlets to smaller retailers. However these relationships were often complex; for example, they subcontracted some of their larger orders to other overseas manufacturers and some of their wholesale outlets also sold direct to the public.

Dominique reflected on her briefing meeting with the managing director.

'Keep it simple', he had told her. 'We are dealing with an eternal fashion garment, and it's the under twenty-five-year-olds who drive fashion. Whatever we do, we must maintain our saleability to that age group.'

But a number of factors made Dominique uncomfortable with the tried and tested approach. First, the age group that they had historically relied upon had decreased in number. In the late 1980s there were nearly sixteen million fifteen- to twenty-four-year-olds in the UK, but numbers had fallen to twelve million by the turn of the century. Second, there were signs that the new generation of that age group would neither want the same clothes, nor buy them through traditional outlets. An increasing demand for 'environmentally friendly' jeans made of organic fibres and natural fabrics was one sign of change. Dominique also recognised that the youth market was the most likely group to adopt new behavioural patterns as a result of advances in information and communications technology. Buyers under twenty-five already formed a significant percentage of Internet shoppers. Clothing was a fast-developing ecommerce purchase category, although it still lagged behind favourite online products – CDs, DVDs, books and computer items. Could jeans manufacturers afford to be driven by this increasingly volatile section of the market when other groups

▶

Jeans cover the age ranges in different colours and styles

© PHOTOALTO/ALAMY

such as children under fourteen and the over-forty-five-year-olds had become more numerous?

The nature of competition was also changing. Kitwell, like other surviving manufacturers, had side-stepped the cheaper imports by concentrating on shorter runs of the latest styles. Now other producers in Europe – particularly the Republic of Ireland, France, Belgium, Italy and Malta – were taking an increasing share of this market. The leading brands increasingly adopted a global approach to their marketing, competing in North American and European markets with the same products and promotional strategies. At the same time they multiplied the number of products on offer. Jeans were no longer the standard blue denim of the 1960s as colours and finishes proliferated. Darker shades in looser fits currently prevailed over the tighter look of the 1990s. Dominique also noted that one of the leading brands had launched a range of corduroy jeans. Could it be that the market for the basic five-pocket denim jean had peaked? She recalled that earlier in the 1980s the sale of jeans had declined sharply as other types of casual trousers had become more popular – until the re-launch of Levi's 501 jeans through the famous 'launderette' advertising campaign had revitalised the whole market.

Their direct customers in the wholesale and retail trade were also becoming more demanding. For example, the delivery time for supply of new lines to some multiples had become shorter and shorter as the retailers tried to stay on top of the shifts in consumer demand. Dominique recalled the exasperation on the face of Kitwell's manufacturing manager as he had explained to her his difficulty in changing production lines from the 'distressed, ripped' look to an 'antique' finish in a matter of days. There was also a trend for manufacturers to become retailers as some of the well-known names had begun to open up their own outlets selling direct to the public.

Dominique knew that she would have to come up with something special if they were to survive in a market in which a declining number of key consumers were being chased by too many competitive products.

QUESTIONS

1 Consider the needs and wants of customers in the jeans market. What is the underlying customer need that jeans are fulfilling? What do different types of customers want when they buy a pair of jeans? *See sections 3.1 and 3.2*

2 Examine the structure of Kitwell's market. Who are their direct customers and what benefits do these customers seek from their suppliers? (It may be useful to draw a diagram of the various types of customers in the chain between manufacturer and consumer). What business should Kitwell consider themselves to be in? *See sections 3.3 and 3.4*

3 Analyse the competitive forces in the jeans market. What is the state of development of the market and what are the trends among existing competitors? How will the relative power between the buyers and suppliers influence developments? How great are the barriers that may deter new entrants? What are the likely threats from substitute products? Are these factors likely to improve or depress the profitability of the industry? *See sections 3.5 and 3.6*

4 Suggest some marketing strategies that Dominique could consider.

that we have used three different terms in this sentence – *want*, *demand* and *need* – to indicate the rationale for the supply of products and services to customers. Each has a complementary but different significance in the role of marketing.

3.1.1 Needs

What do we *need* to survive and thrive in this life? This fundamental question is perhaps more relevant to philosophical debates on the meaning of life than to a book on marketing, but its significance here lies in the distinction that can be made between our needs and our wants.

If you were asked to write a list of everything you wanted and a list of everything you needed, which would be the longer list? The chances are that your list of wants is longer than your assessment of your needs. Although we tend to *want* many things, our basic *needs* are relatively few. The American psychologist Abraham Maslow (1954) narrowed them down to five key needs, arranged as a series of steps, or a 'hierarchy of needs', from the most fundamental to the most difficult to obtain (Figure 3.1).

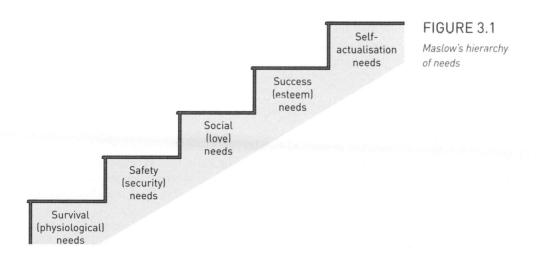

FIGURE 3.1

Maslow's hierarchy of needs

- *Survival (or physiological) needs* are the basic biological requirements for the survival of our bodies. As they include such fundamental needs as food, drink and sleep, we cannot consider other desires until these are met. If we are very hungry and tired, our concern for other needs is minimised until we have eaten and slept. We tend to take the fulfilment of these needs for granted in affluent societies, until the means to gratify them is removed. Threats to survival such as ill health sweep away our concerns for other needs, as anyone who has suffered serious illness will testify.

  Once we have satisfied one level of need, we progress to the next. According to Maslow, 'man is a wanting animal. As one desire is satisfied, another pops up to take its place.' When it does, we tend to lose interest in the fulfilled need and concentrate our energies on the next level of need. Once our physiological needs for survival are met, we tend to take them for granted as we seek to fulfil other needs higher up the ladder.

- *Safety (or security) needs* are next in the hierarchy. Included here is the need for some guarantee that our physical needs will be met in the foreseeable future – that we will have shelter and some form of income. We like to have the security of knowing that at least our basic needs can be met for some time to come.

- *Social (or love) needs* indicate our desire to belong to a group where we are accepted and receive affection. This may be represented by family, friends, workmates, a sports team or social club. The use of solitary confinement, a punishment that deliberately excludes the possibility of social contact, illustrates the significance of this need.

- *Success (or esteem) needs* include our desire for achievement to improve our self-image and enhance our status as perceived by others. Whilst Maslow recognised our need for prestige, he also observed that the healthiest self-esteem is based on deserved respect and not the external symbols of success.

- *Self-actualisation* completes our hierarchy of needs. It means developing ourselves to our full potential, 'to become everything that one is capable of becoming'. It is a measure of the unique contribution each individual can make and the extent to which they feel they have made it, a reflection of the belief that 'what a man can be, he *must* be'.

Maslow's classification of needs has been widely used as a basis for understanding more about human motivation. It contributes to marketing theory by illustrating that relatively few basic needs motivate our acquisition of seemingly countless products and services. We buy products as a means to the end of fulfilling these needs, not as an end in themselves. Although Maslow's hierarchy represents only a psychological interpretation of our needs, it demonstrates that we can only understand what customers want by looking at what lies behind a purchase decision.

3.1.2 Wants

Wants represent the means of fulfilling needs and can be innumerable. Take a child into a toy store and they will usually express many different wants. The child may be expressing a single need in their social desire for play, but they will see many ways of meeting that need on display in the toyshop. A shopper in a supermarket will buy many items as they translate their physiological *need* for food into *wanting* various food products.

Our wants represent how we wish a need to be fulfilled, as conditioned by our past and present environment. As a need can usually be satisfied by a number of alternatives, we choose how we wish a need to be filled and 'want' that particular option. A child's social needs can be met by a range of options from wooden toys to computer games. Our need for food can be met by a huge choice from pork chops to chop suey.

Which of the alternatives we choose is conditioned by our past and present circumstances. As well as current economic circumstances, our social and cultural background plays an important role. We would expect the food contents of a shopping basket in Manila to be very different to one in Manchester. These and other factors lead to a preference for a specific alternative, and this choice constitutes a 'want'.

3.1.3 Demand

Wants are not always translated into actual purchases of a product or service. We may want many more products than we can afford. A demand for goods can only become effective when it is linked to an ability to obtain them, usually by paying for them. The economic concept of *demand* for a certain product assumes that those who want it can also afford its price.

Thus *effective demand* represents *affordable wants*. If we want a product but are unable to purchase it because we cannot afford it or for another reason, then this represents a *latent demand* for a product. I may need a drink and want a glass of champagne, but I cannot afford it (latent demand) so I buy a glass of wine instead, thereby adding to the (effective) demand for that product.

In considering all of our possible wants, we give them some sort of priority order and satisfy them until our available resources are depleted. The problem for suppliers is to make sure their product is high enough up the priority list of sufficient potential purchasers. This is the role of marketing.

In summary:

- A *need* is something necessary for the maintenance of life at either a basic or more evolved level

- A *want* is a choice of how that need is to be fulfilled

- *Demand* is made up of the total number of those wanting a specific product who are also prepared to pay its price

FOR EXAMPLE

Do you want to become a space tourist?

Do we need to travel outside of the Earth's atmosphere? There have been some significant commercial benefits from our ability to send objects into space. The worldwide satellite industry has sales of over £50 billion and employs a quarter of a million people. It remains a growth industry because it meets our basic need for better and easier communications here on earth.

Access to space has also contributed to the development of human knowledge in revealing the nature of the universe. Space travel has allowed us to place scientific instruments and observatories in orbit and to send robot probes to the planets, fulfilling the human need articulated by Aristotle: 'All men by nature desire to know.'

Recent developments have been more controversial. Private space travel could in future meet the needs of the human spirit for self-fulfillment. According to surveys by the Space Transportation Association, a majority of Americans would take a trip into space if they could afford it. One person who could afford it was Anousheh Ansari, an Iranian-born telecommunications entrepreneur who became the world's first female space tourist in September 2006. She blasted off from Kazakhstan on a flight in a Soyuz capsule accompanied by a US-Russian crew who were starting a six-month shift at the international space station. She returned to Earth ten days later with the outgoing crew. She is one of only four space tourists so far who have all paid over £10 million for their seats. The need? She claims it was to 'fulfil her childhood dream' but she also plans to use her experience to help with a project to develop suborbital spacecraft. The aims of the project are to make space travel more affordable and accessible to more people.

© YURI KOCHETKOV/EPA/CORBIS

Anousheh Ansari before her flight to achieve her childhood dream

CHECKPOINT

If you could afford it, would you want to become a space tourist? If yes, which of your needs would you be fulfilling?

3.2 MARKETING MYOPIA

The significance of understanding these terms is more than just an appreciation of definitions. The role of marketing, at the interface between supply and demand, is to interpret our needs and make available wanted products and services that we can afford. However, there is a danger that marketing can develop a myopic view about what is needed by customers. In supplying the existing demand for a product it is possible to believe it is 'needed', when in fact it is only 'wanted' until something better comes along.

3.2.1 Levitt's drill bits

Theodore Levitt (1960), the well-known management writer, called this 'marketing myopia', giving the example of a supplier of drill bits. Because drill bits have been in demand for so long,

MARKETING MISTAKES

THE NORTH AMERICAN RAILROADS

Levitt demonstrated how this 'myopia' applies to whole industries, citing the example of the American railroads. The development of the steam engine revolutionised transport systems during the nineteenth century. The North American railroads were instrumental in opening up the whole continent and setting the USA on course to becoming the richest economy on earth. The railroad companies shared in that growth and by the twentieth century they had become one of the most prosperous and powerful industries in the country. Their decline was as spectacular as their rise; half a century later the industry was in ruins with services drastically reduced, often only surviving through government subsidies.

Levitt's judgement on their rise and fall is that railroad owners and managers mistook wants for needs, believing that people would always need their services, when in fact they needed the most effective, convenient, economic transportation system available. The invention of the internal combustion engine and the development of air transport provided alternatives to meet that need that became more and more attractive – and therefore wanted – in preference to rail.

MARKETING MISTAKES

THE UK COAL INDUSTRY

Many major industries, such as coal mining in the UK, have followed a similar pattern to the North American railways. Coal was the dominant form of energy when the Industrial Revolution began to transform manufacturing and communications in the nineteenth century. Mining companies struggled to keep up with demand and concentrated their efforts on becoming the most efficient extractors of coal. Alternative forms of power were soon to remind them that they were in the energy business, not the coal extraction business as first oil, nuclear power and then North Sea gas eroded their share of the market.

a supplier can be forgiven for believing that their products were 'needed' by all their seemingly loyal customers. However, those customers do not 'need' drill bits. They need what the drill bits produce – holes. Customers 'want' drill bits, but only so long as there is not a better way of producing holes. Once an affordable, superior product becomes available – a hand-held laser drill perhaps – then demand will shift to that product which will then become 'wanted' by those who 'need' holes.

One of the keys to avoiding myopia is first to go back to the basics of defining the consumer need that your product meets, and from this position define the competitive marketplace that you are in.

FOR EXAMPLE

······································

MTV

MTV was the pioneer in the music TV category and has enjoyed dominance for most of its life, but now there are more than twenty music channels available on the Sky platform. MTV's biggest broadcast rival is Emap, whose TV brands include *The Hits*, Magic, Kiss, *Smash Hits* and *Kerrang*. According to the British Audience Research Bureau figures, MTV networks has a 53 per cent share of the music channel viewing audience compared with Emap's 35 per cent.

MTV has expanded its offering into the general entertainment field, although still focusing on the youth market

As MTV has moved from being a pure music channel to a more general entertainment offering with its flagship shows such as *Pimp My Ride* and *The Osbournes*, it has encountered additional competition. E4, for example has launched E4 Music and Trouble, both of which are trying to snatch MTV's youth audience. Trouble also has a user-generated community site, Homegrown.

In a digital marketplace, TV channels are by no means MTV's only competitors, with Napster and iTunes presenting an obvious challenge. MTV also faces competition from brands that want to align themselves with music using digital technology. Online brands are also hunting down exclusive music content; AOL, for example, offered Instant Messenger interviews with high-profile bands and coverage of events such as Live 8 to get closer to its customers.

Mobile networks are also adding to the competition. The phone network 3 had the exclusive on downloading a Madonna video. The company gains revenue from music on its phones and is aiming to create a community through its mobile TV channel See Me TV. MTV has just followed suit with its online community channel Flux which brings it into competition with established players such as MySpace and YouTube.

MARKETING, 2 AUGUST, 2006, PAGE 30.

3.2.2 Overcoming myopia

Levitt's interpretation of the demise of once-great industries like the railroads has been criticised because it does not necessarily indicate what can be done to correct decline. Even if the railroad owners had recognised early enough that alternative transport systems would develop, what could they have done about it? Alternative successful strategies are not obvious. However, some important management concepts emerge from this example that influence how we think of customers and the demand-and-supply equation.

■ Customers are loyal to the capabilities of a product to fulfil needs, not to the products themselves. They buy the end result, not the means to achieve it. The MTV example above illustrates how consumers may want to listen to music but they don't care how it is delivered.

■ Products are wanted only for a limited time before demand shifts to other products which represent a preferred means to the same end. Music can now come via vinyl, audio cassettes, CDs, music channels, mobile phones and MP3 players. Each technology has superseded the other without completely replacing it. The consumer is only interested in the end result.

■ Any organisation which limits itself to a product that represents only one means of achieving the desired result is therefore limiting its own life expectancy. Companies in the music market need to take a broad view of the competition and focus on the final consumer needs that they wish to meet.

We will discuss each of these propositions in turn in the next section on matching benefits and customers.

3.3 MATCHING BENEFITS TO CUSTOMERS

3.3.1 Features and benefits

As customers, we want products that fulfil our identified needs, and we buy them because of their capability to meet our needs. We buy products because of what they can do *for us*. In other words we are really interested in the *benefits* that a product offers us, not in the product for its own sake. We buy drill bits because we need holes, not because we like drill bits. We choose a particular type of drill bit in preference to another because it offers benefits that are appropriate to what we want: it is longer lasting and can make holes in masonry, for example.

Salespeople are trained to distinguish between the *features* of a product and its *benefits* for the very reason that we buy a product for the benefits that it offers us, and not to acquire its features.

■ The *features* of a product describe its characteristics. For example, a mountain bike has the features of a sturdy frame, thick tyres and fifteen gears; a business loan account has the feature of a fixed rate of interest

■ The *benefits* of a product describe the value that its features provide to a customer. For example, the features of a mountain bike give it the benefit of being able to travel more easily over rough hilly terrain and withstand this type of use for longer; the feature of a fixed rate of interest gives this type of business loan account the benefit of predictable repayment amounts and therefore more certainty in planning cash flow

We want products only if the benefits offered match what we need. If we want a bike in order to travel over rough terrain we will be attracted by the benefits of the mountain bike. If, however, we want a bike for use only on flat roads then some of these benefits disappear and become disadvantages. We may prefer less sturdy but lighter bicycles. Similarly, if our business needs the lowest possible rate of interest then we may not see an account with a fixed rate as beneficial and prefer a more flexible type of account. Our loyalty to a fixed interest rate account lasts only whilst it fulfils our particular need.

3.3.2 *Product mortality*

If customers buy benefits rather than the products themselves, then the demand for a product is determined by its success in providing the benefits that customers prefer to those offered by alternative products. However, changes to both supply and demand restrict the length of time that those benefits will be preferred.

■ The supply of new or improved products quickly makes existing products obsolete when superior benefits are offered. For example, the microchip offered benefits to electronics manufacturers through superior performance and smaller size which could not be matched by the transistor components which had hitherto dominated the industry. Just as the railroads offered benefits of speed, economies of scale and comfort over the stagecoach services they replaced, so they in turn were dislodged by the superior convenience of the automobile.

■ The demand for products or services may also decline because of changes in the market environment. For example, a decline in the consumption of beers and lager in Europe has been caused not by the emergence of a new product but by changes to the age profile of the population, greater awareness of the problems created by alcohol abuse and tougher laws on drinking and driving.

Like living organisms, products seem doomed to an inevitable cycle which foresees eventual decline after initial phases of growth. This so-called *product life cycle* is described more fully in Chapter 7, as it is an important concept in the management of the product ingredient in the marketing mix. Customers are fickle and owe no loyalty to products themselves, only to the benefits that they provide.

3.3.3 *What business are we in?*

If an organisation aligns itself closely to *the means* of fulfilling a need (for example, a specific product), rather than to the need itself then it is linking itself to the same inevitable cycle of growth and decline. Levitt's railroad managers myopically saw themselves in the railroad business, thus tying their fortunes to that one particular means of fulfilling our transportation needs. Their business declined with the product.

In order to avoid the same myopia, some guidelines are recommended:

■ Organisations and companies define their activities by asking '*what are we really here for?*' or '*what business are we in?*' It is important that the answers refer to customer needs, *not* specific ways of meeting them. The drill-bit supplier is in the business of providing a means of making holes not the business of manufacturing drill bits. Many organisations in the public as well as in the private sector have drawn up statements of 'mission' or organisational objectives for this reason.

■ Organisations need to know what their customers are seeking *in terms of benefits.* They also need to know if the benefits their products offer are still relevant and how they rate compared to competitors.

■ This process of matching product benefits to what customers want is a *continuous* one as changes to both supply and demand are inevitable.

CHECKPOINT

Think of a product you have purchased recently. Analyse the wants and needs that prompted your purchase. In what other ways could you have fulfilled the same need? What specific benefits prompted you to fulfil your needs this way rather than the alternatives?

3.4 WHO ARE CUSTOMERS?

We have so far referred to customers as if they receive products and services directly from the original suppliers. We have also assumed that the purchaser of a product is also the user of the product. This oversimplified view of the exchange of product or service between producer and user is in reality a long and complex chain involving many parties and influences.

3.4.1 Customers or consumers?

Customers are not always the *consumer* of the product that is purchased. Shoppers buying food do not necessarily eat it all themselves; the person paying for the contents of a supermarket trolley is unlikely to consume it all alone. We buy many products that we share with others or offer to them as gifts. Parents frequently purchase goods that are used by their children. This applies not only to products such as toys and clothes but also services such as education and leisure activities, which are often chosen by parents for their children.

This complicates the question of needs and benefits. Whose needs should the supplier aim to meet – the purchasers' or the users'? Who determines which benefits are most important – the child demanding fun and excitement from their toy or leisure activity, or the parent looking for safety and economy?

Both sets of demands are important in assessing how to match product benefits with customer choice. The role of marketing is to take into account all the important influences on the decision to purchase or to use a particular product or service.

3.4.2 Customer chains

Before a product is finally 'consumed' it usually passes through several stages of manufacture, preparation and distribution. At each stage, suppliers pass on products to the next customer down the line until they reach the final consumer. Customers exist in chains that stretch from raw material producers to High Street shoppers.

FOR EXAMPLE

A CHAIN OF PEAS

Even a relatively simple product such as a tin of peas passes through several types of supplier and customer. Farmers may sell their crop of peas directly to one customer, a canning factory. The canner is under contract to their customer, a national company marketing tinned food products,

FIGURE 3.2 *Changing benefits in the supply chain of a tin of peas*

which in turn sells the product to a national supermarket chain via their wholesaler. The whole-saler distributes the product to the retail store where the final consumer or end user buys the product.

Any assessment of customer needs and the matching benefits to be offered has to take account of the benefits required by the next link in the chain and the needs of their customers further down the chain, as well as the requirements of the ultimate consumer. This is illustrated in Figure 3.2.

■ The farmer has to meet the needs of the canning company, which has specified what it will accept in terms of the size and tenderness of the crop. The farmer decides that the benefit most appreciated by the customer is the dependability of producing regular crops matching the required standards of pea size and tenderness.

■ The canning factory has been guided by its customer, the food company for whom it has to meet specifications relating to canning and labelling operations. It believes it was awarded the contract by the food company because it offered the benefit of the lowest price for production according to the specification.

■ The national food company convinces the supermarket chain to stock its product because it provides benefits to both the wholesale and retail divisions.

■ The wholesale division of the chain wants to be assured of the ease of handling the finished goods. It is happy because the packaging offers convenient storage and efficient distribution.

■ The retail division wishes to stock only those items that sell quickly, so it prefers products that are supported by promotions and priced competitively. It benefits from the high turnover of this fast-moving product which contributes to their profit objectives.

■ The supermarket chain believes that its customer, the end user, selects his or her preferred product on the basis of taste and brand name at an affordable price. It therefore offers its shoppers the benefit of reliability of quality associated with purchasing a nationally advertised brand of peas.

The 'chain of peas' example is a simplified version of the many influences on customer choice at each stage of the chain. Its purpose is to illustrate that customers and the benefits they are seeking represent 'moving targets' depending on their position in the chain. The farmer's perspective of what his or her customer wants and the benefits to be offered is different to that of others in the chain, although all the links influence each other and depend ultimately on the preferences of the final user.

FOR EXAMPLE
....

AN UNUSUAL BENEFIT FROM A TIN OF PEAS

For a food tin, the inexpensive can of mushy peas illustrated here provides an unusual benefit. It raises money for charity every year. At a charity auction in Bergen, Norway a framed tin of mushy peas was first offered for auction in 1998. The successful bidder re-donated the tin for the following year's auction. The next year's successful bidder did the same, and so a tradition was established. The total raised over seven years exceeds £10,000 and the framed tin permanently resides in a hospital in Bergen to remind patients and visitors of the generosity of the charity auction guests.

This can of mushy peas has so far raised over £10,000 for charity

3.4.3 Complex chains

Many chains are much more complicated than the tin of peas example given above, which uses relatively few stages of production and distribution. For example:

■ Some *manufacturing customer chains* are extensive and complicated. The various products that make up a car, from the rubber for the tyres to the electronic components for the ignition system, pass through lengthy and complex chains of suppliers and customers.

■ The *distribution chain* of a finished product can also involve several customers in different stages. A car assembled in one country and sold in another passes through various levels of exporters, importers, agents and distributors before reaching the end user.

■ *Subsidiary chains* exist to provide goods and services to the organisations in the main customer chain. The car manufacturer requires equipment and machinery, which is supplied by a subsidiary chain of design engineers, equipment manufacturers and suppliers.

Each link in a customer chain buys other products or services to help them fulfil their role in the chain; they become someone else's customer. In the example of the pea chain, the farmer is the customer of fertiliser producers and farm equipment manufacturers. The canning factory buys pre-formed cans and labels. The food company is the customer of an advertising agency. The supermarket is the final customer in a chain of architects, surveyors, planners and building contractors whose end product is a new out-of-town retail store.

The relevance to marketing lies in understanding the impact of these complex relationships on customer needs. The producer of fertiliser has to understand the needs of other customers in the chain of a tin of peas in order to understand the needs of their direct customer, the farmer. The farmer needs to provide the benefit of a dependable pea crop to their customer, the canning factory, and they judge the fertiliser they buy on its ability to help deliver this benefit. The problem for the fertiliser producer is that other customers have different priorities. For example, other farmers may put freedom from harmful environmental effects as top of their list of required benefits, as this is demanded by the customers in their particular chain.

3.4.4 Internal customers

Customers can also exist within an organisation. Internal relationships may be organised on the basis of suppliers and customers.

■ Larger businesses sometimes trade between operating divisions by treating the receiver of goods or services as a customer. For example:

— The management of a factory manufacturing electrical goods regards the overseas company responsible for assembling and selling its products in a particular country as its customer even though they are both part of the same multinational corporation. This decentralised approach attempts to overcome complacent attitudes towards captive markets of internal customers who have no choice of supplier.

— The wholesaler and retailer in the 'chain of peas' example may be owned by the same supermarket group, which has organised its operations on the basis of arm's-length trading between units, treating each other as customers or suppliers in the normal way.

■ Changes to many public services has attempted to create supplier–customer relationships. Reorganisations have separated 'providers' from 'purchasers' of services within the same public authority.

FOR EXAMPLE

— Doctors within the National Health Service (NHS) are allocated money to purchase the healthcare needed by their patients. Although they are likely to specify their local hospital, they can opt to send a patient to other institutions for treatment. So a hospital now has several types of 'customers':

— Purchasing agents within the NHS (e.g. GPs) that buy a range of healthcare services from the hospital on behalf of the residents of a certain area

— Other purchasers external to the NHS, such as health insurance companies (e.g. BUPA) that pay for private patient services in the hospital

— The end user (or patients) who are the consumers in the sense that they receive the care that has been purchased on their behalf

■ Organisations have an internal market of 'stakeholders', or people with an interest in the organisation (as we have seen in Chapter 3). These interest groups act in some ways as customers because they influence how much income, investment or other resources an organisation receives even though they do not directly pay for or receive products or services from the organisation. For example:

— The board of directors of a company decides which of its operating divisions receive major investments for new projects or equipment. Divisions make 'bids' to the board by putting forward their case for an allocation of money in a similar way to making a sales presentation to persuade a prospective customer to spend money on certain products.

— The elected councillors of a local government body allocate taxpayers' money between the various services for which they are responsible. Such services as education, highways and the fire brigade compete for funds on the basis of the benefits they provide to the taxpayer. The Council decides which benefits have greatest priority and therefore receive most funds, just as an individual spends his or her income by deciding which benefits, via products and services, they most wish to purchase.

CHECKPOINT

Take an industry of which you have some knowledge (even if only as a consumer, such as the food or clothing industries). Draw a picture of the customer chains that exist within it, specifying the industrial, intermediary, government and consumer markets. What are the characteristics of these markets (in terms of their immaturity or maturity, relative numbers of customers, purchase frequency, etc.)? Are there any signs or past examples of 'marketing myopia' amongst the suppliers?

3.5 MARKETS

3.5.1 Markets old and new

Markets originated as places where buyers and sellers met to exchange goods. The term is now used in a variety of ways to describe:

■ A grouping of customers with similar needs (for example, the 'teenage market')

■ The total demand for a certain product, service or process (the 'jeans market')

■ A combination of the two (the 'teenage jeans market')

In marketing, the term also has some important derivatives.

3.5.2 Market share

The demand for one particular product as a percentage of the total demand of the market is an expression of that product's *market share*. It is a particularly important measurement of success in marketing. Competitors seek to become the *market leader* by enjoying the largest percentage share of a market. A large market share for a product indicates a high level of customer acceptance which in turn can give the supplier several advantages, including:

■ Lower production costs through longer runs

■ Cheaper raw materials and components because of bulk purchasing

■ Other economies of scale because fixed costs such as rent are apportioned over more units sold, thus lowering the cost per unit

■ Greater product awareness in the marketplace because of high sales

■ Greater influence over other customers in the chain to achieve preferential treatment (such as better display in retail outlets)

These and other advantages make the achievement of high market share a very desirable marketing aim. They can be translated into higher profits, or used to increase customer satisfaction by, for example, lower prices or more investment into the research and development of new products.

■ *Potential markets* The role of marketing is to look for potential new customers as well as to satisfy existing ones. This means exploring how to enlarge the total market by adding new types of customers. A high share of one market can provide the resources and incentive to look elsewhere for customers. It can also allow 'blind spots' to develop through over-concentration on a particular group of customers and its needs. The extension of the computer market from business customers to users in the home was not pioneered by the existing dominant forces in the market such as IBM, but by newcomers like Amstrad and Apple.

■ *Immature markets* Markets pass through different stages of development, mirroring the life cycles of the products which are sold in them. New or immature markets tend to be fragmented between many suppliers seeking to benefit from the technological or other change that has created it. In this formative stage, the market provides high growth and high profit margins for the supplying organisations, although this does not usually translate into positive cash flows because of the levels of investment required.

KPMG REPORT, CONSUMER MARKETS AT A CROSSROADS, 2006.

FOR EXAMPLE

Central and Eastern Europe (CEE) is an example of an immature market. This market is emerging, with many retailers and suppliers entering the market, but the simultaneous entry of many multinational retailers has created its own problems and some markets have over heated as a result. For example, Poland has fourteen multinational retailers competing for a share and the Czech Republic has eleven.

However, CEE has benefited from this influx. Those local retailers who have survived have learnt from their foreign rivals. The retailing infrastructure of the countries has improved and the new competition has forced the national retailers to raise their game.

■ *Mature markets* Markets become mature as growth slackens and weaker suppliers are shaken out. Radical innovation of products and services tends to give way to modification and minor improvements as the small number of remaining suppliers fight for market share. Price competition erodes profit margins but cash flows can be positive for suppliers, who often seek to take the benefits of their original investment at this stage.

3.5.3 Organisational and consumer markets

Customers form many different markets but a distinction can be made between two basic types: organisational markets and consumer markets.

Organisational markets

In some markets the customers are organisations such as businesses, public sector institutions or social enterprises. They buy goods and services for use in their own processes, production and service delivery, or for resale to other customers. Most products pass through organisational customers before reaching the final consumer; in some cases, organisations are the final user:

■ The tin of peas in our earlier example passed through several organisational customers before it reached the shopper, including the canning factory, the food company, and the supermarket wholesaler and retailer. The supermarket company was the final customer in the chain of organisations which built the retail store, a 'product' that was only ever involved in organisational markets.

■ A service provided by a hospital, such as an X-ray of a patient, is at the end of a chain of several organisations, including the research organisation that developed the technology of the X-ray process, the manufacturer that built the equipment, the agent who sold it, the health authority that bought it and the hospital that used it.

Organisational markets can be further divided into three main types: industrial markets, intermediary markets and government markets, as illustrated:

■ *Industrial markets* consist of customers who buy products and services that are further processed or used in the production of new products and services. The canning factory is part of an industrial market involved in the processing and packaging of foods. The X-ray equipment manufacturer is part of the industrial market for electro-magnetic equipment and medical supplies.

■ *Intermediary markets* are made up of customers who buy products or services for resale to others. They do not change the products they purchase but add value to them in some other way, often by providing a distribution service. The supermarket wholesaler and retailer, for example, bought tins of peas in their finished form for resale to their customers, to whom they offered the additional benefit of a convenient, centralised shopping facility. An agent sold the x-ray equipment to the health authority because the manufacturer was an overseas company that needed the services of an intermediary responsible for importing and selling in certain markets.

■ *Government markets* consist of public sector organisations that buy products and services as part of their provision of services to the public. School catering services are customers in a local government market, and purchase tins of peas and other food products (probably in bulk from the food company). The X-ray equipment was sold to a public health authority for use in a hospital, both customers in a government market responsible for health services.

Consumer markets

We are all involved in consumer markets as individuals or as part of a household purchasing goods and services. We may be a *direct* consumer, buying for our own personal consumption or an *indirect* consumer, purchasing on behalf of others (for example, purchases of food for a household or gifts for friends). Consumer markets are often broad, with a wide range of customers (such as those who exist for our tin of peas). However some are more specialised, consisting of customers with special interests and needs (stamp collecting or health foods, for example).

Although individual markets vary considerably, organisational and consumer markets exhibit some generalised differences between them.

■ *Demand in organisational markets is derived from other customers in the chain and ultimately the end user.* Changes in consumption patterns further down the chain eventually affect those higher up. For example, the widespread introduction of refrigerators and freezers into households reduced the demand for tinned products as more consumers purchased frozen foods in packets. Retailers, such as the supermarket chains, adjusted their stocks accordingly, which affected the sales of the food company and the canning factory.

■ *Purchasing patterns are usually different.* As consumers, we tend to buy a large number of relatively low-value products on a frequent basis. Consumer markets therefore tend to be made up of large numbers of customers spending small amounts reasonably often. The marketing implications are that the suppliers of consumer markets cannot deal on a personal basis with their customers. They tend to rely on advertising to communicate with customers, and intermediaries such as wholesalers and retailers to distribute their products to the marketplace.

■ *Organisational customers tend to be relatively small in number, purchasing in larger amounts, sometimes on an infrequent or contractual basis.* For example, the market for X-ray equipment is limited to a few customers who do not buy very often but who spend large amounts when they do. The production capacity of the canning factory is sold to a small number of companies who place high value contracts on an annual basis. Marketing to these customers therefore relies on personal contacts, in which long-term relationships are very important.

There are exceptions to these generalisations. Some consumer markets involve infrequent purchases of high-value products by a few customers (e.g. Rolls Royce cars, ocean-going yachts). There are several million business organisations in the UK alone, so products that are used by most of them (e.g. stationery, office furniture) are sold into relatively large markets.

FIGURE 3.3

*Organisational and
consumer markets*

■ *The decision-making process is often different.* Customers in consumer markets tend to make individual decisions, with only the most important purchases referred to more than one person (e.g. buying a house). Organisations frequently involve more than one person in a buying decision of any importance. The composition of a decision-making unit (DMU) varies from a board of directors (for important capital equipment investments) to less formal groups of managers and assistants (for more routine purchases of materials).

How consumers and organisations buy is covered in more detail in Chapter 4. Organisational and consumer markets and some generalised characteristics are illustrated in Figure 3.3.

3.6 NON-CUSTOMER MARKETS

We have seen how organisations can have customer groups that are not necessarily the end users or consumers of their products or services. Some enterprises have internal markets in which one business unit sells services to another. We have also noted (in Chapter 3) that other organisations in the marketing environment, such as suppliers, have an important influence on marketing strategies. Theories of relationship marketing emphasise the importance of these non-customer groups that can be described as types of markets in which an organisation operates. The aim of relationship marketing is to build a supportive network around an organisation through partnerships not only with customers, but also with influential groups in these other markets.

3.6.1 The six markets model

In non-customer markets, there are six types of markets that potentially play an important role in determining an organisation's success: customer markets (as discussed in section 3.5.3), internal markets, recruitment markets, suppliers, referral markets and influence markets.

■ *Customer* markets remain a primary focus, although the emphasis is on developing long-term relationships rather than short-term transactions.

FIGURE 3.4

The six markets model

CHRISTOPHER, PAYNE AND BALLANTYNE, 2001.

■ *Internal* markets refer to stakeholders within the organisation, particularly employees. *Internal marketing* has been described as 'the philosophy of treating employees as customers – indeed wooing employees' (Berry and Parasuraman, 1991). As internal communications are frequently cited as a key management issue, 'selling' an organisation to existing staff is becoming more important.

■ *Recruitment* markets consist of potential, new employees. Companies, particularly those in service industries, have become dependent on attracting and retaining motivated staff. Influencing the best people to apply for vacancies is a key marketing task.

■ *Suppliers* can be crucial to an organisation's ability to meet customer demands because they control access to equipment, components, materials, services and finance. They are also an important source of market intelligence.

■ *Referral* markets include anybody who is likely to make recommendations about the organisation's products or services. Referrals are an important source of new customers for many companies – often *the* most important source of new business, especially for smaller firms. Recommendations can come not just from existing customers, but also other organisations in the marketing environment (e.g. accountants, solicitors, bank managers, friends and acquaintances). The Internet has added a new dimension to such 'word-of-mouth' marketing as positive and negative recommendations can be communicated widely through chat groups, email and networking websites such as MySpace and Facebook.

■ *Influence* markets are made up of organisations and individuals able to influence the marketing environment of an organisation positively or negatively. They include central and local government, pressure groups, consumer watchdogs and trade associations.

3.7 COMPETITIVE FORCES IN THE MARKETPLACE

3.7.1 *The five forces model*

Markets vary in their attractiveness to supplying organisations. Some seem to provide healthy profits or resources for any well-managed supplier. Other markets are supplied by organisations who are all struggling to survive. The underlying economic structure of the market and the

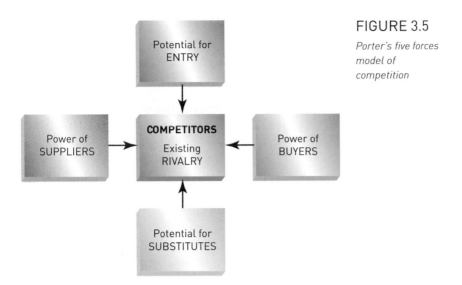

FIGURE 3.5

*Porter's five forces
model of
competition*

intensity of competition within the supplying industry cause these differences. Analysing the forces that affect the competitiveness of the marketplace is an important step in deciding on appropriate marketing strategies.

The management writer Michael Porter (1980) put forward a model of competitive forces which is widely used. In this, five basic forces determine the state of competition in an industry. These are illustrated in Figure 3.5.

These forces of entry, suppliers, substitutes, buyers and rivalry, govern the intensity of competition in an industry and of organisations' abilities to meet profit or other objectives. It should be noted that these forces go beyond the common definition of competition, which is normally restricted to rivalry between the existing suppliers. Porter's idea of 'extended rivalry' includes not only potential new entrants into the marketplace and substitute products, but customers (buyers) and suppliers as well. This reflects the fact that if customers or suppliers have a relatively powerful position they can strongly influence the profitability of the market by, for example, driving down prices or increasing costs.

The focus of power shifts in different markets and industries.

FOR EXAMPLE

- The power in the food industry has tended to centre on the buyer power of the large supermarket chains. Their influence over suppliers is the dominant force influencing marketing decisions on products, pricing and promotion rather than the direct competition among rival food producers.

- In the early days of office copiers, Xerox's patents prevented anyone else from marketing plain paper copiers. This unique position as a supplier gave them the necessary power in the marketplace for their marketing strategies to predominate. Customers had so little influence that they could only rent and not purchase machines outright, allowing Xerox to use long-term rental schemes to prevent them from switching to another supplier.

The relative power of each of the five forces is determined by a number of characteristics, which we will now examine.

3.7.2 Potential for entry

New suppliers entering an industry increase competition and affect the viability of the existing organisations. Some markets are relatively difficult to enter and tend to be dominated by a small number of larger companies. Other markets are relatively easy to enter and tend to be supplied by a high number of small firms. Car manufacturing is an expensive market to enter and therefore dominated by a few international companies whereas it costs relatively little to set up as a consultant, hence the large numbers of consultancy firms.

The potential for entering a market depends on the barriers to entry that exist. These barriers to market entry include:

- **Economies of scale**: If significant cost reductions are available from high levels of output in an industry, new companies will find it difficult to compete because they start from low output levels. In the 1960s, it was believed that the increasing existence of such economies in mass markets would lead to the inevitable decline of smaller firms. In many manufacturing industries this has proved to be the case.

- **Product differentiation**: Established suppliers build up loyalty with customers who identify with their particular product. This differentiation takes a considerable investment in time (to prove the reliability and quality of a product) and money (for branding, advertising, packaging) and therefore represents a significant barrier for any new entrant to overcome. Some companies have attempted to overcome this barrier to entry by using the loyalty to the brand name of a product in one market to enter a different market. For example, Mars used the well-established name and look of Mars chocolate bars when they entered the ice-cream market in order to compete with the differentiated products already offered by suppliers such as Walls.

- **Capital requirements**: A very tangible barrier to entry into some markets are the large set-up costs involved. Some industries, such as banking and insurance or heavy industrial goods, are dominated by long established, larger firms for this reason.

- **Switching costs**: When users change from one company's products to another, they may incur one-off 'switching costs'. These may be in the retraining of staff – in the change over from one computer system to another, for example. Existing stock may become obsolete – for example, if a manufacturer changes from one raw material to another. Where significant switching costs exist, they present a barrier for any new entrant who has to offer more than just marginal benefits to replace an existing supplier. Manufacturers know the importance of keeping a distribution pipeline filled with their stock in order to create switching costs for any retailer who is thinking of changing over to a different supplier. For example, Letraset distributed their patented rub down lettering products through specialist graphic art shops. The marketing strategy was to develop the distribution system as fully as possible whilst their products were protected by patents so that when the patents eventually expired new entrants would still find it difficult to enter the market because the retailers were fully stocked with Letraset. This deterred new entrants and limited the progress of those that did enter the market.

- **Access to distribution channels**: Unless they can sell direct to the user, new entrants need access to the established methods of distributing products. Distribution channels may not be readily available, or they may already be filled (e.g. where the graphic art retailers were already stocked with Letraset products). The competition for shelf space in High Street retailers is fierce and new products have to win the right to be displayed. Failure to secure display in the major newsagent chains such as WH Smith and Martin would effectively block the launch of a new magazine, for example.

■ *Other cost disadvantages*: Some cost advantages enjoyed by existing suppliers are independent of scale. For instance, a manufacturer may benefit from a plentiful local supply of cheap labour, which makes new entrants from outside of the area uncompetitive. An established supplier may have advantages of 'economies of experience' because they have learned the most efficient ways of making products over a significant period of time, a learning curve that will have to be replicated by any new entrant.

■ *Government policy*: Certain markets are controlled by national or local government regulations that create total or partial barriers to entry. For example, regulations control the number of outlets allowed to serve alcohol in public places; new entrants have to overcome the barrier of satisfying local magistrates and police of the need for an additional outlet and their own suitability to run it. Lifting government restrictions can provide business opportunities. For example, postal services have been opened to new entrants and the Royal Mail has gradually lost its position as the monopoly supplier.

3.7.3 Rivalry among existing firms

Familiar forms of competition, such as promotional campaigns, special offers, new product launches, or opening of new distribution outlets, are evidence of existing rivalry between established firms. This rivalry tends to intensify when:

■ The market is divided between competitors of roughly equal size

■ The market is maturing, involving a shake-out of existing rivals

■ New entrants or market changes have created excess capacity

■ The industry has high fixed costs and suppliers prefer to maintain their capacity, even at lower prices

■ The industry has high 'exit barriers', which keeps existing rivals fighting to the bitter end; these exit barriers include the high cost of closing down some types of production, redundancy costs or emotional attachment to a particular industry

FOR EXAMPLE

Competition among the large breweries illustrates several of these points. The market for beers and lagers has matured with demographic and social changes. There is over-capacity among the small number of big brewers who dominate the market. The high fixed costs of brewing creates a powerful financial incentive to maintain capacity, and exit costs are increased by the integration of the brewers into the pub trade. Major brewers such as Bass and Whitbread attempted to exit the industry by selling their brewing operations, although they met with shareholder opposition.

Competition within industries can be divided into two main types: *primary* or *real* competition and *secondary* or *peripheral* competition.

Primary (real) competitors operate in the same market as each other. They target the same consumers with similar products. Secondary (peripheral) competitors may operate in the same product category but have different product offerings.

FOR EXAMPLE

In the car market, who is the primary competition to BMW? It is probably Mercedes, Volvo or Saab, as these manufacturers fall into a similar price band and offer similar benefits such as reliability and

safety. However, if we look at the product category in general there are many more other potential competitors. These may be viewed as secondary competition that may not make the same type of cars currently but they might do in the future. For example, BMW now markets Minis, extending their prestige 'executive' image to enter a different target market of younger, more fashion-conscious car owners. Companies need to monitor primary competition very closely but also keep an eye on secondary competition in case they start to infringe on their market.

The Mini has moved a long way from its original functional image under the ownership of BMW

3.7.4 Threat of substitute products or services

Suppliers compete not only with products similar to their own but also with substitute products. Substitution can come in a number of ways:

- *A substitute product that performs the same function*: American railroads eventually competed with other types of transport such as road and air, which met the same need. Coal has been substituted by other forms of energy such as gas and nuclear power. Theatre audiences were offered a substitute form of entertainment with the introduction of the cinema, which in turn was threatened with substitution by television and home videos.

- *A substitute way of spending money*: Competition for the disposable income in consumers' pockets comes from widely differing products and services. Theatres compete not only with cinemas, television and videos, but a whole range of other leisure opportunities from restaurants and wine bars to evening classes and sports clubs. They also compete with very different uses of disposable income, such as vacations and hobbies.

Industries where there are fewer real substitutes (e.g. basic food such as bread) tend to be more stable than those that can be easily substituted by other products (e.g. forms of leisure) or those that rely on disposable income (e.g. tourism).

3.7.5 The power of buyers and suppliers

Buyers, or customers, 'compete' with suppliers by trying to get the best deal from them. They try to negotiate discounts, additional services, higher quality, more after-sales support and other benefits that are added costs to the supplier. Suppliers naturally try to resist efforts of buyers which reduce their profitability. In some situations buyers have the upper hand; as a supplier marketing to Marks and Spencer your options are limited because of the power of this buyer. In other circumstances suppliers have more power; manufacturers of patented products have the opportunity to recover their development costs by charging high prices to customers as the monopoly supplier. This changing balance of power between buyers and suppliers varies depending on a number of factors: the concentration of buyers or suppliers, differentiation and switching costs, relative importance, and backward or forward integration. Each are dealt with below.

Concentration of buyers or suppliers

If buying power is concentrated in the hands of a few organisations or individuals who are dealing with a relatively large number of suppliers, buyers tend to have more control. Conversely, if a small number of suppliers sell into a market of many buyers, then the suppliers have more power.

FOR EXAMPLE

The DIY market was a fragmented industry with a proliferation of independent retailers, builders' merchants and ironmongers' stores. In these circumstances the suppliers had power to specify products and prices. The supply of paint, for example, was concentrated in the hands of a small number of large suppliers such as ICI who made marketing decisions on colour range, packaging and pricing in isolation from the retailer. The emergence of large out-of-town retailing chains such as Homebase and B&Q has concentrated buying power in the hands of relatively few organisations that now have much more influence over important marketing decisions. By introducing their own ranges of branded products these buyers have further increased their power over suppliers, who are now forced to manufacture in-house brands to the retailers' specification or lose business.

Differentiation and switching costs

A supplier who has developed differentiated products or ones with high switching costs can exercise more power over the buyer. However, if products are relatively undifferentiated and can be easily switched from one supplier to the next, then buyers have greater negotiating power.

FOR EXAMPLE

Xerox once dominated the office copier market, as we have already noted. Their power stemmed from the differentiation of their patented plain paper copiers to competing coated paper machines and the high switching costs created by their marketing strategy of long-term rental agreements. In these circumstances they were able to charge premium prices and create a highly profitable business. Today, office managers have more buying power because other manufacturers entered the market on the expiry of the Xerox patents, offering a variety of products available on flexible purchase and lease terms.

Relative importance

Some purchases are crucial to the success of an organisation or the well-being of an individual (e.g. the purchase of new premises or a house). In these circumstances the buyer is likely to shop around for the best possible deal and exercise their buying power to the full. In other situations, where a purchase is of relatively low value to the buyer and does not have any major impact on their organisational or individual welfare (e.g. the purchase of paper clips or confectionery items), the buyer is unlikely to use their powers to the full and will accept the supplier's terms more readily.

Backward or forward integration

Buyers and suppliers are usually arranged in chains as we have seen (in section 3.4.2 above). This can give suppliers the opportunity of fulfilling the role of the next link forward in their chain themselves if they are dissatisfied with their immediate buyers. Likewise buyers can threaten to perform the role of the link before them in the chain if they feel their suppliers are not doing the right job. For example, a supplier selling through wholesalers to retailers may threaten to sell direct to the retailers if the wholesale terms are not acceptable (*forward integration*). A buyer who does not like the terms of their supplier may threaten to manufacture the product themselves (*backward integration*). The power that such threats carry depends on their credibility as realistic options for the buyer or supplier.

3.7.6 A summary of competitive forces

An analysis of the competitive forces at work in the marketplace helps an organisation identify its own strengths and weaknesses in relation to the competitive structure and evaluate the opportunities and threats that may be revealed. Figure 3.6, a summary of characteristics that determine the nature of these forces, can be used as a checklist for carrying out such an analysis.

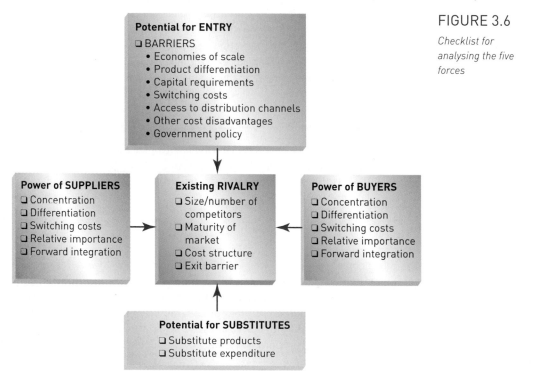

FIGURE 3.6

Checklist for analysing the five forces

ENTREPRENEURIAL MARKETING

Entrepreneurs recognise that some industries are more suited to new ventures than others. Large firms have considerable advantages over small firms in some industries. In other sectors, however, larger organisations will have little natural advantage, and the common form of business unit will be small, allowing more opportunities for entrepreneurs to operate. A number of factors influence the likelihood of fragmentation of an industry into smaller businesses:

- **Low entry barriers**: Most industries with a large population of small firms have low entry barriers. These include many of the service sectors where small enterprises predominate, such as training, recruitment and secretarial agencies, household services and the construction industry.
- **Diseconomies of scale**: Where customer preferences necessitate constantly changing products and styles, smaller, more flexible firms can be more efficient than larger, bureaucratic companies. The fashion industries have many small firms for this reason.
- **High creative content**: Architects, interior design firms and specialist product development companies tend to be small as it is often more difficult to produce conditions of high creativity in large organisations.
- **Personal service**: Where an individualised, personal service is required, for example in consultancy or photography, then small firms are able to offer more responsive, tailor-made services than large firms.
- **Close local control**: Restaurants, bars and night clubs are examples where the close local supervision of an owner-manager often works better than the absentee management of a large company.
- **Newness**: An emerging industry can be fragmented because entrepreneurs are still developing market share with no-one able to dominate the others yet. Technological innovations or shifting consumer needs that create these newly formed industries are often exploited first by newly formed small businesses.

In some markets, franchising is used to overcome some of the forces towards fragmentation. For example, where economies of scale potentially exist in production or purchasing, an industry may still remain fragmented because the marketplace demands personal service or local sources of supply. The brewing industry, for example, overcame this problem with an early form of franchising, retaining centralised production but using tenants with some autonomy to manage the local outlet.

CHECKPOINT

Consider a leisure attraction that you have visited recently, or with which you are familiar (e.g. the local cinema, sports centre, a theme park or national attraction such as Madame Tussauds or Disneyland). Analyse the competitive forces in which it operates using Porter's Five Forces model. Does your analysis indicate this is a favourable or unfavourable market to enter with new products?

3.8. SUMMARY

- Customer needs represent long-term necessities, which Maslow categorised as survival, security, social, success and self-actualisation needs. They are not the same as 'wants', which are how we wish a need to be fulfilled as conditioned by our past and present environment.

- Organisations can suffer from 'marketing myopia' and mistake what customers currently want for long-term needs.

- Customers buy the *benefits* of a product (what it does for them) rather than its *features* (what it is) and change to alternative products which offer superior benefits.

- Customers are organised in chains that link producers to end users. Benefits required from products change according to the position in the chain.

- Customers are served by markets and the industries or organisations within them. The characteristics of a market change as it develops from an immature to a mature state.

- There are consumer and organisational markets. Organisational markets can be further divided into industrial, intermediary and government markets. Distinctive characteristics of organisational markets include derived demand arising from buyers further down the chain, small numbers of buyers purchasing relatively large amounts and multiple influences in the buying decision.

- Other groups or markets can influence marketing strategies. Relationship marketing theories have organised these into the 'six markets' of customer markets, internal markets, recruitment markets, suppliers, influence markets and referral markets.

- The competitive structure of markets changes according to the balance of power between the five forces of existing rivalry, the potential for new entrants, the threat of substitutes, and the relative bargaining power of buyers and suppliers.

3.9 ACTIVITIES

CASE STUDY

IS THERE A FUTURE FOR THE POSTMAN?

The mail carrier and the local post office have been part of the European landscape for more than a century. Even in remote areas, national postal operators have guaranteed an affordable service for all in return for an almost total monopoly.

But the service is under threat. Complaints are rife – the post is held to be 'unfriendly', slow, unreliable and costly – and technology is eroding the market. Email has slowed the steady rise in business mail over the years, and the Internet is taking yet more of this bread-and-butter business.

Some postal operators have responded pragmatically. They understand that their business is bound to shrink, and are therefore focusing on core activities such as business mail or consumer parcel deliveries. They have started to reduce costs, and are lobbying to raise public concern about the possible loss of the local postman and post office. In France, for example, the government was forced to promise that it would not close a single post office. But the erosion continues. The most attractive business – such as 'dense delivery' areas or business parcels – is being poached by cost-efficient and customer-driven competitors. And as volumes fall, fixed costs per shipment go up, making it even harder for national operators to provide a low-cost service, and easier for competitors to win still more of their disgruntled customers.

Postal operators are threatened by the following developments in particular:

Electronic alternatives If electronic messaging keeps up its current momentum, the financial and business mail that represents nearly half of postal revenues today (see Figure 3.7) will dwindle to almost nothing. The US Postal Service, for example, has seen a 33 per cent drop in the volume of business-to-business mail in five years as a result

The face of European mail delivery is changing

of the wider use of faxes, email, and electronic data interchange (EDI).

Companies are not alone in using email. The number of people using the Internet worldwide has grown from 45 million in 1995 to over a billion in 2006. It is expected that soon 25 per cent of Europeans will pay discretionary bills by electronic means.

More demanding customers Where speed and reliability are vital, many businesses in regulated markets are turning to couriers that can handle their shipments at a competitive price. Couriers offering good service for a relatively low price already exist in Italy, Spain and Greece, and carry mail that was once channelled through the post office. Where low costs are the priority, large mailers are asking postal operators for discounts that often exceed the operational savings that can be achieved by serving big customers. If the operators fail to oblige, they only encourage customers to mail fewer letters. Banks, for example, might send out statements less frequently, develop substitutes such as electronic home banking or turn to the post office's competitors.

FIGURE 3.7 *Postal market composition*

	CUSTOMER NEED	POSTAL SERVICES	TYPICAL PROPORTION OF REVENUE	
BUSINESSES	Financial and business communications	Financial mail Business mail Express documents	45%	
	Advertising	Unaddressed Periodicals Catalogue Direct mail	30%	
	Distribution of goods	Parcels Express Logistics	10%	
INDIVIDUALS	Communications to businesses and individuals	Letterbox mail	15%	

B.L. BOT, I.J.H. BOZON, P.A. GIRARDIN AND C.-S. NEUMANN (1997), 'IS THERE A FUTURE FOR THE POSTMAN?', MCKINSEY QUARTERLY, NUMBER 4.

Some companies have resorted to setting up their own in-house operators to provide a service tailored to their needs. In France, Yves Rocher responded to La Poste's repeated strikes by setting up its own mail-order delivery service, Distri-home. In Germany, seven leading mail-order companies and nineteen magazine publishers joined forces to form AZD (Alternativer Zustelidienste) as a cheaper alternative to Deutsche Post.

Other companies will increasingly expect postal and delivery services that integrate seamlessly into their own operations, perhaps using EDI, and will wish to be able to outsource more of their logistics and communications. Private competitors are rising to the challenge, providing tracking systems for parcel and express shipments, for example, and sometimes sending customers facsimiles of recipients' signatures. They also offer closed packaging systems and will collect at the customer's door instead of from the post office.

Clearly, customers are no longer going to be satisfied with a service that merely gets the goods from A to B. Postal operators will have to offer value-added services as well, such as document handling, company mailroom management, spare-parts storage or even assembly to order. And the more closely a logistics or communications provider works with

The Royal Mail in the UK has operated for hundreds of years but is now under threat from new competitors

its customers, the more important it will be to have an international presence. Customers that operate around the world will require cross-border solutions with uniform service levels and product ranges throughout a region or continent.

QUESTIONS

1 Who are the primary and secondary competitors for postal services?
2 What are the main threats for postal operators in Europe today?
3 How have the demands of customers changed over the last decade?

DEVELOPING A MARKETING PLAN

AN EXTERNAL AUDIT

Complete the next stage towards of your marketing plan by undertaking the external review or audit and answering such questions as:

- ■ Who are your customers? Who will be your customers?
- ■ Why do they buy from you? Why will they buy in future?
- ■ What are the features and benefits of your product(s)?
- ■ What is the competitive environment?
- ■ What are the key structural forces that act in this marketplace?

(See also Chapter 12.)

3.10 FURTHER READING AND REFERENCES

Market needs and analysis

Deng, S. and Dart, J. (1994), 'Measuring Market Orientation: A Multi-factor, Multi-item Approach', *Journal of Marketing Management*, Vol. 10, pages 725–442.
Levitt, T. (1960), 'Marketing Myopia', *Harvard Business Review*, July/August, pages 45–56.
Maslow, A.H. (1954), *Motivation and Personality* (Harper and Row).
Siu, N.Y.M. and Wilson, R.M.S. (1998), 'Modelling Market Orientation: An Application in the Education Sector', *Journal of Marketing Management*, Vol. 14, pages 293–323.

Relationship marketing

Berry, L. and Parasuraman, A. (1991), *Marketing Services Through Quality* (The Free Press).
Cahill, D.J. (1996), *Internal Marketing* (The Haworth Press).
Christopher, M., Payne, A. and Ballantyne, D. (2001), *Relationship Marketing: Creating Stakeholder Value* (Butterworth Heinemann).
Little, E. and Marandi, E. (2003), *Relationship Marketing Management* (Thomson Learning).

Competitive analysis

Porter, M.E. (1980), *Competitive Strategy: Techniques for Analysing Industries and Competition* (Macmillan).

Chapter **4**

BUYER BEHAVIOUR

LEARNING OBJECTIVES

By the end of this chapter the reader will be able to:

- Evaluate the influences on a buyer to make a purchase
- Understand the importance of repeat purchase and the impact of loyalty
- Understand how to classify these influences into those over which business managers have some control, and those over which they have very little control
- Assess the effects of social, personal and lifestyle influences on buying decisions
- Understand the differences in the buying processes of an individual and the buying processes of an organisation such as a business or a social enterprise
- Appreciate the different types of roles that managers may take in a buying decision for an organisation

INTRODUCTION

In the previous chapter, we investigated the needs of customers and the nature of the markets that they create. In this chapter, we examine how these customers behave when they are involved in decisions to buy products or services. We will seek to answer the following questions:

- How do customers make buying decisions?
- Why is it important for a business to understand this?
- What influences customers' preferences?
- What differences are there between buyers as individual consumers and buyers in organisations such as a business?

CASE STUDY

....

FESTIVAL FOODS

'Can I introduce Carlo Vidas from the marketing agency, BFG, who is here today to present their promotional ideas for our hot cereal products?'

David Bracewell, marketing director of Festival Foods indicated his colleagues around the table as he introduced them.

'This is Sal Morrisey, brand manager of "Puritan", our new oats-and-honey porridge, Mazrene Richards, packaging manager for the company and Graham Jamieson, purchasing manager.'

Carlo Vidas began his presentation:

'Our detailed recommendations are in the report before you, but perhaps I can review the main considerations behind our proposals. Our brief was to develop a promotional strategy for your hot cereal product range to improve its sales compared to cold ready-to-eat cereals.'

'Looking at the market data, a number of factors are significant in influencing consumer demand for cereals. The high level of advertising expenditure by cereal producers, which is currently running at around 9 per cent of total sales, has ensured exceptional loyalty to the main branded products. Cereals are purchased by over 90 per cent of households, most of whom still prefer to buy well-known brands so that own-label products have not had the same success in cereals that they have had in other food sectors. However, because the market for hot cereals is relatively small, at around 5 per cent of the total cereal market, promotional spending has been traditionally lower in this sector and more erosion to own-branded products has taken place.'

Carlos flicked onto his next PowerPoint slide.

'Weather is a particular influence on hot cereals, with sales peaking in the winter months and cold periods. There are also considerable regional variations, with sales strongest in Scotland, the Midlands and East Anglia. This contrasts to cold cereals, which are served most often in the South and least often in Scotland. Social groups

also behave differently when buying hot and cold cereals. Cold cereals are the favourite among the more affluent AB social groups and least popular among the poorer groups D and E. Hot cereals, on the other hand, are bought most frequently by group D, semi- or unskilled manual workers. The economic climate does not seem to affect total demand for cereals, although the last recession did help the less expensive products take a larger market share and it also slowed the growth of hot cereals more than cold.'

'The family unit is a crucial influence on all cereals as purchasing is highest among 25- to 34-year-olds, who are most likely to have children. And your own research indicates that children's preferences play a large part in determining which cereals are bought. Hot cereals do seem to have an older user profile than cold ones. They seem to appeal less to younger people – except for the under two-year-olds, where they can be used as a first solid breakfast food.'

'Lifestyle changes have been a mixed blessing for hot cereals. On the positive side, the trend towards more healthy foods has favoured cereals containing oats. There has been considerable favourable press coverage about porridge on health grounds compared to the negative comments from the dental profession on sugar-coated cold cereals. However, the increasing number of working women has hastened the decline of the cooked breakfast. The microwave has helped overcome most of the inconvenience of heating cereals in the morning but the decline in manual work and the increasing numbers of us who sit around indoors at work means that we no longer perceive the need for a big cooked breakfast every day.'

'This leads me on to our proposals. We know that the big, cooked family breakfast is a thing of the past during the working week. But it is more common at the weekend as a special treat and this is the behavioural pattern we can use. We cannot compete with ready-to-eat cereals for our key consumer group – the family – other than at the weekend. So we have designed some on-pack promotions designed to be an activity for all the

►

family, not just individual members. We will appeal to parents by promoting the sociability of a hot, but healthy, family breakfast. The activities on the packs are fun, but semi-educational, and can involve adults as well as children. Like this one – the old card game requiring pictures and words to be matched, except that the words are in Spanish and so it is best if a parent gets involved.'

'What I am saying is that we have to stimulate recognition of a new need in the buying process. Cereals are normally a routine purchase with little time spent on the evaluation of alternatives. But there is variety-seeking behaviour in this market, with families in general, and children in particular becoming bored with a daily routine. The weekend provides an ideal opportunity to break this.'

'We can promote recognition of a new need at breakfast – the benefit of bringing the family together at the beginning of the day in a busy world in which individual family members often dash off to their own particular activity at the weekend and see little of their siblings or parents.'

'As you have the detailed proposals, perhaps I can leave other aspects to questions. Thank you.'

Sal Morrisey, manager of 'Puritan', one of the brands under discussion, spoke first. 'How do these proposals affect individual brands which currently have no standardised packaging?'

'Could I add to that?' asked Mazrene Richards, the packaging manager. 'Some of these on-pack activities are quite complex. Will they fit onto our current pack sizes and have you costed the extra items such as stickers?'

'These are only outline suggestions so we would have to work closely with you to make sure the final design conformed to your packaging requirements', answered Vidas. 'I have included some costings from one supplier although you may be able to negotiate lower prices.'

'Yes, we would certainly want quotes of our own.' The purchasing manager was quick to agree. 'We now have a standard procedure that, once a new item has been specified and agreed between the relevant managers here, we invite suppliers for formal written proposals covering the areas outlined in these guidelines.' He handed Vidas a document headed, *Purchasing Procedures – Guidelines for Suppliers*. 'We then select a supplier and place an order that spells out the terms and conditions according to the procedures. Of course this only applies when we are purchasing a particular item for the first time. Repeat or modified purchases are more routine.'

Carlo Vidas began to realise that selling this campaign to Festival Foods might be even more complex than persuading Southerners to eat porridge on a sunny day.

QUESTIONS

1 What influences on consumer buyer behaviour are illustrated by this case? Classify the examples into:

   i   Controllable and uncontrollable influences. *See section 4.1*

   ii Social and personal or lifestyle influences. *See section 4.2*

2 Consider how individuals buy compared to organisations. What examples of consumer and organisational buying processes are given in this case? What are the differences between them? *See sections 4.3 and 4.4*

3 What roles in the decision-making process concerning this proposed campaign do you expect those present at the meeting to play? For example, who will be the key decision-maker and what type of influence will others have? *See section 4.4*

4 Do you think the proposals made are relevant to the buyer behaviour outlined? What other suggestion can you make?

4.1 A BUYER BEHAVIOUR MODEL

In order to target marketing activity as precisely as possible, managers need to understand who their customers are. Once they know who their customers are, they also need to know as much as possible about how those customers behave as buyers. They need to know what influences them to make a buying decision and what processes they follow to select a product or service. They would particularly like to know how they choose between one product and another – they can then use that information to increase the chances of their own products being selected.

4.1.1 The 'black box' model

Researchers have been trying for many years to find out why customers buy the products and services that they do. The many investigations which have been carried out have helped to suggest some general models of how customers behave, but very few universal rules have been found.

One reason for this is that we all make buying decisions in what has been described as a 'black box', an invisible processor in which the influences on the decision are assessed. As most of this processing takes place in our conscious and subconscious minds, the precise mechanics of the decision making process cannot be observed – hence the mysterious 'black box'. All we can do is observe what is happening around an individual or an organisation at the time of a buying decision and look at what inputs and influences the 'black box' might be receiving. These inputs can then be compared to the outputs from the 'black box' in terms of buying decisions to see what impact the various influences may have had.

This general model of customer behaviour is shown in Figure 4.1.

Inputs, as shown on the left of the diagram in the form of controllable or uncontrollable stimuli, enter the 'black box' for processing. There are other influences on individual and organisational buying decisions, such as the personality of a customer or the structure of an organisation, which are shown as buying influences on the processing taking place in the 'black box'. The

FIGURE 4.1 *A 'black box' model of customer behaviour*

results of this process are outputs in terms of decisions on what type of product to buy, if any, what brand of product, from which supplier, in what quantities and when.

4.1.2 The inputs

Inputs to the decision-making process take the form of stimuli, some of which can be controlled by marketing management, some of which cannot.

The *uncontrollable stimuli* consist of many of the environmental forces that we have already discussed as impacting on the marketing organisation (see Chapter 2). The prevailing social, technological, economic and political climates all affect our likelihood to consider buying certain products or services. These forces are usually beyond the control of marketing management. However, it is important to know how customers may react to changes to this 'uncontrollable' environment.

Interest rates are an important economic factor in the purchase of high-value goods such as cars and houses. Those people considering buying a new car or moving house are deterred by high interest rates if they need to borrow money because of the high repayment costs. They may also be deterred even if they have the cash available because the benefit of a good, risk-free rate of return on their invested money may outweigh the benefits of replacing a car or moving home. A fall in interest rates can therefore act as a stimulus on both groups to consider making a purchase.

Organisations considering investing in, for example, new plant and equipment are similarly affected by this economic stimulus. Not only do lower interest rates encourage those organisations which need to borrow in order to place an order, but they also affect those companies that compare the rate of return of investing in new equipment versus the return of investing cash resources elsewhere.

Political factors which may make an impact in the black box include changes to tax rates such as income tax and VAT. Changes to VAT may be a particularly important input as an increase in rates is directly applied to products and services and therefore acts as a price increase for the final consumer who cannot recover the tax.

The weather can also have major effects on many markets. The drought of 2006 in the UK affected many industries, from garden sprinkler manufacturers to soft drink vendors; some positive and some negative. Forest fires in Greece have had a negative effect on tourism in the Thessaloniki peninsula in particular but also across the whole of Greece – and even in those areas which were unaffected by the deforestation. Floods in New Orleans in the US, caused by hurricane Katrina, affected many local businesses and the tourism on which the city is reliant.

The *controllable stimuli* are marketing factors which are usually within the control of the management of an organisation. Controllable variables include the quality of a product or service, its price, how it is promoted, how it is distributed and other elements of the 'marketing mix' (to be examined more fully in later chapters). These factors are used to stimulate demand for a specific product in the short term (by such methods as special promotions and discounts), and in the longer term (by product development and brand recognition for example). One of the key tasks of management is to assess the effectiveness of these marketing inputs on the outputs of the 'black box' – the all-important decisions to purchase certain products.

The product or service sold is critically important and organisations should have a lot of control over these. Their main constraints are likely to be legal and technical. Sky, the satellite TV company, has recently launched SkyHD, a new high-definition channel. Advances in technology in both television sets and satellites have made this possible.

Price is very important to most consumers. The US grocery giant Wal-Mart owns Asda in the UK but has interests across the world in Argentina, Brazil, Canada, China, Costa Rica, El Salvador, Germany, Guatemala, Honduras, Japan, Mexico, Nicaragua, Puerto Rico and South Korea. Despite the use of different brand names in various countries its pricing strategy remains the same. Its slogan is 'Always Low Prices. Always'. An independent survey in the US claims that shopping at Wal-Mart would save the average household $2,300 per year.

Many people associate marketing with TV advertising and sales promotion, but increasingly organisations are using online strategies. Even charities are becoming involved, seeing the Internet as the way to engage hard-to-reach young audiences. In the UK, the NSPCC (the national children's charity) used the Internet to highlight their 'Don't Hide It' campaign, encouraging sufferers of sexual abuse to speak out. This attracted 440,000 unique users in a six-week period.

Companies can control how they get their products to the consumers. They have a number of different options. Dell computers have opted only to deal direct with their end consumer, in comparison with their competitors such as Sony and Toshiba who deal through retailers such as PC World.

Together these uncontrollable and controllable factors form *inputs* into the buying decisions of customers. As we have seen customers can exist as individual consumers or as organisations and we will investigate the behaviour of these two categories separately in more detail.

4.2 CONSUMER BUYING BEHAVIOUR

Purchases by individuals acting as the consumer are influenced by many factors including their own background and personality. We examine these under two classifications:

■ The influences on the consumer as part of a social group

■ The influence of more individual, psychological characteristics

These can be further subdivided, as shown in Figure 4.2.

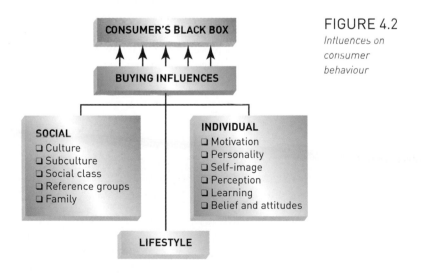

FIGURE 4.2

Influences on consumer behaviour

We will illustrate how each of these influences may operate by using the examples of a shopper buying shoes and a parent choosing a school for their child.

4.2.1 Social influences

Our membership in various types of social groups, ranging from wider cultural groupings to narrower family units, powerfully influences our habits as consumers.

Culture

The society in which we are brought up and the accepted beliefs, values, habits and attitudes which are handed on from one generation to the next as part of its culture are key forces in the marketing environment.

Consumer behaviour is particularly affected by shifts in cultural beliefs and habits which present many opportunities and threats to marketing management.

Our fictional consumer, Owen Polanski, decides that he needs a new pair of shoes for casual wear on informal occasions. His society, like most of Western Europe and North America, has become more concerned about the need for a healthier lifestyle in recent years; this has been reflected in preferences for clothing and footwear products portraying fitness and health. Owen opts to buy a pair of training shoes even though he does not intend to use them for any form of exercise.

Our fictional parent, Susannah Flynn, has three children, the oldest of whom is her daughter, who will soon be five years old. As part of a society whose egalitarian principles make free education available to everyone from five to sixteen years old, Susannah's daughter will soon be sent to a state-funded school. However, recent shifts within this cultural principle of equality have emphasised the responsibility of the individual to make their own choices rather than the collective provision of standard services by the state. In the past, Susannah's mother would have had no real say over which school Susannah attended; now for the first time she has to make a choice of primary school for her own daughter.

Subcultures

Within each social group sharing major cultural influences there are smaller groups, or subcultures, which have distinctive habits and tastes. These may be based on nationality, religion, race, levels of education or other beliefs and situations. These subgroups can have particular needs which create distinct segments of a market. For example, Table 4.1 shows the varying levels of literacy in India. Levels of education tend to create subgroups, particularly at the basic level of literacy. The divide between the 'cans' and 'cannots' in reading and writing can be vast.

TABLE 4.1 *Literacy levels in India*

	URBAN (%)	RURAL (%)	TOTAL (%)
MALE	81	58	64
FEMALE	64	31	39
TOTAL	**73**	**45**	**52**

As this shows, the overall literacy level in India is 52 per cent, but this figure hides a wide variation. The implications for a product targeted at urban males (81 per cent literate) are very different to one targeted at rural females (31 per cent literate). Communications strategies will have to be very different and we will return to this later in the book.

Here are two different examples of subgroups:

Owen Polanski is a vegetarian, a growing subgroup in many countries. As well as avoiding meat products in his food, Owen is also active in promoting animal rights and avoids buying clothes which use animal furs and skin. This extends to his choice of shoes as he does not buy any goods containing leather. His choice of trainers is therefore limited to those made entirely from synthetic substances.

Susannah Flynn and her husband are from families of Catholic beliefs. Although she is not particularly religious, Susannah wants to avoid schools which are connected to religions other than Catholicism. This eliminates for example the local Protestant school and the local Methodist institution. As there is no local Catholic school, Susannah is looking for a secular school with minimal religious overtones.

FOR EXAMPLE

ISLAMIC BANKING

Islamic banking is becoming increasingly popular and is viewed as one of the most important trends in the financial services sector. For example HSBC has launched a division called HSBC Amananah (meaning trustworthiness, faithfulness and honesty) which is committed to Shariah

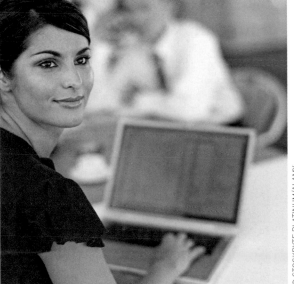

(Islamic law) standards and has a committee of scholars to advise them on appropriate standards. It operates in Saudi Arabia, United Arab Emirates, UK, Malaysia, Indonesia, Brunei and Singapore.

Other major players such as Lloyds TSB have also entered the market alongside the Islamic Bank of Britain. Why?

The Islamic banking industry in 2006 stands at several hundred billion dollars, and consists of more than 300 financial institutions in and outside the Muslim world. There are over 1.5 billion Muslims in the world who look for financial products in harmony with their religious beliefs. At an earlier stage, industry growth was in part a reflection of economic growth in the Islamic world, fuelled primarily by oil wealth. This created a growing middle-wealth segment and hence made banking a necessary service to the larger segment of the population. HSBC's interest is driven

Islamic banking is a popular trend in financial services but faces problems

by the fact that almost a quarter live in countries having Muslim majorities in which HSBC operates. These financial services have been developed to respond to the desire of Muslim customers for Shariah-compliant services, differentiated from conventional financial services.

The most distinctive element of Islamic banking is the prohibition of interest, whether nominal or excessive, simple or compound, fixed or floating. Other elements include the emphasis on equitable contracts, the linking of finance to productivity, the desirability of profit sharing, and the prohibition of gambling and certain types of uncertainty. These parameters define the nature and scope of Islamic banking, as interpreted by the Shariah scholars who work with Islamic financial institutions. As you can see, this is very different from traditional financial services in the West.

Islamic banking is a young industry, growing both financially and geographically. It is indigenous and community-focused: it caters to devout Muslims in indigenous Muslim societies as well as in Muslim minorities in non-Muslim countries. Furthermore, it is inclusive: non-Muslim individuals and communities that seek ethical financial solutions have also been attracted to Islamic banking. This is perhaps one of the most interesting aspects of the growth of Islamic banking; although originally targeted at Muslims throughout the world, its values are increasingly being appreciated by non-Muslims in the West seeking more ethical financial services. In the past several years, increased awareness about Islamic banking has led to conversion from conventional banking and continued high growth (15–20 per cent in key markets).

Another example of a subculture is youth.

FOR EXAMPLE

YOUTH AND TRAINERS

Adidas targeted the youth subculture with the use of graffiti art in the launch of its Adicolor trainer range. The classic white Adicolor line was adapted to include a set of colouring pens, allowing consumers to customise the design of their trainers. The concept was first devised in

Adidas used street art to engage the youth subculture

HÄBERLEIN & MAUERER/ADIDAS

1983 but returned in 2006, supported by ad activity that harnessed the creativity of graffiti. Blank white posters, branded with the Adidas logo, provided a canvas for street artists. Days later, fresh posters were placed over the graffiti, this time with the shape of the Adicolor shoe cut out to reveal the graffiti underneath. This allowed the street art to be incorporated into the campaign, creating a customized shoe on the poster that demonstrated the idea behind the product.

Social class

Social class is a widely used method for classifying people into subgroups. The population can be divided up into 'classes' in which the profiles of individuals tend to coincide. Criteria for making up these profiles include:

■ Income

■ Occupation

■ Education

■ Social status

■ Family background

One common method of social classification is shown in Figure 4.3. Social grade is determined by the occupation of the chief income earner (CIE) in each household (see Table 4.2).

There is a correlation between these groups and their preferences to purchase certain products and the way in which they buy them. The clothes or cars we buy, the type of holiday we take and the use of credit cards have been shown to be influenced by our approximation to one of these social classes. This type of classification is popular because it is used by media such as press and TV. However, other classifications are used and can help with segmentation and targeting, which we will discuss in Chapter 6. For example, the National Statistics Office in the UK uses a different type of socio-economic classification. It is an occupationally based classification providing coverage of the whole adult population. The information required is the occupation coded to

FIGURE 4.3 *Social classes in the UK*

GRADE CLASS	OCCUPATION
A Upper/upper middle	Higher managerial, professional or administrative
B Middle	Intermediate managerial, professional or administrative
C1 Lower middle	Junior managerial, professional or administrative; supervisory or clerical
C2 Skilled working class	Skilled manual workers
D Working class	Semi- or unskilled manual
E Those at the lowest level of subsistence	Casual or lowest grade worker, unemployed, some state pensioners

TABLE 4.2 *Examples of occupations by social grade*

SOCIAL GRADE	TYPICAL OCCUPATIONS	SOCIAL GRADE	TYPICAL OCCUPATIONS
A	Bishop	C2	Foreman with up to 24 employees
	Established doctor, solicitor		Police constable
	Self-employed farmer with 10+ employees		Agricultural workers with special skills (head cowman, chief shepherd)
	Board director, large organisation (200+ employees)		Self-employed unskilled manual workers (1–4 employees)
	Bank branch manager or higher		Bus driver, ambulance driver, AA patrolman
	Police superintendent, Chief constable		Skilled bricklayer, carpenter, plumber, painter
B	Vicar, parson	D	Manual workers, generally semi- or unskilled
	Newly qualified (under three years) doctor, solicitor		All apprentices to skilled trades
	Self-employed farmer (2–9 employees)		Caretaker, park keeper, postman
	Board director, small organisation, senior managers		Fisherman, forestry worker
	Bank clerks with special responsibilities (e.g. chief clerk)		Bus conductor, traffic warden
	Police chief inspector, Inspector		Shop assistant, supermarket shelf-filler, checkout operator
C1	Curate, monk, nun	E	Casual labourers
	Student doctor, articled clerk		Individuals dependent on state benefits or income support for two months or more
	Self-employed farmer with only one employee		Old age pensioners with state pensions
	Foreman with 25+ employees		
	Bank clerk		
	Students on grants		

NATIONAL READERSHIP SURVEYS LTD.

TABLE 4.3 *The National Statistics Office socio-economic classification system of analytical classes*

1	Higher managerial and professional occupations
	1.1 Large employers and higher managerial occupations
	1.2 Higher professional occupations
2	Lower managerial and professional occupations
3	Intermediate occupations
4	Small employers and own-account workers
5	Lower supervisory and technical occupations
6	Semi-routine occupations
7	Routine occupations
8	Never worked and long-term unemployed

the unit groups (OUG) of the Standard Occupational Classification 2000 (SOC2000) and details of employment status (whether an employer, self-employed or employee; whether a supervisor; number of employees at the workplace (see Table 4.3).

The version of the classification, which is used for most analyses, has eight classes, the first of which can be subdivided.

Owen has a middle-class profile in terms of his education and family background. As with all social classes, he is very concerned that the clothes and shoes he wears create the right image. He wants to fit in with his peers. However he does not wish to appear elitist nor emphasise his membership of a 'higher' social class, so his clothes have taken on a more egalitarian look. His lace-up, ankle-length shoes reflect styles traditionally worn by previous generations of working classes. His NSO classification would be 2.

Susannah and her husband have a working-class background and generally fit category C2 in terms of their income, occupation and education. Private education is beyond their income and Susannah has not considered this for her children. However she is influenced by the concept of social mobility and hopes that her children can move to a more middle-class social group. For this reason she is anxious that her daughter attends a school popular with BC1 class parents as well as her own social grouping. Her NSO classification would be 5.

Reference groups

As well as these larger groupings of people, we are also members of smaller reference groups with which we have direct contact. In the case of these groups, we have regular interactions with other group members which can be very influential in our buying decisions. These reference groups are made up of people who are either interdependent on each other or who share common beliefs and values (or both). They can be further divided into:

■ *Primary groups*, which communicate regularly face to face, such as families, neighbours, departments and teams at work, and students in the same class

■ *Secondary groups*, which have less interaction and tend to be more formally structured, such as professional associations, unions, local community groups, religious bodies, and companies

Reference groups are important to marketing because they influence our buying habits in a number of ways including:

■ *The desire to conform to the group norms and 'fit in' fully*: This particularly affects visible products such as clothes which tend to conform to the style of a particular reference group. Many groups have their own acceptable 'uniform', which varies from dark suits to denims.

■ *The transfer of new ideas and habits*: When we change reference group (by changing job, attending a new college, or moving to a new neighbourhood, for example) we encounter new behaviours and lifestyles which may influence our future purchasing decisions. If we change workplace from one where more formal dress is the norm to one where casual clothes are common, we will tend to dress accordingly and buy more casual clothes for work.

The family as a reference group

The family is a particularly important reference group to consider in making marketing decisions. Families, or 'households' as they are sometimes referred to in marketing contexts, form a very common decision-making unit for purchases. Many products or services are bought for consumption by all or several members of the household. It is important therefore to establish exactly who is making the final decision of what to buy.

The married couple as a household unit make decisions in a number of ways which have been classified as:

■ Husband dominant

■ Wife dominant

■ Autonomic (partners make equal numbers of decisions but do so usually without consulting each other)

■ Syncratic (partners mainly make joint decisions)

Families are not static in their composition. They evolve as the various family members grow older and their consumption patterns and buying behaviour change accordingly. Various stages in a common family life cycle can be identified as shown in Table 4.4. The original was designed by Wells and Gubar in 1966 and took account of the variables of age, marital status, career, disposable income and the presence or absence of children. The example shown below is an adaptation of that original but there are many more complex ones. Today's society means that we need to take account of more complex structures which allow for divorce and 'blended families' with half- and step-siblings. Marriage is also not a prerequisite for having children, as in the original model. The example given below gives an idea of the differences that families will encounter at the various stages. The order may vary, for different families.

Owen is single and no longer lives with his parents. He would fall into the Bachelor category and his reference group of friends influence many of his purchase decisions. He has discussed shoes and trainers with them on several occasions and their experiences and opinions form an important input into his decision-making process.

TABLE 4.4 *The family life cycle*

CATEGORY	DESCRIPTION	CHARACTERISTICS
BACHELOR	Young, single, not living at home	Low income but high discretionary income Decisions influenced by peer group Recreation orientated Buys basic kitchen equipment, basic furniture, cars, clothes, holidays
EMPTY NEST I	Couple with no children	Better off financially than they will be soon High mortgage commitment Buys cars, white goods, furniture, holidays and life assurance
FULL NEST I	Couple with young dependent children	Young children (under 6) High debts compared to income Home purchasing at peak Child-dominated household Buys necessities and purchases led by childrens' needs
FULL NEST II	Couple with older dependent children	Youngest child over 6 Income increasing as both parents return to work Relative level of mortgage decreasing Still child-dominated household Buys necessities and purchases led by childrens' needs but categories change with age of children
FULL NEST III	Older couple with dependent children	Older children at work or in higher or further education Exam-dominated household Focus on supporting children's education Buy more tasteful furniture, non-essential appliances and holidays
EMPTY NEST II	Older couple with no dependent children, still working	No children at home Head of household still at work Income increasing but expenditure down Home ownership at its peak Increasing interest in travel, recreation and self education Buys luxuries and home improvement
EMPTY NEST III	Older couple with no dependent children, retired	Cut in income Concern with pensions and savings Interest in hobbies and pastimes Buys medical products and medical care purchases to assist children and grandchildren
SOLITARY SURVIVOR I	Widow/widower, still working	Income adequate but may sell home and move to smaller accommodation Concern with pensions and savings Worried about security and dependence

Susannah is part of a 'Full Nest 1' as she has three young children. As she and her husband both have jobs, they tend to live busy lives. This has lead to 'autonomic' purchase decision-making in which they both make decisions but usually without reference to the other partner as time does not allow for much discussion. Susan has taken responsibility for choosing schools for their children and will inform her husband once she has made up her mind.

CHECKPOINT

Where do you think your family is in its life cycle? Place it in one of the categories in Table 4.2.

FOR EXAMPLE

BT BROADBAND

BT's 2006 campaign features a blended family. It uses a post-divorce family with Adam, played by Kris Marshall, trying to come to terms not only with his new partner but also her previous life with children and an ex-husband.

He has no children but she has, which creates problems he has to deal with. His relationship with the ex-husband is also sensitive. The nuances of this family are used to offer opportunities for BT to emphasise its various products.

4.2.2 Individual influences

As individuals, we have distinct characteristics which influence our buying decisions. Psychological factors such as our personality and attitudes as well as our personal situation are important clues to how we react in certain situations, and how we may respond to marketing stimuli.

Individual motivation

What motivates us to buy the products and services that we do? We are motivated to want products and services because we have needs to satisfy (see Chapter 3). These can be basic physical requirements for food, drink and shelter – needs which override all others if they are not satisfied. Once satisfied, other needs such as our desire to socialise with others, gain respect and status and achieve self-fulfilment can be considered (see the more detailed outline of Maslow's Hierarchy of Needs in Chapter 3, section 3.1).

Owen's motivation to buy shoes was originally the physiological need to avoid the discomfort caused by walking around without them. However, he already has several pairs which can fulfil this basic requirement and his recent desire to buy a new pair of trainers was mainly motivated by status needs to keep up with his friends.

Susannah recognised that in our society education influences not only how we meet our basic needs through our ability to earn money, but also our ability to attain higher needs such as social acceptability, prestige and a satisfying career. She is therefore motivated to obtain a good education for her daughter because of the many benefits which this may bring her daughter and the corresponding satisfaction and esteem which a successful daughter will bestow on her.

Susannah and Owen are motivated – they are ready to act. How they act as individuals is influenced by a variety of other factors, as discussed below.

Trait		Range of types	
Compulsiveness		Compulsive ——— Non-compulsive	
Gregariousness		Extrovert ——— Introvert	
Autonomy		Dependent ——— Independent	
Conservatism		Conservative ——— Radical	
Authoritarianism		Authoritarian ——— Democratic	
Leadership		Leader ——— Follower	
Ambitious		High achiever ——— Low achiever	

FIGURE 4.4

Classification of personality types

Personality types

We are all different from one another in that we are unique combinations of different personality traits, but there are some traits within us that tend to predominate in certain situations. Some people, for example, have a compulsive trait which leads them to respond to certain events in a consistently compulsive way. Others only take decisions after careful analysis of all the factors. Such traits are dominant in that they regularly appear in certain situations. This can mean that we respond to our external environment in a consistent way.

Our personalities exhibit several types of dominant traits which act as a regular influence on how we behave. Many attempts have been made to classify these traits into personality types (sometimes referred to as stereotypes) such as the one shown in Figure 4.4.

If definite links can be established between a person's personality type and their likelihood to purchase certain products or respond to marketing programmes, this could provide valuable information for making marketing decisions. Despite considerable research, correlations have been hard to establish, indicating that personality traits are perhaps only a marginal factor influencing consumer choices. Researchers have, however, proven strong links in some situations.

One investigation into the drinking habits of young men in Britain showed that impulsive, venturesome extroverts consume more beer and cider in public bars and restaurants than more introverted types. This information could be useful to marketing management in a range of decisions, from the selection of advertising for specific brands to the creation of the most conducive atmospheres in pubs.

Self-image

Related to classifications of personality type is the concept of self-image, which sums up how we think about ourselves. We all have complex images about ourselves – a mental assessment of how we look and behave in given situations. We may believe we are better at certain types of activities (such as meeting people or dressing well) than others (dealing with figures, making speeches). These images are made more complicated by an assessment of the viewpoint from which they are taken, such as:

■ *Real Self*: You as you really are

■ *Ideal Self*: You as you would like to be

■ *Looking Glass Self*: You as you think others see you

■ *Self-image*: You as you see yourself

How we see ourselves in this way influences how we react in purchase decision-making circumstances.

Owen Polanski has a gregarious personality and he is very conscious of the image he projects to those he meets. He believes he is a 'modern man' who selects products which make statements about his dislike of overtly materialistic attitudes whilst reflecting the up-to-date fashion tastes of his young age group. He is not at all impressed by one boutique he visits, which has an exclusive atmosphere of thick carpets, luxurious fittings and attentive assistants. He feels relaxed in a more utilitarian shop with only basic furniture and minimal service but a large selection of canvas and non-leather shoes on display.

Susannah Flynn visited the local schools in order to make a choice between them. In each case she met the head teacher. From her own school days she has a strong mental image of herself in a very subservient role to her head teacher; she starts from a position of a poor self-image, which colours how she reacts in these meetings. She is most impressed by one head teacher who makes a deliberate effort to put her at ease and talks to her as an equal. She finds another meeting uncomfortable because the head teacher uses some educational jargon, which she pretends to understand for fear of showing herself up.

Perception

We interpret information received through our senses in an individual way. Our perception will be affected by our ability to selectively perceive, retain and distort events.

Our perception of an event differs from someone else's interpretation of the same situation. Two people listening to the same salesperson, looking at the same product, and sensing the atmosphere of the same shop, end up with different perceptions of this same experience.

Our perceptions are coloured not only by our experiences, backgrounds and personalities, but also our ability to selectively receive only the information or stimuli which interest us. We screen out messages that do not concern us and tune in to ones that do. Parents can sleep undisturbed by the noise of a busy street outside, yet awake at the slightest cry from their baby in the next room. In a similar way we can ignore most of the marketing communications that bombard us every day, whilst retaining the one that triggers a specific interest. It has been estimated that we perceive less than 1 per cent of all the advertisements to which we are exposed.

For this reason, marketing managers often aim for a high number of repetitions of advertisements to make sure that the messages have been received. Similarly, a good salesperson frequently asks questions during a presentation to a prospective customer in order to obtain feedback on their perspective of what has been said so far. It is all too easy to assume that what we say or do is perceived by others in the same way as we perceive it ourselves.

In our example, Owen has a colleague who has recently bought a pair of trainers. Much to Owen's irritation, this person talks constantly about how much these trainers cost, despite the fact that he does no sport. Owen knows that their other colleagues are equally annoyed by his boasting and is determined not to buy the same trainers, however good they are. His perception of the trainers is altered by how other people would see him if he bought them.

Susannah's experience has also coloured her perception. One head teacher confused Susannah with educational jargon during their meeting. He may have perceived that he was demonstrating his professional competence by using specialised language. Susan's perception was that he was probably not a very good teacher as he could not make himself understood even by an adult.

We can also distort information by wanting to hear only things which fit with our personal maps of the world. So we may internally discredit politicians who have views which differ from our own or research which contradicts our views.

Consider Owen, who hears a news report that is very derogatory about men who don't exercise but who wear trainers. The report mentions that the average mileage of a mountain bike is two miles and that 95 per cent of trainers are bought by people who don't exercise at all.

Or think about Susannah, who is a working mother. One report she reads says that this fact will make her children more socially aware and independent, another that they will be dysfunctional lacking a maternal role model. She believes the first and discredits the second – it was written by a childless male, after all.

Learning

We learn from actions and decisions we have taken in the past. Our future buying decisions will be influenced by what we have learned during past buying experiences. Learning theorists believe that much of human behaviour is learned either from direct personal experience of a trial-and-error nature, or through seeking solutions based on a more reasoned approach. The implications to marketing management are that demand and repeat purchasing of products can be built up by reinforcing consumers' positive associations and experiences of a product and correcting any negative ones.

Owen has never purchased a pair of trainers for himself before. However he is favourably disposed towards some brands of trainers, as he has learned about their quality standards by buying other shoes of the same make. He also has a mental picture of some types of trainers that he has either admired or disliked when he has seen them worn by others.

Susannah has never had to chose a school before, but she knows from her own experience as a schoolchild what she would like for her children. She has also talked to friends who have slightly older children so that she knows what to look for when she visits a school.

Beliefs and attitudes

Through our background and experiences we build up beliefs and attitudes that influence our buying behaviour.

A *belief* is an opinion or viewpoint we hold about something. It may indicate a degree of like or dislike which conditions our purchase decisions.

Owen holds some current beliefs about trainers – specific thoughts about some of the products and the images they project. He will tend to act on these beliefs unless specific marketing activities change them. An advertising campaign may shift his opinions or a sales assistant in a shop may be able to influence his beliefs about a certain make.

Susannah also has beliefs about schools that have led her to have views about which schools would be best for each of her three children.

Similarly our attitudes towards different brands will affect our reaction to their shortcomings. Consider the following fictional story about the impact of our perceptions on brands:

Sejal leaves work at lunchtime in search of an egg sandwich, her favourite type of lunch.

She goes first of all to Marks and Spencer. It is not her preferred store but it is nearest. She can't find any egg sandwiches and stops a shop assistant who tells her that all the egg sandwiches have been sold. Disappointed and hungry, she stomps back to work and complains to anyone who will listen about Marks and Spencer's general incompetence, and how hopeless it has become.

The next day she walks past Marks and Spencer in search of a much-wanted egg sandwich. She walks another 200 metres to a Pret a Manger store that she adores. She still can't find any egg sandwiches so she asks the woman behind the counter where they are. Once again she is told that they have sold out. She smiles at the assistant and says, 'Sorry it's my fault, I should have come earlier'.

An *attitude* is a body of opinions which represent a way of thinking or an outlook on life. This body of opinions acts as a framework on which we build our thoughts and beliefs – likes and dislikes – about specific products. We may have an attitude that top-quality products always cost more, or that it is always desirable to buy a particular brand. This influences our belief about the quality and desirability of certain products.

Attitudes are harder to change because they represent a mindset of beliefs and opinions that require several adjustments to alter.

Owen's attitude, for example, is that trainers are the right shoes for him and that the brand is really important to convey the appropriate image of him.

Susannah's attitude is that education is a serious business, which requires firm discipline and hard work. In looking around schools, she tends to like those that are quiet, with children working purposefully at their desks. She particularly dislikes one, which is full of noise and bustle even though the teacher explains that they encourage this more natural atmosphere to make learning fun and stimulate creativity.

4.2.3 Lifestyle

So far we have looked at both social and individual influences at work in the 'black box' where consumer purchase decisions are made. Marketing commentators have relied heavily on the disciplines of economics, sociology and psychology to help explain these forces. Marketing researchers have developed one concept which combines these various approaches under the heading of 'lifestyle'.

Lifestyle is a summary of how we live. It includes our activities, interests, opinions and aspirations. The concept of lifestyle goes beyond the separate influences of culture, social class, personality or attitudes, yet combines them all. People of the same subculture or personality type do not necessarily share the same lifestyle, although these factors do influence which one they choose.

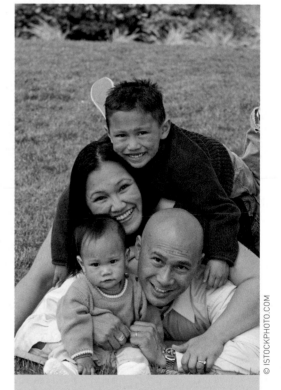

The Quiet Family Man

Psychographics

Psychographics, the technique of measuring lifestyles, has developed several classifications of lifestyle groups. Once identified, these groups can be targeted with products and communications designed to appeal to their composite profile.

For example, one psychographic study divided men into eight lifestyle categories:

- **The Quiet Family Man**: self-sufficient, shy, focus on family life, shuns community involvement, high TV viewing, marked fantasy life, practical buyer, low-level consumer

© ISTOCKPHOTO.COM

The Traditionalist

The Discontented Man

The Ethical Highbrow

The Pleasure-orientated Man

- ■ *The Traditionalist*: secure, high self-esteem, conventional, respectable, altruistic and caring, conservative shopper, selects known brands

- ■ *The Discontented Man*: dissatisfied at work, feels bypassed by life, dreams of better things, distrustful and socially aloof, price-conscious buyer

- ■ *The Ethical Highbrow*: concerned, sensitive, puritanical, content with family friends and work, interested in culture and social reform, buys quality and prepared to pay the price

- ■ *The Pleasure-Orientated Man*: emphasises masculinity, self-image as leader, self-centred, seeks immediate gratification of needs, impulsive buyer, likes products with masculine image

- **The Achiever**: hardworking, dedicated to success, prestige, power and money, adventurous hobbies, stylish, likes good food and music, status-conscious consumer, discriminating buyer

- **The He-Man**: gregarious, likes action, excitement and drama, bachelor-type even if married, buys products with 'man of action' image

- **The Sophisticated Man**: intellectual, socially concerned, artistic and intellectual achievements, wide interests, wants to lead, attracted to unique and fashionable goods

© ISTOCKPHOTO.COM/JELANI MEMORY

The Achiever

© ISTOCKPHOTO.COM/JIM JURICA

The He-Man

© ISTOCKPHOTO.COM/EVA SERRABASSA

The Sophisticated Man

4.3 THE BUYING PROCESS FOR CONSUMERS

We have examined some of the many influences on consumer buying decisions from the marketing inputs to group and individual factors. This section looks at how consumers make decisions – the processes that are followed in order to buy a product or service.

4.3.1 Types of decisions

The process of deciding what to buy is affected by the importance of the decision to the consumer. Some decisions become routine and automatic (e.g. buying a loaf of bread or a postage stamp). Others are irregular and more impulsive, triggered by a sudden desire (e.g. buying an ice-cream from a street vendor or a bar of chocolate on display at the checkout of a supermarket). Others require more selection, but are regularly carried out (e.g. buying some types of clothes such as socks and underwear, selecting a magazine or purchasing fruit from a street market). Some decisions are infrequent and require more thought even though the value may not be high (e.g. presents for a friend, books, some types of clothes such as a pair of shoes); other, infrequent, decisions become even more significant to the purchaser because of their high value (e.g. buying a house, choosing a holiday, arranging a pension).

These types of buying decisions differ in the amount of involvement the consumer has in the process. In some there is very little active involvement; in others there is a high degree of participation. This can be represented as a spectrum ranging from high to low involvement in the decision-making process, as shown in Figure 4.5.

We do not necessarily become more involved as the value of the purchase item increases. A present for a friend may not cost very much but takes a long time to select. Involvement changes through:

- **Familiarity**: as purchase decisions are repeated they become quicker and simpler

- **Significance**: important decisions that have a greater significance in the purchaser's life go through a more elaborate process (although this does not always mean they are better decisions as a result); because we make these decisions infrequently we can make big mistakes

4.3.2 Models of decision processes

Early composite models

Several models have been put forward that attempt to describe the various components in the consumer decision making process. Early models, such as those developed by Engel, Kollat and Blackwell (1968) and Howard and Sheth (1969), amount to complex maps which describe all

FIGURE 4.5 *A spectrum of decision-maker involvement*

Low	BUYER INVOLVEMENT IN PURCHASE DECISION			High
'Routine' ❏ Loaf of bread ❏ Postage stamp	**'Impulse'** ❏ Ice cream ❏ Bar of chocolate	**'Regular'** ❏ Socks ❏ Magazine ❏ Fruit	**'Irregular'(small)** ❏ Presents ❏ Pair of shoes ❏ Books	**'Irregular'(large)** ❏ House ❏ Pension fund

FIGURE 4.6 *The stages of a consumer buying process*

the possible components of a purchase decision. However, these models do not explain how the various components relate to each other, or how they can be measured. They also assume that purchase decisions are a thought-out series of logical events. Whilst this may be true of decisions with high purchaser involvement, it is less applicable to low-involvement decisions.

The stages of a buying process

Models are useful, however, in describing the possible stages that a buyer might go through in making a decision. In some cases, particularly where there is low involvement, stages are missed out or the order is changed. But it is important for marketing management to recognise the possible stages because each one represents an opportunity to influence the outcome of the decision. Figure 4.6 shows the potential stages in a buying process, which we will examine in more detail.

The first three stages represent a decision process before buying; the fourth stage is the actual act of purchase, followed in the fifth stage by a period of usage and evaluation of the product or service. This implies that the consumer is involved in the marketplace before and after buying the product, not just during the actual time of purchase. As we have seen, the level of this involvement varies greatly.

Need recognition

The process cannot begin until we recognise a need. This may be in response to a specific problem (e.g. a broken window, an evening with nothing to do) or a regular and common need (e.g. hunger, companionship, prestige). The need may be triggered by internal stimuli (e.g. a physiological need such as thirst) or external stimuli (e.g. TV adverts, shop displays).

It is important that marketing management understands several aspects of this stage:

■ The factors that may stimulate the recognition of a need for their products

■ How to use these factors to full advantage

■ How to deal with the response to the recognition of need

Think back to how this could play out in our fictional examples. Imagine that Owen's desire for a pair of trainers had not reached a high level of priority among the various needs and wants that competed for his financial resources. However, a shop window caught his attention as he passed by because trainers were displayed in a way that reminded him of his desire to buy this particular product. The retailer had recognised that an interesting window display could prompt recognition of need.

Similarly, consider the response when Susannah was prompted to begin selecting a school for her daughter by a general letter from the local education authority, which reminded her and other parents that a decision on a preferred school had to be notified to them by a certain date. One local school was not prepared for the response that this caused when many parents rang to arrange a visit on receipt of this letter. Susan was initially put off this school as it

FIGURE 4.7 *A range of levels of information search*

required several attempts to get through and when she did the replies to her questions were curt and hurried.

Information search

The recognition of a need may prompt the search for more information. This may be active, or more passive, or in some cases not carried out at all, as Figure 4.7 illustrates.

The level of information search reflects the degree of consumer involvement. At one extreme, the need is recognised but no further information is sought as the consumer moves straight to the act of purchase. If we need a drink, we may go to the nearest store and buy one. At the other extreme, an active search for information is instigated by reviewing product literature, reading consumer reviews, talking to friends or seeing product demonstrations. This is much more likely where there is high involvement, and associated high perceived risk. Buying a car is likely to fall into this category.

Another possibility is that the consumer acknowledges the need but takes no deliberate steps towards fulfilling it. Instead their awareness of products or services fulfilling the need is heightened and they become more receptive to communications about those products, including advertising and promotions, and conversations among friends.

In the case of both active searches by consumers and the more passive state of heightened awareness, the intervention of marketing activities at this stage can be crucial to the decision-making process.

In our example, Owen's awareness of trainers was further heightened as he passed the shop with the interesting display for a second time. He decided to seek additional information on prices and styles available by going inside.

Susannah's search for information on schools is much more deliberate and structured as she considered this to be a key decision in her young daughter's life. She talked to friends of their experiences and recommendations, collected school brochures, and made arrangements to visit those schools she considered most suitable.

Evaluation of alternatives

The consumer processes the information that has been gathered (actively or passively) and in a competitive market evaluates the alternatives. At this stage the consumer is trying to assess which product will best deliver the benefits they are seeking.

Marketing activities that seek to influence this evaluation can only be effective if they focus on the benefits which interest the consumer. If targeted consumers are looking for high quality, it may not be helpful to advertise low prices. If shopping convenience is the highest priority, it may not be appropriate to offer the most extensive range of products if this detracts from ease of access.

An assistant showed Owen several pairs of trainers. He was initially put off some of the brands which presented a sporting image which was not what he wanted. He became more interested when the assistant empathised with his desire for fashionable, non-leather trainers which fitted his self-image of a modern yet caring man.

Susannah evaluated schools primarily on their ability to deliver the basic curriculum of the '3 Rs' of reading, writing and arithmetic, which she saw as the key benefit her daughter needed from her first school. She used word-of-mouth reputation as her main method to evaluate this. She was not impressed by one school where the head teacher continually emphasised the quality of their music teaching, as this was of little interest to Susan.

Purchase choice

The evaluation of alternatives leads to an intention to purchase a certain brand of product or take up a particular type of service. This intention is normally followed by a confirmation of the purchase choice unless new factors intervene such as:

- *The intervention of other people*: Owen made up his mind to purchase a pair of the trainers he had tried on in the shop once he received his monthly paycheque. He told a friend, who warned him of a bad experience regarding the quality of the same type of trainers. Owen decided to think again.

- *The intervention of the unexpected*: Susannah chose a local school and informed the local education authority. She was taken by surprise when she was later informed that her first choice school was over-subscribed and her daughter could not be admitted. Instead she was offered a place at a school lower down her list of preferences.

Post-purchase experience

When a consumer buys a product, they do so with a set of expectations in mind concerning the performance of their purchase. These expectations are derived from their own research and the claims that the suppliers make for the product. They expect it to deliver the promised benefits.

Their level of satisfaction with the purchase is derived from a comparison between these expectations and the actual performance of the product. If it fails to deliver the promised benefits then the dissatisfaction caused can affect future sales in two important ways:

- The consumer does not repurchase that particular product but switches to another make

- The dissatisfied consumer tells other people who are less likely to purchase the product as a result: this is particularly important for services which are difficult to test or experience prior to purchase and therefore rely heavily on reputation to encourage new customers

Research among restaurant users found that dissatisfied customers invariably told their friends but rarely complained to the management of the restaurant. It also found that the most frequent method of choosing a new restaurant was word-of-mouth recommendation, especially from friends. These findings have significant marketing implications: satisfied customers are the most influential form of advertising for restaurant owners. Conversely, dissatisfied customers work as a potent invisible force, deterring new customers and undetected by management until the damage has been done.

The relationship between expectation and performance places a responsibility on marketing management to avoid making exaggerated claims for their products and services. If expectations are raised beyond the normal capabilities of the product by unrealistic or over-enthusiastic marketing communications prior to the sale, then levels of satisfaction are decreased in the post-purchase period, with a consequent adverse effect on future sales. If, on the other hand, product performance exceeds expectations then this is likely to be noticed and have positive effects.

Many retailers now offer a 'no-quibble' refund policy for these reasons. They know that a dissatisfied customer has a potential negative worth far exceeding the value of the lost sale.

Owen returned to the shoe shop and told the assistant that he would not be going ahead with the purchase of the trainers reserved for him because of the quality problems experienced by his friend. The assistant countered by saying that the trainers were now a totally new product which were widely acclaimed for their quality standards, equivalent to much more expensive shoes. Owen was persuaded by an eloquent selling performance and purchased the shoes. Although he did not experience the problems described by his friend, a small defect did develop. This would not normally have bothered him, but because he was expecting perfection following the sales assistant's high praise for the product he was dissatisfied and complained to his friends.

Susannah was pleasantly surprised at the happiness and progress of her daughter in her new school. This was at the level she had anticipated from her first choice of school, but exceeded her expectations for this school which had been lower down her list of preferences. This unexpected satisfaction made her even more enthusiastic when she discussed schools with other parents.

4.3.3 Summary of consumer buying behaviour

We can now summarise the influences on consumer buying behaviour that we have explored in this chapter. These are shown in Figure 4.8.

FIGURE 4.8

A summary of influences and stages in consumer buying

CHECKPOINT

How do you behave as a buyer? Think of some purchases you have made recently. Try to think of examples at either end of the 'buyer involvement spectrum', that is, a purchase over which you took considerable time and trouble, and something you bought without too much thought. Analyse the steps you went through to make each purchase and the factors that influenced you at each stage. How can this information help the organisations marketing the products you bought?

MARKETING MISTAKES

WHAT'S UNDER THE HOOD?

One of the major challenges in marketing is trying to understand target markets that are different from your own experiences. Given that most marketers are middle class and middle aged, urban youth represents a particular challenge. Similarly the grey market (those of retirement age) offers challenges to marketers who are decades younger.

Youth marketing is very lucrative since the sector has great spending power but can seem impenetrable from the outside. For many brands it is essential to connect with youth culture as they can drive trends, fashions and crazes. To connect with this market, the company needs an understanding of this subculture. 'Hoodies', are a much-maligned group that gains energy from rebellion.

Brands such as Sony PlayStation are renowned for their ability to connect with the urban youth market. Despite their consistent performance in this sector, they made a major error when they launched PlayStation Portable in 2006. They hired street artists to spray-paint paintings with graffiti-style images of young people playing with the handset. The campaign attracted derision, with critics accusing Sony of trying to commercialise the credibility of street art. Many of the executions, which ran across cities in the US, were defaced with angry messages such as 'Stop hawking corporate

Sony PlayStation's use of graffiti misfired in their attempt to tap into youth culture

products and big business on our neighbourhood walls' and 'Corporate vandals not welcome'.

For a brand such as PlayStation to get it so wrong is all the more notable since many admire its ability to connect with youth audiences without patronising them. Brands need to be wary about adopting even the most obvious element of youth culture. As one senior marketer of a youth marketing agency said, 'Using graffiti doesn't mean that you understand young people, or that they understand you.'

MARKETING, 18 OCTOBER 2006, PAGE 28.

4.4 ORGANISATIONAL BUYER BEHAVIOUR

In Chapter 3 (section 3.5.2), we saw that markets can be divided into two basic types:

■ Consumer markets of individuals buying mainly for personal consumption

■ Organisational markets in which organisations buy goods and services for business use, further processing or for resale to others; we further subdivided these organisational markets into industrial, intermediary and government markets dependant on the activities of the organisation

Does buying in organisations differ from consumer buying behaviour? Organisations are made up of people who are still influenced by the social and individual forces that we have already explored in this chapter (see section 4.2). However, the nature of the decisions and the processes for decision-making are often different in organisations.

4.4.1 Types of organisational buying decisions

Different types of organisational buying decisions follow different buying processes. Early research in this field (e.g. Robinson, Faris and Wind, 1967) recognised three main types of decision, or 'buy classes': straight re-buy decisions, modified re-buy decisions and new task purchasing decisions. These are dealt with in turn below.

Straight re-buy decisions

Established organisationsal have systems and policies which make some decisions standard and routine. Repeat buying decisions are often made in this way.

In manufacturing companies, the ongoing supply of raw materials may be purchased under contract simply by calling off the quantity of goods required in a specific period. Retailers have automatic re-ordering systems which are triggered when stocks fall to a certain level. Offices often order stationery and office supplies on a routine basis by emailing requirements regularly to one preferred supplier.

The purchasing of services is often on the basis of a straight re-buy from a preferred contractor such as a maintenance company, an advertising agency or a firm of accountants.

Modified re-buy decisions

Sometimes purchasing to meet an existing need is subject to review and buying decisions are modified. The reasons for the review may be discontentment with an existing supplier, pressure to decrease costs, opportunities to buy more advanced products, or simply that it is policy to review suppliers on a regular basis.

For example, consider the following modified re-buy decisions:

■ A manufacturer is unhappy with the consistency of the quality of one of its raw materials and decides to investigate alternative sources of supply

■ A company has a policy of always involving more than one supplier when purchases of any product reach a certain level to protect the security of their supplies and improve their negotiating position

■ A wholesaler is unhappy with the profit margin on one product line and decides to look for an alternative

■ A charitable organisation has a policy of reviewing its major suppliers at least once every three years to ensure that it is still receiving value for money

New task purchasing decisions

An organisation takes a 'new task' buying decision when it purchases a particular type of product or service for the first time. The reasons for this include the launch of a new product or service, the need to acquire a new technology, or an internal reorganisation.

Consider the following new task purchasing decisions:

■ A retailer decides to diversify by adding a new range of products, which involves dealing with a completely different type of supplier

■ A growing business computerises its accounts and payroll systems, which involves investigating software packages for the first time

■ New regulations force a hospital to put a service, which had hitherto been provided in house, out to tender by private sector companies

4.4.2 Stages in the organisational buying process

As in consumer buying, various stages, or 'buy phases', have been identified in the process of buying in an organisation. All buy phases are not always activated in some types of buying decision but the full eight stages are outlined below, with two examples of the process in action.

Problem or need recognition

Many factors can trigger the recognition of a buying need including most of the situations described above (in section 4.3.1). These include internal stimuli, such as dissatisfaction with existing purchases, and external factors such as a visit from the salesperson of a new supplier. Consider:

■ A manufacturer is dissatisfied with the productivity of one of its processes and begins to consider alternatives for improvement

■ A charitable organisation is alerted to a new fund-raising opportunity by the advertising of telephone selling agencies in a magazine

General description of need

Recognition of a need leads to a general description of what is required in terms of the characteristics and quantity of items likely to fulfil the need. The principal benefits from any purchase are identified. For example:

■ The production manager of the manufacturer above identifies some new types of equipment that could make its problem process more efficient and begins an evaluation of the benefits versus the costs

■ The campaign director of the charity organises internal discussions of the fund-raising potential of telephone selling to its supporters and the implications for the organisation

Specification of product required

A specific description of the characteristics of what is required is the next stage, often involving wide consultation with other departments in larger organisations. Using the previous examples:

■ The engineering department of the manufacturer draws up a detailed specification of the type of equipment required after meetings involving production, engineering, purchasing and financial management

■ The fund-raising managers of the charity details the type of telephone sales operation they envisage with cost budgets and revenue targets

Search for suppliers

The next stage in organisational buying behaviour is to look for potential suppliers of the product or service they require. In our manufacturer and our charity examples:

■ The manufacturer's purchasing manager phones equipment suppliers already known to the company

■ A fund-raising manager of the charity is given the responsibility of researching and contacting telephone sales agencies that could meet their brief; this was done largely by searching the Internet and using trade directories

Request for proposals

Buying organisations then normally identify a shortlist of possible suppliers and ask them to submit a quotation to supply the product or service specified. In our examples:

■ The purchasing manager asks for quotations for the supply of the specified equipment from three sources, including details of delivery times, guarantees and after-sales service

■ The fund-raising manager talks to several marketing agencies with telephone sales operations and asks each for a written proposal of the service and the terms they could offer.

Selection of supplier

Proposals and quotations are evaluated and a supplier is selected:

■ The purchasing manager discusses the quotations he receives with the production and finance managers and together they put forward a recommendation to the manufacturing director, who has the decision ratified by the board of directors

■ The fund-raising manager reports back to the management committee of the charity with proposals for a telephone sales campaign and a recommended agency to carry out the work

Specification of terms and conditions

The order is finally placed with the terms and conditions of supply agreed and specified:

■ The purchasing manager signs a contract for the supply of the equipment and organises the leasing finance previously agreed by the finance department

■ The campaign director signs an agreement with a marketing agency for the supply of a specified amount of telephoning selling and the parameters for carrying this out

Performance review

Finally the buying organisation reviews the purchased product or service and evaluates the outcomes against their expectations. For example:

■ Reports from the production manager indicate that the new equipment has improved productivity substantially and recommend the purchase of another machine

■ The fund-raising management of the charity reviews the telephone selling operation and concludes that a combination of poor results and complaints from supporters objecting to being approached in this way indicate that the campaign should be discontinued

4.4.3 A framework for organisational buying situations

The classifications outlined above of the types of buying decisions (or 'buy classes'), and the stages in the buying process ('buy phases') can be amalgamated to form a framework or grid of organisational buying situations. This 'buy grid' is shown in Table 4.5, which also indicates which buy phases are likely to be implemented in each of the buy classes.

TABLE 4.5 *The buy grid framework for organisational buying*

	BUY CLASSES		
STAGES OF BUYING PROCESS	Straight re-buy	Modified re-buy	New task
NEED RECOGNITION	✘	?	✔
GENERAL NEED DESCRIPTION	✘	?	✔
SPECIFICATION OF PRODUCT	✔	✔	✔
SEARCH FOR SUPPLIERS	✘	?	✔
REQUEST OF PROPOSALS	✘	?	✔
SELECTION OF SUPPLIER	✘	?	✔
SPECIFICATION OF TERMS	✘	?	✔
PERFORMANCE REVIEW	✔	✔	✔

✔ = Yes, stage activated ✘ = No, stage not activated ? = Maybe, stage sometimes activated

ADAPTED FROM ROBINSON, FARIS AND WIND, 1967.

4.4.4 The decision-making unit (DMU)

One of the characteristics of organisational buying is that more than one person can be involved in the decision-making process. As a result, marketing to organisations often involves targeting more than one individual. Identification of the membership of the so-called 'decision-making unit' (DMU) or 'buying centre' is a key part of marketing to organisations.

Participation in buying decisions

Several types of decision-makers participate in buying. Some of these have already been illustrated by the various participants in the buying decision of the manufacturer and charitable organisation described above. These include:

■ *Collective bodies*: Boards of directors, management committees, governing bodies

■ *Individuals*: Directors, managers, other delegated decision-makers

■ *Departments*: Department managers, departments (e.g. production, engineering, fundraising)

Participation in buying decisions depends on several factors:

■ *The size of the organisation*: For example, an owner-manager may make all the buying decisions in a small enterprise

■ *The culture of the organisation*: Some entrepreneurial organisations encourage delegation of authority and buying decisions are predominantly individual; other organisations are more bureaucratic and insist that even low-level purchasing is subject to checks and constraints by several participants

The Traditionalist

The Discontented Man

The Ethical Highbrow

The Pleasure-orientated Man

- **The Traditionalist**: secure, high self-esteem, conventional, respectable, altruistic and caring, conservative shopper, selects known brands

- **The Discontented Man**: dissatisfied at work, feels bypassed by life, dreams of better things, distrustful and socially aloof, price-conscious buyer

- **The Ethical Highbrow**: concerned, sensitive, puritanical, content with family friends and work, interested in culture and social reform, buys quality and prepared to pay the price

- **The Pleasure-Orientated Man**: emphasises masculinity, self-image as leader, self-centred, seeks immediate gratification of needs, impulsive buyer, likes products with masculine image

- **The Achiever**: hardworking, dedicated to success, prestige, power and money, adventurous hobbies, stylish, likes good food and music, status-conscious consumer, discriminating buyer

- **The He-Man**: gregarious, likes action, excitement and drama, bachelor-type even if married, buys products with 'man of action' image

- **The Sophisticated Man**: intellectual, socially concerned, artistic and intellectual achievements, wide interests, wants to lead, attracted to unique and fashionable goods

The Achiever

The He-Man

The Sophisticated Man

■ *The type of buying decision*: Some decisions are routine (straight re-buy) and only need one person involvement; other purchases are exceptional, with potential risk to the organisation (new task), and merit careful consideration by several participants

Roles within the decision-making unit

In buying decisions involving several people, the participants play different roles depending on their position in the organisation, their specialised knowledge and personal motivations. These have been characterised as:

■ *The Gatekeeper*: Acts as a filter for information concerning buying possibilities. Gatekeepers include buying departments that receive supplier and product information, people in specialised jobs whose functions include keeping up-to-date data in their area, senior managers exposed to fresh ideas at meetings and conferences and secretaries who filter post.

■ *The User*: Ultimately, the consumer or recipient of the product. Users vary from production managers to post rooms, with varying levels of influence over what is purchased for their use.

■ *The Influencer*: Has a say in the choice of product. This may be for a variety of reasons such as technical expertise (e.g. the engineering department) or because they have the ear of the decision-maker (e.g. a personal assistant).

■ *The Decision-maker*: Takes the actual decision to purchase. As the player of this role changes according to the type of decision, the identification of this key person is an important phase in marketing to an organisation.

These roles are not mutually exclusive. Someone can be both a user and a decision-maker, for example. With small and medium-sized businesses in particular, these roles can be condensed. In very small companies one person may fulfil all roles!

4.4.5 Summary of organisational buying behaviour

Organisational buying behaviour is a complex series of processes. Several models have been developed, but managers marketing to organisations have found it difficult to apply them in practice because there are so many variants.

However, successful marketing and selling to organisations starts with an understanding of the factors which may apply in any buying situation. A summary of those examined above is shown in Figure 4.9.

CHECKPOINT

Imagine you have been appointed as the buyer of casual clothes for a chain of clothes shops. How would you go about selecting your ranges? Explain in detail the activities, such as meetings and visits, you would undertake and the information you would need before making any buying decisions. How could a potential supplier hope to influence your decision-making in their favour?

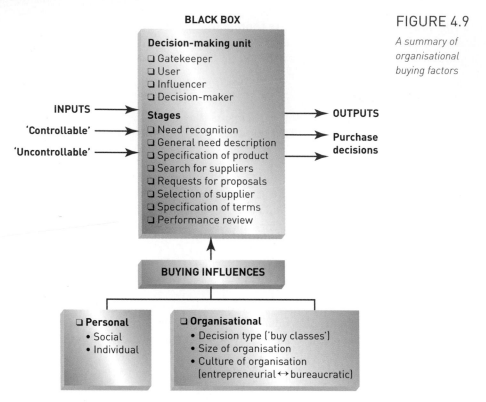

FIGURE 4.9

A summary of organisational buying factors

4.5 SUMMARY

- Customers make buying decisions in a way that cannot be directly observed. However, inputs and influences into the decision-making process can be assessed by the buying decisions that result.

- Consumer buying decisions are influenced by:
  - Social factors, including culture, subculture, social class and reference groups including the family
  - Individual factors, including motivation, personality type, self-image, perception, learning, beliefs and attitudes
  - Lifestyle factors, which combine social and individual inputs and can be classified into psychographic groups

- Consumer buying can be divided into five stages: need recognition, information search, evaluation of alternatives, purchase choice, and post-purchase experience. Some purchases require a lower involvement by the buyer and do not go through all the stages in the process (e.g. routine or impulse purchases).

- Organisational buying can be divided into eight stages: need recognition, general need description, specification of the product, search for suppliers, requests for proposals, selection of supplier, specification of terms and conditions, and performance review.

- Organisational buying decisions are influenced by:
  - The type of decision or buy class of 'straight re-buy', 'modified re-buy' or 'new task'
  - The decision-making unit (DMU) of 'gatekeeper', 'user', 'influencer' and 'decision-maker'
  - The size and culture of the organisation

4.6 ACTIVITIES

STATIUS MANAGEMENT SERVICES LTD

Mark Woods is justly proud of his company, Statius Management Services. He has built it up from nothing to a turnover of £750,000 in fifteen years. He employs five consultants and two telesales operators. The financial situation is secure, but he sees opportunities for growth.

The name comes from Roman mythology: Statius, with his guiding light, was the inspiration for Dante's epic journey from Purgatory to Paradise. In the same way, the principle behind Statius Management Services Ltd is to help clients to make light work of raising standards. They aim to help clients develop their management processes, often with the additional benefit of accreditation of a recognised standard in a relevant field.

Statius' revenue has come from helping client companies to gain this accreditation; there are myriad of standards required by companies operating in the UK and EU. The company helps businesses through the process of getting ISO 9000, Investors in People and many other kite marks. Mark views his consultants as the driving instructors who help their clients get their licences. Basically their role is to help managers run their businesses more effectively. They operate exclusively in the business-to-business field and therefore an understanding of organisational buying behaviour is essential.

Statius' main business has come from a lucrative relationship with the lift industry. As health and safety is a prime issue in that sector, there are strong incentives to have rigorous management practices in place. Mark's experience in the sector means that he knows it inside out. So he is looking for a new challenge. Which industries would need the same skills and have the same incentives?

After extensive secondary research and much filtering, he has come up with two potential targets: Local authorities and construction companies. Local government are becoming increasingly interested in formalised management practices and accreditation with the relevant standards. The same applies to their suppliers, who need

Statius have had success in the construction industry where health and safety issues are paramount

accreditation to even be considered for the short-list to get a contract. A particular issue for them is environment management systems (EMS). As environmental issues move up the national government agenda, so local government follows. Construction clearly has many of the health and safety issues of the lift industry, as well as environmental concerns.

Mark knew that local authorities (LAs) have a very long and protracted buying cycle. Even when central and local governments have targets, buying decisions tend to be very slow. These are large organisations, employing thousands of people and spending millions of pounds. Lots of people are involved in the decision-making process, adding to the time factor. In addition, public accountability means that lots of paperwork is required and managers are very conscious of the audit trail.

Statius put together a detailed report to send to LAs, outlining the background to environmental management systems. How would he get executives and elected councillors on side? Mark was not hopeful as he knew that the large numbers of people involved and the long timescales meant that the report could get lost under a pile of paperwork.

But good news came from a surprising source. A local authority in Essex called about an EMS. Statius were already doing work for Epping Council in a number of other parts of the organisation and gained a reputation doing the ISO 9000 quality work. Also Mark had developed a rapport with the quality manager on the original project as they shared a common interest in classic cars.

The quality manager had passed on Mark's name to a colleague who had identified a need for an EMS. Whilst discussing the project with the council officers, Mark was interested to find that they wanted a system to manage the environment, but not because they had been told to do it, which was usually the case. In this instance, it was being driven externally by a demographic change which was leading to an increase in the numbers of environmentally aware professionals in the council's area. Increasingly, people in this group were asking about the council's processes and environmental credentials.

An additional benefit to Mark from this business was that the contract did not have to go to competitive bidding as it was relatively small. The council's policy was to only ask for bids if the contract was for more than £10,000. Mark knew from past experience that the council tended to take the lowest bid so the fact that this contract fell under that barrier worked in his favour. He effectively had no competition.

Mark moved on to his next target: construction companies. He knew from his secondary research and personal experience that there were literally thousands of owner-managed construction companies. These had grown from the ambitions of one, or perhaps two, key founders. Many companies were still run by these founders who had never got past their 'on the tools' mentality. Now they found themselves having to adhere to quality, environmental and health and safety systems that had not even been considered when they first began trading but were now absolutely necessary. The competition in these instances was often not other consultants but the owners' desire to buy a new van, appoint a new contracts manager, increase marketing spend, add money to a pension scheme or get a new car.

Some, however, were prepared to embrace new systems. One of Statius' previous clients did so and subsequently claimed that they had won £16 m worth of orders because they could demonstrate they had these standards. From Statius' perspective the advantage of this sector is that decisions are usually made relatively quickly, often in a few weeks and almost always within a few months.

Mark had to make a decision. It was his company and his choice. Should he go for both target sectors? Should he prioritise one? And how should he tackle it?

QUESTIONS

1 How do you think that problem recognition might work in the two sectors of local authorities and construction? What is the general description of need?

2 How might the two sectors search for suppliers?

3 Who are the members of the decision-making unit in each sector? What are their roles?

4 How would you decide which buy class these decisions fall into?

5 How might Mark use this information to help his marketing efforts?

DEVELOPING A MARKETING PLAN

SWOT ANALYSIS

Write an initial SWOT analysis of the product or organisation that is the subject of your marketing plan.

■ What strengths and weaknesses are suggested by your internal audit?

■ Which opportunities and threats appear from your external audit?

This initial analysis may clarify some further areas for research. Note what these are as they can be followed up in Chapter 5.

4.7 FURTHER READING AND REFERENCES

Buyer behaviour

Belk, R.W. (1988), 'Possessions and the Extended Self', *Journal of Consumer Research*, Vol. 15, pages 139–168.

East, R., Vanhuele, M. and Wright, M. (2007), *Consumer Behaviour: Applications in Marketing* (Sage).

Engel J.F., Miniard, P.W. and Engel, J.F. (2007), *Consumer Behaviour*, 10th edition (Thomson Learning).

Solomon, R. (2004), *Consumer Behaviour: Buying, Having and Being*, 6th edition (Prentice Hall).

Chapter **5**

MARKETING RESEARCH

LEARNING OBJECTIVES

By the end of this chapter the reader will be able to:

- Understand the role of marketing research in different contexts
- Appreciate the scope of marketing research in such areas as customer and product research
- Understand the process of research through several stages
- Distinguish between the various research methods including qualitative and quantitative research
- Find secondary data for research
- Collect primary research data

INTRODUCTION

Marketing research is a specialised skill – one of the tools in marketing's bag of management techniques. It plays a key part in the analysis stage of the marketing process. This chapter explores marketing research by asking:

- What is the role and scope of marketing research? When is it useful?

- How is marketing research carried out? What are the processes involved?

- What are the various methods used in marketing research?

5.1 THE ROLE OF MARKETING RESEARCH

5.1.1 Marketing information

In previous chapters we looked at the various contexts in which marketing decisions are made, from general environmental and behavioural factors to specific market forces and trends in customer demands. A common theme throughout has been that marketing plans are made and

CASE STUDY

....

FAST FOODS

Ray Greenwich had decided to open a fast-food restaurant in the large urban area where he lived. As a specialist in the catering trade, he was attracted by the continued growth of this sector at a time when more traditional restaurants had seen a fall in their custom. However, he had a number of choices to make before deciding on the exact form of his business.

First he had to decide on the type of food he would offer. He was considering the relative merits of traditional take-away foods like sandwiches or fish and chips against more modern offerings such as burgers, pizzas and pastas, chicken or ethnic foods, stimulated mainly by developments in North America. He felt that whilst sandwiches could offer the stability of the largest existing customer base with around 30 per cent of the market, pizza might offer more potential, if perhaps more risk, as it was a fast-growing sector.

He was also undecided on location. Should he go for a High Street location where customers and competition abounded? Or should he try to attract travelling customers with a concession near the motorway or the railway station, or try a drive-through outlet?

He also had to make a decision about the type of service to be offered. Whilst he was keen to emphasise fast food, there were considerable variations on this theme. Take-aways were always popular, but should he also offer table service? He had read that home delivery was a particular growth area.

The size of the menu was a further issue. He was unsure whether to target the core market of fast-food customers or attempt to attract other, more specific groups. He knew, for example, that vegetarians had become a significant market, with sales of non-meat food growing fast. Concern for healthy eating and for environmentally friendly preparations and packaging was increasing, particularly amongst the younger generation. Should he offer the very limited menu of most fast-food outlets or look to a more extensive menu, which some of the established chains seemed to be developing? This led him to consider his pricing policy, because some outlets offered the cheapest possible food whilst others seemed to justify higher prices by offering something different.

Finally he was considering whether to go it alone or take up one of the many franchises offered by either the large franchisors or more limited, innovative operators.

He decided to discuss these issues with Margaret deSilva, a marketing research consultant.

'The trouble is', he told her, 'that most of the information available relates to the total market rather than the local picture. I know that nationally the main consumers of fast food are young – three out of four sixteen- to twenty-four-year-olds eat fast food at least once a month for example. Over thirty-five-year-olds seem to prefer to eat in more formal restaurants. But how does that help me here?'

'Yes, there is a lot of data from government statistics and other sources on the fast food market', she agreed. 'The market grew very rapidly in the 1990s and although it has slowed down today, it has become very large nationally. However, there are some warning signs as young people are not only the largest customer group but the biggest element in the labour force as well – and sixteen- to twenty-four-year-olds are a shrinking proportion of the total population. It will be useful to build up a picture of national and regional trends. But you are right – we will also need some other research to see how this information applies locally.'

QUESTIONS

1 Consider the role that marketing research can play in this situation. How can research help Ray Greenwich and what types of information does he need? *See sections 5.1 and 5.2*

▶

2 Assume you are Margaret deSilva. Outline the research plan that you would suggest to Greenwich:

  i   What objectives would you set and what areas would your research cover? *See section 5.2*

  ii What research methods could you use? *See section 5.4*

  iii What existing secondary sources of information would you use? *See section 5.5*

  iv What new primary data would you collect and how would you collect it? *See section 5.6*

3 Draft a questionnaire with the objective of profiling the local consumer of fast food in Greenwich's area. *See section 5.6.3*

executed in a complex world subject to constantly changing influences. As a result, the marketplace is full of uncertainties that can influence the outcomes of marketing programmes. These uncertainties stem from various sources, from large-scale cultural or lifestyle shifts and economic trends to specific market forces, competitive activity and customer changes.

The role of marketing research is to reduce this uncertainty as far as possible by providing relevant data and information as a basis for marketing intelligence.

Data, information or intelligence?

Marketing research uses several terms that need further definition as they carry different emphasis in their meanings:

- ■ *Data*: A collection of facts (e.g. purchases recorded at a supermarket till)

- ■ *Information*: Data which has been selected and sorted so that it can be analysed for a specific purpose (e.g. sales as recorded through the till of one particular brand compared to other brands)

- ■ *Intelligence*: The interpretation given to the information through analysis (e.g. recorded sales of the brand show an above-average increase compared to competitive brands, which correlates to a period of special promotion; the results of the promotion are quantified to provide a key input into future promotional decisions)

A marketing intelligence system (MIS)

Marketing research is part of an organisation's marketing intelligence system (MIS), which uses data and information from internal and external sources to better understand the interface between the environment and marketing activities. This is illustrated in Figure 5.1.

FIGURE 5.1 *Marketing intelligence systems*

Environment		Marketing information	Marketing activities
Micro-level	*Macro-level*	• Research	• Product development
• Customers	• Social	• Internal records	• Pricing
• Competitors	• Technological	• External sources	• Promotions
• Suppliers	• Economic		• Distribution
• Intermediaries	• Political		

There are numerous sources for marketing intelligence to work on:

- Marketing information from internal sources such as the sales force
- Marketing information from external sources such as trade fairs, conferences, and the trade press
- Accounting data from internal sources such as invoicing records and credit control reports
- Accounting information from external sources such as the reports and accounts of competitive companies
- Information derived from public information (e.g. government reports)
- Market intelligence reports on specific industries or market sectors, which can be purchased
- Information from the Internet, such as competitors' websites, online reports and newsgroups (online forums)
- Marketing research that is privately commissioned to report on a specific problem or opportunity

Marketing intelligence is used to tackle a wide spread of organisational issues including:

- *Strategic long-term decisions* (e.g. Which market should we be in? What growth can we anticipate?)
- *Tactical short-term decisions* (How do we promote this product in that market? How can we improve the coverage of our distribution?)
- *Ad hoc decisions relating to one-off problems* (What do we do about this new competitor? How do we counter this price discounting?)

5.1.2 The application of marketing intelligence

Organisations use marketing intelligence in different ways with varying degrees of intensity. We will consider how marketing intelligence is used by large companies, non-profit organisations and industrial organisations.

Large companies

Marketing research is widely used by large companies, who allocate substantial budgets to the collecting and analysing of information. Some make extensive use of consumer research before deciding their marketing strategies, which in turn determines the strategic direction of the entire organisation.

FOR EXAMPLE
....

The banking sector has changed at great pace, stimulated firstly by the reduction of artificial barriers which used to separate such institutions as banks, building societies and insurance companies, and secondly by innovations such as telephone banking and the Internet which have reduced banks' dependency on High Street premises. When it was given the freedom to offer a more complete range of financial services, the Trustees Savings Bank (TSB) reacted by carrying out extensive research into its traditional customer base of social categories C2DE (see Chapter 4). From this information it developed products and services appropriate to the financial needs of these types of customers. It was able to target some specific market areas such as senior citizens and fifteen- to nineteen-year-olds. For example, its research indicated that young people were not particularly motivated to open bank accounts by the free gifts given out by most of the High Street banks. Free banking and value for money services proved a better draw for young people with limited funds than free folders and fancy cheque books, and the TSB took an increasing share of the school leavers market. Consolidation in the banking sector made TSB a natural partner for larger banks with a more middle-market profile, so that it is now part of LloydsTSB.

Other companies carry out less formal market research but rely on more informal methods for gathering market information.

FOR EXAMPLE

Hi-Tec Sports became a significant player in the sports and leisure shoes market by closely associating the company with its marketplace. One of the key strands of its corporate strategy is to be 'better informed and wider awake than the competition'. They achieved this by more informal intelligence processes, scanning their environment by paying close attention to expert opinion and competitors' activities. An understanding of lifestyle changes is crucial in their market but Hi-Tec have preferred a 'street-wise' approach to keeping up with fashions rather than use of formal market research. For example, it has developed strong links with the squash market through involvement with top players and sponsorship which helps the company to develop appropriate products as well as promote its image.

Hi-Tec used informal intelligence processes to understand lifestyle changes

Non-profit organisations

Although market research is traditionally linked to large private sector companies, non-profit organisations increasingly justify expenditure on research. As public services and charitable organisations have been exposed to competitive pressures and market forces, so they have responded by seeking fuller information about their clients, customers and supporters.

FOR EXAMPLE

A successful campaign by Help the Aged was based on research that revealed that old people are commonly abused by their relatives.

The charity Help the Aged wanted to raise public and professional awareness of the issue of abuse of old people in the UK. Before they mounted their campaign they gathered the following market research information:

- 500,000 elderly people are believed to be abused at any one time in the UK

- 39 per cent of the general public have never even heard the term 'elder abuse'

- 46 per cent of people responsible for abuse are related to the person they are abusing, but only 1 per cent who abuse are the primary carer

A successful campaign by Help the Aged was based on research that revealed that old people are commonly abused by their relatives

- A quarter of those who abuse are sons and daughters
- 78 per cent of abuse is perpetrated against people who are over the age of 70, with 16 per cent of that abuse affecting people over the age of 90
- Those between 80 and 89 are the most vulnerable to abuse
- Two-thirds of abuse is committed at home
- In 37 per cent of situations, two types of abuse occur simultaneously
- In a third of circumstances, the abuse is perpetrated by more than one person in collusion

Help the Aged used this research to design an effective campaign. The result was a very successful integrated marketing communications campaign around the theme of 'I will', which aimed to encourage commitment to ending elder abuse. It combined a viral teaser campaign by email, national press advertising, radio, door drops, inserts, direct mail, PR and activity in the charity shops.

The campaign was successful in raising awareness amongst its various stakeholder groups. It gained over 26,000 names for its petition and £190,000 in funds.

Industrial organisations

Marketing research is carried out not only by those organisations involved in consumer markets, but also by those marketing to other organisations or professions in the industrial or public sectors. Primary research of buyers in a business context can be difficult because samples are often hard to recruit. A company selling goods to large organisations will have difficulty in getting

WWW.HELPTHEAGED.ORG.UK, MARKETING DIRECT, OCTOBER 2006.

access to the buyers of its products for research purposes. It would be impossible to undertake focus groups with buyers of competing organisations, who would not want to discuss confidential information and are also unlikely to answer surveys. Companies have to rely more heavily on secondary data and informal data-gathering to help their marketing decisions. The sales force can be an important source of information – provided there are processes in place that allow for the systematic collection of data.

FOR EXAMPLE

As a graphic artist himself, Dai Davies did not need to research the market when he invented Letraset, a convenient and quick method of producing high-quality lettering that replaced traditional, time-consuming hand lettering for professional display layouts. He knew about customers' problems from his own experiences as a working professional. However, when the original product idea for Letraset turned into a high-growth international business, the managers of the company needed other ways of staying in touch with their customers. Letraset's products were distributed through agents and retail outlets so end-user contact was maintained by insisting that their own sales forces regularly visited the graphic artist consumer as well as customers in the distribution network. The marketing intelligence resulting from these regular visits backed by some selective market research enabled Letraset to dominate its market. However, it did not help to prevent its market disappearing altogether when a new technology from outside the industry – computer graphics – made its 'instant lettering' products obsolete.

ENTREPRENEURIAL MARKETING

Research among successful entrepreneurs suggests that they develop a rich mental map of their environment. They know their customers well; they watch competitive activity; they are aware of underlying social, economic and technological trends which could affect their business. They achieve this not by commissioning research, which they often regard as too expensive and time-consuming, but by developing extensive networks of contacts within their trade and by keeping an ear to the ground in their chosen marketplace. Researchers have further suggested that the survival of a fledgling business depends on how quickly new owner-managers properly understand their environment and then learn from their experience of dealing with it. For example, In the early 1970s a young couple decided to open a restaurant in a small seaside town. 'Paddingtons' restaurant opened in Littlehampton on the Sussex coast with a menu that reflected the backgrounds and concerns of its owners. It offered healthy food with many vegetarian dishes and Italian touches (vegetarian lasagne and quiches). Unfortunately the local market lagged behind the owners' early conversion to a healthy diet and customers stayed away. Rapidly reacting to this market information, the owners changed their menu to suit the mood of the times and were soon running a successful American-style burger restaurant. The restaurant owners were Anita and Gordon Roddick, who had to wait a few more years before their awareness of environmental issues developed into a more successful business venture when they opened the first Body Shop in 1976.

CHECKPOINT

Think of a time when you were approached for market information. For example, you may have been stopped by a researcher in the street or asked to fill out a questionnaire by post or email. Or you may have been asked for feedback as part of your studies.

What do you think was the objective of the researchers? What sort of decisions were they looking to assist? How successful were they in gaining useful information from you?

5.2 THE SCOPE OF MARKETING RESEARCH

Whether the information-gathering process is formal or informal, it has to start by asking the right questions. These questions can be divided into five major areas for marketing research, as illustrated in Figure 5.2.

5.2.1 Market and customer research

Market and customer research looks at the size and structure of a particular marketplace and the behaviour of buyers or operators within that market. First the business must determine the size and structure of the marketplace:

■ What are the parameters of the marketplace?

■ What sort of customers are in it?

■ Where are customers located?

■ How customers are there?

FIGURE 5.2

Scope of marketing research

These are the kinds of questions that TSB had to ask about their customers before they could make decisions on developing their banking business. They discovered that their customers were concentrated in the C2DE social categories, a group who were potentially growing faster than the ABC1 categories who were the traditional customers of the main High Street banks, such as Lloyds, TSB's eventual partner.

The business must then assess the competition by asking:

■ What are the competitive forces in the market?

■ Who are the direct competitors and who provides substitute products?

■ How successful are the competitors and what are their strategies?

Hi-Tec, for example, has managed to challenge the leaders in a highly competitive market by carefully monitoring every move of the major players such as Adidas and Nike.

Businesses must also assess the behaviour of buyers in the marketplace:

■ What are the behavioural characteristics of those involved?

■ How do the buyers in the marketplace behave?

■ Who makes the buying decisions and how do they do it?

■ What are the principal benefits they are looking for?

Research has been carried by various agencies into buyer attitudes into queuing. Visa UK has calculated that consumers spend 273 days of their lives waiting in queues. It takes thirty-five- to forty-four-year-olds about twelve minutes in a queue to get seriously annoyed; forty-five- to fifty-four-year-olds take two minutes longer. Watchdog PostComm conducted an undercover survey into Post Office queuing time. The longest it found was twenty-one minutes in Cambridge. The Post Office aims to serve 95 per cent of customers in five minutes or less.

5.2.2 Product research

New product ideas and concepts can be tested on a limited scale before they are put to the ultimate test of acceptance in the marketplace. The failure rate for new products is very high; nine out of every ten new product launches fail according to one estimate. To minimise this risk, concept testing is used to establish likely levels of demand. Improvements to existing products or changes to the packaging and presentation can also be tested for acceptability.

The lessons of failure often provide some of the secrets for future success. The Roddicks' abortive venture as a health food restaurant provided them with valuable insights into consumer behaviour before they opened the Body Shop. Such insights can sometimes be less painfully and more quickly learned through research into the marketplace prior to launch.

5.2.3 Promotion research

Research provides important feedback on the impact of marketing activities. Marketing management needs to know the effect of marketing interventions such as advertising in order to be able to plan future campaigns.

All forms of marketing communications can be made more effective by careful research and analysis of the results of past marketing efforts. For example:

- Research among panels of TV watchers checks the impact of advertising campaigns
- Analysis of the response rates to test mailings provides statistical evaluation of direct mail programmes
- The effectiveness of special offers is researched before future activities are decided

FOR EXAMPLE

Halifax uses marketing research as a way of reducing the risk in management decisions about advertising. Halifax's corporate strategy relies on a strong association of values with their well-established brand name. Its advertising has focused on the 'x' in Halifax to aid brand recall. One campaign used the theme of groups of people arranged in various shapes such as houses and wedding cakes to create the desired image. Extensive research showed that consumers find the idea of the Halifax as a 'human' organisation attractive. The creative solution was to use real Halifax staff as the focus, and the 'Staff as Stars' campaign was launched. The first advertisement featured Howard from the bank's Sheldon branch whose rendition of a version of Tom Jones' song 'Sex Bomb', re-worded as 'X-Bomb' to reinforce the brand, was an immediate success. Other members of 'staff as stars' followed.

Research also continuously tracks the effectiveness of this advertising. For example, the sales results from the 'X-bomb' campaign were known to be impressive, with Halifax's share of current account switching increasing from 8 to 25 per cent. This, in turn, informed decision-making about the creative content of future advertisements, as well as how much should be spent on them and in what media.

© HBOS PIC

The Howard campaign was the result of extensive research by the Halifax

5.2.4 Pricing research

The acceptability of pricing levels can be researched in a number of ways. Experiments to assess the effect of changes to the price of a product give an indication of the relationship between price levels and sales. Attitude research among customers can be the basis of an organisation's pricing strategy. Pricing is a difficult area to research as respondents tend to give responses which encourage lower prices. However, prices need to be assessed in the context of overall costs to the consumer, as they include not only the money paid but also the convenience and timing of the purchase.

FOR EXAMPLE

Letraset's research into the buyer behaviour and attitudes of graphic artists found that purchases of instant lettering were not very sensitive to higher prices. As the rub-down letters actually reduced the time taken for a design, they were regarded as a cost saving and in any case the common practice was to pass on the cost of materials such as Letraset to the client who commissioned the work. Competitive products offered at substantially lower prices were regarded as poorer quality. Research confirmed that graphic artists worked to very tight deadlines so they needed the benefit of immediate availability of a high-quality product rather than low prices. This information formed the basis of Letraset's strategy of pricing the product high and using the additional profits generated to improve the quality and availability of their products.

5.2.5 *Distribution channel research*

Research can provide crucial information affecting the physical distribution of goods and services, or intangible channels to market such as the Internet. Feasibility studies into alternative methods of distribution may involve:

- *Analysis of the structure of the marketplace*: What are the current distribution practices in this market? What is the best option for distributing this product – agents, wholesalers, or directly through the organisation's own operation?
- *Research into store location*: What is the optimum location for this retail outlet – prime High Street, secondary off-High Street, back street or out of town?

FOR EXAMPLE

Tesco have become one of the world's leading online delivery services. Tesco Direct was originally set up as a home delivery service for its grocery products. After careful research into the logistics of establishing a reliable delivery system, it was decided to pick orders directly from existing Tesco stores, rather than follow the model of separate, centralised distribution centres. With a high average order value, this localised delivery operation has been one of the keys to the company's successful growth. It has been extended to include non-food products such as electrical goods, furniture and school wear.

- *Research into information channels*: Channels to market may involve developing new methods of getting information to customers as well as physical goods.
The development of the Internet has given companies new opportunities to reach the marketplace. However, these often need careful investigation to make them effective.

WWW.WARNERBREAKS.CO.UK, *MARKETING DIRECT*, NOVEMBER 2006, HITWISE.

FOR EXAMPLE

Warner Breaks used research to understand the Internet habits of 'silver surfers'.

Warner Breaks offer holidays for the 'over fifties' in historic character hotels and coastal resorts. It is notoriously hard to reach their target market of the more mature consumer and their email newsletter proved ineffective. The company used research to help them uncover the behaviour of 'silver surfers' (i.e. Internet users over fifty-five years old). This indicated that users in this age group accounted for 16 per cent of all those online and was set to increase. Their most popular websites mirrored the rest of the population, with Google at the top, followed by MSN Hotmail and eBay. Travel and cruise sites attracted the largest percentage of silver surfers.

As a result of this research, the company designed a new online marketing programme that featured new email templates, tailored emails, and competitions run through third party sites. This improved online bookings from 11 to 20 per cent and their email database increased from 90,000 to 260,000 customers.

Warner Breaks' research allowed them to target the hard-to-reach over 50s effectively

© ISTOCKPHOTO.COM/SEAN LOCKE

CHECKPOINT

Imagine that you are the owner of an independent record company. What market information would you need on a regular basis in order to maximise the music sales of your contracted bands?

5.3 THE MARKETING RESEARCH PROCESS

Marketing research is a process of several stages. These stages depend on each other; the neglect or unsatisfactory completion of one stage affects the quality of the entire research effort. An overview of the process is shown in Figure 5.3.

5.3.1 Setting the objectives

The initiation of marketing research usually arises from management awareness of a problem or an opportunity: Why are we losing ground to competitors? How do we enter this new market?

FIGURE 5.3 *Process of marketing research*

SETTING THE OBJECTIVES	PLANNING THE RESEARCH	IMPLEMENTING THE RESEARCH	ANALYSING THE RESULTS	USING THE INFORMATION
Definition of problems and opportunities to be researched	Proposals for the collection of information	Collecting the data by the appropriate methods	Analysis and evaluation of the results	Presentation of findings and taking action on recommendations

The translation of this awareness into a clear research brief or statement of objectives is not always an easy step. If research professionals are carrying out the work, the understanding between these researchers and managers commissioning the research is crucial in defining the problem to be investigated. Often managers do not have a clear idea of the issue that requires research; indeed the need for research may arise because problems are not understood.

FOR EXAMPLE

Levi's wanted to move into the higher-priced clothes market as a way of diversifying away from the saturated market for jeans in the United States. They planned to introduce a range of high quality men's suits, jackets and trousers called 'Tailored Classics' under the umbrella of the Levi's brand name. Research in the form of group discussions tested the acceptability of the new range. Although this reported that target customers did not perceive the Levi's name to be in keeping with suits, the company decided they could overcome this problem by concentrating on separate jackets and trousers. The new range was not a success. Levi's marketing management had misread the market's fundamental objection to the Levi's name on more formal, upmarket clothes. Their research objectives had not focused on this key issue as the diversification strategy aimed to maximise on the goodwill inherent in the Levi's brand.

5.3.2 Planning the research

The next stage is to plan how to meet the research objectives. This normally requires defining the following areas:

■ *The customer groups or markets to be investigated*: Which customers do we want to find out about? Which products are being considered?

■ *The measurements to be made of these groups*: Do we want to know the value of their purchases, their attitudes to our products and the competitors, their decision-making processes, their buying patterns, or their exposure to various media?

■ *The methods to be used*: How will we collect the data? What information already exists? Which research instruments, such as surveys or observations, will we use? Do we need to select a sample and if so how will this be done?

■ *The costs and time involved*: How much is it going to cost? How long will it take?

In a formalised process involving professional researchers, a *research proposal* summarises this information.

5.3.3 Implementing the research

The implementation stage initiates the selected research methods and fulfils the collection of the required data. These are discussed more fully in section 5.4.

5.3.4 Analysing the results

The data collected in the implementation stage is of little value without some processing to turn it into relevant information. Some data such as reports on markets or competitors may only require the selection of the relevant information. New data requires more processing involving such stages as:

- Editing of survey answers to check for inaccuracies or omissions
- Coding of answers to help with the analysis
- Tabulation of data into an understandable form – this can be assisted by computer processing

5.3.5 Using the information

Once the collected data has been converted into management information, it can be communicated in a way that is appropriate to the situation and the organisation so that it can be effectively used. The form of this varies from informal briefings to written reports and presentations.

Research can only aid marketing decisions. It cannot make or implement those decisions, but it can ensure they are better informed. Ultimately the value of the research depends on specific actions, which are guided by its results and recommendations.

FOR EXAMPLE

....

Although market research can only analyse what has happened, not what is going to happen next, it does provide companies like Halifax with information to make their advertising work harder in the next campaign. Their research is presented not only internally but it is also shared with the advertising agency that created it. Halifax management agree criteria on which the advertising is to be judged with their agency and later review the campaign using research to see what went well or less well. By analysing how their current advertising is working, they hope to learn how to make it even more effective in the future.

CHECKPOINT

You have decided to set up a DJ business, offering your services to various different music venues in the area. You need information on exactly what to offer. Who would you research? What could be the objectives of such research?

5.4 RESEARCH METHODS

5.4.1 Qualitative and quantitative research

Marketing research methods can produce qualitative and quantitative data.

Qualitative research

Qualitative research explores attitudes, perceptions and ideas. It seeks to find out why people make the choices they do, and what they believe their future needs may be. As it asks for opinions which are hard to quantify or reduce to simple questions, it usually involves face-to-face interviews with individuals or small groups. The most common qualitative methods are in-depth interviews or group discussions (see section 5.6.)

Quantitative research

Quantitative research seeks to measure or quantify factors for statistical analysis. It asks how many people buy certain products and in which ways. As it tries to build up a statistical picture of the marketplace, it usually involves taking data from many people in order to draw general conclusions from a sufficiently large sample. Common quantitative methods are therefore large-scale surveys and observations.

In practice, qualitative and quantitative research overlap, and are often used in tandem in a research design. The wider sampling of quantitative data can reveal trends which more detailed qualitative research methods can try to explain. For example, quantitative data may show an unexpected increase in market share, and qualitative research can be used to find out why.

5.4.2 Primary and secondary data

Methods of collection depend on the type of information required. Two distinct categories of data exist:

- **Primary data**: New data specifically collected for the project through field research; generates information specifically for the project at hand

- **Secondary data**: Data that already exists and can be collected by desk research; information relevant to the project, and which already exists somewhere else

This distinction is illustrated in Figure 5.4.

- **Desk research** is a passive form of marketing research. There is no interaction with the customer. Information is collected without the researcher leaving the desk. The researcher looks at both public sources, such as central and local government reports, and private sources, such as the internal accounts of the organisation or data from a trade association.

- **Field research** is actively involved in the marketplace. It may be continuous research in which several organisations participate, such as omnibus surveys. Alternatively it may be one-off ad hoc research commissioned by one organisation to investigate a specific problem through discussions with a group of consumers.

The comparative advantages and disadvantages of each type of data is shown in Figure 5.5.

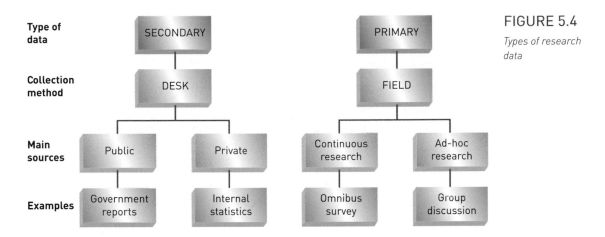

FIGURE 5.4

Types of research data

FIGURE 5.5 *Comparative merits of primary and secondary data*

CHECKPOINT

If you wanted to predict the results of the next general election, would you collect mainly qualitative or quantitative data? What would be your main difficulties in accurately predicting the result?

5.5 SECONDARY DATA

Marketing research starts with desk research for secondary data. An evaluation of the many types of existing data may make further primary research better informed or even unnecessary.

A variety of sources exist for secondary marketing information, including internal sources, competitor sources and external secondary sources. These are described in turn below.

5.5.1 Internal sources

The internal records and knowledge base of an organisation can provide unique, low-cost data. There are several places to look for this including:

- Internal marketing information, such as the reports of salespeople in the field or market surveys previously commissioned

- Accounting, production and other internal records – the records kept by an organisation usually contain statistics on existing customers, potential customers, sales by region, product line, and time period, and the costs of specific products and processes

- Informal sources – the knowledge and opinions of staff, particularly those dealing directly with customers, form an important information base. This is frequently accessed through informal communications, although more formal research methods are used as well. Advice from management gurus encourages managers to leave their desk and practise 'management by walkabout', recognising the value of gathering such information by observation and talking to others within an organisation

5.5.2 Competitor sources

Organisations communicate constantly with their customers and their financial audience. This gives competitors information about the organisation and its strategies. Websites, promotional literature, advertising campaigns, press releases, financial reports and accounts and statutory returns provide data which other organisations can analyse in an effort to interpret their competitors' strategies and forecast their future activities.

5.5.3 External secondary sources

Many external bodies publish information which is relevant to marketing. These are usually available electronically, although not necessarily free. (See Further reading and references at the end of this chapter for examples of electronic databases and online reports).

- Official information is regularly published by governments at national and international level. In the UK, for example, the government provides a 'Monthly Digest of Statistics' on the population, housing manufacturing and other key indicators. 'Business Monitors' summarise business statistics from a large database. The DTI publish a weekly guide to industrial trends and many other market reports. Summary statistics from the 2001 population census are available free of charge. These and many other official reports and statistics are often available online or through the Central Statistical Office and libraries.

- The press is a regular source of information for any organisation whether it is the general press for financial and management information, or specialist publications reporting on specific trade sectors or professions.

- Trade associations and professional institutions, from the Confederation of British Industry (CBI) to local Chambers of Commerce, are potential sources of information.

- Commercial sources also publish a wealth of information. Many research agencies, such as Mintel, the Economist Intelligence Unit, Key Note Publications, Kelly's and Dun and Bradstreet, sell reports and directories of markets and industrial sectors, either online or as hard copies.

MINTEL'S HOUSEHOLD CLEANING PRODUCTS REPORT, JULY 2006

FOR EXAMPLE

A basic type of secondary information is market size, share and trends.
Table 5.1 is an example published by Mintel on household cleaners.

TABLE 5.1 *Mintel survey on household cleaners*

		2006		2004		2004–2006
		£m	%	£m	%	Percentage change
1	RECKITT BENCKISER	97	17	96	17	1.0
2	SC JOHNSON	73	13	76	13	−4.0
3	UNILEVER	63	11	64	11	−1.6
4	JEYES	53	9	56	10	−5.4
5	PROCTER AND GAMBLE	48	8	49	9	−2.0
6	SARA LEE	9	2	11	2	−18.2
	OTHER	73	13	76	13	−4.1
	OWN LABEL	148	26	146	25	1.7
	TOTAL	**564**	**99**	**574**	**100**	**−1.7**

CHECKPOINT

If you were a marketing manager for a household cleaner, what would these figures mean to you?
What other secondary information would you need in your job?

5.6 PRIMARY DATA

5.6.1 Research approaches

There are four different approaches to collecting primary data:

- Observation
- Experimentation
- Surveys
- In-depth interviews and focus groups

Observation

Research in many fields, from anthropology to zoology, uses observation as the basic method of investigation. Marketing research uses observation in a number of ways such as:

- Mechanical observations, which count activities like the number of shoppers in a street or the quantity of cars using a road

- Behavioural observations, which note how people go about buying or using products by, for example, watching how people select brands in a shop or use products in the workplace

- Informal observation, which keeps a 'weather eye' on the marketplace by, for instance, attending exhibitions and noting the activity level on competitive stands

- Internet observation through 'cookies', or small files inserted into end-users' computers, enabling websites to identify users and track their future behaviour; organisations can identify visitors to their website and build a profile of that visitor by observing their future Internet activity

Experimentation

Experiments can assess the impact of variations to the elements in the marketing mix. Prices, promotions, packaging or other aspects of the product (e.g. taste, colour and size) are varied under controlled conditions to estimate the impact on buying preferences.

For example, retailers operating a chain of shops experiment with promotional discounts in one outlet and compare the impact on sales to outlets where the offer is not made. Organisations that use direct marketing test response rates by mailing three different letters to separate samples of the same list.

Surveys

Surveys that collect data through the use of questionnaires are the most common method of primary research. They can be used to collect both quantitative and qualitative data depending on the structure of the questionnaire and the contact methods chosen.

A market survey asks questions of a number of respondents selected to represent the target market. Through the questionnaire, researchers can measure many factors such as:

- Buying patterns and trends (e.g. Have you purchased product X in the last 12 months/ 6 months/1 month?)

- Competitors' performance (e.g. Which of the following products have you purchased in the last 12 months?)

- Expectations related to products and services (e.g. Rate the following reasons for buying this type of product in priority order)

- Attitudes to products and brand names (e.g. How do you rate the performance of product X in terms of this benefit?)

- Media exposure (e.g. Which of the following newspapers do you read regularly/ sometimes/never?)

Surveys use personal contact, telephone and the post. (We look at the relative merits of each of these in section 5.6.2.)

In-depth interviews and focus groups

For qualitative research, in-depth interviews probe more deeply for attitudes and motivations.

■ *Individual interviews or 'depth interviews'* are informal and more conversational than the traditional questionnaires, allowing the respondents to talk about the subject in a less constrained way. They may use techniques to open up respondents' deeper attitudes by asking them to project their feelings into hypothetical situations. These 'projective techniques' include word association and sentence completion tests. For example:

— 'What do you associate with the word Halifax?'

— 'Halifax is . . .'

— 'Halifax ought to . . .'

— 'Halifax ought not to . . .'

■ *Group discussions, or focus groups*, guided by a trained leader can be both informative and creative. A small number of people (typically five to eight) from the target market are invited to discuss certain topics, concepts and products. The discussion leader may guide the group through their views on a specific market, its environment and the competitors before introducing a new product concept for reaction and comment.

FOR EXAMPLE

The wide use of focus groups, not only by consumer researchers but also by political parties, has attracted critical comment. The Association of Qualitative Research Practitioners estimate that focus groups now account for two-thirds of qualitative research expenditure. This has prompted concerns that focus groups may be used inappropriately and have become part of a research 'methodolatry' or '. . . a preoccupation with selecting and defending methods to the exclusion of the actual substance of the story being told' (Denzin and Lincoln, 1998). Focus groups are not just a convenient way to get the outlook of a wider number of people. Their main advantage relies on the concept of group synergy – the group process generates a wider, more creative range of information than would result from a comparable number of in-depth interviews. Their main disadvantage stems from the tendency towards group consensus; a few, dominant members of the group may over-ride the opinions of other, quieter members. Much depends on the skill of the moderators – researchers who lead and control the discussion. They walk a tightrope between allowing a free-flowing, creative discussion, and controlling conversations by reducing the participation of self-opinionated participants in order to encourage the more introverted group members to have their say.

When deciding between these different research methods it is important to consider the research problem that is being addressed. Qualitative research, such as in-depth interviews, involves asking questions in a lot of depth to a relatively few people. It is particularly well suited

TABLE 5.2 *Comparative merits of research contact methods*

CRITERION	CONTACT METHODS		
	Mail/email	**Telephone**	**Personal**
QUANTITY OF DATA	Poor	Good	Excellent
INTERVIEWER EFFECT*	Low	Average	High
CONTROL OF SAMPLE	Excellent	Fair	Poor
SPEED	Poor	Excellent	Good
RESPONSE RATE	Poor	Good	Good
COSTS	Fair	Fair	Poor

*This refers to the possibility of bias in the results because of the preconceptions of the interviewer.

to exploratory research and to researching sensitive subject areas. Quantitative research, such as surveys, asks a lot of people relatively simple questions, which have usually been scoped out by previous qualitative research.

5.6.2 Contact methods

Primary research is conducted by contacting a sample of respondents by mail, telephone or in person. Each method has advantages and disadvantages which are summarised in Table 5.2.

Mail

Questionnaires by post can be inexpensive and reach geographically dispersed samples, but low response rates normally limit the effective size of the sample. Biases in the data are also possible because non-response is not a random process.

FOR EXAMPLE

Ten per cent of people respond to a mailed questionnaire and all of them state they are very satisfied with a specified product. Does this mean that they are a representative sample and that 100 per cent of people are satisfied? Or is it possible that those dissatisfied did not bother to reply and therefore only 10 per cent are satisfied? The truth is probably somewhere in between, but a mailed questionnaire cannot find out more precisely without further investigation.

Telephone

Telephone surveys have become popular as they can provide fast, convenient access to a relatively large number of respondents. The anonymity of the caller may induce more open response, although the lack of visual clues and body language does hinder the collection of qualitative feedback.

Computer-assisted telephone interviewing (CATI) can be used to guide the interviewer through the sequence of questions which appear on a screen and answers keyed directly into the computer system for analysis.

Email

The use of electronic communication methods for data collection is growing. Survey data can be collected by email to known addresses, or more passively via websites that ask visitors to volunteer information. Increasingly email and websites are used in conjunction, with email directing traffic through a link to a survey hosted on a website. As it has been collected digitally on a website, the data can then be downloaded directly into a statistical package for analysis if required.

Website-hosted surveys can also be used in conjunction with other contact methods; for example, agreement to complete a survey form may be made on the telephone or by post, but the questionnaire can be delivered and completed electronically. Whilst it can provide a convenient and fast method of data collection, research by email is constrained by the limited number of email address lists currently available. It is more frequently used to collect data from organisations rather than consumers because of sampling issues arising from the inconsistent patterns of email usage in domestic households.

Online purchasing is very measurable as websites collect visitor information, click-through rates and time and value of purchases made.

FOR EXAMPLE

....

ONLINE MARKETING BOOMED AT CHRISTMAS TIME

According to research carried out by Experian's email marketing firm CheetahMail, there was a 5.9 per cent increase in click-through transactions for the month of December 2006 peaking at 24.3 per cent on New Year's Eve. The report also found that shoppers were still ordering online on Christmas Day and Boxing Day, when 2.4 per cent of click-throughs resulted in transactions averaging £36 per sale.

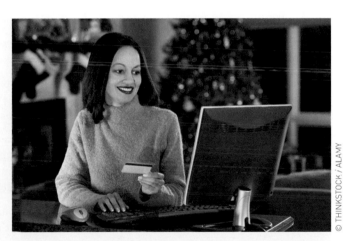

Email marketing boomed at Christmas time

BRAND REPUBLIC, 9 JANUARY 2007.

© THINKSTOCK / ALAMY

Personal

Personal, face-to-face interviewing is still the most popular method of collecting data for surveys. Although it can be expensive because it is time-consuming, personal interviewing provides the opportunity for obtaining large quantities of high-quality data.

Face-to-face research ranges from the highly structured interview with predetermined routes through a planned sequence of standard questions to more open-ended discussions around the relevant topic. In either case the social interaction between the interviewer and the respondent is important for a successful outcome to the interview.

5.6.3 The Questionnaire

The construction of a questionnaire in terms of what questions to ask and their form, wording and sequence determines how useful the resulting data is going to be.

What questions should be included?

If questions are to be kept to a minimum, they are restricted to two types.

■ *Those that qualify the respondent in some way.* Before proceeding with the rest of the questionnaire, the interviewer needs to find out more about the respondent (e.g. Do you own a house? Do you live within twenty miles of here?). Interviews are directed into a different route through the questionnaire depending on the response or in some cases terminated early. (If the questionnaire is about mortgages, the answer to the enquiry on house ownership determines whether to proceed to questions on attitudes to mortgage interest rates, for example.)

■ *Those that contribute to meeting the research objectives.* In a well-designed questionnaire, every question has a purpose in line with the overall objectives of the research and is capable of contributing meaningful data.

What type of questions should be asked?

The form in which a question is asked influences the response. Questions can induce either an open or a closed response.

■ *Open questions* leave the respondent free to choose how to answer; they invite an opinion (What do you think of *x*?), or personalised information (Which books have you read recently?). Open questions are needed for qualitative surveys exploring attitudes and motivations.

■ *Closed questions* attract only a limited response such as yes/no, or a rating on a scale. (Do you own a car? How do rate our service – good, average or poor?). Closed questions are easy to ask and convenient to process afterwards. They are used for quantitative data collection, qualifying respondents or as multiple-choice questions.

■ *Multiple-choice questions* are closed in the sense that answers are predetermined, but they introduce more open elements by offering a longer list of responses than just yes or no.

Rating scales help to quantify opinions and attitudes that might otherwise be too imprecise if left totally open to the respondent. These take several forms, for example:

1. What is your general impression of the picture framing service of 'The Frame Centre'?

Expensive	☐ ☐ ☐ ☐ ☐	Cheap
High quality	☐ ☐ ☐ ☐ ☐	Low quality
Friendly	☐ ☐ ☐ ☐ ☐	Unfriendly
Fast	☐ ☐ ☐ ☐ ☐	Slow

2. Indicate in order of preference the features you would expect to find if the 'perfect' picture framing shop existed near your home:

    A Discount prices

    B Wide choice of materials

C Good design advice

D Quality workmanship

E Easy to get to

F Any other reason (state below)

1st ☐   2nd ☐   3rd ☐   4th ☐   5th ☐   6th ☐

What should the wording be for questions?

The wording of a questionnaire requires careful thought to avoid bias or confusion in the response. Questions are best kept simple and direct avoiding the obvious pitfalls of:

- *Leading questions* (e.g. 'Does inhaling other people's harmful smoke in a public place concern you?' – the wording predisposes the respondent to answer positively even if it is not of great concern)

- *Confusing questions* (e.g. 'What is your favourite dinner-time meal?' – 'dinner time' to some is 'lunch time' to others)

- *Assumptive questions* (e.g. 'Do you prefer pizza or pasta dishes?' – the respondent may not like either of them)

- *Ambiguous questions* (e.g. 'Do you eat out frequently?' – definitions of 'eating out' can vary from a restaurant to a sandwich in the park, whilst 'frequent' to some is 'infrequent' to others)

What should the sequence be for questions?

The order in which questions are asked is important for two reasons:

- The overall structure can influence the social interaction between the interviewer and the respondent. Questions which seem to be aggressive or intrusive in the early part of the interview – 'Why do you live in rented accommodation? How much do you earn?' – can make respondents less than open in their later responses.

- Most questionnaires have a logical sequence that builds on data from previous questions. The need to ask irrelevant or inappropriate questions is eliminated if the order is carefully considered.

'Funnelling' is a common structure that starts off with wider, general questions, often with closed responses to relax the respondent. Narrower, specific questions, especially those inviting more open responses, are left to the end.

5.6.4 Sampling

In some instances, information about an entire population is collected by a census (e.g. the UK Census of Population or a census by a small number of specialised manufacturers). However, most research is designed to draw conclusions about a larger group by studying a smaller sample that is taken to be representative of the whole. For qualitative data, samples are used with less concern for accuracy levels than in quantitative research. Qualitative samples tend to be small and chosen for the way in which they may *illustrate* key issues in the research brief (e.g. urban versus rural consumer opinions; manufacturing versus services management attitudes). For quantitative data, the sample has to be selected in such a way that it can be taken to *represent* the larger whole (e.g. percentages of rural dwellers shopping in urban centres; number of manufacturers buying a particular service).

Sampling involves a number of decisions involving the sampling unit, size and procedure.

Sampling unit

Who is to be studied? Who in the decision-making process is to be interviewed – the user, the purchaser or both?

FOR EXAMPLE

A manufacturer wishes to research the market for personal computers. These include domestic and commercial users. In the home there are several influences, including husbands and wives and other family members. In the office there are also several potential decision-makers and influences. Which people are interviewed?

Sample size

How many people should be interviewed? How many activities should be observed? If properly selected for statistical validity, quite small samples can be chosen to be representative of a wider population or 'universe'. The exact number depends on the amount of variations within the population being studied (e.g. age ranges; sizes of firms), and the accuracy and confidence level required in the results produced. Formulae can be used to calculate the sample numbers needed, which are based on the smallest group in the sample to be analysed separately (e.g. an age range; manufacturers in a particular region). Normally, this would be at least one hundred in the sub-group, depending on which technique you are going to use for analysis.

Normally the larger the sample size the better, but there are exceptions to this. The quirks of statistics can mean that small variations can appear statistically significant when actually they are just variations in the data. Also size is not everything, as the example below shows. A lot depends on how you analyse and interpret the data.

Sampling procedure

How should the sample be chosen? There are some options.

■ *A probability sample* is chosen at random from the whole population being studied. To be truly random, every member of the population under consideration has an equal chance of being selected. It could therefore be expensive to conduct personal interviews of a random sample as they could be geographically distant from each other. A random sample may be modified by *clustering* into a small number of geographic areas in order to minimise this problem. A random sample may also be *stratified* to ensure it matches the population under study in some key respects. For example, target numbers of interviews can be set for particular age groups of people or sizes of firms within a sample in order to ensure that group is correctly represented.

■ *Quota sampling* is the most commonly used method for quantitative consumer research. It involves selecting individuals who meet certain criteria (e.g. age, gender, social group), so that the complete sample matches known characteristics of the population. The interviewer

MARKETING MISTAKES

Coca-Cola has had the same formula since 1886. It is generally viewed as the most famous product on the planet, and in most rankings comes out as the world's most powerful brand. Interbrand, a consultancy which specialises in valuing brands, ranked Coca-Cola as the No. 1 Global Brand in 2006, followed by Microsoft and IBM. It placed the value of the brand at $67 billion.

In the 1980s top management at Coca-Cola became increasingly concerned by the success of the Pepsi challenge. Although Coke outsold Pepsi 2:1, Pepsi was starting to make inroads into its arch rival's market share. Pepsi's sales promotion consisted of blind tests (i.e. ones where the consumer did not know which brand they were tasting and had to chose which they preferred). When consumers were unaware of the brand, they tended to chose Pepsi. Coca-Cola replicated these tests and found the same results. It appeared that consumers did actually prefer the taste of Pepsi. At this point senior management became even more worried. It seemed that Pepsi's success was based on fact.

Scientists at Coca-Cola started work on a new formula, eventually finding one that outperformed Pepsi in blind testing. Because of the sensitive nature of the idea of changing the taste of Coke, the market research was carried out in secret. Over 200,000 secret taste tests were carried out, covering the breadth of the United States from New York to California. The results were overwhelmingly positive. Not only did consumers prefer the taste of New Coke over the traditional Coke, even more importantly, they preferred it over Pepsi.

New Coke was launched with so much fanfare and expensive advertising that within two weeks of

Even marketing giants such as Coca-Cola can misread market research

IMAGE COURTESY OF THE ADVERTISING ARCHIVES

the launch more Americans knew that Coke had a new recipe than knew the name of the US president. Yet despite the extensive quantitative research and enormous promotional spend, New Coke was a failure. Consumers travelled miles to get stock of the original Coke and even set up protest groups. The company had ignored the emotional commitment of their market base. Within sixteen weeks Coca-Cola had to re-introduce the original formulation, labelling it Classic Coke. Over time, they withdrew the new Coca-Cola and Coca-Cola reverted to its original taste.

is then given a quota of individuals who match these criteria (e.g. females between fifteen and twenty-four years old in a certain town) to find and interview. Although quota sampling is less expensive than random sampling, it is also less accurate as bias can enter the selection procedures (e.g. the interviewer may look for fifteen- to twenty-four-year-old females in a shopping precinct, approaching only those that looked willing to spend time on an interview. In this manner, the interviewer therefore excludes not only anyone that does not normally shop there, but also those in a hurry that day).

FOR EXAMPLE

Despite its popularity, quota sampling has its critics. It was widely blamed when the polls forecasting the results of the 1993 UK general election got it wrong. Days before the election, all the main opinion polls were predicting a narrow victory for Labour under Neil Kinnock. In the event, John Major became prime minister with a small Conservative majority. A key problem for the opinion polls was that Conservative voters were reluctant to declare themselves, and were therefore less likely to be selected for interview.

■ *A convenience sample* selects respondents on the basis of ease of access. It may be used in low-budget, qualitative research where representation of a wider population is relatively unimportant. For example, an interviewer may select on the basis of contacts already available, or may use the snowball technique of asking one respondent to recommend another. It is also widely used by students in their research. As long as the respondent is not personally known to the interviewer, for example, a friend of a friend of a friend, then this should not be a problem.

5.6.5 *Continuous research*

Time frames for research depend on the information requirements but there is a choice between two basic types: ad hoc and continuous surveys. Surveys can be ad hoc or one-off pieces of research for a specific purpose, whereas some research is conducted on an ongoing basis. Within continuous surveys, there are various methods used:

■ *Omnibus surveys*: Organisations can share in research by participating in an omnibus survey. Research agencies offer regular surveys of consumer groups of a consistent sample size. Participating organisations share general data and can also insert their own individual questions if they wish. Omnibus surveys are based on large samples which may use any of the different ways to segment markets. These will be covered in more detail in the next chapter but may be demographic (e.g. ABC1 adults), geographic (e.g. Europe), behaviouristic (e.g. car owners) or psychographic (e.g. lifestyle).

■ *Panels*: Panels representing individual, household or industrial customer groups are set up and regularly asked for information about their buying behaviour. By reporting regularly on what products they have bought and when, or what advertising they have seen with what effect, these panels provide data on trends in purchasing patterns and the influences of marketing efforts. The advantage of a panel is that you can track the purchasing habits of the same people over time. This is called a longitudinal study. A disadvantage is that the sort of person who has time to do this is unlikely to be representative of the market as a whole (e.g. they tend to be cash poor and time rich). New technology helps with the data collection – for example, respondents now have key-fob barcode scanners which allows them to monitor consumer purchases outside of the home.

FOR EXAMPLE

The trade magazine *Marketing* (www.brandrepublic.com) carries out frequent studies as part of their Adwatch series. They conducted research in December 2006 as part of their twice weekly OnLineBus omnibus survey. They questioned 1000 adults aged between 16 and 64 with the aim of finding out the UK's most irritating advertisement from 2006. The question asked was 'Which of the following TV commercials irritated you most this year?'

The results are shown in Table 5.3.

www.cillitbang.co.uk

BANG AND THE DIRT IS GONE!

Cillit Bang was one of the most irritating ads of 2006

TABLE 5.3 *Results of the most irritating TV ad*

POSITION	BRAND	PERCENT
1	InjuryLawyers4U	57
2	Cillit Bang	53
3	Picture Loans	51
4	Sheila's Wheels	48
5*	Phones4U	41
5*	Iceland	41
7	Gaviscon	40
8	Daz (Cleaner Close)	37
9	Halifax (New Stars)	33
10	Kellogg's Frosties	32

* Tied in 5th place.

CHECKPOINT

What are the advantages of this type of research?

What are the problems with the way this research has been conducted? What might be the potential sources of bias?

■ *Retail audits*: Another way of regularly assessing demand is through retail audits in which research organisations analyse sales of various product lines in a sample of shops at regular intervals. Retailers now generate huge amounts of data on the purchasing behaviour of their customers through computerised recording of product barcodes through their tills. Researchers also go into stores to check that products are in stock. 'Out-of-stocks' can be a big problem in periods of peak demand. Prices are also often checked as retailers often want to make price comparisons.

■ *Loyalty cards*: The data collected from loyalty card usage is used by retailers to analyse the behaviour patterns of their customers. Although this provides a very accurate record of consumer purchasing, there are two main problems. The first is data overload – the number of purchasing records runs into billions a day for major grocery retailers; as a result they only use a sample for analysis. The second problem is that this research only tells the retailer what is spent with them, so the 'share-of-purse' (or wallet) remains unknown.

Continuous research is particularly important for tracking the effectiveness of marketing activities. The impact of promotions, price offers, product changes and distribution efforts can be measured more effectively through regular surveys of the same sample to give comparable 'before and after' data.

5.7 A SUMMARY OF RESEARCH METHODS

We have examined many types of qualitative and quantitative research methods using primary and secondary data. These are summarised in Figure 5.6.

> **CHECKPOINT**
>
> How could marketing research help you to develop the next steps in your career or personal life? Develop a research brief to answer this question. Suggest a plan for the research that includes objectives, who or what is to be investigated and research methods to be used.

5.8 SUMMARY

■ Marketing research collects data from a variety of internal and external sources and analyses it, providing information to provide marketing intelligence.

■ Research varies from the formalised marketing intelligence systems that larger organisations use to track changes in their environment and the effects of their marketing campaigns, to the informal networking of entrepreneurs keeping an eye out for opportunities.

■ Research can provide information on customers and markets or feedback on products, promotions, pricing and distribution issues.

■ The research process first sets clear objectives before planning and implementing the research, which can then be analysed and used.

FIGURE 5.6 *A summary of marketing research methods*

■ Research methods can produce qualitative or quantitative information from primary or secondary data.

■ Secondary data already exists and can be collected from internal sources, such as accounting records, or external sources such as competitors' publicity or government statistics.

■ Primary data is collected to meet specific research objectives through observation, experimentation, surveys or in-depth interviews.

■ Respondents to surveys are contacted by mail, telephone or in person, on an ad hoc or continuous basis.

■ Samples are used to represent (in quantitative research), or illustrate (in qualitative research) the population being studied. Methods include probability, quota and convenience sampling. Samples can also be clustered or stratified.

■ Questionnaires use open, closed and multiple-choice questions, carefully worded to minimise bias, confusion or ambiguity.

5.9 ACTIVITIES

FOOD, FAMILIES AND FEMALES

David and Susan Fernandez were discussing their future after ten eventful years as business partners. When they had purchased their first free house pub, they had not foreseen that it would expand into the present, fast-growing chain of twenty outlets. The expansion had been born partly of the need to survive in a market that had seen considerable change over the previous decade or so. From the traditional male-dominated, drinking-dominated venues, pubs had been forced to adapt and become family-oriented centres in which food and females played an increasingly important part. The growth of in-house entertainment, demographic change and government deregulation had not only shaken up the industry but also given the couple opportunities to grow their business. They had turned their pubs, which served some food, into restaurants or 'gastro-pubs' that reflected their pub origins but focused primarily on serving interesting food in a themed environment. Now they had a crucial decision to make. What should the future theme of their outlets be and how could they attract people into them on a consistent basis?

The industry Government intervention during the 1990s had aimed at breaking down the monopoly of the large breweries. The Monopolies and Mergers Commission's investigation into the brewing trade, and the ensuing 'Supply of Beer Orders' had forced the major brewers to release half their public houses, over a 2,000-pub minimum, from a tie to the brewery. It had the effect of giving the sector a major shake-up, although in some areas it had actually decreased competition as an estimated 500 pubs per year had closed in the 1990s, many in sparsely populated areas. Since the orders came into force, more than 14,000 pubs had been sold, increasing the numbers owned by the independent sector.

The beer industry was also hit by demographic problems as the population aged and the peak beer-consuming group of young males had declined in numbers. Competition for alcohol sales became fiercer as sales declined and the remaining pubs fought for survival. By 1996, the total number of pubs had declined to an estimated 65,000 compared to nearly 68,000 at the end of the 1989.

By contrast, other sectors of the catering industry were faring better. During the 1980s, the numbers of restaurants and snack bars had increased by over 40 per cent and although the recession at the beginning of the 1990s halted the expansion, the second half saw accelerating growth in the restaurant sector. The conclusions for publicans were inescapable: diversify into food or risk failure. Pubs became increasingly targeted at specific demographic groups. Some, such as the Firkin chain, retained the focus on drink by aiming at the youth and student market. Others concentrated on food sales which became the dominant product of the outlet. Chains owned by the major brewing groups such as Whitbread's Beefeater and Bass's Harvester aimed at value-for-money, family eating. Other outlets, such as the All Bar One chain, targeted younger, professional women by providing low-fat foods in smoke-free, clean environments. Whitbread was one of the most successful groups at implementing a strategy of targeting pubs at segments of the market, following their 'three Fs' policy that emphasised 'food, females and family'.

So successful were the pubs in diversifying that they now sell more food than restaurants. In 2006, pubs served nearly 1.1 billion meals, compared with 642 million served in restaurants. In the past ten years, food sales in the UK's 30,000 managed pubs have risen by 165 per cent, and even faster in its 30,000 smaller tenanted pubs. Some 80 per cent of all British pubs now offer food, compared with about half in the mid-1990s, with the number of pub diners now outstripping the number of pub drinkers. The ban on smoking in pubs has only helped to promote food sales.

The business Susan's background in the hotel and catering industry made it even more obvious to her that they should diversify away from reliance on 'wet' sales when they purchased their first pub. She began by offering a select menu, specialising in seafood, ordered from the bar and served in a separated seating area. This had proved popular and given them the confidence to look around for opportunities to grow. Because they had access to finance from a small group of private investors, they were able to buy free houses and other pubs at bargain prices for a few years. Their single pub expanded to a chain of twenty. They were constantly looking for more, not to run as traditional pubs serving food, but as a new brand of outlet – the themed gastro-pub.

The Jolly-Boat Inn They had developed two distinct themes in their chain. Some of the earlier acquisitions were in large, coastal towns where Susan's original seafood concept seemed a natural theme for this new chain of 'Jolly-Boat Inns'. The essential character of the traditional pub was evident, with decor reflecting the seafaring name. Outside, play boats and pirate activity areas provided safe but noisy playgrounds for children. The profits came from a seafood menu chalked on a large board with daily specials from the local catch. The average price was £12 per head, although lower-priced mini-meals such as mussels and chips were also popular. They opened thirteen of these, mainly along the south coast and in the west country.

Although they were very popular, this part of the chain suffered from consistency problems. It was difficult to reduce the cooking of seafood to a formula, making the quality of the food and service variable, as the couple knew from the complaints they had received. Seasonal factors did not help either – some of the pubs became overcrowded in popular holiday times making it uncomfortable for diners wanting a serious meal. Because of the variable cost of seafood, margins were also less predictable; the average gross margin of 65 per cent on food could show wide variations according to the outlet and time of year. However, a Jolly-Boat Inn developed loyal customers, particularly amongst middle-aged men, who liked eating there for lunch, and families enjoyed it on a day out in the summer.

Tai-P'Inn Their fastest growing concept was 'Tai-P'Inn', a hybrid that David had developed during his time living in Hong Kong. It aimed to combine the sociability of the English pub, the service concept of the American bar-diner and the growing popularity of Oriental cuisine. The name was adapted from James Clavell's well known novel, 'Tai-Pan' (Chinese for 'ruler') set in the historical context of English trade and rule in Hong Kong. The bars reflected this background with lavish decorations along the theme of 'where east meets west'. Framed sayings of Confucius competed with British imperial memorabilia; model Chinese sampans with naval frigates. The menu borrowed heavily from Thai cuisine, but Fernandez had not been afraid to dilute it with other popular, eastern dishes. The average spend per head on a meal was around £15, but he also emphasised value for money with set menus and special offers for off-peak dining.

Business performance The turnover of the two chains and overall group profitability is shown in Table 5.4.

The first Tai-P'Inns had proved very popular in their largely cosmopolitan catchment areas in larger towns and cities. After the first year, David O'Brien thought he had found the formula on which to base the rest of their expansion. But Susan pointed out one worrying trend from their marketing information. Customers were not as loyal to this type of outlet as they were to the Jolly-Boat. Despite their problems, each Jolly-Boat Inn had built up a following who returned regularly for their fresh seafood. Tai-P'Inns attracted many curious customers, some who returned but often after a relatively long gap.

Market information In order to understand their business better, the couple invested in some research. First, they studied some secondary sources of market information and found that population changes were still having a significant impact on the pub-restaurant market.

The consumer Drinking in pubs used to be the preserve of younger, single men and older, working men. The population profile in Table 5.5, which shows significant growth in the older age bands, and the increasing importance of females in that older population, helps explain why pubs have to make a broader appeal to survive.

TABLE 5.4 *Sales turnover*

SALES TURNOVER (in thousands of pounds)				
	2000	Number of outlets	2006	Number of outlets
JOLLY-BOAT INNS	4,800	(12)	5,400	(12)
TAI-P'INNS	1,500	(3)	3,500	(8)
TOTAL SALES	**6,300**	**(15)**	**8,900**	**(20)**
NET PROFIT	**870**		**1,400**	

TABLE 5.5 *UK population by age group and gender (000s), 2000–2005*

Age range	2000		2005		PERCENTAGE CHANGE 2000–2005	
	Male	Female	Male	Female	Male	Female
15–24	3,718	3,518	4,018	3,855	+8	+9
25–34	4,403	4,205	3,933	3,963	−11	−6
35–44	4,486	4,387	4,576	4,667	+2	+6
45–54	3,890	3,903	3,816	3,896	−2	0
55–64	3,009	3,100	3,448	3,577	+15	+15
65+	3,881	5,473	4,143	5,506	+7	0

Women are just as likely to eat in a pub as men, with the habit most popular in the over-twenty-five age ranges, as shown in Table 5.6.

Children in pubs Legislation concerning the admission of children into pubs was relaxed through the introduction of Children's Certificates. A pub with a certificate can admit children of all ages into the bar area if accompanied by an adult.

Tourism Tourism can have a major impact on pubs as tourists are more likely than the normal consumer to need food as well as drink. The number of UK families taking holidays in the UK has steadily increased, and with it the demand for pub food and lodging.

Primary research The partners tried to find out how their own customer base compared to the national picture by commissioning both quantitative and qualitative research.

TABLE 5.6 *Pub food customers*

AGE RANGE	PERCENTAGE OF AGE RANGE
15–24	65
25–34	76
35–44	73
45–54	68
55–64	68
65+	51

A demographic profile was taken of a sample of 500 customers in both chains of restaurants with the results shown in Table 5.7.

Qualitative research Second, they undertook qualitative research in the form of discussion groups in order to find out more about the attitudes of customers and non-customers. (The findings are documented in the Appendix below.)

The problem The problem for the Fernandez partners was first to interpret the results of their market research in relation to their future marketing strategy. If they were to capitalise on the current wave of interest in eating out, they knew they had to act quickly and expand. The shareholders had agreed to fund an ambitious plan to open a further fifty outlets in three years. They needed a marketing formula for these outlets that they could replicate consistently around the country, confident that it would work without constant supervision. 'We need to take the consistency of McDonald's into pub-restaurants', David Fernandez told the board of directors. 'When you eat in one of our outlets you know what to expect whether it's in the north of Scotland or the south of England. We need economies of scale in our marketing efforts by using national campaigns for a recognised brand that we know will work for every outlet.'

The Fernandez's immediate task was to decide the specifics of a marketing plan for the business. They not only had to decide the strategy in terms of target market and type of pub-restaurant, but also how to market these outlets to existing and potential customers to maximise sales and profits on a consistent basis.

TABLE 5.7 *Sample of 500 customers*

PERCENTAGE OF CUSTOMERS		
Age range	Jolly-Boat	Tai-P'Inn
15–24	10	19
25–34	13	23
35–44	22	21
45–54	30	20
55–64	14	10
65+	11	6
Social group		
AB	24	19
C1	32	28
C2	19	24
D	14	20
E	11	9
Lifestyle		
Pre-family	16	42
Full nest I (young children)	25	13
Full nest II (older children)	17	21
Empty nest	34	18
Solitary survivors	8	6
Gender		
Male	56	47
Female	44	53

APPENDIX TO CASE STUDY

QUALITATIVE RESEARCH RESULTS FOR CASE STUDY ON GASTRO-PUBS

Aims The aim of the research was to investigate people's attitudes to eating in gastro-pubs. In particular the Fernandez partners wanted to know how the linkage between pub and restaurant was perceived. They also wanted to obtain views on themes and menus of pub restaurants and compare the attitudes of male and female customers.

Methods In total, ten groups of six people each were organised. Four of the groups were made up of people who had not been customers of either Jolly-Boat Inns or Tai-P'Inns. The rest were divided equally between Jolly-Boat and Tai-P'Inn customers. Five of the groups were all male and five were all female.

Findings Most of the participants claimed that they eat out at least once a month, although everyone stressed that this did vary and 'averages' were hard to estimate. The main reason for choosing pub-restaurants rather than other restaurants was their perceived informality and good value for money. For a number, convenience in terms of access (parking, near to home or work) was also a feature. Reservations about pub restaurants included the atmosphere, which was perceived to be more noisy and smoky than in restaurants – a concern particularly expressed by the female groups. There was also a feeling that the food, whilst likely to be acceptable, was unlikely to be excellent except in rare circumstances.

Typical comments included:

- 'It's not the sort of place you would go for a gourmet supper.'

- 'Good for families, when you're paying the bill for four or five people but not the place you would go for a romantic evening or to impress an important visitor.'

- 'If you get a table away from the bar, ok. Otherwise be prepared to have smoked everything and not much conversation.'

Pub restaurants were also seen as good places for lunch-time eating, away from the office.

- 'I usually eat in one at lunch time, as it's quick, not too expensive and they have draught beer – but the lunch menu is a bit restricted if you don't like ploughman's or sandwiches.'

The women groups particularly mentioned the need for more vegetarian food and facilities for children.

- 'I always seem to be choosing from only one or two vegetarian dishes.'

- 'My daughter is vegetarian so we have to be careful there is enough choice for her. I don't like to eat red meat either if I haven't bought and cooked it myself – it's not worth the risk these days.'

- 'We went to a pub which had a play area for the kids. As soon as they had eaten, they were gone; my friend and I could relax and talk to each other without worrying about whether they were eating properly or quarrelling.'

Concerning Jolly-Boat Inns specifically, the customers liked the freshness and variability of the food. Some did comment negatively on the service; others enjoyed its idiosyncrasies.

- 'There's always something special on the menu even if you eat there more than once a week.'

- 'I had to wait over an hour for my food but what do you expect when they have to go out and catch it!'

- 'I complained once that my fish was undercooked because it had red streaks in it. The chef came out personally and told me that red mullet always looked a bit bloody – the "Woodcock of the sea" he called it. He certainly knew what he was talking about – I thought he was going to throw me out for questioning his cooking!'

Tai-P'Inn customers enjoyed the experience and the service, although the food was seen as rather specialised. These outlets seemed particularly popular amongst women and older families.

- 'The atmosphere is great with all that memorabilia from different places. It kept the kids interested for ages. Definitely worth a visit.'

- 'The food is very interesting. Too spicy for my kids some of it but they need to taste something different now and again.'

- 'I always get my husband to take me there for our anniversary treat.'

- 'They cater for women. The loos are clean, and the bar stools low, so we don't mind sitting down on either of them.'

QUESTIONS

1 Analyse the current position using the information given in the case. In particular:

   i Summarise the key features of the market

   ii Summarise the strengths and weaknesses of both the Jolly-Boat and Tai-P'Inn, particularly in relation to trends in the marketplace

2 Comment on the appropriateness of the marketing information given.

3 Make suggestions of what else you would need to find out. Define your future research needs, objectives and the methods you would use.

4 From the information provided, recommend how the chain can meet the Fernandez's future marketing objectives.

DEVELOPING A MARKETING PLAN

THE RESEARCH PLAN AND IMPLEMENTATION

The analysis stage of your marketing plan has looked at existing information and evaluated this as a SWOT – strengths, weaknesses, opportunities, threats – analysis. Now consider how marketing research could help your project. This may fall into several areas such as:

■ What other secondary information about the market and the competition do you need to complete your analysis? In what areas do you need more data to help clarify issues?

■ In what areas is primary research required to clarify issues? What would be the objectives and methods of such research?

■ What research methods would you use to evaluate the results of your marketing activities?

When you have considered these and any other opportunities for research, decide which you can implement as part of this project and plan how and when you will do this.

5.10 FURTHER READING AND REFERENCES

Marketing research

Chisnall, P.M. (2001), *Marketing Research*, 6th edition (McGraw Hill).
Denzin, N.K. and Lincoln, Y.S. (1998), *Strategies of Qualitative Inquiry* (Sage).
Gordon, W. (1999), *Good Thinking – A Guide to Qualitative Research* (Admap Publications).
Hardaker, G. and Graham, G. (2001), *Wired Marketing* (John Wiley & Sons), Chapter 3.
Hooley, G.J. and Hussey, M.K. (1999), *Quantitative Methods in Marketing* (Thomson Learning).
Kent, R. (2007), *Marketing Research: Approaches, Methods and Applications in Europe* (Thomson Learning).

McGivern, Y. (2006), *The Practice of Market and Social Research: An Introduction* (FT Prentice Hall).

Oppenheim, A.N. (1992), *Questionnaire Design, Interviewing and Attitude Measurement* (Pinter Publishers).

Proctor, T. (2000), *Essentials of Marketing Research* (FT Prentice Hall).

Webb, J.R. (2001), *Understanding and Designing Market Research* (Thomson Learning).

Wilson, A. (2006), *Marketing Research, An Integrated Approach*, 2nd edition (FT Prentice Hall).

Research information websites

Mintel:	http://www.mintel.com
MORI:	http://www.mori.co.uk
Economist Intelligence Unit:	http://www.eiu.com
AC Nielsen:	http://www.nielsen.com
Euromonitor:	http://www.euromonitor.com
Key Note:	http://www.keynote.co.uk
UKOP (UK Official Publications):	http://www.ukop.co.uk

Part 2

THE IMPLEMENTATION OF MARKETING STRATEGIES

Chapter **6**

MARKETING STRATEGY

LEARNING OBJECTIVES

By the end of this chapter the reader will be able to:

- Understand the difference between strategy and tactics
- Assess the basis for segmenting markets
- Evaluate strategies for targeting selected markets
- Assess techniques for positioning products and services
- Appreciate strategies that create competitive advantage
- Understand the concept of the marketing mix

INTRODUCTION

Strategic marketing management involves decisions in three key areas:

- Selection of customer groups, or segments of the market, that are relevant to an organisation's activities
- Targeting of market segments in which an organisation can offer competitive benefits
- Adoption of an appropriate market position that appeals to the selected segment

These decision areas of segmentation, targeting and positioning form the basis of a marketing strategy. Once defined, a marketing strategy aims to gain a competitive advantage to be sustainable. It is implemented through the activities of the marketing mix – the methods through which marketing objectives are met.

6.1 STRATEGIES IN MARKETING

6.1.1 Corporate strategy

A strategy can be defined as a plan or pattern that brings together the objectives and activities of an organisation into a cohesive whole. It sets out the direction and the scope of an organisation over the long term.

CASE STUDY

....

BICYCLES

Over the last half-century, the British bicycle industry has experienced mixed fortunes. Not only has the bicycle become a much less-often used form of personal transport, but also the centre of production has shifted to the Far East. In 1955, the UK manufactured 3.5 million bicycles, of which two-thirds were exported. Producers in Hong Kong, Taiwan, Thailand and China, assembling mainly Japanese components, have since taken over the world's mass markets. Today more than 100 million bicycles are made each year, but very few in the UK. Despite losing its share of global production in the marketplace, the British cycle industry has recovered from the relegation of the bike to a very secondary mode of transport. First the BMX (bicycle moto-cross) craze showed the nation's youth that cycling could be fun and fashionable. Next, the mountain bike, or ATB (all-terrain bike), appealed both to teenagers seeking more excitement and to the over-thirty-year-olds looking for healthy and environmentally friendly recreation. By 2000, ATBs accounted for over two-thirds of all bicycle sales in the UK. Today, the UK market is worth £300 million with purchases of around 2.4 million cycles a year.

Although cycling has made a comeback, with one-third of the population now owning a bike, its penetration varies demographically. More men own bicycles than women (38 per cent of men against 29 per cent of women). Ownership is highest amongst 15- to 19-year-olds (55 per cent ownership) and the 35- to 44-year-old group (40 per cent ownership), with dips in the intervening years and a considerable decline from 45 years on. The AB and C2 social groups own more ATBs than other groups. Ownership is highest where the terrain is flatest (Anglia and the South) and lowest in hilly areas (Scotland and Wales) and urban centres where cycling is more dangerous (London).

Bicycles are owned for a variety of reasons. Exercise and recreation are the most common uses today, ahead of making local trips such as shopping and travelling to work. A more varied product range attempts to meet the needs of the different customer groups. The ATB or mountain bike with its rugged frame and wheels and up to twenty-one gears has a more adventurous image than the conventional sports or touring bike that has thinner wheels, lighter frame and dropped handle bars. But a new hybrid 'town and trail' variety has become increasingly popular. It combines some of the features of the ATB such as multi-cog gears and sturdy appearance with a more comfortable, efficient ride, recognising that most bicycles are still ridden primarily on roads. ATBs have also become the popular form of children's cycle, superseding the junior BMX, although more conventional,

Bicycles are owned for a variety of reasons

small-wheeled cycles and 'trikes' are still sold to the youngest riders. Specialist road and track bicycles cater for the growing number of participants in the sport of cycling, which received a welcome boast in the UK from the success of local riders and cycles in the Olympics. Other specialist products include the folding bike that can be put in the boot of a car, and tandems and tricycles.

All of this was common knowledge to Rob McIntyre, managing director of one of the leading UK cycle companies as he considered the strategic options that had recently opened up to his business. McIntyre had just concluded a deal with a major Japanese producer of cycle components to test-market a new gearing system in the UK. The new product had ten gears, sufficient for most uses, but it was totally enclosed in the hub that protected it and made it easier to maintain and use. The producers claimed that it combined the benefits of the older hub gears and the newer derailleur, 'chain-jumping' systems popularised by the ATB. Although tests on the new product convinced McIntyre that it met these claims, his long experience in the bicycle trade also warned him that there would be resistance to it.

'Cyclists perceive the hub gear as rather old-fashioned and utilitarian compared to the excitement of all those cogs and levers of derailleur gears, however impracticable they may sometimes be', he explained to his fellow directors when they met to consider their marketing strategy for the new product. 'External gears are seen as an essential part of the ATB, and it may detract from its macho image if we give our range an internal gearing system. So we have to look carefully at the various sections of the market and decide where to target this innovation. Should we target buyers of our more traditional sports and touring cycles, as the gears are more in line with their image? Or should we go for the larger market of ATBs and try to reposition the enclosed gear in the marketplace as a technological innovation, far removed from the older systems? Perhaps the benefits of the new product have particular relevance to some types of cycle user above others and can help us develop new markets. We should be quite clear about which segment of users we are targeting and what particular position we wish to adopt in order to appeal to those customer groups. Whatever we decide we should remember that this product only gives us a short-term technological lead. For once, we are ahead of other overseas manufacturers who do not have immediate access to this product, but it will only be for another year or so. We must use our window of opportunity to the full.'

QUESTIONS

1 What do you think McIntyre means by a 'marketing strategy'? How does it differ from marketing 'tactics'? Give examples of strategic and tactical marketing decisions in this case. *See section 6.1*

2 Consider the different customer groups that exist in the bicycle market. In what ways could you divide this market into segments and sub-segments that might be meaningful to cycle manufacturers? *See section 6.2*

3 Evaluate the options open to McIntyre for targeting customer groups with the new product. What targeting strategy would you recommend? *See section 6.3*

4 Evaluate the likely market perceptions of cycles using the enclosed hub gear compared to the open, multi-cog, derailleur variety currently used on mountain bikes. How would you position the new product in relation to existing ones in the marketplace? *See section 6.4*

5 In what ways could the Internet have an impact on the marketing of an established product such as a bicycle? *See section 6.5.2*

6 What marketing methods would you use to support the position of the new product in the marketplace, and how would you do this? *See section 6.5*

Marketing strategies play a significant part in the formulation of an overall strategy for an organisation and it is difficult to treat them in isolation.

Strategic decision-making represents a key stage in the translation of analysis and objectives into specific plans and activities. If we wish to climb a mountain, we start with research into likely conditions and optional routes in order to fulfil our objective of reaching the summit. We finish with the specific climbing and walking activities to get us there. In between we make strategic decisions such as the route to take; for example, we make a strategic choice between a direct assault up the steepest face or a more indirect approach. Similarly, corporate strategy determines the overall direction that an organisation takes to reach its declared destination. Often the corporate strategy is articulated by the company's mission statement.

FOR EXAMPLE

Starbucks is probably the most famous speciality coffee shop chain in the world. It offers whole bean coffees, espresso beverages, confectionery and bakery items in its retail stores. It has also diversified into ice creams and teas.

Its mission statement has the following objective and guiding principles:

Objective: establish Starbucks as the premier purveyor of the finest coffee in the world while maintaining our uncompromising principles while we grow.

The following six guiding principles will help us measure the appropriateness of our decisions:

- Provide a great work environment and treat each other with respect and dignity

- Embrace diversity as an essential component in the way we do business

- Apply the highest standards of excellence to the purchasing, roasting and fresh delivery of our coffee

- Develop enthusiastically satisfied customers all of the time

- Contribute positively to our communities and our environment

- Recognize that profitability is essential to our future success

Starbucks have a comprehensive mission statement

Statements of corporate strategy such as this inform the marketing strategy. (For more on corporate strategy, mission statements and marketing objectives see Chapter 12, section 12.2.1.)

6.1.2 Marketing strategies and tactics

Marketing strategies are an integral part of an organisation's overall corporate strategy because they deal with the all-important interaction with the marketplace. Marketing strategies are sometimes indistinguishable from corporate strategies.

Marketing decisions can be at a strategic or tactical level:

■ *Marketing strategies* define a continuing basis for determining how an organisation interacts with the marketplace to achieve its broad objectives (e.g. Starbucks' marketing strategy of emphasising customer and employee satisfaction is very close to its corporate strategy).

■ *Marketing tactics* are short-duration actions adapted to specific situations to achieve limited objectives in line with the general strategy (e.g. Starbucks has installed automatic espresso machines to speed up service and offers prepaid cards to cut transaction costs in half. It has launched Starbucks Express which allows customers to order and pay through the website, so they can arrive in the store to find their drink ready, with their name printed on the cup. Starbucks have also provided high-speed Internet connections in their outlets to attract younger customers).

Characteristics of strategic marketing

The difference between strategic and tactical decisions depends to some extent on levels within an organisation – what is tactical at senior management level may become strategic at a junior management level, for example. However, strategic marketing decisions have some distinguishing characteristics that seek to answer three particular questions about the relationship of customers to the organisation:

1. *How can customers be grouped according to their needs and buying patterns?* The answer requires analysis that defines the scope and nature of an organisation's marketplace by *segmenting* the market into customer groups.

2. *What benefits do these particular groups of customers look for and how can we provide them?* This leads to matching the activities of an organisation to the market in which it operates by *targeting* selected customer groups.

3. *What do we have to offer this customer group that is special in some way?* This involves matching the strengths of an organisation to the needs of a customer group by adopting an appropriate market *position*.

These strategic considerations of *segmentation, targeting* and *positioning* are the subjects of the next three sections.

CHECKPOINT

Consider a project you have recently completed – perhaps a journey, a work assignment or a sporting event. What was the overall strategy that you adopted to make things happen? What were the tactics you used during the project?

6.2 MARKET SEGMENTATION

6.2.1 Buyer groups

Markets are normally made up of buyers who have different needs and expectations from the products they buy. We are all buyers in the food market and the clothing market, but our diets and our wardrobes are not the same because our particular needs and wants are unique.

However, some people show similarities in what they choose because of their age, lifestyle or other distinguishing factors. The wardrobe of one teenage girl resembles that of another teenage girl in many respects and is certainly very different to that of a middle-aged man. The refrigerators of vegetarians contain many similar items and will differ from the food-store of the average meat-eating family. Different groups of buyers have broadly similar needs and wants from what they buy in specific markets.

Segments

Markets can be divided into distinct groups of buyers in this way. Each group has similar needs or expectations from the products or services they buy, which are different to other groups buying the same type of product. These distinctive buyer groups are referred to as *market segments*.

FOR EXAMPLE

The book market is made up of groups of buyers with different requirements including:

■ 'Recreational' buyers reading for pleasure and relaxation who choose easy-to-read fictional novels
■ 'Knowledge' buyers wanting information on specific topics who buy non-fiction reference books
■ 'Display' buyers who regard books as a symbol of sophistication and culture and buy them for show in their homes or places of work

Sub-segments and niches

Market segments are often broad categories of consumers that can be further subdivided into narrower *sub-segments*.

FOR EXAMPLE

The book market segments described above can be broken down further. 'Knowledge' buyers consist of sub-segments including:

■ Parents who buy reference books such as encyclopaedias for their children
■ Students who need textbooks for a particular course of study
■ Hobbyists who buy specialised information about their hobby

FIGURE 6.1 *Possible segments, sub-segments and niches in the book market*

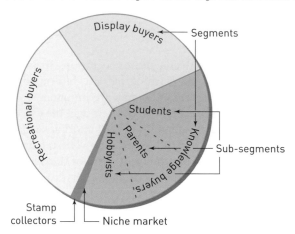

Some sub-segments contain groups of buyers who require very specialised products or services which sets them apart as a *market niche*.

FOR EXAMPLE

....

Some hobbyists form niche markets. Stamp collectors buy specialised books, a market niche served by Stanley Gibbons, who have developed a range of catalogues and reference books specifically for the serious philatelist as well as the more amateur collector.

Markets divided into segments, sub-segments and niches are sometimes represented by pie charts, such as the one representing the above examples in Figure 6.1.

6.2.2 The advantages of market segmentation

Market segments, sub-segments and niches form separate markets which require distinctive marketing strategies. Not only do they need different products but they may also respond differently to pricing policies, promotional approaches and distribution coverage.

FOR EXAMPLE

....

Parents, students and hobbyists, the sub-segments we identified in the book market, all require different types of publications. Student textbooks usually command lower prices than hobby or reference books and their promotion and distribution may be through specialised university bookshops.

The manufacturer or supplier might see this as an inconvenience as it can lead to a multiplication of product lines and fragmentation of efforts in trying to reach the market segments.

However, market segmentation offers the following important advantages to supplying organisations:

■ *Closer matching between what is offered by the organisation and customer needs.* It is possible through a combination of research and experience to develop a good understanding of the needs of a well-defined segment of customers and offer appropriate products and

FOR EXAMPLE

With over 2,000 outlets throughout the country, Arcadia Group Ltd is the UK's largest clothing retailer, reaching its customers through eight brands. Instead of trying to be all things to all people, it has developed and acquired different brands for different target markets.

TABLE 6.1 *Successful branding*

BRAND	SEGMENT
BURTON	25–35-year-old man who is fashion aware but not fashion leader. Confident with his own style but may require some guidance.
DOROTHY PERKINS	18–60-year-old woman with the average customer age in her middle thirties. Likes to look fashionable and interested in keeping up with latest trends. Little time for herself. Always busy, either working or with children. Trusts Dorothy Perkins to deliver styles that suit her and give her outfit advice on how to put the latest look together.
EVANS	25–55-year-old woman of more generous dimensions. Brand aims to celebrate curves. Sizes 16–32 combining fashion and value.
MISS SELFRIDGE	18–24-year-old woman who is feminine, stylish, individual and self-assured. Fashion-aware and confident, experimenting with her own style and expecting value for money. Makes reference to celebrities and style leaders but has her own opinion and unique style.
OUTFIT	25–45-year-old woman. Many have children and want a wide range of affordable fashionable clothing for herself and her children. Outfit operates in selected out-of-town sites and stocks all Arcadia brands plus Rubicon-owned Warehouse and Principles. Desires convenient hassle-free shopping and sees Outfit as a supplement to, rather than a replacement of, the High Street.
TOPSHOP	TopShop girl is style-conscious, independent and addicted to fashion. Goes shopping every week in pursuit of her latest fashion fix. Customers include industry insiders, including stylists, models and musicians.
TOPMAN	Young fashionable male. Uses talented young designers and has won numerous awards including Menswear Design of the Year.
WALLIS	Individualistic, aiming to be deliberately different. Produces own designs with a team of five designers creating ten looks per season. Distinctive dressing.

services to them. It is difficult to get close to customer groups that are widely defined as their needs have fewer common factors. In trying to please diverse types of customers, it is possible to end up pleasing none.

■ *Concentration of resources on areas of greatest advantage.* By identifying closely with one segment of the market, an organisation can concentrate its resources on meeting the needs of that customer group in the fullest possible way. Larger organisations have learned that the key to success in competitive markets is to focus decentralised business units on specific segments. Smaller firms with limited resources survive by concentrating on what they do best for a targeted group of customers.

FOR EXAMPLE

The Body Shop was developed from the humble beginnings of one shop in Brighton founded by Anita Roddick in 1976. Its appeal was to a group of women opposed to the hype of the 'impossible dream' of perfect beauty symbolised by the advertising and packaging of the conventional cosmetic companies. Started with a small £4,000 bank loan, the new business concentrated its meagre resources on a rapidly growing segment of female buyers who desired more natural and less synthetic products. Hitherto, the established cosmetic companies had dominated the market with expensive packaging and extensive advertising. The Body Shop broke their stranglehold by concentrating on developing totally new products with exotic names such as Seaweed and Birch Shampoo, and Honey and Oatmeal Scrub Mask. There was no money for advertising and fancy packaging, but environmentally concerned customers preferred the Body Shop's plastic bottles and simple labels. Anita Roddick's limited resources in those early days focused the Body Shop on its greatest strength – the simplicity and naturalness of an organisation which respected rather than exploited the environment. By playing to this strength, the Body Shop found a gap in the market. Rather than take on the whole body care market on the terms of the existing dominant suppliers, Anita Roddick concentrated her resources to develop a marketing mix appropriate to a new, fast-growing segment. The Body Shop maintained its focus by franchising its original concept throughout the world. By 2006, thirty years after its founding, the Body Shop was an international organisation of over 2,100 stores trading in fifty-five countries.

■ *Market leadership through domination of a narrowly defined market.* It is becoming increasingly difficult to achieve and maintain leadership in large global markets as competition increases. One way to achieve leadership is through specialisation. If an organisation can spot a viable sub-market, it can concentrate on the needs of that segment and establish high customer loyalty and a position of market leadership.

FOR EXAMPLE

A retailer that has successfully adopted a specialist strategy is Mothercare, a widely recognised brand name around the world, and a market leader in retailing to expectant and new parents. Mothercare sells everything that a new parent needs, from car seats and pushchairs to feeding accessories and toys.

Mothercare offers e-catalogues and an extensive website which, as well as covering their comprehensive product range, offers pregnancy and parenting advice plus their own credit card (appropriately named Mothercard). Since 1984 Mothercare has also operated outside the UK, working with international franchise partners. These stores use the concept of the UK stores, offering the same products, store design and level of customer service. Over 170 Mothercare stores can be found in more than thirty countries around the world.

Mothercare has successfully adopted a specialist strategy

■ *Key to profitability in competitive markets.* The segmentation of markets is fundamental to establishing an edge over competitors. Arcadia's success is due to its spread of risk, the Body Shop carved a new segment away from the dominant cosmetic suppliers and Mothercare quickly dominated their market niche. Research has also confirmed that segmentation is the key to profitability in competitive markets. Long-term profitability is associated with those companies that achieve leadership positions in viable segments or market niches.

6.2.3 The criteria for market segmentation

The need for segmentation arises when markets are neither totally homogeneous nor totally heterogeneous. Markets can be seen as a continuum between these two extremes of uniformity and non-uniformity, as illustrated in Figure 6.2.

FIGURE 6.2 *A continuum of market types*

BENEFITS SOUGHT	BUYER BEHAVIOUR
❑ Low price	❑ Purchase rates
❑ Reliability	❑ Loyalty
❑ Safety	❑ Purchase methods
❑ Convenience	
❑ Status	
PSYCHOGRAPHICS	**GEOGRAPHY**
❑ Lifestyle	❑ National
❑ Social grouping	❑ Regional
❑ Personality	❑ Urban/rural
DEMOGRAPHICS	**END USE**
❑ Age	❑ Applications
❑ Sex	❑ Product types
❑ Culture	
❑ Family life cycle	
❑ Company size	

FIGURE 6.3

Possible criteria for segmenting markets

Some specialised markets fall into the extremes at the end of the continuum:

■ *Homogeneous markets* exist in commodities trading where traders seek to buy undifferentiated raw materials, such as metals (e.g. silver, copper) or basic foodstuffs (e.g. sugar, coffee) at the lowest possible prices

■ *Heterogeneous markets* exist in industrial buying situations when one organisation is a large enough buyer to be considered a market by itself (e.g. a manufacturer of aeroplanes might regard each major airline and each significant government purchaser as a separate market)

However, most markets can be segmented in one of several ways. There is no single method of segmenting markets. A number of variables are possible in both consumer and organisational markets. These can be classified as illustrated in Figure 6.3.

Benefit segmentation

Benefit segmentation looks for the major benefits that are given priority by a significant number of customers and then seeks to identify with that group through consistent marketing efforts. Some organisations seek to identify with segments attracted mainly by the best value for money (e.g. Asda), others with those seeking status (e.g. Rolex). It is often a long-term process to build the reputation of a company to the stage where it can be readily associated with a key market benefit.

FOR EXAMPLE

Volkswagen have carried out one of the most successful long-term campaigns to segment a mass market by focusing on only one of the benefits sought by car buyers. The original Beetle had several major disadvantages over its rivals: it looked strange and did not go very fast. But it offered an important benefit over more complicated, larger cars – it was reliable. Advertising over several decades has consistently majored on this theme so that the Volkswagen name and reliability have become synonymous. Early advertising showed a VW starting first time on a wintry morning and travelling through a snow-covered landscape, with the caption 'Have you ever wondered how the man who drives the snowplough drives to the snowplough?' Later even the unchanging looks of the Beetle had become a dependable virtue in an era of change; one advert showed the lunar landing module of the Apollo moon mission with the caption: 'It's ugly but it gets you there.' Advertising for other VW cars, after the demise of the Beetle, continued the same theme. The emphasis switched from car to driver in scenarios depicting a variety of human problems from gambling to divorce, but the message was the same: 'If only everything in life was as reliable as a Volkswagen.'

VW used the strapline "It's ugly but it gets you there"

Another car manufacturer has used benefit segmentation with similar success. Volvo selected safety as the key benefit to offer and established itself as the market leader for a segment of buyers concerned about safe motoring rather than the high performance and style promoted by other manufacturers.

Behaviour segmentation

Buyers can be grouped according to their purchasing patterns and behaviour.

- *Purchase rates* vary among customer groups. Markets are usually divided between a small number of heavy users and a large number of infrequent purchasers.

  The 'Pareto effect', or '80/20 rule', is a common phenomena in both industrial and consumer markets. This expresses the tendency for a small number of customers (as few as 20 per cent) to be heavy users of a company's products and account for a high proportion of sales (maybe as much as 80 per cent). The converse of this is that the majority of customers (the other 80 per cent) are lighter users making up a small percentage of sales (20 per cent). These segments of heavy or light users create a strategic choice for supplying organisations.

FOR EXAMPLE

....

A flooring contractor specialised in commercial contracts. Their marketing strategy was to focus on the heavy user segment of large company contracts and big office developments. Although the sales from successful tenders for these contracts were high, the market was extremely competitive and so prices and gross margins were very low. The company therefore investigated an alternative strategy of focusing on the more fragmented market segment of smaller businesses where there was less competition and higher prices to compensate for the problems of many lower-value orders.

In consumer markets, mail-order marketing concentrates on the frequent buyer, making repeated offers to those who have already bought by direct mail, in the knowledge that they are the most likely group to use this purchase method again.

■ *Loyalty to brands or companies* is another way of segmenting markets, as some customers exhibit great loyalty to one supplier, whilst others switch more easily. By studying and identifying existing loyal customers, an organisation can target marketing efforts to groups of a similar profile.

FOR EXAMPLE

Insurance companies found that teachers represented a group of very loyal, long-term customers. They did not pay the largest premiums and therefore did not fall into the heavy-user category, but their loyalty made them a segment worth targeting.

Identification of existing customers can also help prolong their loyalty. Season tickets have long been used by rail companies and football clubs to recognise and retain their regular customers. More sophisticated techniques are also now used to encourage repeat purchasing through promotions and loyalty programmes.

FOR EXAMPLE

Information technology has helped organisations to pinpoint their loyal customers. Previously, shoppers remained largely anonymous to the larger retailers such as supermarket chains. Smart cards now record the details and buying behaviour of individual customers (with updates at every purchase). Shoppers now receive inducements to use a shop card because retailers allocate points for purchases, which reward their loyal customers through extra discounts or special offers. These loyalty programmes use information from the cards to monitor response rates, making them sophisticated exercises to lock customers into one retailer.

Charities are very dependent on their regular donors. They aim to encourage regular giving by making it easy to Give As You Earn (GAYE) through deductions from pay packets and by direct debit. This is very important to charities as the regular donations allow them to plan their activities because their finances become more predictable. These regular donations are also very tax-efficient as the charities can claim back the tax on them from the Inland Revenue.

■ *Purchase method* is a way of segmenting organisational buyers. Some organisations, such as local authorities, purchase by asking for tenders on specific projects. Some purchase through committees, whilst others delegate to individual buyers. Each of these methods requires a different selling approach.

FOR EXAMPLE

The work of central government has been opened up to private-sector competition. Companies are now invited to bid for contracts to service Whitehall departments in such areas as information technology and computer services. This represents a large market segment for private-sector companies that are forced to adopt distinctive marketing approaches to take account of a central government purchasing culture. For example, Cap Gemini, a large supplier of professional and IT services, has units dedicated specifically to public services which, typically, adopt a procurement approach of asking for bids on a detailed specification of requirements and accepting the lowest price.

Psychographic segmentation

In Chapter 4, we looked at the many social and individual influences on consumer behaviour, from personality types and self-image to perceptions and attitudes (see Chapter 4, section 4.2). Psychographics, a technique for classifying lifestyles, attempts to draw together some of these influences to describe 'typical' consumers who can then be regarded as segments of the market.

FOR EXAMPLE

One classification of lifestyle groups includes a category described as 'the sophisticated adult' – intellectual and socially concerned people who like to lead and are attracted by unique and fashionable goods. This segment is the target market for ranges of exotic soft drinks, including Aqua Libra, a herbal drink of 'pure fruit juices, vegetable aromatic extracts, aqueous infusions of sunflower and sesame seeds, fresh tarragon and Siberian ginseng'. There are many others, including 'Original Norfolk Punch' and a revamped Lucozade competing in this growth market segment of sophisticated adults looking for interesting, healthy alternatives to alcohol.

Geographic segmentation

Geographic boundaries naturally divide many markets. Suppliers or customers determine geographic segments:

- Suppliers may decide to limit their market coverage to a geographically discrete area. Most companies only sell within their home nation and many within a more limited area such as a town or county. Small firms tend to operate on a limited geographic basis and very few export goods or services. Public sector organisations are usually limited by statute to a specific region; healthcare, education, social services and law enforcement are provided on a regional basis. Industrial marketing companies often segment their customers by dividing them geographically into sales areas.

- Customers may be divided into geographic segments on the basis of different localised needs or wants. This is most obvious on a national basis where cultural or climatic differences lead to different demands. Cool, blonde lagers were for a long time confined to hotter European and Antipodean climates whilst warm, dark beers were preferred in the UK.

■ Geography can operate on a number of levels. For a small business, the geographic limitations may be quite narrow. A local supermarket may be limited to only one village. The narrowness of the scope does not mean that that this will be an unprofitable strategy. Customers may be willing to pay a premium price for the convenience of a local supplier.

Larger organisations may have a regional segment. Local county councils operate in their local county, by definition. Companies may be national but most large organisations are becoming increasing global in defining their markets.

Demographic segmentation

Demographic variables are a widely used basis for market segmentation. In consumer markets the demographic variables frequently used are age, gender, occupation and income. Industry classification and company size are often used in organisational markets. There are two main reasons for the popularity of demographic variables as a basis for segmentation:

■ Customer needs often vary according to demographic differences; for example, age and gender clearly differentiate demand in many markets including clothes, magazines and body care products.

■ Demographics are usually well defined and above all, measurable. We know what proportion of the population are over sixty years old, male and live in East Anglia. Government publications identify the numbers of organisations by industry type and region. Demographic statistics are widely available and a major source of quantifiable market data. They are also normally available as secondary data, and therefore quick, inexpensive and easy to gather.

End use

The same product may be used for different applications, or specific types of the same basic product may be developed for distinct end uses.

FOR EXAMPLE

An office copier may be used by one customer group for large runs of the same original, and by another customer for many one-off copies of different originals. Although their total copy volume per month is similar, the needs of these customers in terms of equipment and costs per copy are not the same.

CHECKPOINT

You have been asked to advise on the marketing strategy for your local leisure centre, cinema, museum or another local attraction with which you are familiar.

What would you recommend as the basis for segmenting the marketplace?

6.3 TARGETING STRATEGIES

6.3.1 Alternative market strategies

What strategies can be used to direct marketing efforts following an analysis of the market and its possible customer segments? Three basic strategies can be considered, as illustrated in Figure 6.4.

Undifferentiated marketing

An undifferentiated marketing strategy takes no account of market differences and applies the same marketing effort to the whole market. It relies on one basic product and marketing programme to attract sufficient buyers. This strategy has the advantage of lower costs because it can provide economies of scale in production or administration and lower distribution and marketing costs.

- In consumer markets, an undifferentiated strategy may rely on mass advertising and distribution methods. Guinness, Coca-Cola and the Ford Motor Company are examples of companies that originally offered only one product to their respective markets, relying on its unique, universal appeal, backed by extensive advertising and wide availability.

- In business to business markets, unbranded, commodity-type products are often marketed in an undifferentiated way. Suppliers of electronic components such as transistors, capacitors and resistors sell identical products to different markets using the same strategies.

Undifferentiated strategies are increasingly vulnerable to competitors willing to match the needs of segments more closely. Guinness, Coca-Cola and Ford have all launched new products that recognise the importance of trends in segments of the market. Guinness is now sold in cans for the growing numbers drinking at home. Coke offers numerous variants including Diet Coke, Caffeine- free Coke, Coke with Lemon and Coke Zero for various segments with different pack formats such as cans, glass bottles, plastic bottles and draught. Ford have expanded their range from the original black Model T to a huge range of potential combinations of model, colour, trim and options such as radios and sun roofs. In industrial markets, large users of undifferentiated products, such as electronic components, try to become segmented by negotiating lower prices.

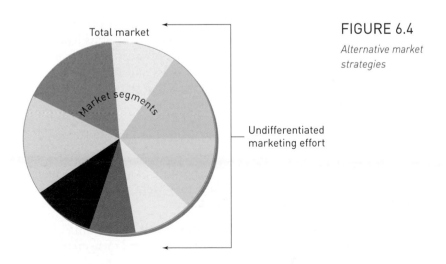

Total market

Market segments

Undifferentiated marketing effort

FIGURE 6.4

Alternative market strategies

Differentiated marketing

A differentiated marketing strategy targets *distinct customer groups* using marketing efforts appropriate to each segment. This may involve developing different products or offering different mixes of pricing, promotion or distribution arrangements.

A strategy which recognises the need for a differentiated approach benefits from the advantages of segmentation discussed above (see section 6.2.2). It has the disadvantage of additional costs in developing new products and implementing diverse marketing programmes to match individual segments. These should be recovered through the additional sales that a targeted approach brings, but there are limits; some segments may be too small to generate the additional income needed to justify a segmented approach.

FOR EXAMPLE

Differentiated marketing is not restricted to the private sector. Many public services are now targeting their efforts at distinctive sub-markets. Secondary schools differentiate between their policies for eleven- to sixteen-year-old pupils and their approach to sixth-form students with different patterns of attendance, dress requirements and the facilities provided. This has been stimulated partly by competition from sixth-form and technical colleges which offer a different environment for the sixteen-plus age group. Similarly, hospitals and universities develop centres of excellence in a particular medical field or academic area, in recognition of the need to demonstrate specialised expertise to attract public funding.

Concentrated marketing

If resources are limited, an organisation may decide to limit its approach to only one segment of the market and follow a strategy of *concentration*.

Specialisation has the advantage of effective use of resources. Most small businesses need this focused market approach in order to survive the start-up period, as the Body Shop ably demonstrated.

There are risks in total reliance on one segment of the market, however. Mothercare, for example, is very dependent on the trends in birth rate. As the birth rate is now at its lowest for some time, it is vulnerable. It has responded to this by expanding its product range from just baby clothes and maternity wear into categories such as child car seats and recently financial services with its Mothercard. A compensating factor for Mothercare is that the increasing age of mothers means that their customers tend to be more financially secure.

6.3.2 Choosing target segments

How does an organisation choose which segments to target? The purpose of targeting a segment is to use marketing resources and effort more effectively than if they were applied to a wider base. Several criteria determine just how effectively this can be done:

- ■ *Can the segment be identified?* If a sub-segment is hard to identify it will also be difficult to measure and quantify for analysis. Targeting relies on precise definition and measurement, without which it becomes inexact and uncertain.

FOR EXAMPLE

....

In the 1990s, many young people attended secret 'rave' parties and were influenced by an underground rave culture. Although stories abounded about what rave culture involved, it remained elusive and ill-defined because of its secretive nature. Some attempts were made to target this lifestyle segment by using psychedelic or irreverent advertising. But despite estimates that up to one-third of all under twenty-five-year-olds had experienced a rave party of some sort, this segment proved extremely hard to access using traditional marketing campaigns.

Today 'flash mobbing', where people organise over the Internet to meet at a specified public place to carry out an absurd or surreal act, has become a craze. The first UK event took place when 200 people met up at a London furniture store, admired the sofas and disappeared, much to the bemusement of the store manager. The bizarre events are usually kept secret, with directions and instructions being given to participants at the last minute. Other examples include a mob tweeting like birds and crowing like roosters in Central Park, New York or gathering outside the American Embassy in Berlin – to drink a toast to 'Natasha'.

■ *Is it a relevant segment?* Effective segmentation is based on criteria that are relevant to the buying decision of that subgroup of customers. There is no point in differentiating between customers on a basis that is irrelevant to how they make particular purchase decisions. A population segment of left-handed people is probably not relevant as a basis for segmenting the clothing market, for example.

■ *Is the segment large enough?* A market segment has to be capable of providing a satisfactory return on the investment made in it. Markets can be over-segmented into small groups of customers whose purchasing power does not warrant a distinctive marketing approach. An organisation can only survive if it is based on a segment which proves to be a viable commercial size in the long term.

FOR EXAMPLE

....

Although we live in an age of increasing specialisation, a slackening of economic growth exposes suppliers who base their existence on a narrow marketplace. When highly specialised retailers, such as the Sock Shop and Tie Rack, first emerged to target a sub-market in clothes accessories, they were among the first to feel the effects of a recession in the High Street, resulting in the closure of many branches.

■ *Is the segment accessible?* Targeting relies on accessibility. Marketing efforts can only be applied if customers in a segment can be reached through channels of distribution and communication in a cost-effective way. The rave lifestyle segment of the population has no established mass media or distribution outlets and so cannot be easily reached, for example.

6.3.3 Targeting segments in practise

In practise, organisations use a number of segmentation variables at the same time to target a marketplace. For example, geography and demographics (sometimes referred to as geodemographics) are used to pinpoint socio-economic groups living in a given district. This is often used in targeting in direct marketing so that mailings go to appropriate addresses. The science of geodemographics is based on the idea that 'birds of a feather flock together' so they cluster households together.

Examples of consumer and organisational market strategies show a number of possible approaches: targeting consumer market segments, targeting industrial market segments and targeting public service market segments. These are dealt with in turn below.

Targeting consumer market segments

Managers marketing to consumers use a series of variables to target customer groups, often starting with demographic and geographic segments but recognising lifestyle and other differences within them.

FOR EXAMPLE

Arcadia (see for example on page 179 and Table 6.1) started life as the Burton Group. The Burton Group learned the lessons from their undifferentiated marketing to the menswear market in the 1960s and 70s. Under a new chief executive, Ralph Halpern, the company began to adopt a much more targeted approach by carefully segmenting the markets for both men's and women's clothes. A new chain of shops, TopMan, specialised in exciting fashion clothes for the younger man, to complement the successful TopShop outlets for young women. Shops still using the Burton name concentrated on a more mature segment of the menswear market and Dorothy Perkins provided good value fashion for twenty- to thirty-five-year-old women. By the 1980s the group recognised the significance of an increasingly fashion conscious group – the baby boomers of the post-war years. Although they were now aged thirty to forty-five, this large segment of the population had been teenagers in the swinging sixties and still tended to look for more style from their clothes than preceding generations. Principles and later Principles for Men were launched to cater for the lifestyle needs of this segment, who had moved on from the brashness of boutiques and now wanted more sophisticated shopping and higher-quality garments, without compromising on fashion and design. Market coverage of this older segment was further increased by the acquisition of Debenhams department stores to give a 'family' feel to the group.

The Burton Group's strategies proved extremely profitable for a while, but the inherent dangers in a highly segmented approach proved to be the downfall of Halpern, who resigned in late 1990. The recession in High Street sales and the slump in commercial property values caught The Burton Group over-exposed in both markets. Demographics affected sales as the teenage population began to fall. TopShop and TopMan were shrunk in size to reflect the decrease in importance of the younger segment of the market. The Burton Group's aim of complete market coverage through targeted outlets proved not only costly but unwieldy in adapting to changes, and the group found themselves over-concentrated on a shrinking youth market. In 1998, the Burton Group de-merged with Debenhams, and renamed itself Arcadia. It has undergone a further restructuring with the sale of hundreds of its shops.

In 2002, Arcadia was acquired by entrepreneur Philip Green and family, and now forms part of the largest retailing group in Europe. It operates through seven of its original brands: Burton, TopShop, TopMan, Evans, Wallis, Miss Selfridge and Dorothy Perkins with the addition of Outfit as an eighth brand. Each brand continues to target distinct segments with leading positions in their respective markets (see Table 6.1). Its history provides a timely reminder that changes in the business environment can erode the effectiveness of a segmentation strategy. The business has succeeded in the longer term because it has recognised that the composition of the segments that make up the clothing market constantly shift, as do the aspirations of the consumers in each segment.

Targeting industrial market segments

Larger organisations selling on a 'business to business' basis frequently use a succession of segmentation variables to target the various markets in which they operate. The structure of the salesforce often mirrors the adopted segmentation approach. Personal selling, like other aspects of the marketing effort, requires different approaches according to the targeted segment.

FOR EXAMPLE

A reprographics company selling a range of printing machines, office copiers and speciality reprographic equipment targeted its markets by enduse, customer type and geographic region. This is illustrated in Figure 6.5.

This organisation first differentiated its marketing efforts according to the end use of the products sold. Separate divisions sold equipment suitable for printing, office copying, and for special applications in the design and artwork processes.

The office copying division targeted its sales force according to customer type and by region. One sales force concentrated on the public sector such as national and local government departments, and the police, health and education authorities, as these customers required special contractual terms. Another sales force targeted national accounts; these large companies operated from a number of premises but still bought office equipment centrally through purchasing managers who required strong personal relationships with their suppliers.

FIGURE 6.5 *Target market segments for a reprographic company*

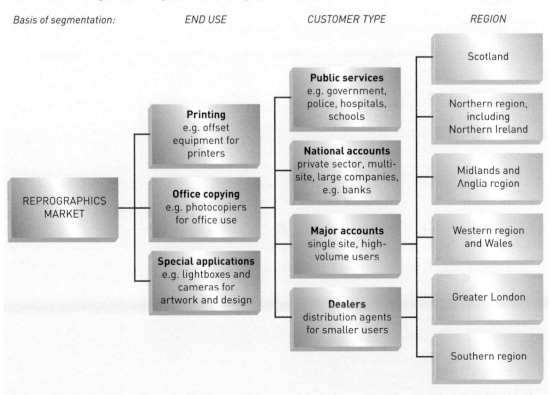

Major accounts were the customer targets of another sales force because they represented heavier users but purchased locally in a decentralised way. Distribution agents or dealers bought stocks of equipment for forward sale to smaller users. Finally both the major accounts sales force and the dealers were organised into six geographic regions.

Targeting public service market segments

Public services increasingly use differentiated strategies in order to meet the requirements of their markets. As one service competes with another for limited funds, public service managers have important internal markets to consider, as well as the external markets made up of the users of their services. These internal markets include stakeholders, who can influence the amount of resources dedicated to that service. Stakeholders include taxpayers and their representatives (politicians and pressure groups), local and central government bodies, employees and their representatives (unions, federations) and quasi-government organisations (ombudsmen, regulatory authorities or watchdogs). Internal and external markets have different needs and therefore require differentiated marketing approaches.

FOR EXAMPLE

A hospital first segmented its markets into different types of stakeholder, including those influencing the level of funds for healthcare as well as the patients requiring healthcare. Patients were further divided by the priority and type of treatment required. These segments are illustrated in Figure 6.6.

FIGURE 6.6 *Possible target market segments for an NHS hospital*

Stakeholders include direct fundholding agencies such as Primary Care Trusts and doctors' practices, the local Community Health Council, taxpayers and their local and national political representatives. These groups all have an influence on the well-being of the hospital, but have different requirements from it that justify separate marketing approaches. The Primary Care Trusts, for example, may be mainly concerned with efficiency and economy, whilst watchdog groups will be more concerned with the effectiveness of the services provided.

Patients form different demographic markets, based on their age and sex, which are recognised in the way the hospital caters for them. They also differ in the priority of the services they need, from emergency to non-urgent care, and in the types of treatment they require from surgery to nursing care. The achievement of high-quality services depends on recognising the different needs between these and other segments of patients.

6.3.4 Targeting and databases

The power of information technology now enables even the largest enterprise to have a close relationship with individual customers or segments of the market. By using computerised databases, information can be acquired and stored on customer buying habits according to selected criteria. Marketing activities can then be focused on a specific group of customers by, for example, sending fully customised offers or information to individuals based upon an understanding of their past buying behaviour.

Database marketing involves building up a database of such information on actual and potential customers. Legal use of databases containing personal information in Europe requires an understanding of national laws, Europe-wide directives, the use of suppression files and company actions. In the UK, both the Data Protection Act (1984) and Freedom of Information Act (2000) are important in ensuring consumer protection (Fell, 2002).

Some of the advantages of using customer databases include:

- *It develops relationships with existing customers.* It can cost up to six times more to recruit a new customer than to retain an existing one. Database marketing helps to develop relationships with existing customers as well as to acquire them. It emphasises the *lifetime value* of a customer by collecting data on their purchases over a long period of time.

- *It allows a bottom-up rather than a top-down approach to marketing.* Market segments can be defined by groups of existing customers who have similar characteristics according to customer records. This is in contrast to segmentation based on information about the whole market, which is often difficult to obtain.

FOR EXAMPLE
....

Tesco's Clubcard has facilitated the collection of data on millions of customers and their purchases. This has been analysed to define groups of customers who are then sent various offers and promotions. Tesco overtook Sainsbury at the top of the supermarket league, not by gaining new customers, but by reducing the attrition rate amongst existing customers, who stayed loyal to Tesco for longer once they had the card. Top-spending customers have been invited to special events to keep them coming back. Competitive threats, such as the opening of other stores, have been monitored by looking at the purchasing patterns of the highest-spending Tesco customers. Those whose spending has declined sharply are assumed to be trying a competitive outlet and specific offers can be made to woo them back. The most important benefit for Tesco was the acquisition of sufficient data so that they could define the needs of their target markets according to their own customer base.

6.3.5 *Targeting customer retention*

Strategies targeted to *retain* customers by the development of long-term relationships can be conceptualised as a hierarchy of customer loyalty, as shown in Figure 6.7.

- **■ *Prospects*** represent the target market. Traditional marketing strategies have tended to focus at this level of converting prospects into customers.

- **■** A ***customer*** in this model is someone who has done business with an organisation once or occasionally. The aim is to develop customers into clients.

- **■** A ***client*** is a regular, repeat customer, however, they may not think positively about the organisation, but come back merely through inertia or because of high switching costs. They are obviously vulnerable to competitors who can overcome these issues.

FOR EXAMPLE

....

Historically borrowers rarely switched from one building society or bank to another once they had established a mortgage because it was an elaborate and costly procedure. Fierce competition amongst lenders has simplified procedures and financial incentives have been offered to existing borrowers to move their mortgages. Retaining existing clients has become a key

FIGURE 6.7

A hierarchy of customer loyalty

marketing objective for building societies and banks who traditionally have only marketed to new buyers (prospects) or existing customers about to take out a new mortgage because they are moving.

Retaining clients it is important in order to convert them into 'supporters'.

■ A supporter *thinks* positively about the organisation and is pleased to be a customer.

■ An advocate *acts* positively about the organisation by recommending it to others. At this level up the hierarchy, the customer is not only more secure from competitive enticements, but also acts as an extra salesperson for the organisation by making recommendations through word-of-mouth communications.

■ Partnerships of suppliers and buyers are at the pinnacle of this particular marketing model as organisations and individuals work together as partners to identify further ways in which mutual advantage can be gained from the relationship.

CHECKPOINT

Your initial advice on the marketing strategy for a local attraction (see Checkpoint on page 186) recommended the basis for segmenting the market.
    Which of these sub-markets would you now recommend the management to target – and why?

6.4 POSITIONING

6.4.1 Positioning strategy

Customers perceive organisations and their products in a certain way. This perception is usually a simplistic impression: some products are perceived as 'upmarket' and expensive (e.g. Rolex watches, Porsche cars); others are 'downmarket' and inexpensive (Timex watches, Seat cars). Some companies give an impression of exclusivity (Harrods), technological leadership (IBM) or classic excellence (Mont Blanc).

These perceptions describe the position of an organisation or a product in the marketplace. The 'position' represents a general impression given to customers in relation to competing organisations or products. To many book shoppers, Amazon.com represents convenience through technology whilst Waterstones is a more traditional browsing experience: we tend to position the countless suppliers that compete for our custom through generalisations in our minds such as these.

Positioning can be left to chance. Many companies earn a reputation, which spreads by word of mouth and sticks with them. This may not be to their advantage and can require active steps to change. Jaguar cars were perceived as unreliable until the company took positive steps to change its market position to that of high performance, luxury motoring. The Labour party was perceived as out of date until Neil Kinnock and then Tony Blair repositioned it as modern 'New Labour'. Barnados, a child-focused charity, has moved away from being about children's homes to being more about children's issues in general.

Steps in a positioning strategy

Targeting a market segment involves deciding what positioning strategy to adopt within it and making sure that the perceptions of the customer match the desired position. This involves several steps:

- Deciding the positions that are relevant to the market segment and most likely to influence buying habits

- Evaluating which position the organisation can deliver effectively and which is hard for competitors to match

- Communicating the selected position through promotions and sales messages

---

FOR EXAMPLE

....

Buyers tend to perceive mass-market packaged holidays as commodities. They are most likely to be influenced by value-for-money considerations, with price the key purchase determinant. The UK tour operator and travel agency business consists of four main competitors: Thomas Cook, Thomson Travel, Airtours and First Choice. These companies have achieved market dominance through economies of scale in the supply chain that keep prices low and competitors out. They have acquired travel agents to sell their holidays. They own many of the charter airlines that fly to their holiday destinations. Because they can generate the volume of bookings that enable them to offer prices and discounts that competitors find hard to match, they have taken market positions of economy and value for money in the perceptions of the consumer. They reinforce this position through extensive advertising of their mass-market holidays.

Thomas Cook is an international brand that won a position of quality in the minds of consumers because of its reputation for offering more exclusive holidays. Whilst this was an advantage in some market segments, this position restricted its ability to compete in mass markets, where package holidaymakers perceive Thomas Cook primarily as a retailer of more expensive holidays. In order to expand its operations, the company acquired other operators such as Sunworld, Nielson and Club 18–30 in an effort to reposition the company.

6.4.2 Positioning maps

Products or organisations can be plotted on a market positioning 'map' and compared to the positions of competitive offerings or companies. A simple method is to represent two key customer perceptions on a grid. For example, the market for restaurants can be evaluated against perceptions of price and quality, as shown in Figure 6.8. The choice of variables for the axes is very important; they must be important characteristics in the market and also discriminate between what competitors offer.

Such a perceptual map can be used to plot the position of competitors so that any gaps in the market can be identified. For example, the perceptions of restaurants in a local area can be evaluated to see if there are any unfulfilled market needs. Figure 6.9 is an example which seems to indicate a gap in the 'high' price/ 'high' quality quadrant. However, further research would need to establish if there was sufficient demand to sustain this type of restaurant in the area.

Positioning is not only by price and quality. Other parameters can be used, such as positioning by application, type of use, benefits offered or customer type. For example, the market for chocolates could be evaluated against consumers' perceptions of end use (from 'special occasion' to 'everyday use') and application of the purchase (from personal consumption to

FIGURE 6.8

A positioning map of the restaurant market

FIGURE 6.9

Positioning of restaurants in town x

The positioning of restaurants is critical in terms of perception and location

MARKETING MISTAKES

LITTLE CHEF SLIMS DOWN

Little Chef has been sold again – another chapter in its chequered history, which has recently featured ownership by both Granada and Compass. The People's Restaurant Group (PRG), which owned 234 Little Chef sites, went into administration in January 2007. The administrators sold 193 Little Chef restaurants to Rcapital, saving 3,450 jobs in the chain. However, forty-one restaurants were closed after they were assessed as loss makers and not considered saleable. Nearly 600 staff lost their jobs as a result. The roadside outlet chain was losing £3 million per year despite more than 20 million visits per year.

Reports of the roadside diner chain being forced into administration has stirred a host of childhood memories in people across the nation and it has quickly become obvious that Little Chef remains a much-remembered brand, but one that is suffering from fatigue. Its image appears stuck in the1980s, with many people associating it with fried food. Little Chef has been part of British heritage since 1958. Thousands of parents have rushed in to change a nappy, made late-night breaks to fill up with caffeine or taken those essential early morning breakfasts before a long journey. For many baby boomers it was viewed as a treat to stop off at a Little Chef on a long journey. Little Chef fits the UK motorway network like a glove, with a seemingly enviable list of locations, developed over decades.

Little Chef went into administration after failing to respond to consumer trends

Despite the nostalgia, the brand is now sadly diminished as a result of not adapting its strategy to a changing world. In recent surveys only 13 per cent of the consumers surveyed had anything positive to say about Little Chef. Although 53 per cent of respondents would be sorry to see the Little Chef go, 47 per cent did not mind. There is now a greater offering of roadside eateries available and, with more people holidaying abroad, they have less need to visit roadside diners. Social trends have also worked against the brand. With higher awareness of obesity, there is desire to eat more healthy foods. An increasing number of people are starting families later and lengthening the gap between sharing their Little Chef memories with their offspring. All in all, the new owners have a tough job on their hands.

a gift). Cars might be plotted against perceptions of image (from functionality to high image) and age range of customer types (older/younger). Some possible product positions for these markets are illustrated in Figure 6.10. How do your perceptions fit with those given in Figure 6.10?

Although every consumer has their own perceptual map of the markets with which they are familiar, research can identify some consensus perceptions by aggregating all the individual impressions to give a total picture. This information can then be used to exploit and develop an established position or to change an unsatisfactory one.

FIGURE 6.10 *Possible positioning maps*

6.5 COMPETITIVE STRATEGY AND THE INTERNET

6.5.1 Strategies for competitive advantage

In order to gain a competitive advantage, marketing strategies can attempt to achieve:

- *Cost leadership* through mass-marketing approaches, which drive down costs per unit
- *Differentiation,* by offering unique benefits, such as product performance or something that is priced or delivered in a different way
- *Focus,* by specialising in a particular niche overlooked by larger competitors.

(See also section 6.3.1.)

The result is a marketplace composed of different types of competitors that can be classified as:

- *Leaders*: Organisations with the largest market share, who tend to lead the way in new product introductions, price movements, distribution coverage and promotional expenditure
- *Challengers*: Substantial market share, but second or third largest, who attempt to improve their position by either attacking the market leader or smaller competitors

- *Followers*: Large or small market share, who imitate, clone or modify the leader's products and marketing approaches

- *Nichers*: Small overall market share, but strong position in a selected niche, who target small segments that larger firms have overlooked inadvertently or deliberately

6.5.2 Impact of the Internet

Initially, the Internet seemed to offer ways in which the established order in many markets would be overturned. In the early days, some commentators believed that the relatively low entry costs of selling internationally via the Internet could overthrow some market leaders, whose competitive standing relied on cost leadership. It could also create new market niches for entrepreneurial companies to exploit. In some market places, Internet-related technologies have indeed upset the status quo.

FOR EXAMPLE

The music industry conforms broadly to the competitive structure outlined above. Internationally it is dominated by four companies, the 'leaders' and 'challengers' in all major markets who represent over 70 per cent of music albums sold worldwide. Market positions vary by country. In the UK market, EMI has become the leader, with over 25 per cent of album sales, helped by the acquisition of Virgin and Chrysalis and the success of artists such as the Spice Girls and Robbie Williams. The other big companies, Sony BMG, Time Warner and Polygram represent the challengers, with a further 55 per cent share of the market between them. Independent record labels and music publishers make up only 20 per cent because the big five have tended to buy up any promising newcomers. Independent labels such as Telstar and Beggars Banquet have succeeded either as followers, by promoting new bands in existing markets or as nichers, developing a specialist music genre.

New technology has destabilised these established positions. The development of digital recording techniques and the commercialisation of the Internet is affecting the music industry in a number of ways:

- CDs and recorded music have become very popular online products in their existing, hard copy form. CDs are well suited to online retailing: They are a commodity product with little differentiation except for the musical content; they are small and light and therefore inexpensive to ship and customer selection from the huge variety available is made easier by computerised searching. Yet it is a newcomer to the music business, the e-tailer, Amazon, that has made the inroads against more traditional music retailers.

- Music can be digitised and downloaded onto computers, which means that musical products can be distributed directly over the Internet. Digital recordings of music can be encoded, for example using the MP3 format, and can be compressed and distributed across computer networks and the Internet. This means music can be copied and quickly distributed anywhere in the world. The 'big five' music companies tried to ignore the new technology until Napster was founded in September 1999 to allow users to swap music files amongst themselves. As the service quickly developed a huge following of 70 million users, the market leaders first reaction to this threat was legal action. Napster's operation was declared illegal in 2001 as it violated copyright laws. In 2002, Roxio, the leader in CD burning and digital media software in the US, acquired Napster and re-launched the service as a legal digital music provider by establishing commercial relationships with all top music labels with a catalogue of over 1.5 million tracks.

■ Many in the industry believe the future for music distribution lies in streaming – instant access to any music via pocket computers and advances in telephony. This opens up new opportunities for the music industry and is being exploited by existing organisations and new competitors. A number of global competitors are emerging including Apple's iTunes, Sony Connect and MSN Music, as well as Napster.

It was not only the music industry that seemed destined for a competitive shakeout. The early wave of Internet entrepreneurs setting up innovative new services, such as eBay and Lastminute.com, seemed to indicate that tried-and-tested competitive strategies would be insufficient to save traditional organisations in many sectors. Since then, the pace of change has slowed. The domination of markets by existing brands and organisations now seems less at risk for a number of reasons:

■ Although rising quickly, Internet retail sales still take a small share of the total market. The most rapid growth of e-commerce is in business-to-business transactions as existing organisations adopt the Internet as a purchasing mechanism. Sales to end users, or business-to-consumer transactions, are still relatively small over the Internet, representing less than 15 per cent of total sales.

■ Existing major brands are popular products on the Internet. Consumers are concerned about shopping security on the Internet, and choose known brands to reduce the perceived risk of buying by this method.

■ Existing companies may not have been the first to realise the potential of e-commerce, but they now take advantage of subsequent developments on the Internet. Well-publicised casualties amongst new technology companies, such as the demise of Boo.com, have made investors more wary of Internet shares. New investment is likely to come from existing competitors buying into the new technology. The music industry model of a market leader (e.g. SonyBMG) supporting an Internet newcomer (Napster) is becoming more common.

The full impact of the Internet on competitive marketing strategies has yet to be seen. Although it is revolutionising the way we do business in some respects, it is also reinforcing some of the principles behind marketing strategies. In particular it is assisting the ability of organisations to accurately target customer groups with customised products and services.

FOR EXAMPLE

The National Society for the Prevention of Cruelty to Children (NSPCC) wanted to reach out to sexually abused children. Through market research, they found that sexually abused children hide behind a mask and pretend 'everything is fine'. The goal of the 'Don't hide it' campaign was to help these children to remove the mask and talk about what was troubling them. The NSPCC wanted to bring across the message that for these children, the face beneath the mask would be more confident and that they would feel better for having disclosed their sexual abuse. To target this sensitive audience, the NSPCC linked their own website (www.donthideit.com) with social networking sites (Bebo.com, Habbo.com and Mykindaplace.com) and 'seeded' adverts in a young peoples' natural browsing area. Very quickly communities sprang up around the campaign. Children gave support, chatted, listened, shared stories, drew pictures – and their 'masks' were removed. Bebo, Habbo and My Kinda place delivered over 7.5 million links. The campaign got more than half a million children and young people talking in just six weeks. Visitors to the site spent an average of 6.5 minutes interacting and the campaign caused an upsurge in sexual abuse-related calls to Childline.

CHECKPOINT

How has the Internet changed your buying habits? Which types of products, if any, do you buy through the Internet? How has the Internet influenced other purchases that you have made? How could potential suppliers target you through the Internet?

6.6 THE MARKETING MIX

6.6.1 The '4 Ps'

Marketing strategies are implemented through management of the *marketing mix*. The marketing mix consists of the controllable variables that marketing management can use to influence customer demand. It represents the methods by which managers seek to meet marketing objectives. Traditionally this mix of marketing methods has been categorised as the '4 Ps':

■ *Products* are more than just physical goods. They include not only intangible products, such as services, but also intangible aspects of physical products, such as image and market position. Product decisions therefore include a range of activities that affect both tangible and intangible factors, from new product development to packaging and branding.

■ *Pricing* decisions can be strategic and tactical. The overall level of pricing is an important strategic ingredient in the positioning of a product, whilst discounts and special offers are used tactically to improve short-term sales.

■ *Promotion* involves communicating to a target market about the benefits on offer. Marketing communications include personal selling, advertising, sales promotions and public relations.

■ *Place* describes how products or services are made available to the target market. It includes decisions on distribution strategy which establish the appropriate channels through which products are marketed (such as agents, wholesalers and retailers). *Location* is a key ingredient in this element of the marketing mix in some cases (for retailers or hoteliers, for example).

6.6.2 Managing the marketing mix

We will explore each of these elements of the marketing mix in more detail in the following chapters. Before examining them individually, it is important to recognise that they are not independent of each other. Each element crucially affects the others:

■ The attributes of a product help determine its price, how it is to be promoted and how it can be distributed

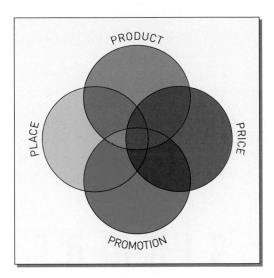

FIGURE 6.11

The marketing mix

■ Price adds to the intangible aspects of a product and may be an important promotional vehicle; pricing levels influence the channels of distribution available

■ Promotions draw on product benefits and pricing strategies and often involve the channels of distribution

■ Place is constrained by product, price and promotional decisions

Rather than distinct elements, the '4 Ps' represent interdependent variables symbolised by the overlapping circles in Figure 6.11.

Strategies bring together an organisation's activities into a cohesive whole. Marketing strategies therefore need to harmonise the elements of the marketing mix into a consistent approach to the marketplace. If the strategy is to adopt a position of exclusivity, this has to be projected consistently by the product, and its pricing, promotion and distribution.

'7 Ps' for services

In many industries and markets, this fourfold classification of the marketing mix represents an oversimplified approach. Some have argued that the particular issues involved in marketing intangible services merit the addition of three extra 'Ps':

■ *People* emphasises the role that the staff play in delivering the service

■ *Process* describes the logistics of service delivery, mapping the players and activities to allow effective production of the service

■ *Physical evidence* is particularly important in services because, by their very nature, they are intangible: some form of evidence of service performance becomes more important as customers seek to address their perception of risk

(See Chapter 7, section 7.2.2 for more on services marketing.)

ENTREPRENEURIAL MARKETING

The limitations of the '4 Ps' and strategic marketing concepts are also evident when we consider the marketing practices adopted by entrepreneurial small business owners. Rather than adopting the planned, structured approach to implementing a marketing strategy as described in this chapter, many entrepreneurs successfully use more informal, intuitive marketing methods. A small business may have very limited resources to use for marketing. However, the development of a strategy through targeting and positioning that is then implemented through a mix of marketing methods can benefit small, medium and large organisations, as the following case illustrates.

Sibmar Sibmar is classified as an SME (small and medium-sized enterprise), although it is no longer that small as it has developed as a successful building contractor with a turnover of about £25–30 million from both public and private sector clients. The business reached a critical stage in its

development and decided to focus on the most profitable sectors to achieve ambitious growth targets.

Segmentation Initially, Sibmar carried out a major customer survey, to establish its strengths and to understand customer needs. From this, it established five potential segments:

1 Public sector: (e.g. social housing/schools/healthcare)

2 Private sector: property developers

3 Private sector: major companies (e.g. Travis Perkins, Toyota dealerships)

4 Private sector: private individuals requiring bespoke work

5 Larger contractors – as a subcontractor

Targeting From an analysis of current and past sales income to Sibmar from each of the segments, it was decided that the focus would remain on the public sector. It is currently the most profitable sector for the company. The company has key capabilities to deliver what the target segment requires as it understands the complex tendering process of local government and is in effect a preferred supplier. Crucially, it can meet increasingly stringent health and safety requirements, a key issue in local government.

Although it was also decided to seek business from key commercial organisations, no work would be accepted on a subcontracting basis or from private individuals as a continuation of the company's past practice. The distance between subcontractor and client often resulted in complications leading to cost overruns and weak margins. For private individuals, projects tended to be carried out in a disorganised manner, causing similar problems.

Positioning To exploit the target markets, Sibmar was positioned as a modern and proactive construction company, fully conversant with the latest industry trends in terms of construction techniques, waste management and health and safety requirements. It was presented as a medium-sized company, with strengths in five specific service sectors:

- Social housing
- Education
- Public buildings
- Private housing
- Commercial

This positioning was underpinned by Sibmar's understanding of the important issues in public sector building activity and the key capabilities required.

Finsbury library (above) and Barth Mews (below) both examples of Sibmar's projects.

The Marketing Mix   The new strategy was supported by a range of marketing initiatives by Sibmar:

- Corporate re-branding to create a company profile that supported the agreed positioning
- Clear communication of the new profile via an enhanced website (www.sibmar.com) and a regular newsletter to its contact base, consisting of current clients, prospects, partners, suppliers and other interested groups
- Installation of a customer relationship management (CRM) process and software support package to manage all customer and prospect communication and relationships on a company-wide basis

Differences in the application of marketing strategies are discussed more fully in Chapter 12. First, however, we will lay the foundation by examining each of the main four elements of the marketing mix in greater detail in Chapters 7 to 11.

CHECKPOINT

Do you think there are differences between marketing in a small business compared to a large organisation? Apart from size of business, what other factors could influence how an organisation could develop and implement a marketing strategy?

6.7 SUMMARY

- A strategy is a plan or pattern that brings together the objectives and activities of an organisation into a cohesive whole.
- Strategic marketing decisions segment markets into customer groups, select target segments, and adopt appropriate market positions.
- Markets can be divided into segments, sub-segments and niches.
- The benefits to an organisation of segmenting its markets include:
  — Closer matching of customer needs
  — Concentration of resources
  — Market leadership of narrowly defined markets
  — Higher long-term profits in competitive markets
- Markets can be segmented on the basis of:
  — A key benefit (e.g. low prices, reliability, safety, convenience, status)
  — Buyer behaviour (e.g. purchase rates, loyalty to brands, purchase methods)
  — Pyschographics (e.g. lifestyle, social grouping, personality)
  — Geography (e.g. national, regional, urban/rural)
  — Demography (e.g. age, sex, culture, life cycle, company size)
- Targeting strategies can be classified as:
  — Undifferentiated (commodities and mass-market products e.g. early marketing of Guinness and Coca-Cola)
  — Differentiated (distinctive marketing approach to segments, e.g. Burtons/Arcadia)
  — Concentrated (a new or small business)
- Viable market segments are identifiable, relevant to the purchase decision, large enough to sustain the products offered and accessible.
- Organisations operating in a variety of contexts, from the private to the public sector, from consumer to industrial markets can target their customer groups through segmentation.
- Customers simplistic impressions or perceptions of a product or company in the market place describe its 'position' (e.g. upmarket/downmarket).
- Positioning strategy seeks to:
  — Identify positions that influence buyer behaviour
  — Select an appropriate, competitive position from which an organisation can deliver
  — Communicate this position through marketing messages
- Competitors in a market can usually be classified as 'leaders', 'followers', 'imitators' or 'nichers'. In some industries (e.g. the music industry), competitive positions are being threatened by newcomers exploiting Internet-related new technologies. However, whilst e-commerce is well established in business-to-business markets, it has relatively low penetration levels in business-to-consumer markets.
- Marketing strategies are implemented through management of the *marketing mix* which can be summarised as the '4 Ps': *product*, *pricing*, *promotion* and *place*.
- Effective strategies harmonise these elements of the marketing mix into a consistent approach to the target markets.

6.8 ACTIVITIES

CASE STUDY

HIT OR MISS?

Introduction At a board meeting of the Revelation Music Company, the directors were faced with a difficult decision. The Internet had promised much for their company, but had so far delivered little. Now they had to decide whether to continue with the new strategy they had initiated or return to more traditional marketing ways.

The Revelation Music Company had had a chequered history. Founded by Johnny Revels towards the end of his performing career, it had traded very close to the brink of liquidation in its early years. Although the company signed up some successful bands and acquired the rights to some popular music, the managers had not been able to turn these assets into regular profits and positive cash flow. Part of the problem lay in the nature of the music industry. Producing and promoting music required considerable up-front expenditure in terms of advances to the artists and marketing costs. Income in the form of record sales and royalties from the music rights took longer to arrive through a complicated chain of intermediaries and collection agencies. It took Revels a few years to build up a catalogue of established music with an ongoing revenue stream.

Although he never fully mastered the details of running a business in this complex industry, he did have the good sense to recruit some managers who did. Whilst he fulfilled the A&R (artist and repertoire) role, acting as the 'ears' of the company listening out for new bands and musical talent, his two senior mangers Juliana Wilson and Dan Chen ran the business. Although they experienced near misses of bankruptcy proceedings, they also had some hits along the way. Groups under contract to them, such as the cult band Devil's Coachmen, sold sufficient records to eventually provide the cash flow to keep the business going. However, their most dependable revenues came from royalties from the performance and broadcasting rights of music. For example, they were fortunate to have signed up Sam Spir who wrote a stream of hits for his own band, Helite, as well as for other musicians.

A sound performance By the late 1990s the company had become one of the largest independent music companies outside of the major corporations such as EMI and SonyBMG. The revenues from its back catalogue of recordings and published music had gradually increased to a size where the company was cash-positive and looked set for long-term survival. It had recording contracts with several well-known bands in niche markets; it published the music not only of its own bands but also of a growing number of other writers who liked the company's informal style but international coverage.

It had developed a specific marketing strategy for promoting its artists and their music that seemed particularly cost-effective. Because it did not have the funds to compete with the promotional campaigns of the major record companies, it had adopted a very targeted approach to its marketing. By attracting artists from narrow musical genres (e.g. scar punk), it could develop relationships with the promoters of that music to ensure their artists achieved the airtime they needed. Instead of using expensive mass media, it promoted to the end users through appropriate specialised clubs and media. The Revelation Music Company seemed set for a long and prosperous future.

The digital revolution Then the Internet began to destabilise the entire industry. Traditional music products such as CDs and tapes proved to be amongst the most popular selling items for new e-tailers such as Amazon. But the new digital technology also meant that musical content could be distributed directly over the Internet. Digital recordings of music were encoded on the Internet using the MP3 format, compressed and distributed across computer networks. Music could be copied

▶

and quickly distributed anywhere in the world. Whilst the big music companies tried to ignore the new technology, Revelation's managers saw it as a major opportunity. Marketing Director Juliana Wilson explained the vision when launching their website www.disconline.com to investors:

'The digital revolution in music has the potential to finally level the playing field in the production and distribution of music. Until now the majors have held all the cards – they have the advantage of economies of scale in the manufacture of records; they can monopolise the distribution channels as many of the chains will only stock the top-selling hits; and they can afford to promote through mass-marketing media. Digital sales over the Internet mean they lose their competitive advantage in each area: we can compete on manufacturing costs because customers can simply download their music, we can bypass the traditional distribution channels, and we can have direct contact with customers, so we don't need to pay for costly advertising in mass media.'

Disconline.com acted as a portal to sell recordings or musical scores of particular artists and songwriters direct to the public. It offered a free download of one track per band, then the option of paying for the rest. This generated revenues through sales of music direct to the end user. But it also created market intelligence on the artists and their followers as downloads, click-throughs and other website activity was closely monitored. This market research could then be sold to promoters and agents on the basis that it made spotting new talent more of a science than the guesswork it had hitherto been.

At least that was the theory. In practice the number of paid-for downloads was very disappointing. Although site traffic was reasonably high, it was achieved at a cost, as traditional advertising was needed to drive visitors to the site. The main problem was the unwillingness of consumers to pay for anything they found on the Internet. Although millions of people were downloading music, not many were paying for it. The Napster phenomenon devalued musical content by providing it free on the Internet. Although Napster's operation had been declared illegal because it violated copyright laws, the damage had been done, and there was a common expectation to get music for nothing.

Another problem was 'artist power'. One of Revelation's bands set up its own website to sell records, which made other artists reluctant to sign up to the company website in case it proved more profitable to do it themselves.

Technologically, Revelation's directors had chosen to exploit downloading musical content onto existing hard format such as CDs and tapes via computer networks. But many in the industry believed the future for music distribution would be streaming – instant access to any music via pocket computers and advances in telephony so that the user did not need to store anything.

Summing up the score The directors of Revelation had to make some fundamental decisions about their marketing strategy Dan Chen presented the key issues to the board meeting:

'It has become clear that online orders are not going to replace sales through our traditional wholesale and retail channels as quickly as we first thought, if in fact they ever do. Disconline.com is still losing money and burning cash at the rate of around £1 million per annum, which means it will eat through our current cash reserves in approximately eighteen months. This leaves us with a number of issues to resolve. First, do we continue to target Internet customers hoping that digital distribution can become profitable within eighteen months? If we do, we will have minimal financial resources to spend on other markets and promote bands through traditional media. Some of our artists are already restless because we have put so much emphasis on Internet sales, so we could have difficulties in signing up new talent. Second, if we do move away from downloading, do we continue to sell traditional products over the Internet, or do we rely on specialist retailers such as Amazon to do this for us? And, as I've said, we already have complaints from managers of bands who say we are not doing enough to promote them, so exactly where do we target our marketing effort in future?' (See Table 6.2.)

TABLE 6.2 *Summary of financial data for Revelation group and Disconline.com*

	REVELATION GROUP	DISCONLINE.COM
SALES	£17.5 million	£1.2 million
GROSS PROFIT	£12.7 million	£0.9 million
OVERHEADS	£9.2 million	£1.9 million
PRE-TAX PROFIT	£3.5 million	(£1.0 million)
CASH RESERVES	£1.7 million	

QUESTIONS

1 How would you divide up the market for the Revelation Music company? Draw a pictorial representation of how you see the various market segments that the business is involved in.

2 What priorities would you place on each of the segments? Rank each of the target markets in order of priority to the company.

3 What positioning strategy would you recommend for each of the top priority segments? Define how you would appeal to the target markets.

4 What would be the most important elements in the marketing mix that you recommend for marketing to these target markets? State the main methods you would use to implement your strategy.

DEVELOPING A MARKETING PLAN

THE MARKETING STRATEGY

From the analysis of the marketing planning process you have undertaken in the activities from Chapters 1–5, what strategies are you going to adopt?

- Which segment(s) of the market will you target (and why)?
- Which position will you adopt compared to competitors (and how)?

6.9 FURTHER READING AND REFERENCES

Strategic marketing management

Dalgic, T. and Leeuw, M. (1994), 'Niche Marketing Revisited: Concept, Applications and Some European Cases', *European Journal of Marketing*, Vol. 20, No. 1, pages 39–55.

Doyle, P. (2002), *Marketing Management and Strategy*, 3rd edition (FT/Prentice Hall).

Hooley, G.J., Saunders, J. and Piercy, N.F. (2004), *Marketing Strategy and Competitive Positioning*, 3rd edition (Prentice Hall).

Ries, A. and Trout, J. (1986), *Marketing Warfare* (McGraw-Hill).

Database marketing

Fell, J. (2002), *How to Keep It Legal* (FT Creative Business), page 12.

Internet marketing strategy

Chaffey, D. (2006), *Internet Marketing: Strategy, Implementation and Practice* (Pearson Education).

Siegel, C.F. (2006), *Internet Marketing: Foundations and Applications* (Houghton Mifflin).

Chapter **7**

PRODUCTS: CHARACTERISTICS AND STRATEGIES

LEARNING OBJECTIVES

By the end of this chapter the reader will be able to:

■ Define a product and understand the terminology for groups of products
■ Appreciate the difference between tangible and intangible products/services
■ Assess the impact on marketing strategy of the different product types
■ Understand the additional benefits that augment the core product
■ Appreciate the power of branding and its development
■ Evaluate brand strategies
■ Understand the concept of the product life cycle and its impact on the marketing mix
■ Assess the strategic modelling of product portfolios

INTRODUCTION

This chapter explores strategies relating to one element of the marketing mix – the product or service on offer. The boundaries of a product extend well beyond physical features to include benefits to consumers and other intangible features. Branding is an important intangible element, key to the success of many products and services. We examine the concept of the product life cycle, emphasising the changing resource requirements of products over time, and some techniques for analysing product portfolios as a way of managing these changes.

CASE STUDY

....

THE PRODUCTS OF A SCHOOL

The Education Reform Act delegated significant powers to individual state schools and their managers in England and Wales. Previously, local education authorities had allocated resources and pupils to individual schools from the centre. The legislation required education authorities to delegate substantial authority and resources to the board of governors and the headteacher. At the same time, parents and children were given greater freedom to choose their school. Theoretically they could choose to attend any state school, although in practice their choice was limited by the places physically available. As annual budgets for each school were allocated mainly on the basis of how many pupils attended the school, education managers were obliged to market their services in order to maximise the resources at their disposal.

Saxon Park School was relatively small for a secondary school. It took pupils from eleven to eighteen years old with a total of 720 pupils, of whom 120 were in the sixth form. Situated in an unfashionable residential area, the former Saxon Park council housing estate, the school lost pupils to larger comprehensives in more affluent parts of town. The local education authority threatened it with closure unless the problem of falling numbers could be overcome, and as a result numbers fell even more as parents lost confidence in the long-term future of the school. Even demographics were working against Saxon Park as 'customers' requiring secondary education were decreasing; there were fewer under-nineteen-year-olds in the region than there had been for decades and numbers were not predicted to rise for several years.

A new headteacher, Jack Shannon, had set about improving academic standards at Saxon with notable success. The tangible outputs of the school in the form of GCSE and A level results were now comparable to the best of the other local schools. 'The issue is no longer one of academic standards', he told a meeting of the governors, 'but one of image. The basic education a child receives here is as good if not better than anywhere else in the area, but parents still associate our name with something inferior. We have removed a fundamental negative and now we need to consider how to give ourselves an edge.'

Shannon was asking the governors for guidance on measures to boost the declining pupil numbers and revenues of the school. To overcome their image problems, one idea was to change the name of the school to The King Alfred School, as the famous Saxon ruler had once held court close by. But Shannon believed that getting the product right was going to be their most important marketing activity, which no amount of clever publicity could equal.

'There are several options we can consider', he told his board of governors. 'We need to achieve a higher share of the local market for the first of our main curriculum areas – subjects leading to GCSE qualifications. For example, almost all our students live nearby, yet we are very close to the train station and bus depot. We should be able to attract more children from the neighbouring villages. We could also consider more mature students – for instance older students re-taking some of their GCSEs, although we may need to modify the courses we offer them. We can consider developing some areas of the curriculum as a speciality. For example, many schools have decreased their sports activities because of timetabling pressures, but we could use our new artificial turf pitch to develop this school as a centre of sporting excellence.'

'A particular issue we have to address is our sixth form, which is small compared to other schools and colleges, so we cannot offer the range of subjects that others can. However some subjects are growing very fast. Science, for example, has always been popular here and we attract quite a few pupils from other state and independent schools because we have excellent laboratory facilities. The subjects are now growing in popularity, so our pupil numbers are increasing quite quickly each year. I'm pleased to see the extra pupils, but on the other hand I worry about the effect on our resources – our laboratories are fully used at the moment so if we increase our numbers we will have to invest in new facilities.'

▶

'I would prefer some growth in our real problem areas of music and drama. We have very few takers for these subjects and no signs of growth, so the courses are not really viable at the moment. In the past we had a poor reputation for social sciences like economics and politics, and many of our students who were attracted to those subjects tended to go elsewhere. But our new head of department has changed all that and from a very small base she is increasing pupil numbers rapidly. Again it means considerable investment, as we have to buy new specialised books and materials.'

'If only we had more subject areas like the humanities – history, geography and the like – which have always been popular here. Numbers are high but reasonably constant because there has been no real growth in demand for some time. We don't have much new investment to make in these subjects because we have all the books and materials we need and they are easier to plan because of the predictable numbers.'

'As we have very limited resources, we have to make some choices to balance both our finances and the portfolio of courses we offer. Your advice would be most welcome.'

QUESTIONS

1   Consider the 'products' or services that a secondary school offers.

   i   What are their main tangible and intangible aspects? *See section 6.1*

   ii   How does Jack Shannon group some of his school's individual 'products' together? *See section 6.2*

   iii   What are the basic benefits which are expected from them? What are some additional benefits which might attract pupils to one school in preference to another? What is the headteacher proposing in this case? *See section 6.3*

2   Do you think the school is right to consider renaming the school to change its 'brand image'? What other branding options should the school consider? *See section 6.4*

3   Evaluate the sixth form subjects according to their growth, market share and use of resources. Classify them according to their attractiveness to the school and suggest strategies for their future. *See sections 6.5 and 6.6.*

4   Do you agree that 'getting their product right was going to be their most important marketing activity'? What types of product strategies would you recommend for Saxon school? *See section 6.6*

7.1 WHAT IS A PRODUCT?

7.1.1 A definition

A product is quite simply anything that is capable of fulfilling customer needs. This broad, basic definition has several important implications.

■ *Some products are more tangible than others.* We sometimes think of products in a restricted way, as objects that have definite physical attributes that can be evaluated by our senses; they can be seen, touched and sometimes heard, smelt or tasted. In consumer markets they can be tins of food, children's toys, bottles of perfume and DVD players. They may be machine tools, chemicals, electronic components or barrels of oil in industrial markets. These represent a subdivision usually referred to as 'tangible products' because they can be touched and appear to have clearly visible boundaries.

■ *Some products are intangible services.* A bank or building society offers consumers a range of services, such as deposit accounts and mortgages. A firm of accountants provides business services, such as an annual audit of accounts or a payroll service. These services are 'products', according to the marketing definition of the word, because they are clearly capable of meeting customer needs. Services like these that are hard to touch because they have no obvious physical dimensions are sometimes referred to as 'intangible products'.

■ *Products are not limited to traditional objects and services that we buy.* Other 'products' include:

— *People*: Pop stars, politicians and sports personalities are all frequently marketed in the manner of more traditional products

FOR EXAMPLE

Tiger Woods has become the biggest sporting personality 'product'. In 2004/5, his annual revenues were over $87 million, and only $7 million was directly from golf. Sponsorship by Nike, General Motors, Rolex, American Express and Disney is worth far more than the prize money that he wins playing golf. However, 'people products' are required not only to excel at their chosen profession, but also to follow exemplary private lives if they are to max-imise their revenue. For example, Shane Warne was hailed as one of the world's greatest cricketers after taking a record 700 test wickets in the Melbourne Ashes Test in December 2006. But despite Warne's place in the cricketing hall of fame, a succession of indiscretions in his private life have limited his marketability and cost him various corporate en-dorsements and offers. Negative publicity following extramarital affairs lost him assignments and spon-sorships, and he has been the subject of parodies and jokes, with a number of songs written about him that focus on his private exploits rather than his cricketing success.

Sportsmen like Shane Warne can earn more from sponsorship than playing their game

© TIM WIMBORNE/REUTERS/CORBIS

'People products' such as cricketer Shane Warne can earn more from sponsorship and endorsement than from playing their sport. But they need to maintain their image as well as achieve sporting success if they are to maximise their earnings.

— *Places*: Towns, counties and countries are increasingly 'packaged' and sold as an entity to encourage tourism or business investment, or to attract one-off events such as the staging of the Olympic Games

FOR EXAMPLE

London dramatically beat four rival cities to win the right to stage the Olympic Games in 2012. Paris was long considered the favourite, while Madrid, Moscow and New York also submitted bids. But after an exhaustive two-year search to find the hosts, the International Olympic Committee members chose London as the all-round 'product' that they wished to buy for that year.

The successful London bid for the 2012 Olympics has opened many business opportunities

— *Organisations*: Many businesses have long recognised the need for a consistent corporate image because they are inseparable from the products they sell; there is effectively a total company 'product', offering a variety of individual products. Supermarket chains such as Sainsbury and Tesco are good examples. Other organisations, from charities and educational establishments to political parties and pressure groups, are now also marketing themselves as a package of 'products' with a consistent presentation. In elections for governments around the world, the different parties offer voters their manifesto of policies in ways that amount to presentations of competing products. Political 'products' share some common names including Conservative, Labour, Liberal, Democrat and Communist.

FOR EXAMPLE

There are many 'Labour' parties around the world. New Labour in the UK, the Australian Labor Party (ALP) and the New Zealand Labour Party are examples of a group which provide for the direct affiliation of trade unions, incorporating them into the structure of the party. The Scandinavian Labour Parties of Sweden and Norway are broadly similar, with local branches of unions affiliated with local branches of the party. Labour parties exist also in Canada, Ireland and Israel.

- *How we perceive a product is related to the benefits it offers rather than the features it presents.* Customers buy benefits, not products (as we have emphasised in earlier chapters). Our perception of a product is therefore coloured not so much by what it can do, but by what it can do *for us*. A large estate car capable of seating seven people may seem desirably convenient to the parents of a large family, but off-puttingly sluggish and hard to park to a single city dweller. We can only define individual products by taking account of customer perceptions of the benefits of that product.

- *Even tangible products have intangible aspects.* The emphasis of our definition is on meeting customer needs, but these are often met by benefits which are intangible, even for products that appear very tangible. As we have discussed in earlier chapters, customers buy for

FIGURE 7.1

The tangible/ intangible spectrum

obvious and not so obvious motives. We need a car to travel from point A to point B but this need alone will not determine our choice of vehicle; other considerations, including our attraction to the 'image' of different models, come into play. Thus even a product as tangible as a car has intangible qualities in the design and brand name which form a significant part of the perceived benefits that it offers.

7.1.2 The tangible/intangible spectrum

Products are thus a mixture of tangible and intangible factors. The relative mix of these factors varies considerably. It can be described as a spectrum ranging from products that are predominantly tangible to those that are mainly intangible, with many different combinations in between. Figure 7.1 illustrates this.

At one extreme are products with tangible features and obvious intangible benefits. Commodities such as coal and sugar, or raw materials such as iron and steel fit this category. At the other extreme are products with only intangible features and benefits. Products such as insurance policies or bank accounts are examples here. In between are products with tangible and intangible features and benefits. A packaged holiday combines intangible services, such as the arrangements for travel and accommodation, with tangible products like the meals served in the hotel. A telephone service requires the tangible hardware of telephone handsets and cabling as well as intangible transmitter and operator services.

> **CHECKPOINT**
>
> Consider the town, city or region in which you live. As a 'product' that might potentially attract visitors, what benefits does it offer? What are the tangible and intangible aspects of what it has to offer?

7.2 PRODUCT CLASSIFICATIONS AND THEIR SIGNIFICANCE

7.2.1 Basic classifications

As well as tangibility, products are classified according to their durability and end use:

■ *Tangibility*: We have seen how products can be divided according to our ability to touch them into

— Tangible products

— Intangible products or services

■ *Durability*: Tangible products are often further subdivided

— *Non-durable goods* are consumed relatively rapidly and usually re-ordered regularly. Food, drink and toiletries are major categories of non-durable products.

— *Durable goods* survive many uses (or should do) and are replaced infrequently if at all. They include so-called 'white goods' such as refrigerators and washing machines, and 'brown goods' such as videos and music stations, as well as industrial equipment from machine tools to computers.

■ *End-use*: A fundamental distinction can be made between products that are intended for the ultimate user and those that will be processed further

— *Consumer products* are bought or taken up by the final consumer for their own use. This is a very wide category, including most (but not all) products that are advertised on television or sold in High Street outlets such as clothes, food, electrical products and banking services. Frequently purchased consumer goods are called *fast-moving consumer goods*, often abbreviated to FMCG. Consumer durables include more infrequent purchases of white goods such as washing machines.

— *Industrial products* are used by businesses or organisations either for further processing or for carrying out their activities. This category includes equipment and raw materials used in manufacturing, and the supplies and services to run an office or a service. It ranges from factories, printing presses and electronic components to farm produce, hospital beds and office copiers.

Figure 7.2 illustrates these basic product classifications.

7.2.2 The impact of product types on marketing strategies

The significance of these classifications lies in the effect they have on marketing strategies.

■ *Consumer goods* frequently have wide appeal, which justifies the use of national advertising media such as television and the national press. In order to maximise demand, indirect distribution channels such as wholesalers and retailers are often used.

■ *Industrial goods* are often more limited in their market appeal and use more targeted marketing methods such as direct selling or exhibitions. This is not always the case, however; there are over four million small and large businesses in the UK alone and products with a generic appeal to all of them, such as office furniture, computers and copiers, enjoy a market bigger than many of the more specialised consumer products.

■ *Tangible goods* are easier to display and demonstrate than intangible products. For these goods, design and appearance can take on more importance than the functioning of the

FIGURE 7.2 *Product classifications*

	TANGIBLE		INTANGIBLE
CONSUMER	Durable	Non-durable	Services
INDUSTRIAL	Durable	Non-durable	Services

product itself. The packaging of a brand of perfume or a child's toy is often *the* crucial marketing decision. In industrial markets, sampling (e.g. of raw materials) and demonstrations (e.g. of office equipment) are frequently used marketing tools.

■ *Intangible goods and services* have several important distinctions:

— *Reputation*: Being intangible makes them difficult to demonstrate or sample. This makes the reputation of the provider of a service a crucial ingredient in the buying decision, and word-of-mouth a powerful advertising force. Professional services offered by accountants, solicitors, medical practices, schools and universities are often selected by personal recommendation.

— *Inseparability*: Services depend crucially on the people that provide them and are often viewed as inseparable from them. Hairdressers, advertising directors and consultants can take their clients with them when they change from one firm to another.

— *Perishability*: Services cannot be stored. They cannot be produced in advance and held in stock until required. An empty seat on a train or an aeroplane is a lost sale forever; an unfilled place on a course or in a school is an opportunity gone for good.

— *Heterogeneity*: Services are often 'tailor made' to suit the customer. Sometimes the product is a unique solution to a customer's requirements, such as a consultant's report, a dental filling or a haircut. At other times the choice is limited to a 'menu' of services on offer, for example a house mortgage, a car service or office cleaning. Even so there is likely to be considerable 'personalisation' of the service to meet an individual customer's requirements: the amount, term and interest rates of a mortgage vary from customer to customer within the overall guidelines of the building society, for example. This lack of standardisation of the final delivered product makes personal contact between the supplier of a service, or their agent, and the customer desirable and often inevitable.

— *Ownership*: Although purchased, services may not be 'owned' in the conventional sense. Services are sold on the basis of access to facilities, information and expertise (e.g. hotels, libraries and legal advice) or the use or rental of items (e.g. passenger transport by train, video hire and bank loans).

Impact on the marketing mix

These characteristics of services have lead some commentators to add three more 'Ps' to the commonly used four of the marketing mix:

■ *Physical evidence*: Most services have a tangible aspect to them which can provide some physical evidence to the potential buyer about the service on offer. The waiting or reception area at a dentist's, solicitor's or accountant's gives an initial impression of the quality of the service provided. Perceptions formed by these physical attributes are particularly important because they are often the only evidence that the customer can easily gain about the service.

FOR EXAMPLE

Parents visiting a primary school to assess its suitability for their children find it difficult to judge the quality of teaching as they walk round. They rely heavily on tangible aspects such as the children's work on display and the condition of the buildings. Marketing activities need to pay particular attention to the impressions formed by any physical evidence of a service. Banking services use the design of cheque books and the colour of credit cards to enhance the image of their services. The importance of letterheads, visiting cards and the layout of reports is recognised by consultants and professional advisers in the selling of their services.

■ *People*: If people are inseparable from the service they provide then they become very important aspects of the marketing of that service. We make decisions about which service to choose not only on our experience of the quality of what is provided but also on our perceptions of the person providing it. The confidence and trust built up by a hairdresser, dentist or solicitor is a crucial factor in how their services are perceived. Restaurants are selected not just on the basis of the food served but also on the people that serve it. Staff selection, training and motivation become significant ingredients in the marketing mix as a result.

■ *Process*: Customers are often involved in the process of delivering a service because they are present when the service is produced and an integral part of it. As customers visit the premises of service deliverers such as hairdressers, dentists, teachers and restaurant owners, the process itself takes on a marketing significance. A happy experience matters as much as the quality of the service in forming the perceptions and future choices of the customer. The way the service is delivered can become as important as the end result. Mistakes and conflicts are difficult to conceal and relationships with a customer may never recover from just one processing error.

This is not the case with tangible products, as the manufacturing process is usually hidden from the eye of the consumer. We do not form impressions of a tin of beans from an involvement in the production process or knowledge of the number of rejects in the system (or if we do it often has lasting effects). Visibility of the process can be used as a positive marketing tool.

FOR EXAMPLE

Some restaurants deliberately make the food production area visible to customers to add to the image of efficiency and hygiene they wish to portray. Others are themed around the concept of involving customers in the cooking of ingredients selected by them. Yo! Sushi is an internationally successful chain that has made the service process a tangible feature of their restaurants. A conveyor belt circulates around the restaurant, carrying a variety of dishes that mix both oriental and western cuisine. Each dish is placed on different colour-coded plates, indicating different prices, and all the empties are simply counted up at the end of the meal for the bill. Drinks can be ordered by pressing airline-style call buttons. An intangible process has been turned to a tangible feature that makes this dining experience different.

YO! SUSHI BLUEWATER, WWW.YOSUSHI.COM

Restaurants such as Yo! Sushi emphasise the food preparation area to make the offering more tangible

Automation and standardisation of some services can become important marketing tools to overcome the problems of variability of service provision. Automatic cash dispensing machines have improved banking services. Hotel groups and car rental companies have built world-wide chains based on the standardisation of services so that the customer knows what to expect no matter the geographic location.

7.2.3 Product aggregations

Organisations offering more than one product sometimes *aggregate,* or collect together, various products into one classification.

- *Product mix or product portfolio*: All the products offered by an organisation (e.g. all the pet products sold by a manufacturer; all the courses offered by a school)

- *Product group or category*: Several related product lines (e.g. all tins of pet food; all GCSE courses offered)

- *Product line*: Several products which are related by specification or markets (e.g. all tins of cat food; all GCSE language courses offered)

- *Product item*: A single, identifiable product or service (e.g. a tin of chicken-and-liver cat food; a French GCSE course)

These groupings may be necessary to facilitate management decisions (a product line or group may be managed by one 'product manager' or their equivalent in other organisations – such as the head of department in a school) or to focus marketing strategies (a product line may be advertised under one brand name or in one marketing campaign).

CHECKPOINT

Consider products you have recently purchased, been given or used. Classify them into non-durable, durable and intangible products. For the intangible products (e.g. a taxi, bank account or haircut), what role did any *physical evidence* of the service play in your decision? Likewise, what role did *people* or the *process* of purchase or service delivery play in your purchase decision or your satisfaction with the service?

7.3 THE AUGMENTED PRODUCT: FEATURES AND BENEFITS

As well as having boundaries that are less obvious than might at first appear, products can be described on several different levels.

- *The core product* describes the fundamental reason for the acquisition of the product. This is the benefit which underlies the decision to purchase a product or use a service. In a competitive market it will almost certainly not be a unique benefit offered by any one product, but rather a generic description of the core benefit of a number of competitive offerings. Although it is the real stimulus for the demand for a product, it is not necessarily the main reason for the choice of one product in preference to another.

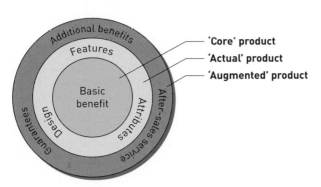

FIGURE 7.3

The layers of a product

'Core' product
'Actual' product
'Augmented' product

FOR EXAMPLE

....

The core benefit for buying a ticket for an airline flight is usually to travel from one place to another quickly, safely and conveniently.

■ *The actual product* describes the key features that a customer expects from a product. It represents the level of quality and type of features that enable a product to deliver the core benefits desired. Therefore, these often represent the minimum required for a product to survive in a competitive environment.

FOR EXAMPLE

....

The actual features expected of an airline flight as a product might be regular scheduling, non-stop flights, good seating arrangements, in-flight services and a reputation as a reliable and safety-conscious airline.

■ *The augmented product* represents additional benefits and customer services that have been built around the basic product, often in an attempt to differentiate it from competitive offerings. These are methods of adding value to the core product, which in themselves do not represent the reason for purchase, but may well be the reason for choosing one product over another. Examples of these are provided in Table 7.1.

FOR EXAMPLE

....

The augmented product of an airline flight might include such extras as:

■ Free transport to and from the airport
■ Discounted travel insurance
■ Refund guarantees on flight arrival times
■ Free extra tickets for regular business-class users
■ Wide choice of in-flight entertainment at no additional charge
■ Reclining, bed-style seats on long-haul flights

TABLE 7.1 *Examples of the augmented product*

PRODUCT	A PENCIL	OFFICE CLEANING SERVICE	DENTAL CHECK-UP
CORE PRODUCT	Enables graphic communications in words or pictures.	Clean working environment with minimum disruption and effort.	Healthy and attractive teeth by prevention of problems.
ACTUAL PRODUCT	Choice of lead hardness. Easy-to-grip barrel. 8 inches in length.	Daily and weekly cleaning routines. Fixed price contract. Self-managed. Honest reputation.	Modern equipment and facilities. Reputation as skilful dentist. NHS patients accepted.
AUGMENTED PRODUCT	Eraser at one end. Personalised message on barrel.	Penalties for non-performance. Security checks. Preventative maintenance.	Free parking. Appointment reminders. Stickers for children.

CHECKPOINT

Consider one product or service you have recently purchased (from the list you developed in the Checkpoint on page 220). How would you describe each according to the three elements of the core benefits, the actual product features and the augmented product of additional features and benefits?

7.4 BRANDING: DEVELOPMENT AND STRATEGIES

7.4.1 The power of branding

The name of a product, and symbols associated with it, can be more significant in determining consumer choice than the product itself. The branding of products to give them distinctive images differentiating them from competitors has turned mundane products into ways of life.

FOR EXAMPLE

'Carbonated drinks' do not sound like the most exciting product category, yet Coca-Cola has turned a fizzy drink into a symbol for the friendship of global communities. The peoples of the world certainly have one thing in common: they all drink Coca-Cola, the world's top brand, sold throughout 185 countries. 'Coke' is now the most recognised word on earth, it is claimed. In the UK it is the biggest consumer brand, with over £1 million worth of Coke consumed every day.

7.4.2 A definition of branding

Several terms are used in conjunction with the branding of products:

- A brand is a combination of name, symbol and design that clearly identifies one product from another

- A brand name is the written or spoken word(s) used to distinguish the brand (e.g. Mars Bar, Kellogg's, Rolls-Royce, Apple Mac)

- A brand mark (or logo) is a distinctive symbol or form of lettering which is always associated with the brand, (the red lettering of Mars, the Kellogg's 'K', the 'RR' of Rolls Royce, and the Mac's multi-coloured apple with a 'bite' out of it).

However, branding means more than just the labelling of products to distinguish one from another. Successful branding has other aspects that make it one of the most powerful tools of modern marketing:

- *It represents an assurance of a level of quality and product performance.* A key objective of branding is to build a relationship with customers that will keep them loyal to the product. Such a relationship can only be based on the consumers' trust that a product will do what they expect it to do. The marketing of branded products builds on an expectation of performance which is known to be relevant to the customer. 'Beanz meanz Heinz' because its taste is appreciated by its target market. As long as the expected performance is consistently delivered, consumers can repurchase the product safe in the knowledge that the satisfaction derived from the last purchase will be repeated. Companies such as Heinz and Mars faithfully reproduce the taste of their products to protect the customer goodwill that it has taken them decades to build up.

FOR EXAMPLE

Supermarkets usually stock around 20,000 different product lines, which gives consumers a be-wildering choice of alternatives. Research indicates that when consumers are faced with a lot of information about competing products, they pay most attention to brand names. Brands are thought to be the best indicators of performance and are purchased in preference to unbranded products unless there are compelling reasons to do otherwise. 'Generic' products – unbranded, simply packaged and lower priced versions of popular products – became more common in super-markets. These were initially successful in taking market share from branded products, but have now become branded products themselves as chains such as Wal-Mart, Tesco and Aldi use their own brand name to endorse products. These 'private-label' brands are now estimated to repre-sent almost 40 per cent of the UK grocery trade as the big retailers have recognised the power of branding their own products to develop consumer loyalty.

- *Brands are selected for what it says about the consumer as well as for what the product does for the consumer.* Brand names have become increasingly symbolic of lifestyle and emotional aspirations. Products are differentiated not only by what they taste like or how they operate, but also by what they symbolise and imply about their purchasers.

FOR EXAMPLE

Kellogg's cereals offer not just a tasty breakfast but the promise of a fun-packed, healthy life as well. Persil washing powders symbolise caring mothers and responsible parenthood. Managers buying Canon office products can be perceived as reliable and rational decision-makers. Rowntree markets Black Magic chocolates to couples aspiring to elegance and romance and Ferrero Rocher to those who want to be associated with gracious living.

7.4.3 The development of branding

The original meaning of the word 'brand' was the mark burnt onto an animal's hide to establish ownership. In this sense products have been branded from the earliest days. For example, ancient potters put a mark on their wares to denote the place of origin. If a potter's reputation grew by word of mouth, then items with their mark on them became more sought after and therefore more valuable.

The explosion of economic activity associated with the Industrial Revolution in the nineteenth and twentieth centuries was accompanied by the rapid development of branded products. Differentiated, branded products of high quality survived and prospered in increasingly competitive markets, particularly when early market growth slackened and weaker products were squeezed out.

Many of the brands developed in those early years still predominate in their markets. Kodak film, Wrigleys chewing gum, Gillette razors, Coca-Cola, Campbell's soup and Goodyear tyres all became established brands in the late nineteenth or early twentieth century. They are still market leaders today, testifying to the value of consistent branding.

Key developments

Legal systems throughout the world have worked increasingly hard to stop imitations of brand names and logos. Trademark, copyright and patent laws have established the sellers' right to protect the intangible value of their products. Enforcement is still difficult. Although the European Customs Code now permits officials to impound suspected goods, there is a thriving trade of counterfeit brands in Europe estimated to be approaching £100 billion. Most established brands have defended their name vigilantly against any impostors in order to protect the intangible value that is at stake. Winners are not always the big brands; the law is there to protect smaller companies as well.

FOR EXAMPLE

Halifax dropped its plans to launch a service offering motor insurance because the High Court ruled it could not use the word 'Halifax' in conjunction with motor insurance policies. A local insurance company, Halifax Insurance Ltd, won an injunction against its more famous namesake, which recognised that it had sold insurance since the 1960s under the Halifax name.

Services as well as tangible products are now branded. For example, suppliers in the increasingly competitive financial services industry such as Halifax, Barclaycard, and Norwich Union have recognised the value of branded products.

Brands have expanded geographically and organically. Coverage has become increasingly global, whilst variety and local choice has developed within brands.

FOR EXAMPLE

....

Coca-Cola expanded rapidly as a single product into almost every country in the world. It then added variations to the main theme with products such as Diet Coke, Caffeine-free Coke, and Cherry Coke. However, in the late 1990s the company ran into problems. Pepsi took market share in the USA and European markets began to react against symbols of uniformity in global markets such as Coke. (See Chapter 5, section 5.6.4 'Marketing mistakes' for how Coke initially responded to Pepsi's challenge). In 2000, a new CEO, Douglas Daft, introduced a strategy of 'thinking local, acting local'. This involved responding to changes in consumer tastes quickly by developing new products as the drinks market becomes increasingly fragmented. Coke now consider that they compete against four categories of products: refreshment drinks (main brands such as Pepsi), hydration products (mainly waters, such as Perrier), energy and stimulation drinks (e.g. Lucozade and Red Bull) and juices and health drinks (e.g. Five Alive). They plan to offer appropriate products in each of these areas, dependent on local tastes. For example a new drink, Alchemy, is targeted at those who want a sophisticated non-alcoholic alternative to traditional cocktails. The ingredients are activated by shaking in a container in the form of a personal cocktail shaker – a far cry from Classic Coke.

The sale of products at low cost on the Internet was initially seen as a threat to the domination of branded goods. However, e-commerce is still full of unknowns, especially in the areas of payment and quality control, and in those circumstances, consumers have opted for the products they already know – the established brands.

7.4.4 Branding strategies

As organisations developed and products proliferated, managers were faced with a choice of strategy over the naming of branded products: should the same name be used for all products to give them an authoritative stamp of approval? Or should products be individually branded and left to develop their own loyal following? Both strategies have been used successfully and less successfully.

'Umbrella' branding

'Umbrella' branding makes the maximum use of a well-established brand name by using it on all the organisation's products. This strategy has two main variants:

■ Use of the company name on all products, often with more descriptive, individual product names

FOR EXAMPLE

Kellogg's Special K, Kellogg's Crunchy Nut Cornflakes, Kellogg's Corn Flakes, Kellogg's Rice Krispies, Kellogg's Coco Pops and Kellogg's Fruit 'n Fibre all use the name of the founder Will Kellogg, who launched the original corn flakes in 1906. The company's simple, focused approach help it to dominate the cereal market in the UK. Kellogg's had five out of the top ten packet breakfast cereal brands in 2005 and three-quarters of the UK population bought a Kellogg's cereal in 2006.

■ Use of one brand name for all products or a group of products which is different to the company name. For example, for many years Marks and Spencer used the St Michael label for all of their own products. However, some organisations take the use of their brand name too far.

FOR EXAMPLE

Bic became a very successful brand name for pens, razors and lighters. When the company diversified into toiletries, the Bic brand was used on a perfume product, this time without success as the cheap, disposable image of the name was not appropriate for a more exclusive, luxury item.

A 'portfolio' of brands

Some organisations are involved in diverse markets that require different brand names.

FOR EXAMPLE

Reckitt Benckiser (formerly Reckitt and Coleman) market a wide variety of household products under many individual brands, many of which have their own variants. They range from health products such as Lemsip and Disprin to cleaning products such as Vanish, Mr Sheen and Dettol. It would be difficult to see how their products – as diverse as Colman's mustard and Harpic toilet cleaner – could be marketed under the same brand.

■ Other companies acquire branded products or develop their own competing brands to maximise their share of one market. In these circumstances, the strategy is to develop a portfolio of different but complimentary brands.

FOR EXAMPLE

Procter and Gamble and Unilever between them dominate the market for washing powders. Both companies market overlapping brands to ensure complete coverage of the market. Procter and Gamble's Ariel, Daz and Bold compete with each other as well as with Unilever's Persil and Surf.

MARKETING MISTAKES

FOR DATSUN READ NISSAN

'Datsun new car' Datsun was the original brand of the first mass-produced Japanese car in the 1930s. By the 1970s, it had become a leading international brand, with flagship 'Z' sports models (the Datsun 240Z and 260Z) that were the best-selling sports car in the world. It competed in the USA and Europe head-on with its main rival, Toyota, and was well ahead of a third Japanese car manufacturer, Honda. Inexplicably, in 1980 the parent company decided to change the Datsun brand to Nissan. After several years of expensive marketing effort, Nissan had lost market share, falling behind Toyota, with Honda rapidly closing the gap. Surveys indicated that consumers' recall of the Datsun name was still as high as the Nissan brand five years after it had been dropped. The brand has now fully established itself, but it does offer a lesson in how attempts to refresh a brand name can be an expensive and perilous operation.

For Datsun read Nissan, but the old brand lived on years after its withdrawal

Consigned to the bin A more recent example of re-branding was so unpopular it had to be reversed. In March 2001 the UK Post Office, founded in 1635, decided to overthrow centuries of history by changing its name to Consignia in order to demonstrate a more modern approach. Just over one year later, the group announced it would be ditching Consignia and re-adopting the Post Office name. The re-branding attempt followed a long line of former British nationalised industries choosing to become less identifiable but more modern, including National Power changing to Innogy, British Steel becoming Corus; and Welsh Water, Hyder. However, the Post Office's change to Consignia was met with outcry from many quarters. Even Post Office workers boycotted the use of the new name, one mockingly demanding that the directors involved in the decision should 'resign-ia'. It did seem an obvious error to discard not only over 250 years of branding, but also many other valuable assets such as the Royal Mail name and the red post box icons that adorn British streets. However, a branding overhaul is sometimes necessary, even after a long distinguished history, and Consignia gave several seemingly valid reasons for the change. First, as the group was expanding internationally, 'Post Office' could possibly be confusing abroad. Second, the Post Office did not fully describe its total business, which also includes banking and retailing. Unfortunately, the new name was even more vague and also potentially confusing, and so offered no real advantage in exchange for dumping a perfectly good brand. The Post Office has now re-instated their name with the strap line: 'for the little things that make the big things happen' – which goes some way to overcoming the problems with the Post Office name.

CHECKPOINT

Can you think of other brands that are no longer marketed? Why do you think they have disappeared?

Discontinuing brands

Although building the value of a brand is an expensive and time-consuming process, many are deleted every year when the costs of reviving a flagging name become greater than the expected returns. But brand names do not always die completely. Some defunct brands are sold on, only to be revived by the new owner. For example Allied Domecq sold off what they considered to be a redundant brand, Plymouth Gin, for 'scrap value' to John Murphy of InterBrand. Within a year he had turned the brand back into a stunning success – much to the embarrassment of Allied Domecq. To avoid such difficulties, many brands are simply left unused on the shelf as an inactive trademark. Trademarks are registered for ten years, after which they must be renewed. If they are not renewed the trademark lapses and anyone can use it. As renewal is relatively cheap, most companies keep their trademarks to prevent a competitor from reviving them. Examples of brands that are no longer marketed include: Marathon, Opal Fruits, Jif, Mercury, Compaq, Line One and BSB. Some are still marketed but under a different name. For example, Marathon is now Snickers, Jif is Cif and Opal Fruits is Starburst. These have been victims of the move towards global branding, which requires names that can be pronounced and understood without negative connotations in any country.

7.5 THE PRODUCT LIFE CYCLE

7.5.1 The life of a product

Products have a finite existence in the marketplace. Many are short-lived fads or failures; others go on for many years before they are overtaken by new developments. However long they last, products, like people, are mortal. They do not live forever; some have a brief moment of glory, others persist in relative obscurity, but they all wax and wane in popularity.

Their 'lives', like ours, can be divided into several distinct stages:

- Products are 'conceived' and developed by their innovators until they are ready to be launched

- They are 'born' and introduced into the marketplace

- They 'grow' to the limits of their sales potential

- They 'mature' as their markets become saturated and more competitive

- They decline and 'die' as demand falls and alternative products are 'born' to begin the cycle over again

This is the concept of the 'product life cycle' (PLC), which is usually illustrated graphically as shown in Figure 7.4.

Not all products follow this classic curve closely. Products can miss out stages or they can be rejuvenated to earlier stages of the cycle. For example:

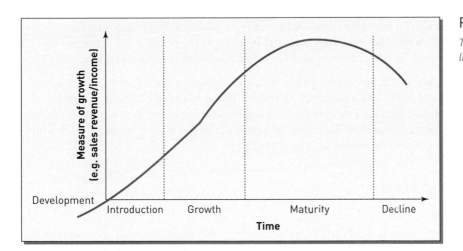

FIGURE 7.4

*The product
life cycle*

- Unsuccessful products may not have any significant growth stage, but go into decline soon after their introduction (e.g. the Sinclair C5 electric car, most music bands)

- Some products exist because of a short-lived fad or craze – the speed of their introduction and growth is matched only by the rapidity of their decline which leaves no time for a period of consolidation and maturity (e.g. the hula-hoop, Rubik's cube, a 'one-hit' pop group, and many children's 'heroes' from the 'Teenage Mutant Hero Turtles' to 'Pokémon')

- Products are sometimes rescued from an earlier decline by revitalisation as growth slackens and markets mature. This could be the result of marketing efforts to re-stimulate demand by re-presenting or re-packaging the product (e.g. the re-launching of 'Marathon' chocolate bars as 'Snickers', the re-packaging of many soap powder brands from 'Blue Daz' to 'Green Persil', the changing images of pop stars such as Kylie Minogue, the enhancement and re-launch of the Star Wars movies). Products are also helped by technological changes that may enhance their demand. Film-making was given a new lease on life through the development of videos and DVDs, which has given many films a second opportunity for generating revenue; the market for watches had matured until the introduction of quartz crystal digital mechanisms created a new growth stage; similarly, domestic demand for computers and peripherals was stimulated by the development of the Internet.

The product life cycle can be used to describe generic classes of products (computers) and their subdivisions (personal computers), or the specific product lines of one organisation (Macintosh PCs) or their individual product items or brands (the iMac). This produces some differences in the application of the concept.

- Generic products tend to have longer life cycles than individual products. Coal as a generic form of energy in the UK has been through a long cycle, lasting hundreds of years; it was introduced during the Industrial Revolution, grew rapidly in the nineteenth century to reach a peak of production soon after the First World War, matured as markets saturated and other forms of energy such as oil, gas and nuclear energy were introduced, and has now suffered a substantial decline in output. Many generic product classes (cars, office copiers, university degrees) stay in the mature stage for a long time because there is no better alternative.

■ Within a generic product's life cycle, subgroups exhibit a variety of different curves. Although the overall market for coal had matured by the 1960s, house coals returned to a phase of modest growth as house owners rediscovered the benefits of an open fire.

■ Individual products are much more susceptible to rapid change in their fortunes because of competitive forces and shifts in consumer preferences. Some branded products survive, virtually unchanged, for decades (Mars bars, Oxo cubes), but these are the exceptions rather than the rule. Most long-living brands change as a product (e.g. Gillette razors, Kodak film), so that the brand lives on in the shape of a new product.

7.5.2 The life cycle stages

The development stage

In the development stage, new product ideas are researched and taken through to readiness for the marketplace. No sales are made during this stage (except perhaps during a market test), so it is an unprofitable, cash-absorbing phase in a product's life. Two aspects of product development need emphasising as they can work against each other:

■ The most important element in the marketing mix is getting the product right in the first place. No amount of clever promotion, sophisticated pricing, or extensive distribution can compensate for a weak product that is not in tune with customer needs.

■ Speed of new product development is becoming more and more important in competitive international markets. It is no longer enough to get there first; continual improvements to existing products are required just to maintain market share.

FOR EXAMPLE

....

The Range Rover was the first rugged four-wheel-drive vehicle to be sold as a luxury car, but the world market has been dominated by Japanese manufacturers who developed newer versions more suited to mass markets. Rank Xerox once dominated the UK office copier market with the only plain-paper machines available. After the expiry of their protective patents, Xerox saw their leadership eroded as competitors, such as Canon, introduced more versatile and compact copiers to give customers the decentralised copying facilities that they preferred.

Given the overwhelming importance of getting the product right, organisations can suffer from inertia in developing new products to take over from successful existing products. The result is that they lose out to more agile competitors. Some companies, such as 3M and Hewlett Packard, have developed deliberate policies to overcome these negative forces. These include:

■ *Keep divisions small*: There is evidence that smaller business units provide a more innovative, working environment than larger groupings.

■ *Tolerate failure*: One success usually comes from many rejected concepts which nevertheless contribute something to help progress an idea. This implies that risk-taking and experimentation is to be encouraged even when it means high failure rates.

■ *Look for innovations, not just inventions*: The two are often confused, but they are not the same. Invention involves creating new ideas; innovation takes new ideas but puts them to practical use as desirable products or services.

■ *Encourage some 'disorder'*: Creativity is often sparked when ideas that are normally not connected are 'accidentally' linked. This is the basis for processes such as brainstorming, which attempt to encourage creative thinking. Unfortunately, most management activities strive for order and predictable policies as the only way of coping with complex structures and markets. 'Thriving on chaos' does not come naturally, particularly to well-established organisations.

■ *Systematically search the most likely sources of opportunities*: New products rarely come as a one-off flash of inspiration. Organisations that are most successful in new product development seek out innovation continuously and methodically. Changes to existing markets and customer habits often leave clues that the innovator can pursue. For example, demographic changes often signal opportunities for new products as well as threats to existing ones. We know, for example, that the UK population profile is set to become older as the percentage of over seventy-year-olds increases. This is already creating opportunities for those offering services such as sheltered housing and nursing homes for the elderly. Conversely, the decline in numbers of young people poses product problems for those dependent on youthful markets (for example manufacturers of fashion clothes, leisure shoes and trainers, alcoholic and non-alcoholic drinks).

In an established marketing organisation, product development usually goes through a number of processes, which take a new idea from a position of unknown risk through to reasonable prospects of success. This is illustrated in Figure 7.5.

FIGURE 7.5 *New product development process*

UNKNOWN RISK	
GENERATION OF NEW PRODUCT IDEAS	Systematic search for innovative opportunities among employees, customers, competitors and other sources, using analysis, research and 'creativity techniques' e.g. brainstorming.
SCREENING OF IDEAS	Unsuitable ideas rejected often by reference to a checklist of criteria for acceptable product parameters and performance.
TESTING OF CONCEPT	The idea of new product is tested conceptually on a group of target customers before it is taken further.
PLANNING OF STRATEGY	Marketing objectives for new product established. Financial and other implications analysed in a business plan.
DEVELOPING THE PRODUCT	Development of a successfully working prototype product.
TESTING THE MARKET	Product is tested and evaluated in the market place by limited exposure in selected areas prior to more extensive launch in the introduction stage.
REASONABLE PROSPECTS	

The introduction stage

In this stage the product is introduced into the marketplace and made available to customers. Most new products are relatively unknown at this stage and, therefore, demand is slow; there are exceptions such as films or West End plays, which use pre-launch publicity to generate the immediate, substantial demand that these products need to be financially successful.

The common themes (although not hard and fast rules) of the introduction stage are:

■ If the product is innovative, competition will be limited

■ The product specification remains basic as refinements are not yet needed and may be undeveloped

■ The need to develop awareness of the product makes promotional effort the highest priority in the marketing mix, whether this comes from advertising, personal selling, PR or other methods

■ Pricing pressures are downward because of increased output and more competition

■ Distribution is widened (e.g. geographically) and deepened (e.g. to smaller retail outlets) to maximise sales potential

■ Financially, growth leads to profits as revenue increases and unit costs decline. This may not be reflected in a positive cash flow, however, as increased debtors and stocks, or other investments necessary to cope with growth, absorb surplus cash. Profits may also be re-invested in product improvement or other marketing activities in order to capture more market share.

FOR EXAMPLE

....

LEVI'S® ECO JEANS FOLLOW THE ENVIRONMENTALLY FRIENDLY TRENDS IN FASHION

For the first time since it started making trousers for miners more than 130 years ago, in 2006 the famous Levi Strauss & Co. clothing company brought out a pair of sustainable jeans to reach out to fashion-conscious consumers interested in high-quality products that demand less from the environment. The well-established company was responding to increasing environmental awareness and a growing trend among consumers to choose and purchase products based on their environmental impact.

The Levi's Eco line of jeans, made from 100 per cent organic cotton, was first launched in the USA in the summer of 2006. Consistent with the company's practice of adapting and developing their global product lines to be relevant to the markets in which they are sold, the version launched by the company in Europe in November 2006 took the Levi's Eco initiative even further.

In addition to using only 100 per cent organic cotton, the button on the waistband is made of coconut shell, there are no metal rivets and the innovative finishing process uses only chemical-free

LEVI'S® ECO LINE

Levi's® Eco follow the environmentally friendly trends in fashion

compounds, including natural indigo, Marseille soap, potato starch and mimosa flower. The jeans are made in Hungary, the cotton comes from Turkey (the nearest available source) and other materials and components are also sourced in Europe, which cuts down on long-distance transport and associated fuel costs. The European version of the Levi's Eco jeans were granted 'EKO Sustainable Textile' certification from Control Union Certifications, and are believed to be the first certified sustainable jean from a major denim brand. Levi's Eco jeans were introduced in two of the brand's most popular existing fits, marked with a few subtle identifiers including an ecru Tab with the Levi's brand name in green, a printed cotton back patch and a hangtag made of recycled cardboard.

All in all, the company appears to be minimising its carbon footprint (at least with this product) whilst maximising a business opportunity.

The maturity stage

As markets become saturated and competition increases, growth peaks and sales begin to stabilise. This is the onset of maturity, the most common stage for products, and one that tends to last longer than other phases. Common themes in this stage are:

- The slackening rate of growth leads to a shake out amongst competitors. At first, competitive activity may increase as rival suppliers try to maintain growth by increasing market share through promotional activities, product improvements and price-cutting. The resulting decline in profit margins usually forces weaker competitors to exit from the market. This may allow for a period of relative stability among the few established organisations that emerge as the final market leaders.

- Products become more refined as rivals seek to gain competitive advantage through improvements to performance and presentation and by the addition of new features. It is in the maturity stage that the added value of the augmented product becomes a more and more significant determinant of demand. Additional benefits, such as longer guarantees, after-sales service, financing deals, give-away extras and incentives are required to attract buyers.

- Promotional activity is no longer targeted at creating awareness but at maintaining loyalty to a brand or product. Some promotions may seek to develop new, secondary market segments.

- Pricing becomes more sophisticated as markets mature. Discounting may threaten margins in the short term, and in the longer term if over-capacity remains a permanent feature of the market. However, suppliers often try to protect margins by offering a more attractive 'bundle' of benefits for the same price.

- Distribution spreads even wider in an attempt to improve sales. It may be at this stage that international markets become more attractive for the first time as demand in the home market slackens. New channels of distribution may be opened up to gain access to different segments.

- Financially, profits tend to decline as sales level off, although they can improve again if a shakeout of competitors stabilises the market. However, the maturity stage can be sufficiently cash-positive for successfully managed products to recoup the investments made in earlier stages. Indeed, it is important to prolong this stage for as long as possible to ensure satisfactory financial returns.

- Managing the mature stage is a key marketing management task, as manipulation of the marketing mix can delay the beginning of decline or stimulate a return to growth.

FOR EXAMPLE

KELLOGG'S ALL BRAN REVITALISED

Kellogg's created All-Bran in the 1930s. Since then the product experienced steady growth, with the company injecting regular promotional spends to support product development. The most spectacular growth was in the 1980s, with widespread publicity for the 'F' Plan Diet from nutritionists and health experts. This diet had an impact similar to that of the Atkins and GI diets in recent years. Following this, the Kellogg's 'bran' range moved into a more mature stage and was in danger of going into decline – it was time to revitalise the brand.

Kellogg's aimed to raise consumer interest by creating a family of fibre-based cereal brands focused around the All-Bran banner in order to create a 'power brand' structure. This umbrella branding added strength to each separate bran product.

Portfolio analysis Kellogg's identified the existing fibre-based products that offered the best return and future prospects and concentrated on them. This simplification made it easier to manage the product portfolio. Managers focused on the common elements of the chosen range and directed marketing activity towards them. This produced management and marketing economies of

The All-Bran umbrella brand forms part of the Kellogg portfolio and has been expanded

scale, although not production economies – the complexity of manufacturing individual products was not reduced.

Research Kellogg's market research showed that, in choosing a cereal product, consumers place high priority on taste. Although they want a healthier cereal, it still must taste good. So Kellogg's decided to develop new 'tastier' products under the single All-Bran umbrella, such as Bran Flakes Yoghurty. Before proceeding with the change, Kellogg's carried out some detailed market research. Qualitative research assessed consumers' perceptions of possible new packaging, obtained their views on the benefits of the product and investigated why they used fibre-based cereals. It also helped Kellogg's to develop the concept of a family of fibre brands.

After the qualitative market research, the concept was tested through quantitative research. This involved using surveys with a much larger sample of targeted consumers to estimate the impact on sales if these changes were put into the market. The market research revealed several issues for Kellogg's to address when launching the bran family:

1 Some respondents found the idea of a 'bran family' confusing

 Response: Packs displayed both the power brand name (All-Bran) and also the product name (e.g. Bran Flakes). To maintain continuity, Kellogg's used consistent type fonts and colours from the old packaging, whilst introducing the flash 'new name, same great taste'. To help consumers understand the new range, the back of each pack featured the different attributes of each of the products in the range. This allowed consumers to make purchase decisions on the basis of taste and the amount of fibre they required in their diet.

2 Consumers saw cereals as a 'natural product', which is a strong selling point.

Response: Feature the ingredients on the packaging so that the All-Bran range can be seen as part of a daily healthy diet. For example, the newest addition to the All-Bran range, Bran Flakes Yoghurty, claimed to promote users' inner health by providing 17 per cent of daily fibre needs.

Promotion   To give the campaign maximum impact, Kellogg co-ordinated television and radio advertising, PR and in-store promotions that encouraged consumers to try out the revamped products. For example, the company introduced the All-Bran 'Feel Great in a Fortnight' Challenge, a campaign designed to make the brand's benefits more relevant to consumers. This message moved the brand away from the outdated 'keeps you regular' message by focusing on the 'feel-good' factors of high-fibre diets that may help people to feel lighter and more energetic as well as aiding the digestive system. So far this strategy appears to have been successful in extending the maturity phase of the Kellogg's bran family and preventing its decline. Other initiatives may be required in the future.

The decline stage

Eventually the sales of an individual product or group of products may go into decline. This can represent a gradual shift or a more rapid decline in demand, caused by the introduction of better or substitute products, or a change in consumer attitudes.

Choices for marketing management include:

■ Maintain the product by concentrating on segments where there is evidence of continued demand

■ Revitalise the product so that it can be re-launched as 'new' in some way

■ 'Harvest' remaining profits from the product by reducing expenditure on it to a minimum

■ Delete the product from the range

FOR EXAMPLE

The thirty-five-year-old Sindy doll was phased out by its makers Hasbro, who withdrew all marketing support. Sindy was the casualty in the battle with Barbie, who proved the more durable doll, and relative newcomer, Polly Pocket.

7.5.3 Effects of the product life cycle on the marketing mix

This description of the PLC illustrates how the evolution of a product changes the use of the marketing mix over time:

■ More emphasis is placed on product changes as the cycle advances. Whereas the basic product is acceptable in the introduction stage, features are added in the growth stage;

additional benefits of the augmented product are needed in the mature stage, and finally the product may be totally revamped in the decline stage.

■ Promotions vary in both extent and objectives. During introduction and growth, extensive promotion may be required to generate awareness and to capture market share. In maturity and decline, promotional activity may be reduced to improve profitability and targeted at increasing customer loyalty. Alternatively it maybe increased temporarily to promote a re-launch of the product.

■ Pricing can be high for innovative products during their introduction but prices are increasingly subject to competitive pressure as the cycle progresses. Substantial discounting may be required to maintain market share in maturity and decline.

■ The 'place' element of the marketing mix can also change as distribution policies reflect a product's fortunes. Restricted distribution in the introductory stage usually gives way to wider geographic coverage and deeper penetration of specific channels of distribution as markets grow and mature.

The implication for marketing management is that the effective use of the elements in the marketing mix varies according to the stage of the life cycle. What works well at one time may fail or be inappropriate at another stage.

> **CHECKPOINT**
>
> Consider products you have recently purchased, been given or used. In which stage of their life cycle would you place each of these products?

7.6 PORTFOLIO ANALYSIS AND STRATEGY OPTIONS

7.6.1 Life cycles of a product portfolio

Most organisations offer more than one product or groups of products at a time. They offer a portfolio of different but often related products. Each of these products has its own life cycle and, at any given time, they will be at various stages of their cycle. Figure 7.6 illustrates the life cycles of the portfolio of products of one organisation. On a specific date – Time *X* – in this

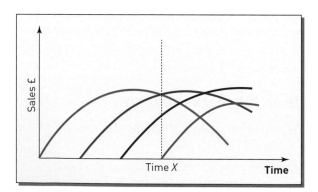

FIGURE 7.6

Life cycles of an organisation's product portfolio

organisation's history, one product is in decline, another has entered maturity, one is growing fast, whilst one is just being introduced.

The potential impact of this combination of life cycles is an important ingredient in the organisation's product decisions.

Resource implications of the product life cycle

Financial and other resources are affected by the PLC:

- *Profits* which are non-existent during development and introduction, should emerge with growth, and may then plateau or disappear altogether in maturity and decline.

- *Cash investment* is required to develop new products and to finance their introduction. Products often remain cash-negative during high growth, only generating a positive cash flow as growth slows into maturity. The decline stage can be cash-positive or neutral if products are well managed and support for them is removed in line with sales; eventually decline inevitably absorbs cash if significant losses occur before deletion of the product.

- *Other resources are also affected by the life cycle.* For example, more management time may be required to cope with the rapid changes likely during introduction and growth than is needed once more predictable patterns have emerged in maturity. The production of a new product probably needs more operator and machine time than an equivalent, established product where 'economies of experience' have begun to be realised.

The implication of this analysis is that an organisation requires a portfolio of products that is balanced in line with the resources available and the growth objectives of the organisation. In order to finance the development, introduction and growth of newer products, a business needs more mature products which provide the necessary cash flow. In order for a business to continue to grow overall, it has to introduce new products to replace the growth lost by mature and declining products.

Competitors, market share and life cycles

The competitive situation is likely to change with the life cycle of the products in the marketplace:

- An innovative new product may have little competition when it is introduced but many competitors emerge as growth of the market is confirmed.

- In the growth stage, a large number of organisations with relatively small individual shares of the market can survive, many of them dependent on the increase in the total market to provide them with new customers rather than any specific competitive advantage.

- As market expansion slows down, the survivors are likely to be those who have gained a relatively high market share because they have demonstrated a competitive advantage. This may come from lower costs which give bigger profit margins to invest in promotions or product development, or to withstand the effects of a price war. Or it may stem from a superior product that is able to differentiate itself from competitors.

- Once markets have matured and become dominated by a few, well-established organisations, it is usually more difficult to gain market share. Market leaders should have a lower cost base as they produce more than their competitors and can benefit from economies of scale or experience. Research and development to produce a superior product can be expensive as competitors have already introduced sophisticated or technologically advanced modifications.

These characteristics imply that taking a relatively large market share in the growth stage can be critical to success and survival in the maturity stage. In an expanding market, growth may be relatively easy to achieve. However, if the growth of a product is below the rate of increase in the rest of the market, this could spell problems later as that product is losing ground to its competitors and may end up with a relatively small market share. Complacency during the earlier stages of a product may shorten its life expectancy.

7.6.2 The BCG growth-share matrix

These influences of growth and market share have been brought together into a matrix by the Boston Consulting Group (BCG), as shown in Figure 7.7. Products are labelled according to their likely impact on an organisation's resources.

- A *star* product is growing fast and has achieved a high market share. Although it generates high revenues and is profitable, it uses lots of cash to fuel its growth and maintain its competitive position. It is well placed to survive and prosper when growth slackens.

- A *cash cow* has a high share of a market which has matured. Because of its dominant market position, it is able to exploit maturity and generate plenty of surplus cash from its sales. Cash cows 'evolve' from the stars of the growth stage and are a critical source of cash and other resources to develop new products.

- A *wildcat* (sometimes referred to as a 'problem child' or 'question mark') is in a growth stage but has achieved a relatively small market share. As this makes the product unprofitable at present and could put it in an even weaker position when the market matures, it requires some changes and probably investment to improve its market position. Wildcats are therefore net users of cash resources. They may be managed into stars but they can also degenerate into dogs if market growth disappears.

- A *dog* has the worst of both worlds, having a low share of a market with no or low growth. It represents a drain on an organisation's resources, often at the expense of other products, and is a candidate for deletion unless it can be transformed through growth into a wildcat.

FIGURE 7.7

The BCG growth-share matrix

The growth-share matrix emphasises the need for a balanced portfolio of products if an organisation is to grow and be self-sufficient in resources. Once the portfolio profile has been established four basic strategies for each product are possible:

- **Build**: Increase market share to strengthen the future position at the expense of shorter-term profits and cash flow, for example turning wildcats into stars.

- **Hold**: Maintain current market share to make sure maximum profit and cash is generated now or in the future, for example by sustaining and milking a cash cow.

- **Harvest**: Increase short-term cash flow even at the expense of longer-term profits, for example by taking profits from stars and wildcats rather than investing in them and milking cash cows dry if market conditions seem set to worsen.

- **Divest**: Cut off a drain on resources even if it means taking short-term losses, for example by terminating a dog.

Critics of the growth-share method of analysing product portfolios point to its simplistic assumption that market share is always the key measure of a product's competitive position and that market growth is always the most important indicator of an industry's attractiveness. In particular, it overlooks the large number of highly successful products that occupy niche positions in larger markets and the diseconomies of scale in providing some services which undermines the value of a high market share.

7.6.3 Market attractiveness–competitive position matrix

To overcome these and other criticisms, different models have been developed to help guide product strategies. In one approach (developed by General Electric and McKinsey), products are rated against two principal dimensions: attractiveness of the market and their competitive position.

- **Market attractiveness** is a measure of the profit potential in a market for all participants, including not just growth but also other factors such as market size, level of competition, historic profit margins, rate of technological change, and the political and legal constraints

- **Competitive position** is assessed not only by market share but also product quality, perceived image, distribution network, management strength, patent protection and other significant factors

This multifactor model can be drawn as a grid as shown in Figure 7.8.

Products are plotted on the grid according to their rating against the established criteria. They can be drawn as parts of circles where the size of the circle represents the size of the total market and the product's market share is shaded. The cells of the matrix fall into three distinct areas:

- Those justifying investment for growth

- Those requiring more selective management and cautious investment

- Those needing a policy of harvesting or divestment because they represent unattractive options

7.6.4 Ansoff's classification of product strategies

We looked briefly at alternative marketing objectives which specify the relationship between products and markets in Chapter 2 (see Chapter 2, section 2.5). This introduced the four basic, alternative strategies of Ansoff's Matrix, which links products to the markets they are targeted to serve, as shown in Figure 7.9.

FIGURE 7.8 *The GE multifactor portfolio model*   FIGURE 7.9 *Ansoff's matrix*

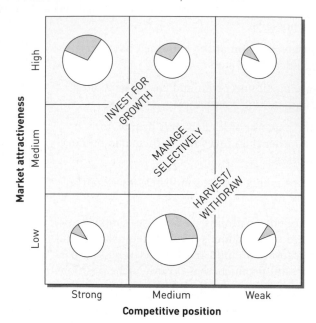

- **Market penetration** develops existing products within existing markets. The underlying assumption is that there is still untapped demand or competitive advantage that can be further exploited without either changing the product or looking beyond existing market segments. This strategy usually involves use of other elements in the marketing mix, such as an increase in promotional effort, more aggressive pricing policies or more extensive distribution. Providing the potential exists, it is the strategy of least risk because both products and markets are known, for example, Kellogg's has encouraged the use of breakfast cereals for other meals, so consumers are encouraged to eat cereal for their lunch or evening meal.

- **Product development** introduces new products into existing markets. It assumes that an innovation will be accepted by the organisation's existing customer group. Product development can be radical, with the introduction of an entirely new product; or moderate, involving only the modification of existing products in some way such as performance, presentation or quality. Many prestige car manufacturers offer a range of merchandise targeted at car owners so that you can buy replica models, clothing and pens.

- **Market extension** takes existing products into new markets. This strategy assumes that existing markets are fully exploited or that new markets can be developed concurrently with existing markets. New markets may be defined geographically (e.g. potential export areas), or by customer grouping (e.g. a different age or social group) or other parameters (e.g. purchasing patterns, industrial classification or sectors). Some market extensions may be counter-intuitive – for example, Guinness, traditionally a drink for colder climates, is now a successful brand in a number of African countries.

- **Diversification** develops new products and offers them to new markets. As it represents a departure from an organisation's existing product and market involvement, it is the strategy of highest risk. Richard Branson of Virgin has often used this strategy with mixed results. His forays into the vodka and cola markets have not been successful. The music stores (sold) and airline have been more successful, but the train company continues to be troubled.

7.6.5 The use of portfolio and product strategy analysis

Although portfolio analysis using these and other models has been much discussed amongst theorists, research has indicated that they are not often used in practice. Some managers have not heard of them, others do not understand them and some have tried them and found them wanting as management techniques.

Defenders of portfolio analysis claim that the tools are frequently misapplied and often too much is expected of them. They are intended as techniques that can help the product planning process by providing ideas on the value of various strategic options, but they are not methods which on their own can determine product strategy.

ENTREPRENEURIAL MARKETING

Irrespective of the merits of the techniques of portfolio analysis, the need for product planning is undeniable. This can be particularly true in younger, high-growth companies that tend to accumulate products as they expand without systematic review of what should be in or out of the portfolio. This places an unnecessary strain on the already stretched resources of a fasting-growing SME. The example below illustrates how one company is conducting a much-needed analysis of its portfolio in an uncomplicated way.

FOR EXAMPLE

Windmill Organics is a fast-growing, specialist supplier of packaged organic food products, sold under four brand names:

- **Biona**: A comprehensive range of quality organic products across most food categories, both chilled and ambient
- **Amisa**: Organic products that fulfil a specific dietary need
- **Biofair**: Organic Fairtrade products
- **Profusion**: Organic products with a specific functionality, such as probiotics, cholesterol reduction or detoxification

A successful new product development (NPD) activity in response to changing health and eating trends resulted in an extensive portfolio of around 650 products. These are spread across the four brands, but Biona and Amisa account for 80 per cent of sales. As well as direct sales to key supermarkets and larger retailers, the range is sold through a network of specialist wholesalers that supply health food and organic retailers.

As an SME, Windmill Organics has few employees – only ten, so the management of this extensive portfolio places considerable demands on the staff. This will increase, as at current rates the range is growing by about fifty products a year. Consequently the managers have decided to conduct a thorough review of the product portfolio to evaluate the products within the main product categories. The aim is to reduce the portfolio to a core of 250 products across the four brand categories, supplemented by a further 200 products that complement these.

The key evaluation criteria for each product will be:

Windmill Organics demonstrate how a high-growth SME has to cull unwanted products even more diligently than large companies

■ Contribution to the revenue stream

■ Importance, in terms of being either a category leader or a 'me-too'; those products that are currently low volume, but in key growth or niche areas will be given special consideration

■ Fit with current and projected trends in consumer demands for organic food related to developments in this market

■ Special consideration will also be given to products that have limited sales but which help to:

— Complete a sub-range that has a particular health or organic focus

— Attain volume discounts by enhancing order values from suppliers

The new product portfolio will be supported by a range of marketing initiatives:

■ Corporate re-branding to create a strong company profile

■ Clear communication of the revised portfolio via an enhanced website which will feature the key products and ranges prominently through a 'flagship' positioning

■ A clear focus on these products in future marketing initiatives

Windmill Organics is demonstrating how a high-growth SME has to cull unwanted products even more diligently than large companies.

More information on Windmill is available on www.windmillorganics.com.

CHECKPOINT

Choose a high street retailer with whose products you are familiar (such as WH Smith, Boots, Woolworths or a local trader).

Draw your impression of the life cycles of one of their product categories (e.g. greetings cards, film processing or confectionery) and consider the implications of this analysis.

7.7 SUMMARY

- A product is anything that is capable of fulfilling customer needs. It is therefore not limited to physical objects, but includes intangible services, people, places and organisations.

- Products are classified into consumer or industrial products, and tangible or intangible products. Tangible products are subdivided further into durable or non-durable goods.

- Individual product items are aggregated into product lines, groups, and finally portfolios or product mix – all the products offered by an organisation or unit.

- Three distinctive elements of a product need consideration: the core product of basic benefits to meet customer needs, the actual product of features which create those benefits, and the augmented product of additional features and benefits (such as guarantees and after-sales service) which often differentiate competing products.

- Branding has become an important, intangible aspect of many products, representing an assurance of quality, and a statement of aspirations of the purchaser.

- Branding strategies can follow an *umbrella* or *portfolio* approach.

- The 'product life cycle' (PLC) concept divides the lifespan of a product into stages of development, introduction, growth, maturity and decline.

- The *development stage* takes new product ideas from concept to market readiness. This development process can be under-emphasised, without deliberate policies to generate, screen and test new ideas that can then be planned, developed and tested as products in the marketplace.

- Typically in the *introduction stage*, a basic product is launched with limited competition, promotional activity, higher prices, restricted distribution and sales and negative cash flow.

- The *growth stage* is typified by rapid market acceptance, more competition, product improvements, additional promotional effort, and downward price pressures. Although profitable, the product continues to absorb cash.

- In the typical *mature stage*, growth slackens, products and pricing becomes more sophisticated, distribution becomes wider and deeper and promotions seek to maintain loyalty. The pressure on profits and market share shakes out weaker competitors, although cash flow becomes positive.

- In the *decline stage* decisions are needed to either revitalise, harvest or delete the product.

- A balanced *portfolio of products* is required to cope with the resource and marketing implications of the product life cycle. The *growth-share matrix* typifies products as 'stars', 'cash cows', 'wildcats' and 'dogs' according to their market share and growth characteristics.

- The *multi-factor model* measures the market attractiveness and competitive position of a product.

- *Ansoff's matrix* classifies product strategies as market penetration, market extension, product development or diversification.

7.8 ACTIVITIES

CASE STUDY

LEGO®: BUILDING A PORTFOLIO

In 1934 Ole Kirk Christiansen, a Danish carpenter, invented an interlocking brick and named it 'LEGO', after the first two letters of the Danish words 'Leg Godt' which means 'play well'. By coincidence the word is also Latin for 'I put together'. From these early beginnings LEGO has grown to be a substantial international brand: on average, every person in the world has 52 LEGO bricks and more than 400 million children and adults spend 5 billion hours a year playing with LEGO. The products are on sale in more than 130 countries, with four LEGO sets sold each second.

The brand name encapsulates the company's philosophy that good play enriches a child's life by stimulating the imagination and creativity. The brick is a very flexible toy. A professor of mathematics has calculated that there are over 900 million different ways of combining six eight-stud bricks of the same colour. The LEGO range contains 2,000 different items, in 55 different colours and 20 different materials. The product portfolio has been developed in such a way that there is something for all ages and stages of development. It caters for consumers who prefer to make things up as they go along as well as those that wish to build from pre-designed models. Fifty years ago there were few alternatives to the little plastic bricks, but the competitive environment for toys has changed. Today children are wooed by electronic gadgets and computer games as well as more traditional toys. LEGO has attempted to adapt the product to the electronic era. Children can visit the LEGO Factory website (factory.lego.com) where they can design their own LEGO models and build them with virtual bricks before ordering the real thing online. LEGO's policy of encouraging lifelong play is reflected in their product mix which is organised in five categories: pre-school, creative building, play themes, licensed products and robotics.

Pre-school products cater for younger children from two to six years old, encouraging them to use their hands and develop their motor skills through creative play. Duplo was launched for this market as 'the big brick for the small hand'. It emphasised safety to parents because the bricks are large enough to prevent swallowing and moulded to avoid smaller pieces becoming detached. LEGO briefly phased this out and replaced it with LEGO Explore. The move was not a success. Revenues in the pre-school market halved in a year as confused consumers believed that LEGO had withdrawn from the market, and DUPLO was reinstated. Today the product line consists of both loose bricks – so that the child can build entirely what comes into their mind, and play themes – for example, an airport or pirates.

Creative building extends the range to older children who can be trusted not to eat the smaller parts. Young builders can use their imagination or follow detailed plans to create structures and scenes from containers of bricks and special parts such as windows, wheels, roof tiles and mosaics. Gender has influenced the development of the category, as research showed that young boys gain enjoyment from the construction stage of play whereas young girls spend more time in the role-playing phase. This led to the launch of LEGO Belville with distinctive pink packaging targeting young girls. Themed sets such as a fairy castle contained more mini-figures so that girls had to spend less time building their scenario and more time playing.

Play themes are those products that can be built to represent scenes ranging from everyday life at a fire station or an airport, to a fantasy world such as the 'Bionicle Universe'. As well as enjoying building, the child can play with the finished models.

Licensed products are play themes based on movies or books for which the LEGO company has acquired the rights to base its products. Playing with licensed products is a question of role play – becoming absorbed in the world already familiar from the movie. Designers recreate the universe and characters in LEGO bricks so that play can continue on the floor at home. For example, LEGO negotiated product tie-ins with Star Wars and Disney. More than one million Hogwarts Castle LEGO sets were sold when the first two Harry Potter films came out. As a result LEGO is refocusing on its core business of open-ended imaginative play.

Robotics attempts to take an essentially low-tech product into the electronic era. LEGO Mindstorms NXT is aimed at armchair inventors, robotics fanatics and LEGO builders aged ten and older to design and build real robots. Robots can be programmed to perform many different operations using the software included in the set. They can be fitted with sensors that control motors and react to light, sound and touch. They can react to the builder's voice or can be controlled via a mobile phone – they are even Bluetooth enabled.

Future plans take account of the need to reduce the time new products take to get to market. New products and lines now focus on the classic LEGO brick using eternally popular themes such as Town, Castle, Pirates and Vikings. This allows the time from concept to final product on the retailer's shelf to be dramatically reduced, with the average period of development at about twelve months.

© THE LEGO GROUP

HARRY POTTER, CHARACTERS, NAMES AND RELATED INDICIA ARE TRADEMARKS OF AND © WARNER BROS. ENTERTAINMENT INC. HARRY POTTER PUBLISHING RIGHTS © JKR.

© THE LEGO GROUP

LEGO uses different products for different targets to build a balanced portfolio

QUESTIONS

1 How is LEGO segmenting the market?

2 How would you categorise LEGO's product portfolio in terms of the multi-factor model or Ansoff's matrix? *See section 7.6*

3 What gaps do you think exist within the customer segments currently targeted by LEGO?

4 What products would you suggest for these targets?

DEVELOPING A MARKETING PLAN

THE PRODUCT STRATEGY

How will your product strategy reflect the objectives and market strategies you have decided to follow?

- What are the core benefits, the actual features and the augmented aspects and other benefits of your principal products?
- What is the anticipated mix of products in your portfolio?
- What is the implication of the mix on resources?
- How will you develop new products?
- How will your products be differentiated from the competition?
- How do you assess the attractiveness of the market?
- What will be your strategy – penetration, market extension, product development or diversification?

7.9 FURTHER READING AND REFERENCES

General texts

Doyle, P. (2002), *Marketing Management and Strategy*, 3rd edition (Prentice Hall).
Gabbott, M. and Hogg, G. (1998), *Customers and Services* (Wiley).
Lovelock, C. (2004), *Services Marketing: People, Technology and Strategy*, 5th edition (Prentice Hall).

Branding

Keller, K.L. (2003), *Building, Measuring and Managing Brand Equity*, 2nd edition (Pearson Education).

New product development

Crawford, C.M. and Di Benedetto, C.A. (2005), *New Products Management*, 8th edition (Irwin McGraw-Hill).

Chapter 8

PRICING: INFLUENCES, STRATEGIES AND METHODS

LEARNING OBJECTIVES

By the end of this chapter the reader will be able to:

- Understand the importance of pricing mechanisms in both private and public sectors
- Assess the impact of internal factors, including marketing and financial strategies, on pricing a product or service
- Assess the impact of external factors, including customers, market and environment, on pricing a product or service
- Define elasticity of demand
- Evaluate different pricing strategies including skimming and penetration

INTRODUCTION

This chapter investigates various influences on another key element in the marketing mix – pricing. Price is a particularly important element of the marketing mix since it determines profitability by its impact on costs and demand. A number of internal and external factors help determine the optimum price for a product or service:

- Internal factors include the marketing and financial strategies of an organisation
- External factors include the type of customers, the state of the marketplace and more general environmental influences such as taxation and the economic policies of the government.

The two generic pricing strategies of market skimming and penetration are examined in the light of these factors. Finally the chapter considers specific pricing methods and techniques under the categories of the '3 Cs' of cost-based, customer-based and competition-based pricing.

CASE STUDY

···

PRICING BICYCLES

Monica Bogaert, product manager for all-terrain bicycles (ATBs, or mountain bikes as they were more commonly known) at one of the top UK suppliers had an important task to complete. She had to recommend a pricing strategy for a new model to be launched by her company. It was a hybrid 'town and trail' bicycle, so-called because it had all the off-road features of a mountain bike but it was comfortable and efficient for on-road use as well. It incorporated some important new features: a super-light aluminium frame to minimise the pedal power required, front suspension forks to cushion the ride, and most innovative of all, hub gears. Unlike the old-three speed variety, which had become outdated by external, cog-changing derailleur gears, the new enclosed hub gears provided ten speeds and were much easier to use and maintain.

The marketing strategy for the new bike was to target some market segments which the existing ATBs in their range had not fully penetrated, notably the over thirty-five female group, whilst having appeal to the core market of fifteen- to nineteen-year-olds and men over thirty-five. Although the new features gave it considerable advantages, the bike's technical leadership was likely to be short lived as the innovations were the result of developments not by Bogaert's own company but by component manufacturers.

To take advantage of advances made by Far Eastern producers and to keep fixed costs to a minimum, all the components of the new product were to be imported with final assembly only taking place in the UK. Bogaert had received estimated costings for the components and manufacturing. Assuming an order for quantities of at least 10,000, the total cost of components approximated to £80 per bicycle, which Bogaert knew to be very competitive considering the new features. Even the price of the lighter aluminium frames had fallen considerably in recent years, although they were still more expensive than the hi-tensile steel models. The costs of setting up each bike in

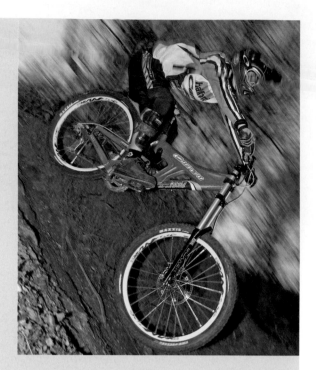

Pricing had to appeal not only to the core market of 15–19 year olds but also to the over 35 female group

the UK would add a further £30. There were fixed costs that would be charged to the new model as well. The promotional budget had been set at £200,000 for the first year to cover advertising and sales promotions and an allocated cost for group publicity such as catalogues and exhibitions. A further allocation to central overheads including R&D, central services and finance costs had been estimated at £300,000 per annum. In any pricing decisions, Bogaert would have to observe the key financial measures used by her company, such as a profit to sales ratio of at least 10 per cent.

The final price of the bike to the user would have to take into account the distributors' margins and of course value-added tax (VAT) 17.5% in 2007. Bicycle distribution in the UK was still very fragmented with most sales going through independent retailers, although superstores such as Halfords had grown in popularity to an estimated 25 per cent of retail bike sales. Most retailers added a mark-up of between 35 and 45 per cent to their buying price, depending on the volume of their purchases and how keenly they wished to price their products.

Over a million adult ATBs were still being sold in the UK, but Bogaert knew that the market had become very competitive. The growth of the ATB market had attracted many competitors and imports of lower-priced bikes had grown steadily. Now 'bargain' ATBs started at £99, with reasonable bikes for the more serious rider in the £199–£250 bracket. Aluminium-framed models continued to drop in price and were now available at £300 and under. For the enthusiast there was a growing choice of mountain bikes over £500 with a top of the range price of £1500–£2000. As growth of the ATB sector had slackened, manufacturers tried to differentiate their products through improved features and the use of branding with names such as 'Dirty Dog', one of Bogaert's own

models that had achieved something of a cult following. Although Bogaert's company and one other supplier controlled over 50 per cent of the UK bicycle market between them, there were a dozen or so other serious competitors offering a variety of models.

'I must decide first what my pricing strategy will be', thought Monica Bogaert. 'Do I take advantage of the technical superiority of my new product and make good profits as quickly as possible by pricing up in the market segments that I know will pay? Or do I look for longer-term profits, keep my price down and broaden my appeal to more segments in the hope that I can take a significant market share?

(Note: this case can also be read as a follow-on from the case 'Bicycles' in Chapter 6, which has additional market information.)

QUESTIONS

1 What types of influences on pricing decisions are discussed here? Are there others that should be taken into consideration? *See sections 8.1 and 8.2*

2 Consider the possible impact of these influences:

   i Which internal influences will be most important and why? *See section 8.3*

   ii Which external influences will be most important and why? *See section 8.4*

3 Consider the questions Monica Bogaert is asking herself about the pricing strategy to adopt. What are the advantages and disadvantages of the alternatives she suggests? What pricing strategy would you recommend? *See section 8.5*

4 What selling price would you recommend for the new model and why?

  What is the break-even volume of sales at your recommended price? *See section 8.6*

8.1 PRICING IN THE PRIVATE AND PUBLIC SECTORS

New products and economic growth in many market sectors have increased the significance of non-price variables, such as branding, advertising and distribution channels, on customer preferences. Maturing markets and economic downturns reaffirm pricing as a crucial marketing tool. The introduction of market forces into the delivery of public services and growing competitiveness amongst other non-profit organisations has also emphasised the importance of pricing as a management function.

In the private sector, pricing has a crucial impact on the profitability of a business. In the public sector, the importance of the pricing mechanism is less obvious because users of public services do not often pay directly for each service received. However pricing is still an important management function in both sectors, although there are differences in its application.

■ **In the private sector,** prices charged need to cover at least the costs of providing products if an organisation is to survive in the longer term. Pricing is unique among the 4Ps of the marketing mix in that it produces income whereas the other elements incur costs. The total income or sales revenue of a business can be represented by the formula:

$$R = PQ$$

where:

R is sales revenue

P is the price per unit sold

Q is the volume or quantity of units sold

Pricing strategies therefore not only represent an important marketing consideration, but also play a direct role in the financial viability of a private sector company.

■ **In the public sector,** organisations receive revenues from a mixture of charges to customers and allocations of public funds from tax receipts. A state-owned corporation such as Royal Mail is expected to cover its costs mainly from prices charged to consumers, with increasing pressure to minimise any subsidies from taxes. Pricing operates in much the same way as it does in the private sector except that it is subject to more political scrutiny. However public services such as the health, police and education services are mainly funded by allocations of tax funding, as there are few direct charges on consumers.

These allocations of government funding are increasingly made on the basis of the delivery of a specific service which therefore takes on a notional price.

FOR EXAMPLE

In the UK, state schools are allocated annual budgets primarily on the basis of the number of pupils attending the school, thereby giving a notional price to the provision of a year's education to a child. Hospitals are awarded contracts for the provision of certain services, which effectively puts a specific price on the provision of those services. Some departments (such as physiotherapy) within a hospital can be used by patients paying directly through a medical insurance scheme and so those services have to be priced separately. Some public services, such as refuse collection, are subject to competitive tendering; if a public authority (such as a district council in the case of refuse collection) wishes to continue to provide the service itself, it must submit a price in the form of a tender for the contract.

Within many public services, there is a division between the purchaser of a service who controls the allocation of public funds and monitors the quality of delivery, and the provider who delivers the specified service for a set price. Managers in today's public services have to understand pricing either from the side of the purchaser assessing competitive bids for a service, or from the context of a provider of services for a specific price.

CHECKPOINT

Consider a non-profit organisation with which you are familiar (e.g. a charity or social enterprise). What role does pricing play in the management of this organisation?

8.2 INFLUENCES ON THE PRICING PROCESS

8.2.1 Fixed and flexible pricing

The setting of prices for products and services varies from a relatively simple to a very complicated process. However, pricing decisions are rarely easy in practice because they are subject to many different, often conflicting, influences and constraints inside and outside of an organisation.

Historically buyers and sellers arrived at a price through a process of bargaining. Both parties searched for a price by making offers and counter offers until they decided on a level acceptable to both, or made no deal. Prices arrived at by this method were often different for each transaction even if the product was essentially the same, reflecting the individual needs and negotiating skills of the bargainers.

Although elements of this process can still be found on the floors of commodity and stock exchanges, where prices for the same item change by the minute, most present-day sellers set defined prices. Retailers normally establish a price for each product and buyers either accept it or reject it. Some organisations do offer differential pricing for the same product: an industrial seller may accept lower prices for bulk or regular purchases; travel companies and hotels offer discounts for off-peak users of their services. However these prices are mostly subject to uniform policies which qualify the buyer. In our society, individual negotiation is the exception rather than the rule, limited to larger one-off deals between organisations (e.g. negotiation of a long-term contract) or individuals (e.g. buying a house). The majority of items sold in the UK are pre-priced before they are offered to the marketplace, with little room for bargaining thereafter. Other cultures have different practices with bargaining seen as the norm. Many local markets, such as the souks in Marrakech, expect negotiation.

8.2.2 Internet pricing

The Internet does allow for more individual negotiation of prices. Auctions have recently been given new impetus by the Internet with the success of Internet auction houses such as eBay. The system of bidding is usually the same as the traditional format, but the Internet makes the process more convenient and easier to join in. Internet auctions have also developed some pricing novelties, for example, a buyer can state how much they wish to pay (e.g. for airline seats) and see if a seller wishes to accept (for example, at eWanted).

Other sites use collaborative buying power to attempt to achieve lower prices for specific items (e.g. LetsBuyIt.com). Some sites act as an intermediary seeking to find the best price on your behalf, whilst on others you can barter for a better price. For consumers, these systems and services are still developing. The key issues to overcome before extensive expansion of individual bargaining are to increase the security of payments over the Internet, and to develop more cost-effective methods of delivery of products. Many individual buyers are still wary of giving credit card details over the Internet, and are cautious about the value of bargains which prove expensive to deliver.

Buyers in organisations increasingly use e-procurement to achieve lower prices. This may be done in conjunction with other companies forming a virtual marketplace of buyers and suppliers (such as the WorldWide Retail Exchange of over 100,000 suppliers and major retail buyers). In most cases procurement is still through an electronic catalogue, so that there is little effect on pricing. However, companies are also using 'reverse auctions': the buying company indicates what it wishes to purchase, and suppliers bid for the order, successively lowering the price. Such methods facilitate communications between buyers and suppliers so that players in the marketplace are better informed. However, pricing decisions are still influenced by a series of internal and external factors, whatever the communication or negotiation mechanism.

8.2.3 Influences on pricing

Pricing decisions are subject to a complex series of influences arising not only from the needs of buyers and sellers but also from the market and general environment around them. Figure 8.1 illustrates some of these influences which might be taken into account by an organisation when pricing its products.

- ■ *Internal* influences include the *marketing and financial strategies* of an organisation. Marketing strategies are likely to stipulate the markets that an organisation targets, the position it takes within them and the marketing mix strategies adopted. Financial strategies dictate the cost base for providing products and services and the returns expected from them. All are fundamental influences on pricing decisions.

- ■ *Customers* influence pricing decisions by their perceptions of the relative importance of price in the marketing mix, which establishes the elasticity of demand for particular products.

- ■ *Market* influences take into account the state of development of the market and the strategies and activities of competitors.

- ■ *Environmental* influences on pricing include the applicable levels of taxation, the state of the economy, existing legislation and current government policies.

- ■ *Pricing decisions* eventually set prices for each item, but they also establish a strategic framework within which the method of selecting individual prices can operate.

Each of these influences in the pricing process is considered in more detail in the following sections.

Internal influences
❑ Marketing strategies
  • Target markets
  • Positioning
  • Mix
❑ Financial strategies
  • Cost base
  • Financial objectives

Pricing decisions
❑ Strategies
❑ Methods
❑ Individual items

External influences
❑ Customers
  • Perceptions
  • Elasticity of demand
❑ Market
  • State of development
  • Competitors
❑ Environment
  • Economic
  • Political/legal
  • Intermediaries

FIGURE 8.1

Influences on the pricing process

Think of a purchase that you make regularly (e.g. confectionery, books) and a significant purchase you have made recently (e.g. clothes, computer equipment). What role did price play in your purchase decision in both cases and how did you evaluate it? What lessons might suppliers draw from your experiences?

8.3 INTERNAL FACTORS: MARKETING AND FINANCIAL STRATEGIES

Prices are frequently determined by a mixture of marketing and financial factors. The price of a product is a key part of the marketing mix and needs to be in line with other elements of marketing strategy if the customer is to be given consistent messages. The price achieved by a product is also a significant ingredient in the financial equation which determines the profitability or efficiency of an organisation. Thus pricing is a function of concern to both the marketing and financial management of an organisation.

8.3.1 Marketing strategies

Different marketing strategies can lead to different pricing decisions. For instance, a strategic objective to penetrate the market as rapidly as possible is more likely to keep prices down than the aim of maximising profits at the expense of growth.

Prices are particularly influenced by the following marketing decisions:

■ *Target markets*: The decision to segment a market into customer groups and target one particular segment with a differentiated approach affects pricing as well as the other variables in the marketing mix.

FOR EXAMPLE

In the early years of passenger travel by air, the airlines differentiated only between those passengers able to pay for first class seats and regular fare payers. However, an important segment of business travellers emerged who expected some of the luxuries of first class without the high price tag. Airlines began to target this segment by charging premium rates over economy passengers for extra comforts and services. Although the basic benefit of rapid transportation from point A to point B was the same for all passengers, the business class segment was offered a package of additional benefits, including the status and comforts of a separate seating area, which avoided the extravagance of a first class ticket but was still priced higher than economy class. Fast-track check-in has also become important, particularly since enhanced security checks have become commonplace and time-consuming.

■ *Positioning strategy*: Customers' perceptions of the position of a product or organisation in the marketplace are influenced by pricing strategies. The exclusive position of cars made by

Rolls Royce or Ferrari is maintained by making sure only a few customers can afford the price. Most organisations do not have such an obvious connection between their prices and market position but still need to establish a clear identity that is created or confirmed by their pricing policies. Often there is a clear correlation between price and quality, with the expectation that if you pay a high price you will get high quality; conversely if you pay a low price you can expect quality to be lower.

FOR EXAMPLE

Woolworths' shops have always aimed at the bargain position in the marketplace. Their original strategy offered shoppers the convenience of extensive ranges of lower-priced products from buttons to bath taps sold in one town-centre store. Large stocks of cheap items no longer made economic sense as the costs of High Street retailing escalated in the 1970s and 1980s and retailing became more targeted. Woolworths refocused its operations in the UK under the umbrella of the Kingfisher group that also included the B&Q DIY chain. The traditional Woolworths shops concentrated on limited popular lines such as toys, children's clothes, music and videos. However they retained their historic position as the bargain basement retailer. Although this proved popular in the recessionary times of the early 1990s, shoppers grew weary of year-round sales and became confused by the variety of in-store promotions offered by all retailers fighting to retain their share of shrinking markets. Woolworths decided to reaffirm their position by a radical, consistent pricing scheme called 'Street Value'. This gave customers the simple promise of the lowest prices on items marked with the 'Street Value' logo. The aim of this price-branding scheme was to position the group as the retailer who offers permanent value for money. Woolworths Group plc returned to independence when it began trading as a listed company again in 2001 after its de-merger from Kingfisher plc.

■ *Marketing mix strategies*: Pricing decisions are part of a marketing mix strategy that can only be effective if all the ingredients blend together. Decisions on price need to be consistent with those made about other elements of the mix.

FOR EXAMPLE

The Arcadia group approach fashion retailing by targeting demographic segments, differentiating between younger buyers of both sexes, and older age groups. This involved changing the proposition of each element in the marketing mix in a consistent way to each market segment:

■ TopShop sells fashion ranges appropriate to the younger female clothes buyer. This age group typically likes to keep their clothes up to date by frequently changing what they wear. Product quality can therefore be compromised as long as prices are low enough to allow the buyer to repurchase relatively quickly. The place of purchase and promotional messages which emphasise low prices for high fashion are also consistent with the lifestyle of the youth market.

■ By contrast, Wallis targets an older female age group, offering individualistic clothes by incorporating distinctive, fashionable designs. Prices are correspondingly higher, relating to the higher-quality merchandise offered in a more sophisticated shopping environment with appropriate promotional communications.

8.3.2 *Financial strategies*

Pricing possibilities are constrained by the financial structure and objectives of an organisation:

■ The financial structure determines the cost base of the products to be priced

■ Financial objectives indicate targeted revenues to be achieved by products through a combination of volume and price

The cost base of an organisation is a particularly important influence on pricing strategies. Whilst the overall level of costs compared to income determines the profitability or viability of an organisation, the *types* of costs within the total cost base are what often determine the pricing strategies adopted. Two basic types of cost can be defined: fixed costs and variable costs.

Fixed costs

Fixed costs refer to expenses that do not vary with the level of products sold or the quantity of service provided. They are overhead costs such as rent, rates, insurance, heating, lighting and management salaries which, within limits, do not change irrespective of whether there is one customer or one thousand.

A manufacturer incurs the same costs to finance its plant and equipment whether they produce ten units per week or ten thousand. A retailer has to pay at least one person to serve in a shop, even if there are no customers for long periods. A school has to pay the same to heat and maintain its buildings whether there are fifty or five hundred students enrolled.

As these fixed costs have to be recovered from sales or income, a crucial element in the pricing decision is the volume of production or quantity of services that can be allocated to cover these overheads, as the following two examples illustrate.

FOR EXAMPLE

....

Two manufacturers of the same product line had identical fixed overheads of £10,000 per week. Company *A* estimated that their sales would average 1,000 units per week, whilst Company *B* budgeted for 2,000 units sold each week. Company *A* therefore allocated fixed costs of £10 per unit when calculating the cost base of a product whilst Company *B* worked on the basis of unit fixed costs of £5. This allowed Company *B* to offer substantially lower prices than Company *A*, or generate more profits from the same prices assuming the forecasts were met.

Two secondary schools had similar fixed costs (which excluded teachers' salaries) of £200,000 per annum. School *X* had 1,000 students on roll but School *Y* was less popular, with 800 students and several empty classrooms. Fixed costs at School *X* were therefore £200 per student, whist at School *Y* they were 25 per cent higher, at £250 per student. The education authority paid each school the same grant for educating one student irrespective of total numbers. Both schools received £2,000 each year per pupil, from which most costs (fixed and variable) had to be met. This meant that School *X* could spend £50 more on each of its students for resources such as books or more teaching hours.

Economies of scale occur when an organisation spreads its costs across more units of production, or quantities of service provided, in this way. Economies of scale mean that the largest seller in a particular market will normally have the lowest costs per item, providing they are at least as efficient as their competitors. This is why gaining market share is such an important objective for many producers. Taking a large share of a market can create economies which provide competitive advantages through a lower cost base. This facilitates lower prices, or it may be transferred into other advantages.

FOR EXAMPLE

Company *B* in our previous example decides to price its products at the same level as its competitor, Company *A*. The economies of scale provided by its higher output means that it generates more profits than its rival. Because it is buying in large quantities, it can get bulk discounts, reducing the unit costs of its purchases. Company *B* reinvested some of this extra profitability in product development and promotional campaigns to give it a more permanent competitive advantage.

School *X* in our previous example was able to spend £50 per pupil more than the neighbouring School *Y* because of the economies of scale from its higher student numbers. The extra teaching resources that it was able to provide helped it to register better examination results and attract even more pupils as a result. School *Y*, on the other hand, found itself in a downward spiral: fewer pupils meant that even more of the per-student financial allocation had to be spent on fixed costs and even less on classroom resources, which in turn meant it was less able to attract students for the future. This vicious circle is hard to reverse.

Variable costs

Variable costs are expenses that do change in proportion to the level of sales or the amounts of services fulfilled. They are the costs of raw materials for manufactured products, the price of stocks sold by a retailer or the materials used by a service organisation.

As activities in an organisation increase, so do the variable costs. The manufacturer has to buy more raw materials to make up finished products if sales increase; a retailer has to buy more stock as items sell; a school has to buy more books as student numbers increase.

FOR EXAMPLE

Viking Direct, a leading supplier of office equipment to SoHos (Small Offices/Home Offices) offer a sliding scale of unit costs based on the volume ordered. Someone ordering lever arch files might pay £2.69 if they are only buying one, but if they buy ten they will only pay £2.29 per unit and, should they order forty, the unit cost reduces to £1.49 per unit.

Profit margins

The relationship between the variable costs and the selling price of a product is often expressed as a mark-up or a gross margin:

■ *Mark-up* expresses how much is added to the variable costs to reach the selling price. It is often given as a percentage of the variable costs.

This can be represented by the formula:

$$\% \text{ mark-up} = \frac{\text{selling price} - \text{variable cost}}{\text{variable cost}} \times 100$$

FOR EXAMPLE

A clothes retailer buys a shirt from its manufacturer for £20 and gives it a selling price of £50. The mark-up is £30, or 150 per cent of costs. In a sale the item is reduced to £40; the mark-up is now £20, or 100 per cent of costs.

Any manufacturer or retailer of shirts needs to consider margins and mark-ups

© ISTOCKPHOTO.COM/MAURICE VAN DER VELDEN

■ *Gross margin* is also an expression of the difference between the selling price and the variable costs of an item. However, it takes the selling price as its reference point, expressing how much of the revenue from the selling price is left after deducting variable costs. It is often given in percentage terms, expressing the difference between price and cost as a percentage of price.

FOR EXAMPLE

The retailer in our previous example who priced a garment for £50 that had been bought for £20 aimed to achieve a gross margin of £30 or 60 per cent (of the selling price). It was sold in the sale for £40 at a gross margin of £20 or 50 per cent (of the selling price).

This can be represented by the formula:

$$\% \text{ gross margin} = \frac{\text{selling price} - \text{variable cost}}{\text{selling price}} \times 100$$

Mark-ups and gross margins are often used to provide guidelines in the pricing process, establishing minimum or budgeted levels.

FOR EXAMPLE

A retailer preferred to work with mark-ups because it was easier to start with the cost of an item, which was always known from purchase invoices. The retailer adopted the policy of always adding at least a 100 per cent mark-up to items purchased as this was the minimum required to cover the fixed overheads of premises and salaries on the current level of turnover.

A manufacturer budgeted for a 45 per cent gross margin on their sales as this had historically been achieved and gave a reasonable profit after fixed overheads were deducted. When pricing new products, the marketing manager knew that they had to achieve an average gross margin of at least 45 per cent.

Flexibility in pricing

Some organisations have fewer pricing options than others because of financial constraints. One important influence is the mix of fixed and variable costs in the total cost base. Where most costs are fixed, there will be more chances to offer differential prices for the same product once the fixed costs are covered. If variable costs are the major cost element and represent a high percentage of prices charged, there is less room to manoeuvre and opportunities for using flexible pricing policies are limited.

FOR EXAMPLE
....

The tourism industry illustrates extremes of flexible and inflexible cost structures. Travel agents receive a commission of approximately 10 per cent for booking holidays provided by tour operators; thus their gross margin on sales is effectively only 10 per cent. They have little flexibility in their prices to customers if they wish to cover their costs, and usually pass on the full prices charged by the tour operators. Customers may also end up with additional costs, such as fuel surcharges and additional taxes which are not negotiable.

Conversely, hotels have mainly fixed costs with a low percentage of variable costs; premises and staff costs remain similar irrespective of guest numbers so the key indicator of success for a hotelier is room occupancy rate. Once fixed expenses are covered, it costs relatively little to accommodate more guests. Special prices offering large discounts can be used to attract customers during off-peak periods. So a hotel that has a significant proportion of business visitors during the week may offer discounts to families over the weekend. It also in the hotel's interests to encourage visitors to stay more than one night as the costs of completely cleaning the room are greater than just the superficial cleaning that occurs when guests stay for several nights.

Financial objectives

As pricing has a direct impact on the financial performance of an organisation, pricing decisions are constrained by financial objectives and policies. Examples of financial objectives and their impact on pricing strategies include:

■ *Short-term profits*: If a company sets ambitious targets for the profits it expects from any investment in new products, then the pricing of those products may have to be aggressively high in order to achieve the financial targets. Because of their limited resources, smaller companies often adopt short-term financial targets for new investments.

■ *Longer-term profits*: Some organisations are prepared to adopt longer-term financial strategies allowing products more time to develop profitability. In these circumstances, prices can be set at lower levels to maximise penetration of the marketplace and build profitability from a position of high market share. Historically, Japanese companies in the automobile and electronic markets have tended to follow this strategy.

■ *Cost recovery*: Successful new products often have to recover the costs of products that fail or were never launched; prices also have to take account of development costs. Pharmaceutical companies, for example, invest heavily in the research and development of new drugs, the cost of which has to be recovered from the profits of the small number of successful new products that are launched.

FOR EXAMPLE

The mobile phone industry was over-burdened by debt because of the introduction of 'third-generation' (3G) telephones. This development offers users exiting new features such as high-speed Internet access and video clips for which the phone operators can charge higher prices. However, companies, including British Telecom, Vodafone and France Telecom, paid over £80 billion to buy the licences to operate the new network in Europe. Technical problems delayed the introduction of 3G handsets that are effectively mini-computers. As a result, the income from the sale of the new product, which is needed to service the debts from the licences, was delayed. This caused financial problems and a pricing dilemma: the 3G phones could either be priced up in order to recover the high fixed costs of the new system, or priced down in order to generate cash as quickly as possible to pay down the debts.

■ *Survival*: In industries suffering from surplus capacity or changes in customer demand, organisations are forced to regard survival as their overriding objective. Normal financial criteria become secondary as prices are cut in an effort to stay alive until the market achieves a better balance between supply and demand.

FOR EXAMPLE

Price wars often erupt when demand in a market sector turns down. Chip makers and personal computer (PC) manufacturers saw the Internet-led boom disappear during 2000/2001. As PC sales declined, they soon became caught up in a price war that reduced the number of players in the marketplace. The battle was triggered when the two largest chip makers, Intel and Advanced Micro Devices, responded to sluggish sales by repeatedly reducing prices. This in turn reduced the costs of PC manufacturing and gave the PC makers an opportunity to join the battle. Compaq became the largest PC maker when it overtook IBM in 1994, but Dell's decision to cut prices by over 20 per cent in early 2001 allowed it to become number one in terms of market share. Compaq responded with cuts of its own, and although the major companies can probably withstand the financial effects of the price war, inevitably there have been casualties as smaller companies are taken over or close down.

■ *Non-profit objectives*: Some organisations, such as charities and public services, do not have the profit objectives of private sector businesses. This does not necessarily make their pricing levels lower. A charity tries to maximise the funds available for its chosen cause, and may therefore even price products it sells at a premium. If public authorities charge for any of their services they are usually required to obtain prices which fully recover all of their costs so that there is no possible hidden subsidy from public funds.

FOR EXAMPLE

Oxfam has been very successful in selling virtual presents through its Oxfam Unwrapped range. For example, for £20 you can buy an alpaca package for a family in a less developed country, which helps farmers to buy and look after the animals – helping them to earn their own living. The money could be used on the animals themselves, what's needed to care for the alpacas – shears, shelter, food and fences – and on training for the farmers to sell the wool. The prices of the gifts – from £5 to £1,700 – reflect the actual cost of delivering that item or service in a poor country. In some cases the money may be spent on a closely related item, to ensure that the funds are used in the most flexible way to meet the needs of people in poverty. These ethical gifts offer the benefit of both donor and recipient feeling good about the gift.

Oxfam offers charity gifts such as buying an alpaca to encourage donation

CHECKPOINT

As a consumer you have probably benefited from economies of scale in suppliers' costs that have influenced prices.

List the times you have benefited from buying more than one of any item. What are the advantages and disadvantages of this to the supplier, and to you?

8.4 EXTERNAL INFLUENCES: CUSTOMERS, COMPETITION AND THE BUSINESS ENVIRONMENT

Whilst influences internal to an organisation establish parameters for pricing decisions, the final judgement on the acceptability of a price is made in the marketplace.

8.4.1 Customers' perceptions and demand

Customers surrender something of value (the price) in order to acquire the product or service that they are purchasing. The level of price they are prepared to pay depends on the value they place on the benefits on offer. Customer-orientated pricing decisions therefore involve an investigation into the customer's perception of the value of the benefits of a product.

In some cases the benefits a customer obtains from purchasing a particular product can be valued directly because they reduce costs in other areas.

FOR EXAMPLE

....

Energy-saving devices can be used in connection with a variety of electrical installations such as lighting. Sellers of these devices target heavy users of electricity and sell their product on the basis of the benefit of lower energy costs. They can measure the savings to be made with some precision and therefore quote customers a sum of money they will gain in exchange for paying the price of the product. Pricing of the energy-saving device is related to this valuation.

In most cases the benefits a customer receives are harder to value in this way. Many products offer benefits that are difficult to evaluate because they are intangible and relate to customers' perceptions of a product.

FOR EXAMPLE

....

The purchaser of a new car buys some benefits that may have an obvious value; for example, the benefit of low running costs can be quantified in comparison to competitive vehicles. Some of the benefits perceived by a customer are intangible, such as the prestige and pride derived from new car ownership. Moreover these perceptions vary from customer to customer; the positive status of ownership of a Jaguar perceived by one customer may be perceived as inappropriate material-ism by another.

Pricing decisions therefore involve an understanding of the motivations behind a purchase decision and how much the customer is prepared to pay for the benefits they perceive.

Elasticity of demand

In some cases customers are prepared to pay almost any price to obtain the benefits they per-ceive. In other cases they are sensitive to even small price movements, which can change their buying decision. The demand for a product is influenced by many factors, of which price is only one. The relative importance of price compared to other factors varies according to the type of product, and the circumstances of the marketplace.

Elasticity of demand measures how much the demand for a product changes with movements in price:

- *Inelastic demand* indicates that quantities sold are likely to change very little as prices move up or down

FOR EXAMPLE

....

Many commodity products, such as milk and bread, are inelastic. Energy consumption also falls into this category because consumers are reluctant to alter their purchasing patterns despite in-creases in gas, electricity and petrol prices. Buyers may cut back on consumption – or at least try to – but they will still need to purchase these products.

- *Elastic demand* indicates that quantities sold are likely to be significantly affected by prices changes

FOR EXAMPLE

Discretionary purchases, are elastic. If the price increases dramatically, we might choose to manage without the product. So if the price of a chocolate bar was to rise significantly, we might decide to give up chocolate.

Different circumstances make customers relatively insensitive to small price changes and therefore exhibit inelastic demand:

- *Products that have few competitors or substitute products.* Lack of direct competitors is not in itself sufficient to produce inelastic demand if there are substitutes. For example, railway companies often enjoy a monopoly service having no direct competition on their routes, but this does not result in inelastic demand. If prices are raised, more customers use substitute methods such as road transport.

- *Exclusive products sold for benefits of status and prestige.* A high price is part of the image of some products, such as perfumes and luxury cars, which are expected to be expensive. Being able to afford these product categories can be an expression of a person's success or worth, and price decreases can even trigger a fall in demand as the perceived value is undermined.

- *Well-branded products.* Some established brands have a higher inelasticity because of the loyalty of existing consumers. For example, this may apply to particular coffee or body care brands.

- *Expenditure on a product is a small part of total costs or income.* When one product represents a very small part of the overall costs of a project, the price of that product has less significance and demand is more likely to be inelastic. This has helped some manufacturers to survive the fierce cost competition from countries such as China because they make only a small part of an overall product or service – for example, manufacturers producing components for specialised products such as scientific instruments.

Demand curves

The relationship between price and the number of units bought can be shown graphically as a 'demand curve'. Figure 8.2 shows the 'normal' demand/price relationship for many products.

In this case, there is a straight-line relationship between price and demand. The higher price (P_2) leads to the lower quantity sold (Q_1); the lower price (P_1) leads to the increased demand (Q_2). Each change in price leads to a corresponding change in demand. This may be the relationship for many non-essential products such as confectionery and magazines.

FIGURE 8.2

'Normal' demand/price relationship

FIGURE 8.3   *Demand curve for essential goods*   FIGURE 8.4   *Demand curve for some luxury goods*

However it is not the relationship for all products. Figure 8.3 shows the demand curve for more essential goods such as certain basic foods (e.g. bread, potatoes).

The lower price (P_1) again leads to higher demand (Q_2) and demand decreases as price levels rise, but in this case the rate of decline slows and eventually stops (Q_1) as demand reaches the minimum required for survival whatever the price (P_2 and above).

In other cases, the curve may be inverted as demand rises with price (see Figure 8.4). This may be the case for certain types of luxury goods (e.g. jewellery, perfumery and 'top-of-the-range' products such as exclusive cars) where the perceived value increases at price levels which make the product a status item.

In this case, demand is smaller (Q_1) at the lower price (P_1) and then increases (Q_2) at the higher price (P_2), before declining again as further price rises put the product beyond the purchasing power of significant numbers of customers.

It is important for organisations to understand the price/demand relationship for their products if they are to optimise their prices. In practice it is difficult to eliminate other influences on demand in order to study the effect of price changes only.

FOR EXAMPLE

A retailer tried to calculate the effect on turnover of its annual sale in which it discounted a variety of goods. Although he knew that turnover had increased during the sale, he was unsure how much of this was due to lower prices and how much due to the increased advertising to promote the sale or improvements to the economic climate. Another retailer with a chain of stores was able to produce more accurate estimates of the relationship between demand and price changes as she could monitor the effect of lower prices in one store against the results in a similar store where prices were not changed.

8.4.2 *Market and competitive influences*

The competitive structure of a market plays an important role in determining prices. Economists have classified markets into different categories according to the type and level of competition:

■ *Perfect competition* exists when many buyers and sellers collectively determine prices at the point where supply equals demand. In this hypothetical situation, no seller has advantages over another as products are uniform and equally available. Sellers cannot therefore charge more than the going rate that buyers are prepared to pay to obtain all they need; nor do they have any incentive to charge less as they can sell all they have at these prices. Although some markets, such as fresh fruit and vegetable and commodities trading, come close to these conditions, this type of pure competition is largely a hypothetical concept as many factors such as product differentiation and shortages or surpluses of supply distort 'pure' competition in the marketplace.

■ *Monopolistic competition* describes the markets in which there is a range of prices for similar products because sellers differentiate what they offer and buyers are prepared to pay different prices for the perceived differences. This is the usual situation in most of our consumer markets, for example, where branded products often command a price premium over non-branded goods because of their higher perceived value.

■ *Oligopolistic competition* exists in markets in which the high cost of entry restricts the numbers of competitors. The small number of sellers compete actively however, often following each other's pricing strategies to protect their customer base. For example, petrol companies and high street banks rapidly adjust their prices and charges to match any competitive movements which look like having an impact on customer demand.

■ *Pure monopoly* means a market in which there is only one seller. This may develop because of government intervention (e.g. the national lottery), or because of patent protection (e.g. Dyson cleaners). Prices are not necessarily high in these circumstances: nationalised industries were subsidised in the past and are now regulated by watchdog committees even after they have been privatised; monopoly private sellers often use their advantage to penetrate the market as fully as possible with lower prices before competition develops.

The level of influence of competitive pricing therefore varies according to market conditions. For example, in oligopolistic markets of non-differentiated products, pricing is a more crucial element in the marketing mix than it is in monopolistic markets of differentiated goods and services.

However significant their influence, competitors' pricing strategies and activities form a key part of marketing intelligence. Collecting information on competitors' prices can be done formally or informally.

FOR EXAMPLE

Retail audits, often carried out by specialised research agencies, collect data on the prices of a wide range of products at the point of purchase. For instance, a confectionery manufacturer may collect information on the prices of competitive chocolate bars on display in retail outlets.

Firms of accountants price their service of the annual audit of a company on the basis of individual quotations. It is therefore difficult for one firm to monitor the prices of other accountants, as the information is not generally made available. Instead they rely on informal information-gathering methods such as talking to customers who have received quotations from other firms.

Environmental influences

Other factors in the external environment influence prices:

■ The state of the economy plays a part in most markets, with prices weakening in recessionary times and hardening as boom times return.

■ Taxes on goods and services such as Value Added Tax (VAT) form part of the price paid by the final consumer and act as a constraint on the flexibility of suppliers' pricing strategies. A

MARKETING MISTAKES

THRESHERS

A plan to use price discounts to reward a select group of suppliers with discount vouchers misfired after it was hijacked by hundreds of thousands of bargain hunters over the Internet during Christmas 2006.

Threshers, the off-licence chain, admitted that its '40 per cent off' discount scheme got completely out of hand when it was leaked onto the Internet. More than a million vouchers were downloaded and the Thresher's website crashed several times because of the huge number of customers looking for their nearest shop. Offers meant only for staff, loyal customers and specific groups of consumers were openly swapped or sold on the Internet.

Threshers sent the voucher, which entitled the bearer to 40 per cent off up to £500 of wine and champagne, as a 'thank you' to a selected group of suppliers. It also invited them to pass them on to 'friends and family'. But once one voucher was placed on a blog of the South African winery Stormhoek, it was quickly copied onto numerous other websites, blogs and chat rooms.

Threshers honoured every voucher but admitted that 'This has got way, way bigger than we thought it would. We sent it out to our suppliers and we included a bit saying, "Feel free to send it to your friends and family". We had absolutely no idea how many vouchers would be downloaded.'

Staff had to work up to four hours' overtime each to cope with demand. They struggled to stock the shelves and had to cope with phones constantly ringing with people asking if the offer was legitimate.

The deal has been compared to Hoover's ill-fated offer in 1992 of a free return flight to New York for anyone spending more than £100. The company eventually had to spend more than £20 million on flights to the US to satisfy demand.

Although Threshers admitted that the sales promotion risked slashing its profit margins it pointed out that it had been offering a three-for-two offer on wine for more than a year – equivalent to a 33 per cent discount.

© FERRUCCIC/ALAMY

Threshers underestimated the impact of their coupon-based price promotion

manufacturer may think again about a planned price rise following an increase in the rate of VAT on their products.

■ Government intervention influences prices directly and indirectly. The pricing levels in some privatised industries such as gas, electricity and telephone services are subject to direct regulatory control by watchdog agencies. Government insistence on increased competition in some markets has a more indirect, but often significant, impact on prices. For example, the enforced loosening of ties between public houses and breweries led to intensified price competition between rival brewers with surplus capacity.

■ Intermediaries in the chain between the manufacturer and the end user have varying levels of influence on prices. Some intermediaries have more power than the manufacturer to determine prices. Large retail groups such as the supermarket chains dictate prices to their suppliers. More fragmented wholesalers and retailers have only marginal influence on pricing levels.

CHECKPOINT

You have just taken over a pizza restaurant and need to price your menu. How would you go about this? Suggest some prices for menu items with your reasons.

8.5 PRICING STRATEGIES: SKIMMING AND PENETRATION

The internal and external influences discussed in the previous sections shape pricing decisions in the context of pricing strategies. Organisations can adopt two generic types of strategy:

■ *Skimming*: a higher price strategy to 'skim the cream' off the market

■ *Penetration*: a lower price strategy aimed at penetrating the market as thoroughly as possible

8.5.1 Skimming

Price skimming aims to develop a market by attracting the least price-sensitive segment of customers first, and satisfying their demand with high prices. If demand begins to fall or further growth is required, then prices are lowered to attract the next segment of customers who are attracted at slightly cheaper prices. This process can be repeated until all potential markets are satisfied, although competition may hasten the development of sales to new customer groups at lower prices.

FOR EXAMPLE

The iPod portable MP3 media player was launched in 2001 by Apple. This has been subsequently upgraded with the sixth generation being launched in 2007/8. Its ease of user interface made it an immediate success and its price has come down successively over the years. It has moved from being an elite product to a more commonplace consumer purchase. Its original skimming strategy has moved to penetration as the distinctive white headphones have become a frequent, rather than a rare sight.

Apple used skimming, then penetration pricing strategies for its iPod

© CHRIS LEWINGTON/ALAMY

Favourable factors for price skimming

Circumstances which favour price skimming strategies include:

■ Products that have unique advantages (e.g. light, portable laptops still command a premium over PCs with a higher specification). High initial prices may be needed to recover the investment in research and development, and the best time to do this may be when competition is likely to be at a minimum.

■ Mature or saturated markets that can be segmented with differentiated products or services. The travel industry is now well developed, with distinct pricing strategies for different customer segments. We have already described how airlines adopted a high price strategy for business class travellers by offering a few extra luxuries (see section 8.3.1). Rail companies have also increased their revenues by charging premium prices for inter-city and peak-hour commuter travel.

■ Suppliers with limited resources who wish to maximise revenues from the capacity they have. This might apply particularly to smaller organisations.

ENTREPRENEURIAL MARKETING

SMALL BUSINESS – SMALL PRICES?

Many small business owners are tempted to compete mainly on price. It often seems the obvious way to attract new customers, especially in the start-up stages of a new venture. Sometimes, a small business with low overheads can compete on price in the longer term, provided they do not grow to a size where central overheads are required. A garage offering a repair service from cheap premises with no administrative staff is always likely to be able to charge significantly less than a specialist dealer with an alluring showroom and office staff to support. However, many small business owners compete on price in an unsustainable way, often based primarily on the cheap labour of the owner. Unless a business has established economies not available to its competitors it is unlikely to gain long-term competitive advantage through pricing policies alone. As economies of scale are not usually available to a small business (because of its size), low prices are most likely to come from short-term cost savings: for example the owner does not expect a market wage, particularly in the start-up phase of the business, or little investment is made in product development or marketing. As other businesses are likely to react by lowering their prices, the small firm may find that the only result of price competition is to reduce the profitability of the total business segment. Under-pricing has certainly been a major factor in small business failures. Conversely, a well-considered pricing strategy based on the needs of the customer can be the foundation of success.

FOR EXAMPLE

A small company built up a reputation as a high-quality printer specialising in relatively short-run jobs such as company reports, which commanded premium prices. They maintained a high price strategy by avoiding the temptation of taking on lower margin work which would keep their presses more fully occupied but detract from the fast, flexible service which they could offer to the higher price segment of the market.

TABLE 8.1 *Potential advantages and disadvantages of skimming strategies*

ADVANTAGES	DISADVANTAGES
Fast payback of investment in new products, research and development etc.	Encourages new entrants into the market.
High profits while less competition.	May produce diseconomies of scale as volumes kept low.
Prices can be gradually reduced.	May limit sales potential
Less investment and resources required, as output limited.	
Positive image and status associated with high prices.	

Skimming strategies have a number of potential advantages and disadvantages which are summarised in Table 8.1.

8.5.2 Penetration

Pricing to achieve market penetration means keeping prices as low as possible to achieve the highest potential level of sales. This may be achieved by taking market share from competitors, or growing the total market rapidly, or a combination of both.

New products

Some new products need to develop rapidly into their marketplace to consolidate their position before competitive products arrive and to achieve economies of scale through larger production volumes. To achieve this, a low price strategy may be chosen.

FOR EXAMPLE

An electronics manufacturer designed an innovative fuel injection system for cars. Although the product had important new benefits, the company priced the product in line with existing systems on the market in order that the major car manufacturers could specify the new product into their existing production of vehicles without increasing their cost base. In this way the company was able to penetrate the market quickly, rather than wait for its product to be specified into new models as they were launched. This rapid build-up of demand overcame the problem of a reduced initial profit margin as it gave the company two important advantages: first, it achieved a high market share which protected its position when competitors caught up with its technology because its product was already designed into existing models. Second, the high production volumes created economies of scale, which eventually improved the company's profitability.

Existing products

Penetration pricing may also be used as a strategy to improve the competitive position of existing products.

FOR EXAMPLE

....

Tabloid newspapers declined in popularity in the 1980s and early 1990s. In July 1993 one of the market leaders, the *Sun,* decided to cut its cover price from 25p to 20p in an attempt to win back lost readers. The strategy had two aims: to improve circulation figures for the total market and to gain market share from the other tabloids. Sales of tabloid newspapers had fallen from a peak of 12.6 million per day in 1983 to 10.6 million by 1993. Rupert Murdoch, chair of News International, which owned the *Sun,* believed that the decline was partly in reaction to the cover price of papers, which had increased by an average of 11 per cent a year since 1983. The industry had believed hitherto that sales of newspapers were price-inelastic and regularly increased prices above the rate of inflation. However, Murdoch had watched the daily sales of the *Sun* decline from 4.3 million in 1989 to less than 3.5 million by 1993, and felt that the market had become price sensitive. The 20 per cent price decrease was designed to tempt back some of those who had stopped buying papers on a regular basis as well as take circulation from competitors, particularly its close rival, the *Daily Mirror.* The *Mirror* responded by taking its own price down from 27p to 10p for a day as a one-off promotion. Murdoch at least proved that newspaper sales are price sensitive: the *Sun* gained daily sales of 200,000 in the first week at its lower price, and the *Mirror* sold an extra 500,000 copies on its special-price day. This price sensitivity will further increase as digital news information becomes more widely available.

Favourable factors for price penetration

Circumstances which favour market penetration pricing strategies include:

- *Markets in which demand is price elastic.* There is no point in offering lower prices if demand is unaffected (which was the collective wisdom of the newspaper industry before Murdoch changed its pricing strategy).

- *Industries that offer economies of scale to the largest producers or suppliers.* The large retail chains and supermarkets look for this benefit when offering low prices because they know that they can replace lost margin by spreading their fixed costs over higher volumes of sales.

- *The launch of new products where rapid adoption and awareness is a key marketing goal.* This may apply, for example, to products expected to enjoy a market advantage for a limited period only.

FOR EXAMPLE

....

Pricing strategies on the Internet have generally followed penetration strategies for this reason. Internet Service Providers (ISPs, such as AOL, CompuServe, BT Internet, Virgin Net and NTL) needed to attract a critical mass of users as quickly as possible. At first, providers such as AOL offered unique online services via the Internet for which they could charge a monthly subscription. However, the Internet now offers far more than single providers can hope to match. Inexpensive Internet access has become the norm, as the ISPs compete for market share and take revenues instead from the telephone companies who make the connection. Market share has become so prized that providers have offered reduced-price and even free phone connections.

TABLE 8.2 *Potential advantages and disadvantages of penetration strategies*

ADVANTAGES	DISADVANTAGES
Fast sales growth.	Reduces profit in short term.
Wide product awareness.	May be difficult to put prices up.
Builds strong market position.	More investment and resources required to build high volumes.
Economies of scale through higher volumes.	
Deters new entrants into the market.	

■ *Markets dominated by a small number of major suppliers (oligopolies).* Price wars are often the trigger to the elimination of weaker suppliers with subsequent gain in market share by the survivors. *Today,* a loss-making title amongst the tabloid press, was closed down – a casualty of the newspaper price war.

The potential advantages and disadvantages of penetration pricing strategies are summarised in Table 8.2 above.

CHECKPOINT

List some recently introduced new products that have been launched using:
1. skimming pricing
2. penetration pricing.

8.6 PRICING METHODS

In this chapter we have so far considered the main internal and external influences on pricing decisions and the generic strategies that can be followed. But how are pricing decisions made in practice? There are a number of methods and techniques that can be used to help determine the optimum price to offer the customer. These are sometimes categorised as the '3 Cs':

■ Cost-based pricing

■ Competition-based pricing

■ Customer-based pricing

8.6.1 Cost-based pricing

Cost-based pricing methods take the costs to produce and supply a product or service as the starting point and add what is considered to be an adequate element of profit, or contribution to revenues, to arrive at the final price. Although cost-based pricing methods have disadvantages, most organisations do take costs into account when setting prices. Even when prices are not calculated directly from them, costs remain a significant influence.

Cost-plus pricing

Cost-plus pricing is a simple and very common way of pricing items. A standard percentage mark-up is added to the variable costs of an item. The standard amount added is calculated in such a way as to cover fixed costs and produce some profit.

The advantages of adopting a cost-plus formula include:

■ It is simple to understand and operate, providing that costs can be calculated accurately

■ It ensures that costs are at least covered, providing sales volume targets are met

However, there are several limitations to this method:

■ It does not take account of competitive pricing or what the customer is prepared to pay, hence there may be a missed profit opportunity

■ It is often difficult to allocate costs to specific products, particularly when costs vary with volume or they are shared with other products

■ It can ignore capital requirements or return on investment criteria

This method is widely used in retailing, where variable costs can be easily identified. Customer preferences and competitive activity can be taken into account by using the system flexibly.

FOR EXAMPLE

A jeans boutique has a standard pricing policy of adding a mark-up of 200 per cent to the cost of garments purchased from the manufacturer. Thus a pair of jeans invoiced at £15 from the manufacturer is sold for £45 to the consumer. The mark-up is £30, or 200 per cent of the cost of the garment to the retailer. Experience has taught this retailer that such a mark-up is needed to cover the fixed costs of running the shop, such as rent, rates and staff wages, and to provide a reasonable profit. Although the 200 per cent mark-up is the rule for normal trading, sales and special offers are used throughout the year to stimulate sales and counter competitive activities. The annual trading accounts of the shop are shown in Table 8.3.

This indicates that the standard cost-plus policy provides a benchmark to arrive at the full retail selling price. This is then adapted to market conditions by offering discounts from the full price.

TABLE 8.3 *Annual trading accounts for jeans shop*

TOTAL SALES AT FULL PRICE	£150,000
DISCOUNTS	£25,000
COST OF GARMENTS SOLD	£50,000
GROSS PROFIT	£75,000
FIXED COSTS	£50,000
PROFIT CONTRIBUTION	**£25,000**

Gross margin pricing

A variation on the cost-plus method is to use a standard gross margin rather than a mark-up as a means of arriving at the final selling price. (If you are unsure of the difference between gross margin and mark-up, review section 8.3.2.)

FOR EXAMPLE

....

Sci-Scope, a manufacturer of scientific instruments, priced its products to give an overall target of a 50 per cent gross margin on its sales. The marketing manager worked within pricing guidelines that required at least a 50 per cent gross margin after taking account of the variable costs. Thus if a selling price of £30 was required, the normal gross margin would be at least £15, or 50 per cent of the selling price, leaving £15 to cover the costs of parts and labour.

   This system was used flexibly, with the gross margin calculation being used to provide a baseline from which to assess other pricing options.

Break-even analysis

One of the problems in the cost-plus methods we have described above is that prices do not reflect changes in the volume of items sold. A break-even analysis helps to add this further dimension because it is a method of exploring the relationship between cost, price and volume.

   The first step is an analysis of fixed and variable costs.

FOR EXAMPLE

....

Sci-Scope are launching a new optical instrument. Fixed costs of £500,000 per annum are apportioned to this new product. Variable costs are £25 per unit, or £25,000 per thousand units. From this information, the total costs per unit at various volumes can be calculated:

1 If 10,000 units are produced, the costs equal:

Fixed costs	£500,000
Variable costs	£250,000
Total costs	£750,000
Total costs per unit	£75

2 If 20,000 units are produced, the costs equal:

Fixed costs	£500,000
Variable costs	£500,000
Total costs	£1,000,000
Total costs per unit	£50

This is illustrated graphically in Figure 8.5.

Point X = total costs to produce 10,000 units
Point Y = total costs to produce 20,000 units

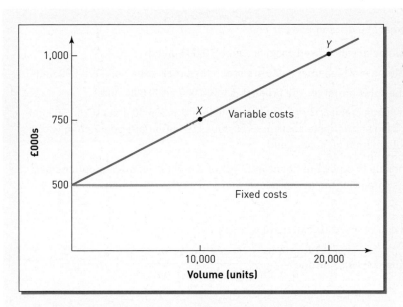

FIGURE 8.5

Fixed and variable costs for Sci-Scope new product

The next step in a break-even analysis is to calculate the sales revenue obtained from certain prices at varying sales levels.

FOR EXAMPLE

Sci-Scope wish to consider the price/volume relationship at a price of £50 per unit. This indicates that at 20,000 units, revenues equal the total costs of £1,000,000 and that at 30,000 units sales reach £1,500,000 – the targeted revenue for the product. A sales revenue line can now be added to the graph to show the break-even point, and levels of profitability at various volumes (see Figure 8.6).

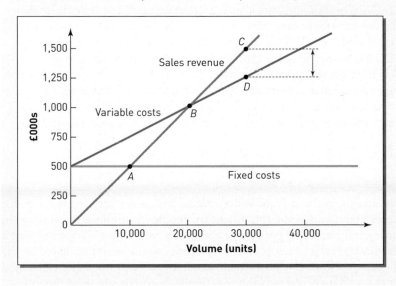

FIGURE 8.6

Break-even analysis for Sci-Scope new product

Figure 8.6 illustrates that at a price of £50 per unit:

■ Point *A* is the sales volume at which fixed costs are met (10,000 units)

■ Point *B* is the sales volume at which total costs are met – the break-even point (20,000 units)

■ Point *C* represented the sales target for the product (£1,500,000 or 30,000 units)

■ The distance between points *C* and *D* represent the profitability at 30,000 units (£250,000 net profit after deducting fixed and variable costs or £750,000 gross profit after deducting variable costs only, a gross profit margin of 50 per cent)

Sci-Scope used this technique to study the financial effect of a number of pricing options before deciding on their pricing strategy for the new product.

The following formula can be used to calculate a break-even point:

$$\text{Break-even volume} = \frac{\text{Fixed costs}}{\text{Gross margin per unit}}$$

Marginal costing

The break-even analysis described above ensures that both fixed and variable costs are covered by the price of a product. In some circumstances, it may be necessary to ignore fixed costs and price products on their variable costs only. A contribution can be made towards profits, providing there is a margin between the selling price and the variable costs and assuming fixed costs are covered by other sales.

FOR EXAMPLE

Sci-Scope's sales of its new optical instrument achieved their target of 30,000 units ahead of schedule through its normal distribution channels. Noting the success of the new product, a major distributor asked Sci-Scope to produce a very similar product for them, but under their own brand name. As the distributor had to make their own profit margin on the product, they asked for a maximum price of £35, compared to Sci-Scope's normal selling price of £50, in return for large orders. A selling price of £35 left Sci-Scope with a gross margin of £10 on their variable costs, or 28.6 per cent – well below their target margin of 50 per cent.

However, the marketing and finance managers advised the company to accept the deal on the basis of marginal costing. The fixed costs were already covered by normal sales of the product and this contract would generate a contribution to profits of £10 per unit, which they would forgo if they did not take the business.

Time and materials

In the public sector and increasingly in the private sector, organisations are offering services for which the most important cost ingredient is the time spent by people in fulfilling the service. In the education and health care services up to 80 per cent of total costs can be the salaries and wages of staff. The pricing of professional services such as solicitors and accountants is dominated by the costs of the time of staff allocated to jobs. In these circumstances, pricing is normally calculated by charging hourly rates for the staff involved plus the cost of any materials spent on the job.

DIRECT RESPONSE, SEPTEMBER, 2006, WWW.PRICINGINPROPORTION.CO.UK, MARKETING DIRECT, OCTOBER 2006.

FOR EXAMPLE

Garages normally price car repairs on the basis of time spent on the work multiplied by an hourly rate plus the cost of any parts used. The hourly rate is calculated to cover not just the costs of the mechanic but also to make a contribution to the fixed costs and profits of the garage. Many other services, from physiotherapy to plumbing, are charged on the same basis.

FOR EXAMPLE

In August 2006, the Royal Mail changed the way that mail is priced in the UK to reflect their costs more accurately. They introduced a new pricing system called Pricing in Proportion (PiP). Previously, postage prices were based upon the weight of the item. The heavier the item, the higher the price. Pricing in Proportion takes into consideration the physical size and thickness of the item as well as the weight.

Royal Mail changed their pricing strategy because they were losing money on larger envelopes and items. Large and irregular shaped packages take up more space in postbags and vans and cost more to sort, handle and deliver. This meant that most light but bulky items were priced below cost, whereas smaller, heavier items were generally overpriced.

Many customers will be affected, but Royal Mail estimated that over 80 per cent of mail would not change in price. To help companies deal with the change, Royal Mail set up a new website (www.pricinginproportion.co.uk) and its first-ever interactive digital TV site (iDTV) to help customers understand the new structure. The interactive discussions incorporate illustrations and movement in order to give practical advice. The website details which services are affected and which are not.

This pricing strategy change has implications for businesses that rely on direct marketing. For example, charities that regularly send out free pens with mailings are testing flattened versions. Cancer Research UK has tested alternative formats of their mailings but will reduce either mail sizes or volumes to keep their costs the same. The Direct Marketing Association has redesigned its brochures for its annual events to fit a C5 envelope. One home shopping firm considered getting rid of their catalogues in favour of a sole web strategy but found that customers preferred to browse through a book and then order online. Toyota has seen a benefit from PiP, with brochure fulfilment prices falling as most consumers request information on more than one model, allowing them to take advantage of PiP's heavier weight limits. Lexus has reconfigured its brochures to get similar benefits.

8.6.2 *Customer-based pricing*

Consumers rarely judge the price of a product by attempting to work out what it may have cost to make. We tend to assess prices on the basis of what products are worth to us. We have a perception of the value to us of the benefits of a product, and we compare its actual price to this perceived value.

Customer-based pricing uses this notion of perceived value as the starting point and attempts to set prices on the basis of what the market is prepared to pay. This may be more influenced by either the circumstances under which the product is sold, or the particular environment in which it is offered, rather than a generalised idea of the value of the product itself.

Product shortages or restrictions on supply may create circumstances in which demand exceeds supply, if only on a temporary basis, and suppliers increase prices to a level at which available stock can be sold.

FOR EXAMPLE

The Morgan Motor Company produce their specialised cars at a rate well below market demand. The length of time between placing an order for one of their new, hand-built cars and taking delivery extends at times to several years. This tempts some buyers to sell their newly delivered cars at a quick profit to someone lower down the waiting list who is prepared to pay more for an earlier delivery. The family-owned Morgan company was criticised by John Harvey-Jones in one of his *Troubleshooter* television programmes for not raising its prices to reflect the perceived value of customers rather than their own costs, nor automating its production to meet the higher levels of demand. But the company prefers its traditional methods to more commercial practices.

In other situations, the environment in which a product is sold add to, or detract from, its perceived value.

FOR EXAMPLE

The price of a cup of tea varies considerably. A tea bag in a plastic cup from a vending machine may cost 50p. The same product sold in a railway station café may be priced at 90p or £1.20 if it is purchased from the buffet car on the train. In a family teashop, a pot of tea normally costs over £1. In an upmarket restaurant, the same product could be priced well over £2. Why the differences? Variables other than price establish perceived value differences to the consumer. These may be product quality perceptions (e.g. the difference between a tea bag in a plastic cup and a silver teapot with china crockery), or they may be related to the environment in which the tea is consumed (standing on a railway platform or sitting comfortably in a restaurant).

© DAVID MUSCROFT/ALAMY

The price of a cup of tea is more dependent on where it is poured than how it tastes

Customer-based pricing relies on finding out how much customers are prepared to pay for the product or service on offer. Although market research can help to understand the value in a customer's mind of various products, in practice experimentation is often used to align prices with what customers are prepared to pay.

Psychological pricing

Psychological factors are often used in advertising prices to customers. These include:

- *Price-break points*: Some prices points form important psychological barriers which suppliers try not to break. £9.99 or £9.95 is a much more common price than £10, or £10.05. One company has moved away from this trend. ASDA introduced a claim of every day low pricing (EDLP), with prices such as £1.34 to emphasise that they are passing on all possible savings to the customer without regard for psychological pricing points.

- *Discounts*: Many customers place great importance on receiving a discount on the original price of a product. We see this in many sale offerings where the emphasis is on the amount off rather than the actual price. This is a technique favoured by kitchen companies such as Magnet and MFI. Some suppliers pitch their initial pricing high in the knowledge that they can enhance the perceived value of their offer by bringing prices down at a later date. This is particularly common in business to business (B2B) negotiations.

- *Loss-leaders*: Pricing can be used as a promotional tool to gain customers by offering them low prices for one product on which little or no profit is gained in the hope that they will buy other products. For example, direct mail companies use this technique in offering 'continuity programmes' of reference publications and other products in which the first instalment is priced at a fraction of the price of subsequent instalments. Retailers use the same ploy to tempt customers into their premises.

8.6.3 Competition-based pricing

Costs may fix the minimum price for a product, and customer demand may reflect the maximum price that can be charged, but competitive pricing acts as a third influence, which often sets prices somewhere between these two extremes.

Direct competition between a limited number of suppliers often results in the most aggressive use of pricing as a marketing tool. We have already described two industries in which the leading suppliers competed directly on price: the tabloid newspapers who tried to win over customers by reducing their cover prices, and the major PC manufacturers attempting to cope with a downturn in the telecommunications market. In both cases a small number of major suppliers tried to gain a larger share of a market by reducing their prices.

Price competition may also be indirect. Customers may select among products which are not the same, but which offer similar benefits.

FOR EXAMPLE
....

Cinemas used to compete directly with similar establishments in the same town. Except for larger towns and cities, it is now rare for more than one cinema to exist within a convenient geographic area. Far from representing a cosy local monopoly, cinemas fight for their customers with a host of other forms of entertainment and price is a major determinant of demand. Video hire or streaming is a form of direct competition which costs less than cinemas, but is less immediate in offering the latest films. Theatres tend to be more expensive, but offer live entertainment. There are also a whole host of alternative ways of spending money on leisure and entertainment from eating out to concerts. In selecting their choice of entertainment, customers consider the value to be gained from the various options, even though they are in some respects dissimilar.

FOR EXAMPLE

In response to the Pricing in Proportion initiative by the Royal Mail a number of different carriers have responded with their own offerings. DHL claim to typically reduce costs by between 5 and 20 per cent. UK Mail claim have 'Large Letter' prices at least 10 per cent cheaper than the Royal Mail Standard Tariff.

FOR EXAMPLE

Mobile phone companies compete by offering different deals to encourage consumers to use their network. They design pricing packages to appeal to different consumer segments, for instance, some deals favour young consumers who text a lot, whilst others favour older consumers who may talk more.

CHECKPOINT

Investigate the different prices charged in your local area for essentially the same product (e.g. a pair of jeans, a pizza, a cup of tea, or a fizzy drink). What is the range of prices and what justifications can you give for this?

8.7 SUMMARY

- Pricing is a key ingredient in the marketing mix of private and public sector organisations and one that has a direct financial effect.
- The Internet has increased the potential to lower prices through improved communications between willing buyers and sellers. Consumers can benefit through the development of individual bargaining (e.g. through auctions), and organisations through virtual marketplaces and reverse auctions.
- Prices are derived from a mixture of internal and external influences.

■ Internal influences include:
   — Targeting, positioning and marketing mix strategies
   — The cost base of fixed and variable costs
   — The financial objectives of the organisation
■ External influences include:
   — Customers' perceptions of the value of a product and elasticity of demand
   — The competitiveness of the marketplace (defined by economists as perfect, monopolistic and oligopolistic competition, and pure monopoly)
   — Environmental factors, such as the economy, taxes, government intervention and the power of intermediaries
■ The two generic pricing strategies are:
   — *Skimming,* which has the possible advantages of fast payback, high profits, possibility of price reductions, less investment and an upmarket image; and the disadvantages of encouraging new entrants, diseconomies of scale, and limitations on sales volume potential
   — *Penetration,* which has the possible advantages of fast sales growth, wide product awareness, strong market position, economies of scale, deterring new entrants; and the disadvantages of reduced profits, difficulty in increasing prices, and more investment required
■ Pricing methods include:
   — Cost-based pricing using break-even analysis
   — Competition-based pricing
   — Customer-based pricing

8.8 ACTIVITIES

CASE STUDY

MAURITIAN SCUBA DIVING

Richard Gill has made a decision to leave his lucrative job as a successful marketing consultant and return to Mauritius to follow a life-long ambition of running a scuba diving centre in one of the most exclusive hotels on the island. His old school friend Michel Frederick operates a number of diving schools on the island and has offered Richard an opportunity to invest in a new centre.

Even in exotic locations such as Mauritius, pricing decisions are crucial

The annual costs of renting premises from the hotel, including pool hire, is £10,000; employing two dive leaders costs £20,000 each, and a boat handler £10,000. Additional salaries of £15,000 will be required to hire temporary staff to cover holidays and sick leave. Richard will pay himself a basic salary of £8,000 per annum and pay Michel Frederick a royalty payment of 15 per cent of the annual revenue and 5 per cent of the annual profits to the hotel. Richard will retain any profits.

The total costs for purchasing capital equipment to run the diving school are shown in Table 8.4.

The average yearly fuel cost to run the compressor and boat is estimated to be £2,000.

Additional maintenance costs for servicing equipment are estimated at £6,000 annually.

For safety reasons there can only be a maximum of two dives per day. Richard has also been advised to write off approximately 20 days a year for potential bad weather. The total cost per dive is relatively constant but the number of divers can vary significantly from zero to well over the maximum capacity of the boat (10 divers). As the centre is new, there is no way of estimating average numbers for any one dive.

According to research undertaken by Michel, there are potentially four types of customers, as shown in Table 8.5.

QUESTIONS

1 Identify the cost elements of the proposed dive business and classify them according to their different cost categories.

TABLE 8.4 *Capital equipment cost for Mauritian scuba diving*

EQUIPMENT	PURCHASE COSTS	DEPRECIATION (yearly)
COMPRESSOR TO FILL TANKS WITH AIR (replace at five-year intervals)	£2,000	£500
DIVING EQUIPMENT (replace at five-year intervals)	£18,000	£3,000
BOAT (replace at ten-year intervals)	£20,000	£2,000

TABLE 8.5 *Customer types for Mauritian scuba diving*

CUSTOMER TYPE	PERCENTAGE OF DIVERS	NEEDS
TYPE I – *COMPLETE NOVICES*	50	Require extensive pool training, fitness assessment and supervision on open water dives in the sea
TYPE II – *RECENTLY QUALIFIED DIVERS*	30	Require significant supervision
TYPE III – *QUALIFIED DIVERS*	15	Wish to increase their experience by taking further professional course at the school
TYPE IV – *QUALIFIED AND HIGHLY EXPERIENCED DIVERS*	5	Want to dive by themselves with a good guide

CHARTERED INSTITUTE OF MARKETIN.G.

2 Making any necessary assumptions, calculate how much a dive is likely to cost Richard regardless of whether or not he has any potential divers.

3 As Richard is likely to get different customer types at different times in different numbers, first identify the ways in which he might manipulate the marketing mix to allow for differential pricing. Then evaluate the likely impact that different prices would have on the value perceptions of different divers who are technically paying for the same service.

4 Prior to setting an optimal price for each segment, Richard would like to consider the potential competition threat for the business. Advise him on how he should define the competitive environment and the factors to be considered in developing a competitor audit.

DEVELOPING A MARKETING PLAN

PRICING STRATEGY

Define your pricing strategy taking into account the appropriate internal and external influences. Will you use a skimming or penetration strategy?

How will you price your product(s)? What methods will you use? What will be your recommended prices? What is your break-even point?

8.9 FURTHER READING AND REFERENCES

Pricing strategy

Nagle, T. and Holden, R. (2001), *The Strategy and Tactics of Pricing*, 3rd edition (Prentice Hall).

Internet pricing

Chaffey, D. (2006), *Internet Marketing: Strategy, Implementation and Practice* (Pearson Education).
Siegel, C.F. (2006), *Internet Marketing: Foundations and Applications* (Houghton Mifflin).

Chapter **9**

PROMOTIONS I: MARKETING COMMUNICATIONS

LEARNING OBJECTIVES

By the end of this chapter the reader will be able to:

- Evaluate the issues involved in how messages are communicated
- Understand the stages of the marketing communications process
- Assess the elements of the promotional marketing mix in order to select the appropriate mix
- Understand the impact of the Internet on marketing communications
- Appreciate the role of personal selling as a marketing tool and the variety of selling situations
- Use the stages of conducting a face-to-face sales meeting as the basis for personal presentations
- Evaluate components of field marketing such as exhibitions, trade fairs and experiential marketing

INTRODUCTION

Marketing communications – the promotional element of the marketing mix – need to be understood first as a general model of how we send and receive messages. An understanding of the processes of how we communicate, and the issues associated with this, underpins all successful marketing messages. There are many types of marketing communications: some are delivered personally (e.g. direct selling), and some are delivered impersonally via various forms of media (e.g. the Internet or television). This chapter looks at 'personal promotions' that require direct interface between sellers and buyers, including direct selling, exhibitions and trade fairs, and experiential marketing. These activities are sometimes given the umbrella title of 'field marketing'. A second chapter on marketing communications (Chapter 10) considers the non-personal aspects of marketing communications, such as advertising, sales promotion, public relations and direct marketing.

CASE STUDY

....

'INSURING' THE MESSAGE

For once Ali Montana sat down in front of his television specifically to watch the ads. Normally he would 'zap' the commercial breaks with his remote control, but tonight was different. His company, one of the largest sellers of insurance and pensions in Europe, was screening its first UK TV advertisement for several years. As sales director, Montana had a particular interest in watching this opening instalment of a campaign that would include £10 million of media advertising, supported by mailings of special offers, new-look leaflets, press releases and sponsorship deals. All would feature a consistent theme, as market research had revealed confused and contradictory consumer perceptions of the company and its products.

Positive marketing communications were much needed after a run of bad publicity for both Montana's company and the insurance industry as a whole. Accusations of sharp practice by insurance salespeople had culminated in allegations that the regulatory standards had been breached consistently in the selling of personal pensions to people transferring from occupational pensions. The decision to set up a single personal investment authority to regulate the whole industry had helped overcome some of the problems and Montana believed that the UK government's stakeholder pension scheme had restored some confidence. But selling insurance was hard enough without adverse publicity, and a general suspicion of the insurance and pensions industry still persisted. Customers now received sales approaches from their banks and building societies to add to their weariness of the hard sell from conventional insurance companies. Direct selling of policies by telephone and over the Internet was also threatening the tradition role of the salesperson offering face-to-face information on pensions and insurance.

Montana had organised a conference to launch the new campaign to his salesforce. He was particularly concerned to ensure his salespeople reinforced, rather than undermined, the themes of the campaign. This was especially true after the expressions of public unease over standards in the insurance industry. The size of the company made this a daunting task: over £10 billion funds under management, over one million customers and a 3,000-strong direct sales force. Each one of those salespeople had their own way of communicating with clients; that could mean very fragmented messages about the company. The conference would attempt to unify their overall communications, without stifling individual styles. As well as suggesting answers to some of the more common objections arising from the bad publicity, Montana would be insisting on a more consultative sales approach by his salesforce.

Although he did not want his salespeople to learn scripted presentations, he had decided to give his version of a sales presentation of one of their products. He chose their new 'Personal Property Protection Policy' insurance scheme to demonstrate the new corporate image. The policy was designed to provide insurance for the loss of any personal possessions inside or outside of the home, and included a scheme for protecting credit cards, chequebooks and mobile phones against false use after loss. A special feature was the databank of customer's possessions, credit- and bank-card numbers, passport and other important details so that the relevant authorities could be notified immediately from one central point in the event of loss. In his presentation, Montana would try to present the benefits of the product in a way that would generate attention, interest and desire for the policy so that a prospective customer would action his or her purchase willingly – without being pushed.

'I wish I could reach millions of homes with a consistent communication like that,' Montana thought as he watched the advert, 'but I have 3,000 different voices speaking to over one million customers and delivering the appropriate message every time is not going to be easy.'

▶

QUESTIONS

1 Consider the marketing communications process in the insurance market. How do prospective customers receive information and other messages about the policies available? Why is Montana so concerned about developing a consistent message? *See sections 9.1 and 9.2.*

2 Montana's company is using several different types of promotional methods in its campaign. What are these? What will be the different objectives of each type? *See section 9.3.*

3 The image and professionalism of selling are subject to widespread concern in this marketplace. How would you advise Montana on developing a more professional approach amongst his own salesforce? *See section 4.4*

4 How would you structure the sales presentation on the Personal Property Protection Policy that Montana will make? Explain what you consider to be the basis of a sales presentation for this product to a prospective customer. *See section 4.5*

9.1 COMMUNICATION OVERLOAD

For most of our waking hours, we are subject to an almost constant bombardment of marketing communications.

FOR EXAMPLE

As you sit down to breakfast, your attention is drawn briefly to the free offers and nutritional information on the packets of cereal brands before you on the table. In the background, a radio jingle repeats the sponsor's message before an announcer reminds you of forthcoming programmes. You open the newspaper, scanning reports of the election campaigns of the political parties, before turning to the sports news and Tiger Woods' latest golfing victory. Checking texts on your mobile, you are irritated by a company that has spammed you with an unsolicited offer. You make a note in your diary that boasts the name of a pharmaceutical company on the front cover, writing with a pen embossed with the sponsor's name. As you prepare to go out, even the label on your coat discreetly reminds you of its maker. You leave the daily delivery of mail shots on the floor, to be opened or thrown away later.

Your journey takes you past rows of shop windows inducing you to buy the merchandise inside, and even the refuse bins in the street carry notices reminding you of the activities of the local council. You walk into the station past poster hoardings recommending that you eat fruit and vegetables as part of a government health initiative. Avoiding the attention of a salesperson offering you a leaflet from a mobile exhibition stand, you are advised on the cheapest train ticket for your journey by a station assistant whilst another employee of the rail company explains changes to departure times over the public address system. As you wait for your train, a friend chats to you about how long they have waited to see the consultant at the local hospital, the problems with their new car, and a film that they recommend you see. Your day has hardly begun and already you have been inundated with a profusion of marketing communications.

CHECKPOINT

There are at least sixteen different types of promotional activities in this everyday example. Can you list and categorise them? (See Figure 9.4 on page 292.)

We cannot escape this daily bombardment. Promotions have infiltrated every aspect of our lives. Hospitality tents and sponsors' logos have invaded even the most traditional of sporting events. Public toilets are now seen as appropriate places in which to advertise, whilst telephone and Internet selling penetrates the privacy of home life. Branded products are not only promoted overtly but are seen more subtly as props in films and television programmes as a result of product placement.

This promotional saturation has led to two conflicting concerns:

- *Social concern* that advertising is ruining the environment whilst it brainwashes us into buying what we do not need and cannot afford. The Advertising Standards Authority, the regulatory body in the UK, does have powers to prevent misleading or unfair advertising but they cannot limit its extent.

- *Marketing concern* that the competition for consumers' attention has become so intense that extreme measures are required in order to be noticed. One study indicated that a typical consumer was exposed to 550 advertisements in one day and yet paid attention to less than 1 per cent of them. Some advertisers are using more sensational advertising to get their message heard.

FOR EXAMPLE

Benetton, the retailer of colourful fashion clothes, achieved some notoriety and considerable publicity for their series of controversial posters depicting graphic scenes such as a newborn baby, oiled seabirds, a man dying of Aids and the horses shown on the right. All are aimed to shock to gain attention in a busy marketplace.

In an over-communicated world, shocking images can be used to gain attention

FOR EXAMPLE

Entrepreneurs such as Richard Branson and Anita Roddick who have a natural flair for publicity have become even greater assets to their companies as the competition for air space has intensified. Some companies still overdo it; for example, the Advertising Standards Authority upheld complaints against a poster campaign for International Distillers and Vintner's Cockspur Golden Rum. The headline ran: 'She can take my jeans, she can take all the duvet, but she can't take my Cockspur.' The complaint was on the grounds that it emphasised the strength of the drink in the deliberately ambiguous final clause.

Marketing communications have become such an integral part of everyday life in our society that they are often inseparable from other types of communication – partly because they work in a similar way.

9.2 MARKETING COMMUNICATIONS: THE PROCESS AND OBJECTIVES

9.2.1 A communications model

Marketing communications flow from an organisation to its customers, potential customers and other groups who may influence its success. They involve many types of communications: some deliberate (e.g. advertising), others unplanned (e.g. personal recommendations). The communications may be supportive (e.g. personal selling) or critical (e.g. adverse press comments). In total, these communications form an overall impression, or image, which determines how people think about an organisation and how they may act in relation to its products.

Whatever their origin and effects, marketing communications work like any other forms of communication: they are concerned with *who said what, in which way, to whom, and with what effect.*

This process can be represented as a model with a number of components, as illustrated in Figure 9.1. This shows how any message might be transmitted – whether it is a message in a bottle from a shipwrecked sailor, a mail shot from a charity or a sales presentation by a manufacturer.

■ The *Sender* ('who'): The person or organisation sending the message:

— A shipwrecked sailor

— A national charity

— A manufacturer of office equipment

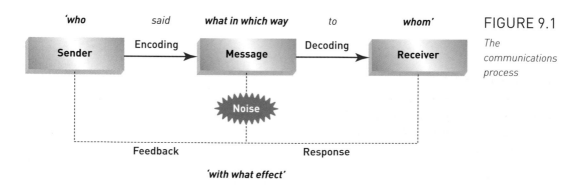

FIGURE 9.1

The communications process

■ *Encoding* is the process of putting abstract ideas into a form that can be understood by others – the process of putting thoughts into words or pictures:
  — The shipwrecked sailor writes a message on a piece of paper asking for help
  — An agency working for the national charity puts together a mail shot asking for donations to a specific cause
  — A sales representative of the office equipment company prepares a presentation to a prospective customer

■ The *message* ('what'): The written or spoken words, pictures and other symbols that are actually transmitted:
  — The sailor keeps it simple and writes 'Help!' with an indicator of his position
  — The charity uses its well-known name to authenticate the written message that is reinforced with photographs of those in need
  — The salesperson gives a verbal presentation supported by visual aids and a demonstration of the product itself

■ The *media* ('in which way') – the channels of communication that are used to take the message from the sender to the receiver:
  — The sailor uses the traditional bottle thrown in the sea
  — The charity employs direct mail – a letter and leaflet sent through the post
  — The salesperson delivers the message in person and leaves a written report and quotation to reinforce the verbal message

■ *Decoding* is the process by which the receiver interprets the message encoded by the sender:
  — Someone spots the bottle, takes out the paper and reads it
  — The direct mail shot is opened, the name of the charity recognised and the letter read
  — The presentation is watched by committee members who also consider the written report and quotation

■ The *Receiver* (to whom): The person or group of people who receive the message:
  — A passer-by who finds the bottle
  — A supporter who is on the charity's mailing list
  — The committee with responsibility for a particular office equipment purchase

■ *Response* represents the attitudes and actions of the receiver in answer to the message:
  — The passer-by cannot decipher the message in the bottle and throws it back in the sea
  — The charity supporter is sympathetic and makes a mental note to make a donation
  — The committee defers their decision because they find they have spent their allocated budget for the year

■ *Feedback* is that part of the response which is received back by the sender of the message:
  — The sailor waits in vain for a response to his message in a bottle
  — The charity receives a returned coupon and donation from the supporter
  — The salesperson hears that the committee has postponed making a purchase until next year

■ '*Noise*' can interfere with the message that is being sent, and distort or block out the original communication:

— Water leaked into the bottle and made the message illegible

— The supporter received many requests for donations from a variety of charities and ignored all but a few of their requests

— The sales presentation was interrupted by an urgent phone call to one of the audience, whilst other committee members were distracted by their own preoccupations

9.2.2 *The objectives of marketing communications*

Communication processes aim to establish a common understanding between the sender and receiver. The term 'communication' means to make ideas 'common'. Information is transferred between the parties with the objective of establishing a 'commonality of thought' between them. Some communications take this a stage further by trying to establish not only understanding but also response from the receiver: the sailor wanted not just an awareness of his predicament but some action to save him. Similarly, marketing communications provide a stimulus aimed at inducing a desired response. In the examples above, the charity's objective was to obtain donations and the salesperson was seeking an order.

Not all communications can go this far. Although the ultimate objective of a marketing communications process is to induce a purchase (or its equivalent, such as a donation), some advertising, or sales calls, have more limited initial objectives. It may take several types of communication to achieve a sale. In our example, the charity may have used marketing communications in the form of information to the press to create a favourable reception for the mail shot by heightening public awareness of the need for their work. The salesperson had to make the appointment for the sales presentation by letters, phone calls and other communications. Even impulse purchases, such as buying a bar of chocolate at the checkout point of a supermarket, are preconditioned by advertising, which creates recognition of a brand.

Marketing communications have a wide range of objectives.

■ In *consumer* markets, the objectives of marketing communications may be to:

— Introduce a new product (such as the launch of a new brand of cereal or the opening a new retail outlet)

— Remind customers of the product's existence (by in-store displays for products or street signage for shops, for example)

— Encourage repeat purchases (by offering points towards gifts and other 'loyalty' promotions)

— Give information about special offers (such as three for the price of two or free credit deals)

— Correct misunderstandings and problems (explaining the withdrawal of products and actions taken to replace defective goods, for example)

— Improve a company or product image (by corporate or brand name advertising)

— Educate customers (for example 'social' advertising about drinking and driving or healthy eating)

— Give information and advice (as given by shop assistants or product leaflets)

■ In *organisational* markets, the objectives of marketing communications may be to:
— Obtain the name of the decision-maker (often by 'cold' canvassing)
— Make an appointment with the decision-maker (by personalised letters, email and other approaches)
— Arrange a sales presentation (usually through telephone calls or personal visits)
— Provide follow-up information and advice (for example a detailed quotation or after-sales service)

9.2.3 Communication stages

The choice of tasks for marketing communications depends on the stage the customer has reached in their decision-making process towards a purchase. In some cases, customers have made up their minds about what they want and only need further details from a sales assistant to complete the purchase. In other circumstances, the consumer is not even aware of the existence of a particular product, let alone of their need for it, until they see an advertisement which arouses their interest.

In Chapter 4, section 4.3.2, Models of decision processes, we listed the five stages of a consumer buying process as:

■ Need recognition

■ Information search

■ Evaluation of alternatives

■ Purchase choice

■ Post-purchase experience

During this process of making buying decisions, customers adopt various attitudes, or are in various states of mind, in relation to products on offer. It is the job of marketing communications to influence these attitudes or states of mind so that the customer completes the process in favour of a particular product. As this state of mind changes through the buying stages, so the nature and objectives of marketing communications change to match.

The AIDA model

Various models of the stages of the communications process have been advanced to illustrate these changing objectives as the consumer progresses from a position of unawareness of a product to one of willingness to purchase it. The simplest of these is the AIDA model, in which marketing communications seek:

■ First to gain **Attention** (an awareness of the benefits of a product)

■ Second to create **Interest** (by an understanding of those benefits in relation to a personal need)

■ Third to arouse **Desire** (when the benefits are wanted to fulfil a need)

■ And finally to obtain **Action** (by arranging for the customer to acquire the product)

The model does serve to illustrate the objectives of the various stages in the communications process, along with some possible barriers to effective communications, as shown in Figure 9.2.

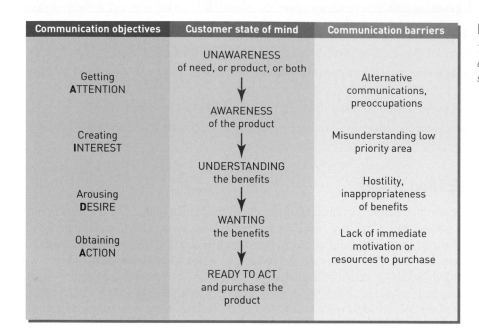

FIGURE 9.2

The AIDA model of communication stages

The AIDA model can be illustrated by the three examples we have already used:

- The message in the bottle gained attention from someone who was unaware of the sailor's need. Although this led to interest, which we know because the bottle was opened, the communication process did not go any further as there was lack of common understanding between sender and receiver.

- The charity mail shot obtained attention when it arrived, and created interest when it was read, by developing awareness of a problem and an understanding of how it could be tackled. This induced a desire to help which was finally translated into the action of making a donation. A number of obstacles were overcome in this process, including indifference to the cause and inertia to do anything even when the benefits of acting had been accepted.

- The office equipment salesperson's communication process stalled at the last stage of translating desire into action. Although the communications convinced the committee of the need and the desirability of the benefits on offer, they could not overcome the lack of resources to make the sale at that time.

Alternatives to AIDA

More elaborate models have been suggested to describe how marketing communications work. These include the five-step adoption model of *awareness*, *interest*, *evaluation*, *trial* and *adoption* used particularly in new product marketing. The common theme is that marketing communications need to be staged to match the progression of the buyer through his or her decision-making process. These are 'hierarchy of effects' models that assume that the buyer moves sequentially through the stages identified. They have an obvious weakness: low-involvement products such as chocolate or chewing gum may be bought on impulse that collapses these stages into one decisive action. They also focus on the trial or initial purchase of a product, whilst most markets survive on repeat purchases encouraged by marketing communications.

AIDA is also described as the 'strong theory' of marketing communications as it assumes that the power of promotions is always sufficient to convert non-buyers into buyers. An alternative

FIGURE 9.3

The ATR model of communication stages

model that seeks to address this issue is the Awareness-Trial-Reinforcement (ATR) model. This represents the 'weak theory' of promotions in that it assumes that marketing communications are considerably less powerful and should aim to:

■ First, gain **A**wareness of the benefits of a product

■ Second, encourage **T**rial (by nudging the customer towards a first purchase)

■ And finally provide **R**einforcement (by giving reassurance after the first purchase)

This model suggests that most marketing communications are intended to keep consumers doing what they are already doing by providing reassurance and reinforcement. This is certainly true for many low-involvement categories such as fast-moving consumer goods (FMCG).

9.2.4 *The flow of marketing communications*

So far, the communications models presented have assumed direct contact between the sender, or source, of the marketing communication and the intended receiver, or audience. In practice, the process is more complicated as intermediaries often interpret marketing messages for others. The influence of 'opinion leaders' whose views we respect, and 'word-of-mouth' communications that we believe to be impartial, are particularly important.

■ *Opinion leaders* and their effects were recorded by researchers who carried out a famous study during the 1940 presidential elections in the USA that investigated the influence of the mass media on voting intentions. They discovered that messages about the candidates did not always travel directly from the media to the voter but often went via an intermediary or 'opinion leader' who filtered and interpreted messages and influenced others for or against the candidates. Although the existence of opinion leaders has been confirmed by other research, they have proven very difficult to identify as a group that can itself be targeted by marketing communications.

Opinion leaders are those that others turn to for opinion and advice. They owe their influence to:

— *Who they are*: They may personify certain values which are looked up to by others (e.g. social and family values)

— *What they know*: They may have knowledge in certain areas, which is highly regarded by others who see it as more impartial than other expert advice

— *Who they know*: They may need extensive personal networks to obtain information and to be influential they need to be accessible to lots of people

■ The influence of word-of-mouth communications from family members, friends and neighbours stems from their assumed impartiality. Our natural suspicion of anything we are told when we believe there is an ulterior motive is an important barrier for all marketing communications to overcome. We are naturally resistant to accepting information that we believe to be part of a selling process. Independent, but often amateur, advice from acquaintances is more trusted than expert recommendations from those in the business. One study even found that if subjects believed they were 'merely overhearing' a message, they were more likely to be influenced by it, as the senders could not be suspected of ulterior motives.

FOR EXAMPLE

Some agencies now employ people to go around talking about products to create a pseudo word-of-mouth effect. So students might be employed to talk about a new lager whilst socialising in public places to encourage young people to trial the product.

These two factors – the influence of opinion leaders and the perceived impartiality of word-of-mouth recommendations – help to create a *diffusion* of marketing messages as communications are passed on from one person to the next, rather than a direct flow from the sender to the intended audience.

FOR EXAMPLE

A new bar opens in town amid a fanfare of publicity in the press and special offers to entice the first customers through the doors. Those that try the bar like the atmosphere and tell their friends, who also made a visit and pass on favourable comments to other acquaintances. It becomes known that some of the minor celebrities of the town are seen there, which further improves the bar's popularity – almost to the status of a cult. Even those who are not in the habit of drinking in such bars feel obliged to make a visit to find out what they were missing.

This *diffusion process* has been used to explain how new products become accepted. A small percentage of people are more likely to try innovative products. These so-called 'early adopters' are likely to be opinion leaders and therefore a prime target for marketing communications

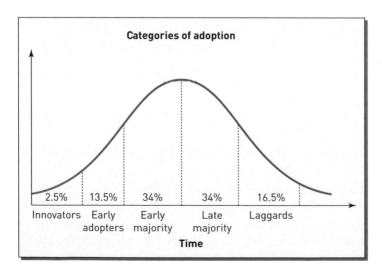

FIGURE 9.4

The stages of adoption of a new product

aimed at introducing new products and ideas. Early adopters are likely to be young, socially mobile and of high education and income. They influence the 'early majority' of other users, who adopt the product before the 'late majority', together making up about two-thirds of all final users. The final category of 'laggards' then adopts the product.

9.3 THE COMMUNICATIONS MIX

9.3.1 Controllable and uncontrollable communications

Organisations communicate with their publics and consumers through many forms of marketing communications. Some they control directly themselves; others are less controllable. Some communications are delivered personally by representatives of an organisation, or other people who talk about it; other messages are delivered by impersonal methods in print or other media. This 'mix' of marketing communications is summarised in Figure 9.5.

Uncontrollable communications

The image of an organisation and the demand for its products are affected by communications outside of the control of its managers. These may be directly communicated (face to face), by email, text, telephone or letter, as customers discuss their experiences of dealing with an organisation. They can also be impersonal communications, such as news reports in the media or messages posted on an Internet newsgroup site. These uncontrollable communications can be very

FIGURE 9.5 *The marketing communications mix*

influential, as we are more likely to believe them than communications received directly from the supplying organisation. However, such communications do not always promote the cause of the organisation under discussion in a positive way.

FOR EXAMPLE

A well-known restaurant chain launched a promotional campaign to attract new customers and improve declining sales. Press advertising, leaflets and posters offered free bottles of wine to couples dining in the evening and discounts to families eating lunch. The campaign was evaluated through market research among users and non-users. The campaign seemed successful as sales in the group's restaurants increased during the campaign, but the follow-up evaluation revealed deeper problems. The research revealed a high level of dissatisfaction amongst customers over the standards of service, particularly the waiting time before food was served. Further research revealed an even more damaging picture, for although only a small minority of customers actually complained to the management about the poor service, a majority mention it to their friends and acquaintances. One customer had even posted advice to avoid the restaurant on an Internet newsgroup about eating out. This implies that potential customers are more informed about the problems than the restaurant managers! Any plans for further promotion are stopped until the service problems are overcome because the management realise the disadvantage of attracting large numbers of new customers who are likely to act as a negative marketing force among their friends.

This example illustrates some important truisms about marketing communications:

- Uncontrollable communications (which may or may not promote a product) are more powerful in many cases than controllable promotions. Many causes have been lost through bad publicity, and many organisations have succeeded by relying only on word-of-mouth recommendations. Small enterprises often rely on word-of-mouth recommendations to increase their customer base: research has consistently shown that the vast majority of small firms cite recommendations as their number one method of attracting new customers.

- Word-of-mouth marketing communications are no longer restricted to face-to-face conversations between friends and neighbours. The telecommunications revolution means that people exchange views on their buying experiences in a number of new media, including text messaging and email. Internet newsgroups (online discussion forums) now involve millions of people around the world exchanging news and views over a huge range of topics. This often includes positive or negative stories about buying experiences or a product's performance. The scope for uncontrollable, word-of-mouth marketing communications on the Internet is enormous.

FOR EXAMPLE

Usenet news (http://groups.google.com) is a network of over 85,000 discussion groups, each dedicated to a specific topic. These range from the serious (e.g. tips on mortgages and pensions) to the weird (e.g. messages from aliens). Usenet users often react against attempts to use their site for commercial purposes by 'flaming' anyone who posts overt advertising, that is by sending them abusive messages in return. However, users frequently make positive and negative recommendations about products and services. Some entrepreneurs use groups to subtly inform others about their business (e.g. by contributing informative postings, and signing off with a website address and contact details).

■ Advertising and promotions have helped a large number of organisations to become successful, but it is not enough on its own. Even the most intensive, well-conceived advertising campaign cannot compensate for a deficient or unwanted product. The Sinclair C5 electric car and the De Lorean sports car both received enormous publicity when they were launched, yet both failed because they were found wanting in other crucial respects.

Controllable communications

An organisation can choose to use various forms of promotions, such as personal selling, advertising and special offers to try to influence the demand for its products and services. The organisation's management pays for and controls these communications by selecting the type, quantity and timing of the promotional methods. In subsequent sections of this chapter and Chapter 11 we will look at the various types of promotions in more detail.

However, promotions are not the only element in the marketing mix to communicate to an organisation's customers. Product, pricing and place strategies also communicate messages that form part of the overall image projected by an organisation:

■ A tangible product's design and packaging communicate important impressions. Intangible products communicate through the physical evidence of their delivery. For example, a credit card projects an image of the banking service that is behind it.

■ Pricing can communicate a variety of messages from exclusivity or high quality to cheap and cheerful or value-for-money images. For example, the bargain air travel prices of EasyJet and Ryanair are a crucial part of the 'power to the people' message inherent in their strategy of opening up short-haul routes to a wider customer base.

■ The place in which a product is sold or distributed communicates further images. For example, the waiting room of a surgery often leaves a lasting impression in a visit to a doctor (often because the most time is spent there).

Communication strategy

An organisation has to consider several aspects of marketing communications if it is to have an effective strategy for communicating to its customers. These include:

■ *Consideration of uncontrollable communications*: How to use word-of-mouth recommendations as thoroughly as possible and how to limit the possibilities of damage done by negative communications

■ *Planning controllable communications*: How to ensure that all the elements of the marketing mix are giving consistent, not conflicting, messages to the public

■ *Use of the 'promotional mix'*: How to optimise the use of specific promotional opportunities and techniques available to an organisation

9.3.2 The promotional mix

The term 'promotion' is used in a variety of contexts and meanings. Here we are using it to describe controllable communications to customers or potential customers which, in conjunction

FIGURE 9.6

The promotional mix

with the other elements of the marketing mix, support the marketing objectives of the organisation.

Promotions have a 'mix' of their own because wide choices of promotional methods are available. Most organisations employ a variety of these methods in differing mixtures.

Major categories of the promotional mix can be classified as:

- **Personal selling, including field marketing**: An umbrella term that involves the use of staff to represent a product or service to potential buyers 'in the field' – the marketplace. It includes many different activities that involve direct contact between suppliers and buyers such as sales calls, exhibitions and trade fairs, merchandising, retail auditing and 'experiential' campaigns, such as roadshows and consumer sampling.

- **Advertising**: A paid form of non-personal presentation, using various media such as the press, TV, radio, cinema, posters and the Internet. Advertising agencies sometimes refer to these methods as 'above the line' (ATL) promotion.

- **Sales promotions**: Inducements or incentives outside of the normal terms of trade to encourage sales within a specific time period. This non-media, or 'below the line' (BTL) promotion, includes loyalty cards, free gifts, competitions and other special offers which add value to the original product.

- **Public relations (PR)**: Attempts to gain favourable, unpaid publicity, usually in the media, and to limit any potentially unfavourable comments or activities. PR is concerned primarily with influencing as far as possible the various 'uncontrollable' communications that affect the image of an organisation.

- **Direct Marketing (DM)**: Direct communication to a customer or business designed to generate a response in the form of an order, a request for further information, or a visit to a store or other place of business. This may be direct mail or e-marketing.

A promotional campaign may embrace several or all five elements in an integrated effort. This is called integrated marketing communications (IMC), where all elements contribute in a different way to meet the same objective.

FOR EXAMPLE

....

British Airways uses a combination of PR, advertising, sales promotions, personal selling and direct marketing to counter competitive activity and launch new services. The company suffered considerable adverse publicity following revelations of a 'dirty tricks campaign' by BA against Richard Branson's Virgin Atlantic. This allegedly included accessing computer information relating to Virgin Atlantic flights and poaching passengers at airports. BA's public relations department worked hard to minimise the damage in the media by emphasising their corporate pedigree and popularity with customers. More recently, the airline sought to gain a competitive advantage by focusing on premium customers through an integrated communications campaign involving TV and press advertising, direct mail, sales promotions and personal selling. BA's business service was upgraded with the introduction of bed-seats. The changes were advertised in the press, on BA's website and on TV. Frequent travellers were mailed newsletters detailing the new service. Sales representatives visited and telephoned travel agents to encourage them to sell the benefits of these new services to their customers.

9.3.3 Promotional mix decisions

Decisions about which element(s) in the promotional mix to use are affected by the type of purchase, the objective of the communication process and the product life cycle.

Type of purchase

In general, personal methods of promoting such as personal selling and exhibitions are more suited to communicating to markets made up of a relatively small number of large customers. Conversely, impersonal methods of communicating are more appropriate to promoting to a large number of relatively small buyers. A complex, infrequent purchase is more likely to need personal attention than a simple, frequently made one. These variables can be shown as a spectrum of purchase types: at one extreme, in-depth personal contact is needed; and at the other extreme, impersonal communications such as advertising influence the buying decision.

This means that the order of preference of promotional methods changes, particularly between organisational and consumer markets:

- In consumer markets, advertising and sales promotions tend to receive most resources, followed by direct marketing, personal selling and public relations.

- In organisational markets, personal selling is usually the most-used method, followed by direct marketing, sales promotions, public relations and advertising. Depending on the market, exhibitions may also be widely used.

Objectives of the communication process

As buyers progress along their decision-making process, marketing communications seek to achieve different objectives. As we discussed in section 9.2, Communication stages, these objectives can be summarised as: attention, interest, desire and action – the AIDA model (or awareness, trial and reinforcement in the ATR model). When awareness of a product is low, communication is required in order to gain attention for the product, so advertising and public relations are often the most effective at this stage. PR and sales promotions, as well as advertising, are widely used to generate interest in a product. When awareness and understanding of the benefits on offer are higher, sales promotions, direct marketing and personal selling are the more effective methods to increase desire, whilst some form of direct marketing or personal selling may be required to complete the necessary action to make a purchase.

FIGURE 9.7

*Types of purchase
and the
promotional mix*

The relative effectiveness of each category of promotion in the stages of the AIDA model is illustrated in Figure 9.8.

Product life cycle

The stage a product has reached in its life cycle influences the choice of promotional method.

■ In the introduction stage, personal selling is important to introduce the new product to the supply chain to gain exposure. Advertising and public relations are used to generate awareness and understanding of the product. Sales promotions are used to attract the 'early adopters' to try the product.

■ In the growth stage, sales promotions and selling may be needed less as advertising and PR maintain the momentum.

■ In the maturity stage, the product is usually well known so that the level of advertising may be cut back with more reliance on sales promotions to provide a stimulus to sales.

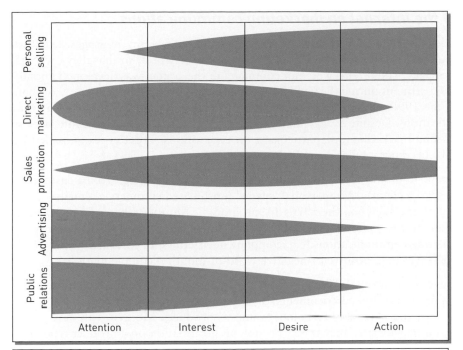

FIGURE 9.8

Communication objectives and the promotional mix

■ Shaded areas indicate relative effectiveness of the promotional method to achieve that objective of the communication process

■ In the decline stage, expenditure on promotion is usually reduced to a minimum, although sales promotions may still be used to prop up sales.

FOR EXAMPLE

....

These various influences on the composition of the promotional mix can be seen at work in the launch and subsequent management of new products. For example, a large company launched a new brand of toothpaste. A special conference trained and motivated the company's own sales-force to introduce the product into the toiletry trade so that it receives good display and shelf space, particularly in the large multiple retailers. A TV advertising campaign attracted the attention and interest of the target buyer groups. Free samples and discount coupons, some given away by company representatives during in-store promotions, introduced customers to the product. Press releases told the story of the new product to the trade and national press. The strong growth and continuing national advertising of the toothpaste maintains the retail trade's interest in stocking the product, so the level of selling activity is reduced as the brand achieves its market share targets. When growth slackens, the company cuts back on their advertising budget in order to maximise profits from the product. Market research reveals a high level of consumer recognition and acceptance of the brand, so promotional activity concentrates on coupon offers and competitions to win free holidays as a means of stimulating demand.

9.3.4 *Impact of the Internet on marketing communications*

The Internet provides a variety of new ways of communicating marketing messages. It allows computers to communicate with each other from anywhere in the world, so that they can both send and receive messages. The origins were not commercial; the system was developed initially by the US Defense Department during the Cold War, and adopted by academics as a way of sharing information. In the 1990s, business managers began to realise the potential of the Internet for commercial applications. Despite exaggerated expectations in the late 1990s, the Internet has emerged as an important marketing tool, particularly for promotions. Three types of marketing communications have become popular over the Internet:

■ *Email*: Email can be in the form of personalised marketing messages (e.g. from a customer service department to a client), or impersonal 'spams' (unsolicited commercial email, apparently named after a sketch in the 1970s TV programme *Monty Python's Flying Circus*, in which everything on the menu was the same: Spam). Email can be used formally for controllable marketing communications (e.g. company newsletters) or informally for uncontrollable messages (e.g. positive or negative word-of-mouth recommendations).

■ *Websites*: The development of the Web has made the Internet user-friendly. A website is typically a collection of interlinked documents, or web pages, which might contain, for example, information and news about a company and its products. Most sites are now interactive; for example, a visitor may order, or look up information on a product type on one visit to a website and be presented with tailor-made information on related products on a subsequent visit. In some cases, customers gain access to an organisation's intranet via the website in order to answer specific questions about the status of their order or other information hitherto provided by a customer services department.

   For marketing communications, the Web offers a remarkable combination of international coverage with individual targeting: it is already used by over 300 million people around the world, yet it is also able to deliver messages targeted at one individual. A website can also provide information on its effectiveness as a communications medium; small files, or 'cookies', inserted into hard drives by a web server, track data on the numbers and activities of visitors to a site.

   The problem with the Web is that it is extremely difficult to get noticed. Millions of companies and countless individuals have websites in a relatively uncontrolled, unstructured system. The first marketing issue is to ensure that potential customers find your site before the competition. When looking for information about products and services on the Internet, most buyers and consumers use search engines (e.g. Google, AltaVista) to help users find web pages on a given subject. The search engines maintain databases of websites and use system devices (referred to as 'spiders' or 'robots') to collect information, which is then indexed by the search engine. Similar services are provided by 'directories', which maintain ordered lists of websites (e.g. Yahoo!). If your site is not listed in the first page or so of results of keyword searches relevant to your product, it is unlikely to be visited. As the number of sites expands, such listings are increasingly difficult to achieve. Many companies are now using traditional marketing communications such as advertising and direct mail to 'drive' visitors to their sites.

■ *Newsgroups*: Newsgroups are online discussion forums of people exchanging news and views on their particular areas of interest over the Internet. They have become informal yet important ways of spreading positive and negative word-of-mouth recommendations communications about products and services. (See also the example on Usenet in section 9.3.1 on Uncontrollable communications, page 293.)

These new forms of marketing communications are evolving constantly, creating new forms and nuances as they do so. Some represent controllable communications from websites and banner advertising. Others are less controllable messages via chat rooms and emails. They have become particularly important because of their ease of access for all types of business; creating a website and sending marketing messages on email has become relatively straightforward and inexpensive.

We will now consider each of the five major categories of the promotional mix in turn. The rest of this chapter looks at the more personal, face-to-face methods involved in field marketing – that is, personal selling, exhibitions and trade fairs, and experiential marketing. Chapter 10 considers the non-personal promotional methods of advertising, sales promotions, public relations and direct marketing.

CHECKPOINT

When using the Internet, evaluate the different types of promotional marketing that you see and the forms that it takes. How many types of promotions that are involved with search engines such as Google make money?

9.4 PERSONAL SELLING

9.4.1 The sales stereotype

Until sales are made, a business cannot be sustained. Sales in many organisations depend at some stage on a personal presentation of the product. These simple facts ought to make personal selling a cherished and respected role. In fact, selling has fallen into such disrepute that many of those doing the job have stopped calling themselves salespeople and adopted euphemistic titles such as 'account representative', 'national account manager', 'field engineer' or 'customer service executive'. Other business professions, such as accountancy and production management, have become more respected than personal selling, which developed a reputation not as a profession, but as a manipulative activity carried out by fast-talking extroverts. Selling is one of the largest professions in Europe and North America, but it still has fewer specialist journals or societies devoted to it than other, less numerous professions – an indication of its low esteem.

Factors that have fuelled this poor image of selling include:

■ *Sales orientation*: Many organisations have concentrated on finding as many new customers as possible irrespective of the underlying needs of the market. Sales training has focused on teaching salespeople techniques to get new orders at any cost rather than to improve the level of service to existing customers. Successful salespeople have been judged on their ability to sell 'anything to anybody' – the proverbial 'refrigerators to Eskimos' – rather than on their efforts to meet customer needs.

■ *Polarisation of salespeople and customers*: This emphasis on sales at all costs by suppliers has created a protective reaction from potential buyers. Fearful of falling prey to persuasive selling, customers have made themselves less accessible to the sales approach. Hostile receptionists and professional buyers have put up barriers to the now-unwanted sales call. Salespeople have risen to the challenge and looked for new ways to break through. Seller and buyer have become adversaries as salespeople adopt aggressive tactics to 'find the weak spot' and deliver the 'knock-out blow' to clinch the deal.

- *Wide range of selling situations*: 'Salesperson' is a term applied to many different sales situations, ranging from shops to international negotiations. This has not helped the profession develop a consistent image capable of attracting the most able recruits. Instead, selling has been perceived less as a profession and more as a trade to be fallen back on if qualifications are inadequate for other jobs.

- *Characteristics of successful salespeople*: Countless different personality types enjoy successful careers in selling. Whilst attempts to correlate sales success and character traits have failed generally, research in North America indicate that salespeople differ from non-salespeople in the following respects:

— Salespeople are more likely to persuade rather than criticise

— They act on intuition rather than analysis

— They are more energetic

— They are more motivated by money, prestige and power

These characteristics can, of course, be interpreted positively or negatively. Some salespeople have not always been good advertisements for their profession and live up to the stereotypical image of the charming, adaptable, fast-moving performer always ready to take your money. However, more salespeople differ from the popular stereotype than conform to it because selling is a complex and demanding job that relies on positive personal qualities as well as organisation and technique. Unfortunately, the low status image is hard to change and helps to perpetuate the myth by making recruitment into the profession harder.

9.4.2 The changing face of selling

There are signs that the relatively low status of selling is improving, helped by some changes to the sales environment:

- *Increased costs of personal selling*: Increased labour costs have reduced the numbers involved in selling at the retail level and have forced manufacturers to look for maximum productivity from their sales force. The 'jack of all trades' role has become more sharply focused as organisations count the cost of making a sales call.

    For example, the total annual costs of a salesperson, including their salary, commission, travel and other overhead costs may range from £30,000– £100,000 p.a. The effective selling time of a salesperson may represent 200 days in the year, once time has been deducted for holidays, training, internal meetings and administration. In one day, the number of sales calls that are possible varies according to industry and market from one per day for complex sales

FOR EXAMPLE

GlaxoSmithKline, the pharmaceutical giant, owns Lucozade (the energy drink) and Ribena (the blackcurrant drink) amongst its stable of many brands. It wanted to increase the point-of-sale visibility of these two brands by improving the retailers' understanding of consumer trends. It produced sales presenters and recruited a team of 130 temporary sales staff who were trained to call on the UK's top 22,000 independent retailers. Market share rose over 2 per cent and the brands accounted for over 94 per cent of total soft drinks growth.

TABLE 9.1 *Range of costs per call*

COSTS PER ANNUM	COSTS PER DAY (based on 200 days per year)	CALLS PER DAY	COSTS PER CALL
£30,000	£150	10	£15
£40,000	£200	7	£29
£50,000	£250	4	£63
£60,000	£300	2	£150
£100,000	£500	1	£500

(such as sophisticated industrial equipment) to ten or more per day for simpler calls (such as merchandising to retailers). This gives the range of costs per call shown in Table 9.1.

With costs ranging from £15 to £500 per call, selling has had to become a more focused, specialised activity to justify its expense.

The alternative for many companies is to outsource at least some of its sales activities. This is true even for some of the biggest companies in the world.

■ *Increased buyer power*: Buyers have become more powerful in certain markets as their purchasing power has increased. For example, the concentration of retail sales in the hands of fewer companies and outlets has placed more emphasis on negotiating larger contracts with multiples and retail chains, rather than one-off local sales, with a commensurate increase in the level of skill and knowledge needed from the salespeople involved.

■ *Increased competition*: National and international markets are becoming more and more competitive. Salespeople are no longer 'order-takers', but 'order makers' who have to win business in the face of local and overseas competition. The increased emphasis on quality standards and agreed minimum specifications means that products are often similar in performance, price and other respects. The main differentiation is the relationship with the selling organisation and in particular their representative – the salesperson. This has put more pressure on organisations to recruit, train and retain high-calibre sales professionals.

■ *Professional involvement*: The growing influence of market forces in the public services and professions such as accountancy and law has brought selling into some unfamiliar environments. Bank managers, accountants, solicitors and architects now make sales presentations to secure clients. Head teachers openly acknowledge their selling role when they show prospective parents round their school. The acceptance of selling into these more traditional surroundings has helped legitimise it as a professional activity.

9.4.3 Types of selling

Personal selling can be defined as the personal presentation of the organisation and its products to customers or prospective customers. This can take many forms, from the doorstep deliveries of the milkman to the presentation of computer equipment to a multinational corporation, as illustrated in Table 9.2.

TABLE 9.2 *Types of selling situations*

DESCRIPTION	AIMS	EXAMPLES	POSSIBLE CUSTOMERS	JOB REQUIREMENTS
Delivery selling: The delivery person who also sells	Increase sales to the existing customer base by using customer visits that are already being made	Milkman, van drivers	Receptionists, stay-at-home parents	Friendly personality, a driving licence
Retail selling: Serving customers who visit the company's premises	Show customers what is available, offer advice and complete the transaction	Sales assistants in shops, waiting staff in restaurants	Shoppers, visitors to showrooms	Some product knowledge, patience and stamina
Trade selling: Selling products into the relevant distribution chain	Ensure adequate, well displayed stocks are held at the wholesale and retail level, provide promotional assistance with in-store displays and point-of-sale merchandising	Sales representatives for food and drink companies	Shopkeepers, buyers for multiple chains	Limited technical knowledge, good understanding of customer practices
Technical selling: Providing technical advice and assistance	Identify, analyse and solve customer problems, develop relationships with existing customers	Sales engineers of electronic or industrial equipment manufacturers	Other manufacturers, public services	Good technical and product knowledge essential
New business selling: 'Creative' selling to new customers or markets	Find new customers for existing or new products, create sales where an established market does not exist	New account executives for advertising agencies, insurance and office copier salespeople	Office managers, public service managers, consumers	Good selling technique and experience, resilience to rejection
'Experiential' selling: Promoting to the end users or specifiers of a product	Create demand by sampling or giving consumers/buyers an experience related to the product/service	In-store sampling of beauty products, medical representatives selling to doctors who prescribe medicines dispensed in chemists	Consumers, general practice doctors	Low pressure selling but to large numbers – therefore articulate and energetic

The role of personal selling

The role of selling and the requirements of the job change according to the situation in which it takes place. The list of selling situations in Table 9.2 illustrates just how different the selling role can be. Two variables in particular have a significant effect:

■ *The complexity of the product or service*: selling a mainframe computer system obviously requires a different approach to presenting a line of confectionery products

■ *The experience of the buyer*: in some markets, the buyers have little or no internal expertise of the product and it is a 'new task' purchase (because of the newness of the product or their newness to the market). In other cases, the buyers are very experienced at purchasing the type of product under consideration as in a straight re-buy or modified re-buy situation (see Chapter 4 section 4.4.1, Types of organisational buying behaviours, for clarification of the terms 'new-buy', 'straight re-buy' and 'modified re-buy'). Again, very different sales approaches are required.

This can be illustrated as four different selling roles, as in Figure 9.9 below.

The changing nature of the selling role influences the skills and types of salespeople required and how they are organised.

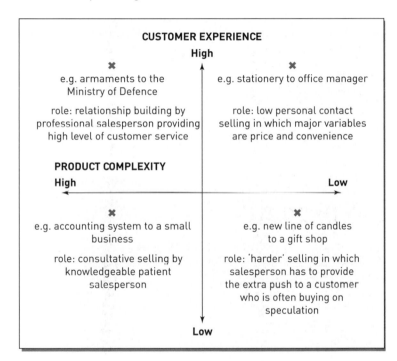

FIGURE 9.9

Selling roles by customer experience and product complexity

FOR EXAMPLE

An electronics company, Deltronix, sells two types of product. The first is custom-made electronic designs that vary according to the needs of individual customers, who are themselves usually manufacturers of consumer or industrial durables. The second is a range of ready-made electronic components, which are stocked by the company and sold to other manufacturers as required. The company is organised into two separate divisions, each with two different types of sales team. One division sells the custom-made products – complex designs using specialised, new technologies of which customers have little experience. Initially, sales engineers use consultative selling approaches to demonstrate the potential benefits of their design and production methods to the technical design departments of potential customers. At this stage, a complex product is being sold to an inexperienced customer. However, once the Deltronix sales engineer has achieved acceptance of their proposal and the new circuit has been designed into the customer's own product, the sales role changes as the customer's purchasing department takes over the ordering of the circuit. Although the product is still complex, the customer has experience of what it is and the quality standards they expect from it. Deltronix builds relationships with these existing customers through a second sales team responsible for technical support. The products of the second division are standard electronic components sold from a catalogue that specifies the performance features of each product type. A 'new business' sales team is responsible for opening up new accounts in a competitive market in which many similar products were available. They therefore rely heavily on sales techniques to introduce their range to companies who are often satisfied with their existing suppliers and have little experience of dealing with Deltronix. Once the new business salesforce has opened an account, they hand over its day-to-day maintenance to a telephone sales team which can deal with regular ordering and enquiries because the product is relatively less complex and the customer has more experience with it.

This example illustrates how sales teams can be organised to reflect types of selling role, as shown in Figure 9.10.

FIGURE 9.10 *An example of organising selling by roles*

9.4.4 Sales management

Sales management involves the planning, implementation and control of salesforce activities. The evaluation of which of the different types of selling effort is required and the deployment of appropriate salespeople and selling resources is one of its key roles. Sales managers make decisions in the following key areas:

■ *Setting selling objectives*: As we have seen, sales approaches have different objectives that are dependent on a number of factors, including the stage customers have reached in their decision-making process. Some companies give their salesforce the complete job of opening, developing and protecting customer accounts. Others divide the sales function into more discrete roles (as in the example of Deltronix). As well as quantifying objectives into sales forecasts, sales managers make judgements about what needs to be achieved in the various stages leading up to the final sale.

■ *Establishing the selling strategy*: Is a consultative, technical selling strategy required, or would a relationship-building approach work better? Does the situation need 'harder' selling or low personal contact? Sales managers determine the appropriate strategic sales approach.

■ *Deciding on the salesforce structure*: Salespeople can be given responsibility for a territory based on geography (e.g. by counties or major towns), on customer types (e.g. in retail selling, customers might be grouped into 'national accounts' of large supermarkets, 'major accounts' of large regional stores and 'standard accounts' of independent retailers), product ranges (e.g. custom made or ready-made product divisions, as in the example of Deltronix above), or a combination of these (e.g. the product range of one division in a geographic area).

■ *Recruiting and training the required salespeople*: Once the objectives are agreed, the strategy set and the structure decided, the implementation of these decisions revolves around selecting the salespeople and training them in both product knowledge and selling technique. This can be done at formal training sessions or in the field. In practice only the larger companies regularly train their salespeople 'off the road'; smaller companies rely on learning on the job.

■ *Motivating and controlling the sales team*: Sales managers are responsible for monitoring and controlling the performance of their salespeople and their selling activities. Selling can be a very lonely job; many salespeople spend over 90 per cent of their time out of contact with others from their own organisation. They can experience high levels of frustration and rejection; they often spend long periods trying to contact a busy customer or waiting for appointments, and when they do finally see someone a high percentage of answers are 'no thank you'. The sales manager's ability to motivate salespeople in these difficult circumstances is crucial to success. As well as personal advice and counselling, managers organise sales team meetings to provide opportunities to discuss common issues. A variety of incentives, from regular commission payments to one-off contests with prizes, can help maintain enthusiasm and momentum.

CHECKPOINT

Evaluate some of your experiences of personal selling as a potential customer. Consider some negative and positive experiences and evaluate the key differences between them. These may have been in shops, dealing with tradespeople, customer services, door-to-door or telephone selling.

9.5 THE SELLING PROCESS

9.5.1 Pre- and post-selling activities

Personal selling is much more than making presentations to customers. Making the sale is the tip of an iceberg of activities which create the opportunity for personal selling to work.

Prospecting for customers

These activities vary with the type of selling but many sales roles are designed to find prospective customers and to make appointments to see them. This so-called 'prospecting' is usually more time-consuming than the actual time spent selling in front of customers (see Figure 9.11).

FIGURE 9.11

An example of activities required to make sales

FOR EXAMPLE

Jack Coltman, a salesman selling office copiers, analysed the average number of activities which he undertook to secure a sale. He found that for every order he took, he made an average of five product demonstrations. For each demonstration made, he averaged two other appointments with customers, equivalent to ten appointments for each sale made. To make those appointments, he used a combination of 'cold canvassing' (or unannounced visits to customers' premises), phone calls, sales letters and mail shots. For each sale, he needed an average of fifteen cold calls, fifty phone calls and one hundred mailings.

Coltman used this information to work out the amount of each type of activity he needed to meet his annual sales targets of fifty copiers. He then broke this down into a daily target assuming he had a maximum of 250 working days a year. He found that he needed to be making an average of one presentation, two appointments, three cold calls, ten phone calls and twenty mailings each and every day – and this did not take into account time for travelling, administration, training, meetings, illness or holidays!

The lessons from this type of analysis are:

- *Selling is a 'numbers game'*: persistence in prospecting for customers is as important to sales success as eloquence in front of customers. In many selling situations, the opportunities to make persuasive sales presentations depend on systematic and regular prospecting. The salesman in our example will meet his sales target if he remembers the 'numbers game' and makes the required number of telephone calls and sends the necessary number of mail shots to give him the right number of appointments and demonstrations to make sales. He can reduce the number of these activities by improving the ratios between them and the final sale, but the most successful salespeople maintain activity levels whilst also improving their effectiveness.

- *Rejection* is a fundamental part of selling: every acceptance is built on several refusals. In our example, for every 'yes' after a demonstration there were four 'nos', and many other rejections during cold canvassing and telephoning. Whilst the new salesperson can become disheartened by this amount of negativity, the experienced salesperson knows that it is part of the job.

- *Time management* is essential to successful selling. The high level of pre-selling effort needed to generate consistent sales can only be achieved by a careful allocation of time to each of the important activities and a minimisation of time spent on non-productive tasks. Travel, for example, often accounts for a high percentage of a salesperson's time but can be reduced if sales calls are grouped geographically.

Post-selling activities

The conclusion of one sale often signals the beginning of other activities.

- *Referrals*: We have already emphasised the importance of word-of-mouth communications in marketing (see section 9.2.4). Successful salespeople make these work in their favour by asking existing accounts for introductions and referrals to new customers.

- *Account maintenance and development*: Satisfying existing customers so that they are prepared to make repeat purchases is usually a more economic and productive way of making sales than finding new customers.

9.5.2 The stages of making a sale

Like other forms of marketing communications, personal selling takes the prospective customer through several stages, or states of mind, before they are ready to buy. Sales trainers frequently use the mnemonic AIDA, which we discussed earlier as a model of the general stages of the communication process (in section 9.2), to illustrate the four basic stages of making a sale.

Attention

The salesperson's first task is to gain a customer's attention so that effective communications can take place. This is harder than it might seem, as buyers are usually preoccupied with their own responsibilities and problems and initially not at all concerned with what the salesperson has to say or show. The impact of a salesperson's opening message has to be strong enough to overcome these preoccupations and to make the prospective customer receptive to his or her communications.

Actual words are not what count most in effective communications. Impact is conveyed:

- *Verbally*: Words only, the content of what we are saying

- *Vocally*: The tone and inflexion of voice, the stresses and pauses in our presentation

- *Non-verbally*: Gestures, postures, facial expressions, and visual aids

This implies that:

- *Non-verbal* gestures and expressions are often the key to gaining attention. A positive, smiling salesperson speaking enthusiastically is more likely to gain our attention than one repeating a prepared script. It is not what is said, but how it is said and the expressions and gestures that accompany it that are important, particularly in the opening moments of a sales interview.

FOR EXAMPLE

The eyes are particularly important in establishing initial contact as they are indicators of trust, as some of our common phrases indicate. 'Seeing eye to eye' implies agreement whereas 'shifty eyes' signify lack of trust. 'Looking a person in the eye' is needed to establish trusting communication. To establish a good level of trust, our eyes should meet the other person's very regularly during a conversation or presentation. However, eyes can also signify hostility if contact is prolonged into a stare, so regular but short bursts of eye contact are desirable.

- *Visual aids* such as demonstration kits, computer-generated presentations, and written material all help to gain attention. These are particularly important in the presentation of intangible products that cannot be physically demonstrated. Insurance salespeople, for example, are trained to draw graphs, present written figures and show newspaper articles as testimonials to support their presentations visually.

Interest

A sales presentation does not keep attention for long unless it also arouses interest. We become interested when we can relate personally to what is being said. Attention, once won, only lives on through the self-interest of the customer who begins to identify with what is being sold. This stage of the sale needs therefore to demonstrate to the customer that the product or service presented is relevant to their problems by identifying the customer's particular needs and matching the benefits of the product to them.

- *Questions* are often the best way to involve and interest the customer, and they also provide essential information when identifying the customer's requirements. In answering questions about themselves, their organisation and its needs, customers have to focus their attention onto the subject of the presentation and away from their other preoccupations.

- *Listening* carefully to the answers is the only way the salesperson can learn more about the customer. However, listening takes many forms and can be shown as a spectrum of 'listening modes', as in Figure 9.12.

In selling, the temptation is to adopt responsive or selective listening modes to think about the next part of the presentation, or the answer to a query, whilst the customer is speaking. To fully engage the customer's interest, attentive, and sometimes 'active' listening is required to help find the benefits that most closely identify with customer needs.

FIGURE 9.12 *A spectrum of listening modes*

Feigned listening	Responsive listening	Selective listening	Attentive listening	Active listening
Attention elsewhere, admiring the view	Use of listening time to compose your response	Attention elsewhere unless signal to give further attention given by speaker	Full attention, 'listening with both ears' to cut out mind chatter	Listening as a mirror, with no pre-judged interpretation, to lead both speaker and listener to a fuller understanding of the problem

■ *Attentive listening* concentrates fully on the words and ideas being presented so that the response will be appropriate and informed. 'Mind chatter' – the ever-present temptation to let the mind wander to topics other than those directly in front of it – is kept to a minimum.

■ *Active listening* takes attention a stage further by adding an element of participation designed to help the customer articulate what they need. The aim is to help both prospective buyer and seller to reach a common understanding of a situation.

FOR EXAMPLE

Jack Coltman, the copier salesman, had an appointment with an office manager and during the course of the meeting, he asked: 'Do you have any particular copying requirements?' The office manager replied: 'We operate to very tight deadlines. Everything has to be copied by a certain time.'

This could be taken as a signal to interest the customer in the product by presenting a time-related benefit with a statement such as, 'Our fastest machine makes ninety copies a minute, which makes sure everything is copied on time.'

But Coltman was experienced enough to recognise he had not got to the root of the problem. He adopted an active listening mode to probe further:

'You have to copy to a deadline?'

'Yes, although we email information to head office on a daily basis, we have to confirm it with signed hard copies every week. The courier has to have all the copies by 6p.m. on Thursday so that they are in Switzerland by Friday. Whatever the problem, they have to be there.'

'What sort of problems can there be?'

'You name it we've had them – from staff sickness to equipment breaking down at the last minute.'

'Your equipment sometimes lets you down?'

Coltman went on to present the benefits of his equipment in terms of its reliability and rapid back-up in the event of problems. He had found out that the real issue of interest to the customer was not the time taken to copy but the critical nature of the deadline. Providing the equipment was working, there was sufficient time to make the required copies, so that copying speed was not the key problem. Keeping the equipment working, however, was essential to meet the deadline. Coltman not only kept the office manager interested by talking about the customer's own problems, but he found out a key area of need which allowed him to pass to the next stage of making the sale.

Desire

Interest in a specific problem has to be translated into desire for a particular solution before a sale can be made. Desire is aroused when the benefits of the product or service on offer are understood and accepted as viable answers to a customer need. For example, Coltman aroused the desire of the office manager for his product by presenting the benefits of its reliability and a guaranteed minimum call-out time in the event of breakdown.

Desire for certain benefits of a product are not always a guarantee of a sale, however, as other constraints and objections may condition the desire.

■ *Objections* are negative attitudes that threaten the conclusion of a sale. They may be fundamental problems, hesitations, or particular problems.

FOR EXAMPLE
....

Coltman convinced the office manager that his product was a preferred solution, but there may have been a fundamental objection, such as the unexpired lease of the existing equipment or the lack of budget for new equipment. Perhaps the office manager wanted to put off a decision to confer with others. Or there may have been a specific issue that still bothered the office manager. Coltman's previous experience told him that desire can decline rapidly after a sales interview, so any objections need to be dealt with as quickly as possible.

■ *Empathy* with the customer's problem is important if objections are to be answered. Empathy is trying to understand the other person's point of view rather than denying it has any validity.

FOR EXAMPLE
....

After agreeing with Coltman's summary of the benefits of the copier, the office manager brought up a new concern: 'Your cost per copy is more expensive than other suppliers.'

Objections like these can be the signal for an expression of disagreement with the customer with a reply such as: 'I think if you include all the relevant costs we are less expensive.' Coltman's training had taught him that winning arguments with customers did not win orders. So his answer tried to show understanding of the customer's problem before answering the objection: 'Yes, if you compare the cost per copy in our price lists, we are more expensive. Our prices include free service and call-outs. Competitors' prices exclude this because they charge separately for maintenance and breakdowns. If the machine never needs attention, we are more expensive. But as reliability and fast repairs are important to you, then our pricing system could well turn out less expensive – as well as giving you a predictable all-inclusive price.'

MARKETING MISTAKES

Sometimes the desire to make a sale can overwhelm an enthusiastic salesperson. Examples of this can be seen in the financial services sector in the UK. We have already seen from the 'Insuring' the Message case study at the beginning of this chapter that there were concerns about the mis-selling of pensions. But the financial industry was hit by another scandal when it was revealed that many householders had been mis-sold endowment mortgages.

The most common way to buy a house in the UK is to take out a mortgage – a long-term loan normally for around 25 years to pay for the property. There are two popular ways to do this: a repayment mortgage or an endowment-linked mortgage. With a repayment mortgage, the home owner borrows a cash sum and pays off the interest and some of the capital each month. With an endowment mortgage, the owner also borrows a cash sum, but only pays off the interest on the sum each month. The capital remains outstanding until the end of the term. Alongside the interest payments, the householder pays into an endowment policy, which is invested in stocks and shares. The advantage for the householder is that an endowment mortgage often has lower initial payments. There is also an implicit understanding that the endowment policy will grow sufficiently to (at least) pay off the capital at the end of the term. Householders were not warned of the risk associated with endowments.

It is estimated that 2.7 million (11 per cent) of households in Great Britain have an endowment-linked mortgage. However, as a result of downturns in the stock market, many of them are facing a shortfall as the endowments fail to give a sufficient return to pay off the capital. This is likely to affect 82 per cent of those with endowment mortgages – or 2.2 million households. The mean debt for these households is £7,200, giving a total shortfall of £16 billion across all householders. This in turn has blighted the reputation of the endowment industry, which has lost share in the mortgage market. An additional side effect is a growth in no-fee no-win agencies dealing with claims of mis-selling. It's an ill wind.

Action

Once desire is aroused and objections dealt with, the last stage of the sales process can begin. Some form of action or 'closing' of the sale is required. Closing a sale is asking for a buying decision. This may seem straightforward, but salespeople often find this the most difficult stage because of the fear of being turned down. Because customers often feel uncomfortable during decision-making, the close can be a difficult moment for both buyer and seller. To help smooth the way to a final decision, several closing methods can help the salesperson test the customer's readiness to buy:

- *The assumptive close*: If all he stages of the selling process are obviously complete, the salesperson may use an assumptive close such as: 'I can arrange delivery of this model next week if we can complete the paperwork today.'

- *The question close*: Questions can provide 'trial closes' which find out how near a customer is to ordering. They are often used in conjunction with an assumptive close such as: 'I can arrange delivery of this model next week. Would this be early enough?'

- *The alternative close*: Another type of closing question is to ask the customer to choose between alternatives such as: 'Do you think this model will cope with your requirements or do you need the high-speed version?'

■ *The testimonial close*: This method refers to a satisfied customer who is already using the product: 'One of your competitors has used this model to transform their office systems. Don't you think it makes sense for you too?'

■ *The direct close*: A direct request for an order is sometimes all that is needed: 'Can I ask you to sign a purchase order for this model as I think we have agreed it is what you need?'

CHECKPOINT

You have been asked by a prospective employer to make a short sales presentation about yourself. Make notes on and practice such a presentation, if possible in front of others. How could you make use of the AIDA model?

9.6 FIELD MARKETING

Field marketing is a general term covering sales activities in the marketplace. As well as the types of selling described in the sections 9.4 and 9.5 above, it covers specific applications of personal promotions, such as forms of experiential selling and exhibitions and trade fairs.

9.6.1 Experiential marketing

Experiential campaigns include the use of roadshows, sampling and other face-to-face activity to engage consumers on behalf of a brand. The idea behind this is that consumers are more likely to remember the brand if they have some sort of direct experience of it. Experiencing a product increases its 'saliency' or how well it stands out from the crowd.

FOR EXAMPLE

TAKE A CATCH

The key to successful field marketing is often combining different elements of the communications mix to achieve the marketing objective. Vodafone used a wide variety of tools to achieve their objective of brand awareness and data capture through a promotional campaign to followers of cricket.

The company sponsors the England cricket team and wanted to maximise their association by building an emotional connection between the mobile phone operator and cricket fans. They achieved this through a strategic alliance with Sky Mobile TV, which helps supporters to stay in touch with sports action no matter where they are. The promotion aimed to help cricket fans feel like an integral part of the game, to the benefit of both companies. A team of ten 'outfielders' (field sales people) engaged with the fans at

Vodafone used cricket to engage consumers and increase brand awareness

Test matches, handing out 60,000 flyers, demonstrating Sky Mobile TV and encouraging fans to take part in a 'Take a Catch for England' experience. This was shown on big screens set up in grounds which were used to drive data capture, rather than just showing brand or content-driven film. Mobile messages were used to invite fans to visit a WAP portal built specifically for the campaign. (WAP allows mobile users with wireless devices to easily access and interact with information and services instantly.) This directed 3G customers to Vodafone live! and linked prospects instantly to the telesales team to upgrade and join Vodafone. (3G is the third generation of mobile phones which is more efficient and allows for the downloading of video clips at very high speeds.) With a total of 70,000 fans viewing the big screens, both Vodafone and Sky benefited from this campaign. Over 20,000 mobile numbers were captured and nearly 3000 took part in the 'Take a Catch' experience. Subscriptions to Sky Mobile's television news, sports and factual package increased by nearly 160 per cent.

9.6.2 *Exhibitions and trade fairs*

Exhibitions and trade fairs feature mainly in business-to-business (B2B) markets where suppliers take stands and aim to get leads from potential buyers. However, there are some business-to-consumer (B2C) exhibitions, such as the Ideal Homes Exhibition and the Boat Show.

Exhibiting at trade fairs can be very expensive and a rigorous cost–benefit analysis of taking part is often neglected. Attendance can become a defensive strategy, as managers feel that they need to be there because their competitors are. However, exhibitions have a more positive role in an integrated communications campaign and can be very effective, particularly for new product launches. Most industries have at least one major trade fair a year.

Potential buyers are given the red carpet treatment at a boat show

© MARK DYBALL/ALAMY

The following tips are helpful when planning an exhibition:

- The stand should be well lit with focal areas highlighted
- Stand design is a three-dimensional representation of corporate identity: what do you want customers to think about your brand?
- Copy needs to be concise and large enough to read from a distance
- Any presentations should be short

FOR EXAMPLE

The horticulture industry has a number of trade fairs, including flower shows at Chelsea and Hampton Court for the enthusiastic amateur. The largest annual trade event for buyers in garden centres is Glee, where each September 25,000 trade visitors meet over three days. It covers three market sectors: gardens, including landscaping and garden care; leisure and sports; and pet care and aquatics. In common with most exhibitions, the exhibiting companies pay for space for their stands, which they set up. They use this opportunity to get sales leads and to reassure their existing customers. Often it is also a chance to launch new products. It allows visitors to find new suppliers and new products. They can network with their existing suppliers, interact with industry experts in seminars and demonstrations and find merchandising solutions.

The exhibition world is becoming increasingly international, with many pan-European and even global trade fairs. For example IFE is the world's leading brand of food exhibitions, with shows in Hungary, America, India, Poland, Russia and the UK. It has agreed with a competitor to consolidate two major food exhibitions into one large annual event that will serve the Balkan and Central European region. The result of this consolidation is IFE Foodapest, taking place for the first time at the end of 2007 in Hungary.

16-18 September 2007
NEC Birmingham UK
gleebirmingham.com

the home of international garden, pet and leisure

Glee is one of the main trade fairs for the horticultural industry

■ Storage space should be included in the design so that the stand does not look cluttered

■ Staff need to trained and briefed

As with any marketing communications, objectives need to be set and evaluated after the event. Often with exhibitions, the objective is to get qualified leads – that is, to obtain contact details of people who are interested in the product or service.

CHECKPOINT

Choose a market sector and find the important exhibitions and trade fairs.
How would you choose which to attend?
Select a well-known brand in your market sector. What brand values would you attempt to communicate and how would this translate into stand design?

9.7 SUMMARY

■ Marketing communications are concerned with *who* (the sender), says *what* (encoding the message), in *which way* (media channels), to *whom* (the receiver), and with *what effect* (decoding, response and feedback).

■ The AIDA model of *attention*, *interest*, *desire* and *action* summarises the stages necessary for successful communications where high involvement in the buying process is evident. ATR (*attention*, *trial* and *reinforcement*) may be more relevant for products where there is lower involvement in the buying process.

■ Marketing messages often travel by a process of diffusion because of the influence of opinion leaders and word-of-mouth communications.

■ The marketing communications mix consists of uncontrollable and controllable communications. Controllable communications form a promotional mix consisting of:

— Personal selling and field marketing

— Advertising

— Direct marketing

— Sales promotions

— Public relations

The selection of the appropriate method depends on the objective of the communication influenced by the product life cycle stage.

■ The commercial development of the Internet has had a major impact on the scope of marketing communications. It offers a number of new media opportunities for promotional activities including:

— Email in the form of personalised marketing messages or impersonal 'spam'

— Websites for information, advertising and online ordering

— Newsgroups (online discussion forums) of millions of people around the world exchanging news and views about products and services

■ Personal selling has suffered from a poor reputation as a marketing tool, but factors such as increased costs and competitiveness are making it a more professional activity.

■ Selling covers many types of activity from household deliveries to complex presentations. Customer experience and the complexity of product sold divide the role required into:

— Consultative selling (complex product, inexperienced customer)

— Relationship building (complex product, experienced customer)

— Harder selling (straightforward product, inexperienced customer)

— Low-contact selling (straightforward product, experienced customer)

■ Sales management involves establishing selling objectives, sales strategy and the sales force structure; and recruiting, training, motivating and controlling the sales team.

■ The selling process involves many time-consuming and potentially de-motivating activities as well as making sales presentations.

■ The stages in making a sale follow the AIDA model:

— Attention is gained non-verbally, vocally and verbally

— Interest comes from careful questioning and attentive or active listening

— Desire has to overcome objections with empathy

— Action means closing the sale

■ Field marketing involves direct communications with customers through experiential marketing, exhibitions and trade fairs.

9.8 ACTIVITIES

CASE STUDY

SPREADING THE WORD

Alnur Dhanani owned an independent hotel, the Commodore, based in central London, near Paddington Station. In his view, it was a three-star hotel with nowhere to go. He wanted to increase occupancy rates but, in common with many small businesses, he had a very limited budget. He knew that small businesses relied heavily on word-of-mouth recommendations for customer acquisition and was looking for a way to harness this.

Three characteristics of his hotel emphasised the importance of word-of-mouth recommendations.

1 The intangibility of a hotel would make buyers likely to seek advice, probably via recommendations, before choosing

2 Guests would be likely to make recommendations (either positive or negative) because of the high involvement of the buyer in the consumption process

3 The small business nature of the hotel meant little formalised marketing was undertaken, and it was therefore reliant on recommendations for customer acquisition

Alnur conducted a two-stage research process to help his business. The first stage was in-depth interviews, which he followed with a survey.

Interviews Client research began with preliminary face-to-face interviews that formed the basis of a customer survey. Five guests were interviewed personally by the owner-manager and asked about their pre-purchase and likely post-purchase behaviour in relation to the hotel: That is, how they chose the hotel, their decision-making criteria, who or what influenced the process, and their likelihood to discuss their experiences (positive and negative), and with whom. Their comments informed the development of the questionnaire used in the second stage of the research.

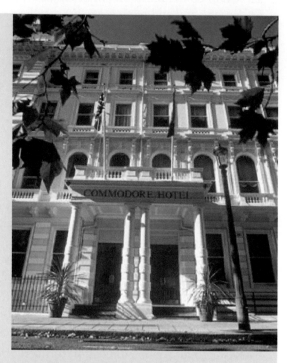

The Commodore is an independent hotel in London, owned by an entrepreneur

Questionnaire Following a pilot survey of fifteen guests, a questionnaire was developed and distributed to 250 clients of whom 121 responded, a usable response rate of 48 per cent. The objectives of the questionnaire followed those of the earlier, face-to-face interviews in seeking to determine pre- and post-purchase behaviour, and the significance and types of word-of-mouth communications in those processes. Tourists, largely from overseas, accounted for 80 per cent of the hotel's occupancy. The owner considered this to be the most difficult market segment to reach by word-of-mouth communications because there were few obvious networks to use for such a widely dispersed group, compared to the second most important market segment of business travellers. The research was carried out in August and September, a time of year when the hotel was occupied mainly by tourists, in order to maximise response from this segment.

Word-of-mouth marketing strategy Following analysis of the results, the owner implemented a marketing strategy which incorporated activities based on his interpretation of the research and the nature of marketing communications concerning the hotel in particular.

Survey of hotel customers Only 12 per cent of respondents had booked directly with the hotel, with 88 per cent using travel agents or tour operators, possibly because most respondents were overseas visitors. The principal factors which influenced them were location, price and facilities.

Input word of mouth recommendations Respondents were asked if the hotel had been recommended to them. Just over half (52 per cent) confirmed that it had. The majority of these (77 per cent) had been recommended by a travel agent. Although it could be argued that these did not represent independent points of view, over 70 per cent of respondents found the recommendation to be the most important, or quite an important factor in choosing the hotel. Travel agents might get paid a commission, but the target audience perceived that they were independent of corporate influence.

Output word of mouth recommendations Levels of satisfaction with the hotel were high, with 92 per cent of respondents stating that they were satisfied with the hotel. This level of satisfaction is reflected in the number of guests claiming that they would make recommendations. All except one respondent agreed that they would discuss the trip afterwards, with over 90 per cent of these agreeing that they would discuss the hotel specifically.

However, a marketing communications issue became evident from the analysis of recommendations made by customers *after* their visit (output word of mouth) compared to the recommendations that had been made to them *before* they used the hotel (input word of mouth). Customers proved most likely to make recommendations to their friends and relatives (70 per cent), whereas this group was a relatively unimportant source of recommendations before a visit. By contrast, only 30 per cent of customers were likely to pass on recommendations to travel agents, who represented by far the largest source of input word-of-mouth recommendations.

Marketing communications strategy From his research, the owner concluded that word-of-mouth marketing could play a significant part in the hotel's marketing communications strategy. He first addressed the imbalance between the high levels of input recommendations received by customers from travel agents, and the relatively low levels of output recommendations returning to those agents as feedback.

He instituted strategies to encourage a larger proportion of guests to tell their travel agents, and for the hotel to communicate guest satisfaction to the travel agents who had originally recommended the hotel. The use of an incentive encouraged guests to fill in comments cards, summaries of which were sent to the original booking source. Travel agents and guests were encouraged to recommend the hotel, by both personal and psychological incentives.

Complimentary room nights for travel agents, travel writers and other gatekeepers encouraged personal visits from these professional sources of recommendations. Travel agents were sent visual 'reminders of England' in the form of a miniature teddy bear (evoking images of Paddington Bear, reminding travel agents of the location of the hotel), followed by regular mailings of honey to feed it.

As Alnur said 'We gave a teddy bear to travel agents that booked x number of times and then they got a jar of honey through the post. . . . Of the people that got it, we got three times as many bookings as from those that didn't. It was a way of permanently generating interest because we regularly sent them jars of English honey. When I stopped sending it for three months to some agents, sales from exactly that segment of agents went down, and then back up again when I restarted it.'

Believing that such visual aids improved the likelihood of positive recommendations, the owner also gave a teddy bear to each guest on departure in the hope of reminding them of the novel aspects of the hotel. He recognised the strength of recommendations in other forms of marketing communications such as press releases and brochures, by quoting comments on value for money, facilities and location by independent sources, including external rating organisations and trade affiliations as well as guests.

The entrepreneurial owner used teddies and honey to encourage opinion leaders to recommend the hotel

QUESTIONS

1 How might Alnur reduce negative word-of-mouth communications?

2 How might Alnur encourage satisfied customers to engage in positive communications, other than the measures he had undertaken?

3 What other marketing communications might Alnur undertake?

DEVELOPING A MARKETING PLAN

PLANNING THE MARKETING COMMUNICATIONS

■ What objectives will your marketing communications have and how will you achieve them?

■ Which elements of the promotional mix will you use and why?

■ How will your marketing communications attract attention, gain interest, arouse desire and generate positive action?

■ What role will personal selling play and what style will you adopt?

9.9 FURTHER READING AND REFERENCES

Marketing communications

Blythe, J. (2006), *Marketing Communications*, 3rd edition (Financial Times Press), Chapters 1, 2, 8 and 11.

Word-of-mouth marketing communications

East, R., Hammond, K., Lomax, W. and Robinson, H., (2005), 'What is the Effect of a Recommendation?', *The Marketing Review*, Vol. 5, No. 2, Summer 2005, pages 145–157.
Rodger, E.M. (2003), *Diffusion of Innovation*, 5th edition (Free Press).

Personal selling

Jobber, D. and Lancaster, G. (2006), *Selling and Sales Management*, 7th edition (Financial Times Press).

Internet marketing communications

Chaffey, D. (2006), *Internet Marketing: Strategy, Implementation and Practice*, 3rd edition (FT Press), Chapter 5.

Customer relationship marketing

Gummesson, E. (2002), *Total Relationship Marketing,* 2nd edition (Elsevier).

Exhibitions

www.exhibitions.co.uk

Chapter **10**

PROMOTIONS II: IMPERSONAL MARKETING COMMUNICATIONS

LEARNING OBJECTIVES

By the end of this chapter the reader will be able to:

- Evaluate the planning and implementation of an advertising campaign
- Assess the merits of the various media used in advertising including television, radio, direct mail, the Internet and outdoor sites.
- Evaluate the roles of sales promotions, public relations, sponsorship and direct marketing as marketing communications tools
- Understand how to set meaningful objectives for a promotional campaign
- Assess how to evaluate the success of a promotional campaign

INTRODUCTION

This chapter looks at further elements in the promotional mix that are non-personal in the sense that they do not necessarily involve face-to-face contact with the customer. These are: advertising, sales promotions, PR (public relations), sponsorship and direct marketing. It describes the five basic steps that can be used to plan and implement a campaign of media advertising. It examines sales promotions that use incentives and inducements to push or pull sales through the distribution system. The chapter also evaluates PR, sponsorship and direct marketing activities that promote an organisation to its various target markets.

CASE STUDY

···

PROMOTING 'KidKare'

Jane Chan was pleased with her latest project. She worked for a marketing agency and had been asked to manage a new client, a charity called 'KidKare' that had been set up to raise £50 million towards the rebuilding and re-equipping of a children's hospital. She looked forward to working for a cause rather than a business, but her investigations soon indicated that this was no easy assignment.

She discovered that charities worked in an increasingly competitive and controversial environment. There were simply too many charities chasing too few donors. Many larger national charities were using aggressive promotional tactics to communicate their appeal and maintain their flow of donations. As charitable giving had not increased in line with national wealth, there was a feeling among some of the smaller charities that they were being forgotten in the deluge of requests for help. Medicine and health was the largest charity sector, attracting about one-third of all funds, but this itself had been subject to some controversy. Some people felt that they were being asked to finance, through charitable donations, what had previously been provided out of taxes. All publicly owned hospitals could raise money from charitable sources, and critics suggested that they were increasingly using fundraising for projects that should be paid for by the government. The National Lottery was an added complication. It did provide an additional source of revenue, but it also created complacency amongst some potential donors, who assumed it was providing all the money required for good causes.

Jane's initial brief was to develop proposals for advertising, promotions, PR and sponsorship. She considered first the market she was targeting. There were three distinct donor groups: individuals, companies and public bodies such as local authorities. She knew from secondary research that the typical profile for sources of funding was as shown in Table 10.1.

She had not been given a total promotional budget. She had just been allocated £25,000 to test promotional approaches. Those that proved cost-effective in bringing in funds could then be used more extensively.

'We are happy to consider any type of promotion to raise money as long as it is in keeping with the values of a professional health service', the director of the charity had told her, 'and we also need some positive publicity for the project to counter some of the criticism aimed at the lack of government funds.'

TABLE 10.1 *Typical profile for sources of funding (charity sector)*

SOURCE OF FUNDING	PERCENTAGE OF FUNDING
VOLUNTARY FUNDRAISING	20
COVENANTS	5
OTHER GIFTS	30
CORPORATE DONATIONS	10
LOCAL GOVERNMENT GRANTS	15
TRADING	5
LEGACIES	15

QUESTIONS

1 What advertising would you recommend? Consider the objectives, the media to be used and the creative strategy. How would you evaluate the results in order to decide what to repeat and what to discontinue? *See section 10.1*

2 Make some proposals for sales promotions in the form of inducements and incentives that could be made to the target markets. *See section 10.2*

3 What PR activities would you recommend? What message would you try to communicate, to whom and how? *See section 10.3*

4 Direct marketing is often used by charities to target donors. How would you approach this? *See section 10.5*

5 Is sponsorship an appropriate avenue for this charity? Justify your answer. *See section 10.4*

10.1 ADVERTISING: PLANNING AND IMPLEMENTING A CAMPAIGN

A leading practitioner of advertising said that advertising should not judged by creativity but by its effectiveness in making people buy the product (Ogilvy, 1995). This practical approach contrasts with the mystique surrounding advertising, which is sometimes perceived as an art form rather than a management tool. Creativity plays an important part but there are other more systematic areas.

Planning and implementing an advertising campaign covers five important decision-making areas:

■ Setting objectives

■ Estimating the budget

■ Deciding the creative strategy and message

■ Selecting the media

■ Evaluating the results

We look at these steps in more detail below.

10.1.1 Setting objectives

The particular objectives chosen for a campaign depend on the overall marketing strategy, taking account of such factors as the target market, the desired product position and its life cycle stage. Advertising can achieve one or more of three main objectives:

■ To inform

■ To persuade

■ To reinforce

Information

Advertising can inform target customer groups and build awareness of the existence of a product or service – a particularly important objective when new products are launched. It can also be used to give out information that could change people's behaviour.

FOR EXAMPLE

Social advertising is often concerned with giving information. Charities engage in marketing communications to pass on a message to their target markets. The BBC World Service Trust and UNICEF put together an integrated communications (TV and radio) campaign to address a number of social issues. These include talking about sex, condom use, and stigma towards people living with HIV and Aids, as well as mother and child health issues such as acute respiratory infections and diarrhoea.

Movie action star and hero Jackie Chan appeared in a television advertisement as part of the campaign to fight HIV and Aids. He is a UNICEF Goodwill Ambassador and appeared alongside the Trust's animated condom character, Loak Chuoy. Loak Chuoy is well known and popular in Cambodia, following numerous star appearances in television and radio advertisements to highlight the safe sex message. Research has shown that the cartoon condom is successful in getting people to talk more openly about safe sex, and using condoms.

Let's fight HIV/AIDS together

BBC WORLD SERVICE TRUST

Social advertising in Cambodia benefited from a campaign featuring Jackie Chan and Loak Chuoy

After this first appearance, Jackie Chan joined the fight against HIV-related stigma by starring in another TV advert alongside a group of Cambodians living with HIV and Aids. One of the campaign's most popular radio spots addresses breastfeeding. The message focuses on the relationship between mother and child. The child sings advice to the mother to the tune of a traditional lullaby. The tune became so successful that it could be downloaded as a ring tone on mobile phones.

By giving people information, this campaign aims to persuade them to change their behaviour. The end-of-campaign surveys on both HIV Aids and maternal and child health issues showed that the work had contributed to positive changes on both issues – and in some cases very large changes over a relatively short period of time.

Persuasion

Once a product has gained the awareness or attention of potential customers, it needs to persuade them to purchase it in preference to anything else. This is achieved by emphasising the benefits that products offer.

There have been claims that the advertising industry dictates what we eat and drink, what we wear, how we spend our leisure time and even who we elect to run our affairs. Advertising certainly can persuade and there have been notable success stories.

FOR EXAMPLE

By the early 1980s, denim jeans had become dated. Their popularity as the symbol of youthful rebellion in the 1950s and 60s had faded over the years as they became more synonymous with middle-aged conformity. Sales dropped, including those of the leading brand, Levi's. After unsuccessful attempts to diversify into other clothing markets to replace the lost sales, Levi Strauss decided to return to their original product and re-market 501 jeans. 501s were first manufactured as hard-wearing, working trousers in California in 1873, the '5' referring to the original factory production line that made up denim cloth, product code '01', into the functional trousers with five pockets that have not changed to this day. The objective of the advertising campaign was clearly stated in the brief to the advertising agency: 'To make 501s from Levi's compulsory equipment, establishing them as the definitive, classic jean.' The target group of 15–19 year old males was to be shown the product in a way that associated the original jean with the beginnings of teenage culture in the 1950s. The result was a series of advertisements that fulfilled David Ogilvy's criteria of success: they sold a lot of jeans. Two years later, 501s were selling at fifteen times the volume of the pre-advertising levels. The campaign has also become part of the creative history of advertising featuring scenes such as 'Launderette', in which a young man waits in his boxer shorts for his 501s to wash to a background of nostalgic 1950s music. The brand continues to be successful today with the launch of many new products, including 'eco-jeans'.

Although the Levi's campaign in the example provided may indicate the extent to which consumer demand can be influenced by advertising, success at this level is the exception rather than the rule. Research indicates that much advertising fails to persuade, that sales do not increase with advertising expenditure. Those products that do respond to advertising are more likely to show small gains rather than dramatic changes.

Advertising can attempt to persuade with a number of end results in mind:

■ *To increase sales by increasing the total market*: Levi's advertising benefited not only its own brand but other manufacturers as well because the total demand for jeans increased (even the sales of boxer shorts went up as a result).

■ *To take market share from competitive products*: British Airways' advertising of its business travel facilities is designed to take away customers from competitive airlines in a market that is constrained by its flight routes.

■ *To persuade a target audience to a point of view*: Advertising is not only concerned with increasing sales of products. It is also concerned with promoting a whole range of social issues, from ideas and attitudes to specific charities and political parties. It can do that by providing information, as shown in the Cambodian case study above and these European examples.

FOR EXAMPLE

The Norwegian government demonstrated how advertising could be used to address social problems when it launched a campaign with the objective of reducing alcoholism among teenagers. Headlines such as 'The average Norwegian 16/17-year-old drank 155 bottles of alcohol last year' achieved record levels of readership, including 70 per cent of all Norwegian parents. The advertising sparked off a national debate and the heightened awareness of the issues helped reduce the upward trend of drinking among teenagers. This type of success has encouraged UK governments to use advertising to promote its policies, from the wearing of seatbelts to the muzzling of dogs.

FOR EXAMPLE

In the UK the government has sought to encourage drivers to reduce their speed with a series of graphic advertisements. They show how likely it is for a child to die at a variety of different speeds. The differences between driving at 30mph and faster are emphasised. The campaign focuses on the emotive picture of a young girl, either surviving the impact or not, depending on how fast the driver was going. A similar campaign uses emotion to demonstrate the danger of using a mobile phone while driving, citing the number of accidents that have occurred when the driver was on the phone.

Reinforcement

Advertising is also defensive in that it attempts to keep existing customers by reminding them of favourable attitudes they have towards an organisation or its products. Campaigns can have the objective of reassuring customers that the choice they have just made is a wise one. For example, research indicates that car advertisements are more likely to be read by existing owners of the promoted model than anyone else; manufacturers use this information to build up repeat purchasing habits by reminding customers of the benefits behind their original buying decision.

Organisations can sometimes arrest the decline of their product by reminding customers that the satisfaction they once gained is still available.

FOR EXAMPLE

By 1990 the end of the milkman seemed in sight. Every year approximately one million customers cancelled their home delivery of bottles of milk and opted to buy the cheaper cartons in their local supermarket. Although a promotional campaign in the mid-1980s had been unable to halt the switching, the National Dairy Council launched a TV campaign in 1991 to remind viewers of what they were giving up. Animated milk bottles emphasised the friendliness and convenience of home deliveries by jumping into milk crates outside people's homes according to personalised milk orders. The award winning advertisement worked, halting the decline of home deliveries of milk at least temporarily. The Milk Marketing Council recently launched a new campaign with the same objective – to reinforce the value and convenience of British traditions such as the milkman.

FOR EXAMPLE

Car advertisements tend to be watched more by people who have just bought the car than those about to buy it. This is because buying a car is a very high-involvement purchase for most people. They have invested time and financial resources as well as emotional energy. They want to be reassured that they have made the right decision, and they know that the advertising will emphasise the positives of the model they have chosen. In psychological terms it reduces their post-purchase cognitive dissonance: 'Have I done the right thing?'

10.1.2 Estimating the budget

Advertising is more difficult to budget than most other costs because it is often difficult to know how much to spend and to quantify the benefits. An organisation has no choice over some costs, such as wages and rent, but how does it know how much to spend on advertising? The decision becomes increasingly difficult as the objectives become less tangible and more long term as, for example, in corporate advertising aimed at building up a favourable image over a number of years.

In practice several different methods are used:

- *Percentage of income*: Because most advertising is aimed at increasing the income received by an organisation, a common method is to set a budget as a certain percentage of existing or expected sales. Percentages vary widely from above 20 per cent of sales for some fast-moving consumer goods, to less than 1 per cent of income for some public services. Whilst this may be a convenient method in stable market conditions, it does not provide resources for opportunities that lie outside of the existing business.

- *Competitive expenditure*: In competitive markets, products often need to ensure they receive an equal amount of advertising as their competitors. This is often called 'share of voice'. Market share objectives can also be translated into an equivalent share of the total advertising expenditure on similar products: a product with the sales objective of a 20 per cent market share could be assumed to need 20 per cent of total advertising expenditure on the product category. This method is reactive, assuming that competitors have got their expenditure levels right, and can lead to an escalation of total expenditure as suppliers all try to increase market share.

- *Objectives and tasks*: Promotional budgets can be set by defining specific objectives, then establishing the tasks required to meet the objectives, and finally costing those tasks as a budget. This logical approach assumes that a relationship between objectives (e.g. an increase in sales) and advertising tasks (e.g. media exposure) can be defined. However this method does have the advantage of linking planned expenditure to the accomplishment of specific tasks so that performance can be more easily evaluated.

- *'What can we afford?'*: Many organisations set their budget based on what they think they can afford rather than any other, more sophisticated measure. This is particularly common among smaller organisations with limited resources.

In reality many organisations use a combination of these methods.

The cost of advertising

Advertising costs can be split into two main types:

- *Media costs*: The price of buying the relevant media space or time. Advertising agencies are normally paid their fee for creating an ad as a percentage (up to 15 per cent) of this media expenditure. Media expenditure varies from millions of pounds spent on a national TV advertising campaign to a few hundred pounds to buy space in the trade press.

- *Production costs*: The costs of producing the final advertisement. For a television campaign, these might include directors, actors, camera operators, location, filming, music and studio time. These costs have escalated as advertisers have used increasingly elaborate productions to attract viewers' attention. For example, the National Dairy Council's advertisement in support of home milk deliveries cost £5.1 million to make.

10.1.3 *Deciding the creative strategy and message*

Once objectives and budgets have been set, the next two steps of deciding the creative strategy and selecting the media can be implemented. Although we treat them separately here, in practice these two steps are simultaneous rather than sequential because the selection of the message and the media influence each other and cannot be treated in isolation.

A creative strategy is designed to fulfil the advertising objectives in the selected media by transmitting the appropriate messages to the target audience.

The approach selected depends on the aims of the campaign in relation to the target audience:

- ■ *If it is to inform*, then a straightforward, factual strategy may be used. The message may give target customers the information they need to use the product or service, for example the dates and hours in which Buckingham Palace is open to the public. It can sell more overtly by offering information as a unique selling proposition (USP) that makes the product more competitive.

FOR EXAMPLE

This headline appeared in the national press: 'Stay in a Forte city centre hotel on business and wake up with 35 per cent off your bill.' The Forte hotel group were running a summer promotion to attract the business traveller and stated the benefit in a clear and direct way, which informed the reader of what was on offer in the headline whilst the copy went on to explain where and when.

- ■ *If it is to persuade or reinforce*, a more subtle, psychological approach may be necessary. Advertising uses images of lifestyles and emotions to appeal in a more indirect way. Levi's communicated nostalgia and teenage non-conformity to sell 501s. The National Dairy Council reminded us that the friendly milkman delivering bottles to our doorsteps is part of the British heritage, a valuable national institution that we throw away at our peril.

  Persuasive advertising offers attractive lifestyles, but ones which need to be in tune with the aspirations of the target audience if they are to work.

FOR EXAMPLE

British Airways business class advertising took a new creative approach in its re-launch of its business class service. Previous promotions had focused on the theme of the 'office in the sky', showing how BA could give hard-nosed business executives a competitive edge over their scheming rivals. Whilst this may have been appropriate to the enterprise culture of the Thatcher years, BA's research indicated that a softer approach was now needed. A new campaign conjured up images of comfort and relaxation as the business traveller used flying time for personal reflection rather than clinching deals. This theme was continued in the launch of BA's bed-seat service in 2001, which emphasised home comforts whilst travelling.

Virgin Atlantic responded to BA's advertising by revamping its own appeal to business travellers. Originally, Virgin had launched its transatlantic service as a no-frills, cut-price alternative to the major carriers. As airfares dropped generally in response to the new competition and over-capacity on the route, Virgin had to offer something more, particularly to the less price-sensitive business traveller. They launched TV and press ads which conjured up images of a self-indulgent, luxurious lifestyle whilst retaining echoes of their earlier low price appeal with headlines such as: 'You know those rotten, pampered so-and-so's who travel first class? Become one for the price of a business class ticket.'

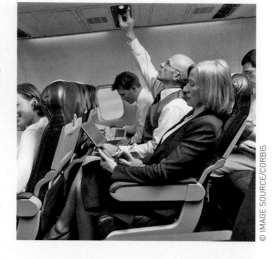

Airlines are constantly seeking a competitive advantage as the battle between British Airways and Virgin shows

© IMAGE SOURCE/CORBIS

10.1.4 Selecting the media

Media selection requires choices not only between different media (e.g. press or outdoor) but also within each medium (e.g. the *Times* or the *Telegraph*; poster site locations).

In the UK, approximately £12 billion (US $25 billion) is spent each year on the different display advertising media. Table 10.2 compares this to other countries.

TABLE 10.2 *Top ten countries by advertising expenditure, 2005*

	1996		2005		1996–2005
	US$m	Rank	US$m	Rank	Percentage change
USA	99,095	1	155,252	1	56.7
CHINA*	2,392	17	38,525	2	1510.6
JAPAN	35,869	2	35,941	3	0.2
UK	13,804	4	25,186	4	82.5
GERMANY	22,714	13	20,689	5	−8.9
MEXICO*	2,419	16	14,268	6	489.8
BRAZIL*	8,432	6	14,161	7	67.9
FRANCE	11,023	5	12,842	8	16.5
ITALY	6,621	7	10,753	9	62.4
CANADA	4,831	9	8,858	10	83.4

WORLD ADVERTISING TRENDS 2006, WWW.WARC.COM.

NOTES

* Data shown are at rate card prices.

Data for remaining countries are shown at discount level.

TABLE 10.3 *Breakdown of expenditure on UK press advertising*

	£m	% OF TOTAL
REGIONAL NEWSPAPERS	1,469	34
NATIONAL NEWSPAPERS	950	22
MAGAZINES – BUSINESS AND PROFESSIONAL	661	15
MAGAZINES – CONSUMER	623	14
PRESS PRODUCTION COSTS	653	15
TOTAL	**4,356**	**100**

ADVERTISING STATISTICS YEAR BOOK, 2006.

Press

Press advertising has a long history dating from the first English newspapers in the seventeenth century. Despite the advent of radio, TV and the Internet it remains popular because it is so flexible. It can be used as a permanent reminder of a small business in Yellow Pages, as a targeted approach to a specific industry in the trade press, or as part of a national campaign in the Sunday papers.

Its share of media expenditure in the UK can be broken down further, as shown in Table 10.3.

Often the attractiveness of such media is assessed by the relative cost of reaching a thousand readers. This may vary dramatically. For example if we take the women's magazine sector, the cost per thousand (CPT) for *Sainsbury's* magazine, a mass market publication, is a reasonable £5.57, whereas for *World of Interiors*, an upmarket interior design magazine, it is a whopping £80.17 (ABC, NRS and Brad, 2005).

CHECKPOINT

What might explain the difference between the CPTs?

If you were deciding which media to use for an advertising campaign, how would you choose between magazines on this basis? How could you refine this measure?

Press advertising has several advantages compared to other media:

■ *Broad, targeted coverage*: The diversity of press publications ensures that they provide a wide yet targeted coverage of customer groups suited to segmented marketing campaigns. National papers offer lifestyle focus (e.g. the Sunday colour supplements); the regional papers give a local, geographic breakdown (e.g. the *Surrey Advertiser*); magazines offer advertisers demographic segments (e.g. *Seventeen*) or special interest readers (e.g. *Gibbons Stamp Monthly*); the trade press targets a profession (e.g. *Physiotherapy*) or an industry (e.g. *Electronics Weekly*).

■ *Permanence*: It provides a permanent record so that the reader can refer to information more than once.

■ *Responsive*: The press can carry coupons for direct response or telephone enquiry numbers, which are more likely to be retained than other media.

The limitations of press advertising include:

- *Limited impact*: Print does not have the same potential sensory impact as multidimensional media such as cinema, TV and the Internet. It is limited to a purely visual impact. However, production values have increased, with more and more publications offering high quality colour.

- *Fragmentation*: The diversity of the press can make in-depth coverage of some customer groups difficult and fragmented across many publications. For example, a consultancy practice wishes to advertise their services to the business community. Do they choose national press for wide coverage, regional papers for local contacts, trade press and professional journals for specific customer segments, or a combination of them all?

Television

Television is a familiar advertising medium to us as consumers, yet a relatively small percentage of organisations use it. Small enterprises cannot afford it and industrial products do not need its wide coverage. TV is heavily used by larger companies, particularly the suppliers of branded consumer goods seeking impact and coverage who can spread the high production and media costs over a substantial turnover.

FOR EXAMPLE

Twelve per cent of the UK population is aged between five and fourteen, a group of around 7.4 million consumers (Annual Abstract of Statistics, 2005). This segment represents the core market for many leading branded products from Coca-Cola and Tango to Sega and Lego. Advertising to this segment of consumer goods such as snacks, confectionery, soft drinks, music, videos, toys and computer games is largely carried on TV. Satellite and cable TV have given advertisers a new option because this group watch more of TV than adults do. It is capturing an increasing percentage of their viewing time, with complete channels such as Sky Kids and Nickelodeon, dedicated to their age group.

The advantages of TV include:

- *Impact*: Sight, sound and motion combine to appeal to our senses and emotions.

- *Reach*: 'Reach' is a measure of how many people in the target market are exposed to a particular advertisement in a specific period. If a promotional objective is to achieve a 'high reach' of a national market, TV is often the most effective answer.

- *Attention*: When we watch TV we tend to be a captive audience absorbing whatever is shown as there are few distractions. However, this situation is changing as more and more people 'zap' between channels and fast forward the ads on recorded programmes.

TV advertising is restricted to under one-third of UK media expenditure because it does have some significant disadvantages:

- *High total costs*: Although it can be a cost-effective media for high turnover products, the costs of production and airtime are prohibitive for products with a more limited appeal. The risks involved if the advertising does not work are also greater.

FOR EXAMPLE

One of the world's most expensive TV advertisements is a three-minute long commercial for Chanel. It cost almost £18m with Nicole Kidman alone costing £2m. The long length of this ad (most are 30 seconds) added to the advertising budget because media costs are based in part on time. Other big budget ads include the Honda Accord and British Airways.

Chanel spent nearly £18m on one of the most expensive ads in marketing history

- ■ *'Clutter'*: Television programmes are increasingly 'cluttered' by advertising. The average number of ads shown by the commercial stations continues to rise and viewers are becoming more immune to promotional messages because of the overload. Remote-control units and video recorders can remove the advertising content of viewing time.

- ■ *Impermanence*: Most advertisements on TV last 30 seconds or less and are rarely stored. This does not make it a good medium for the communication of detailed or complex messages.

CHECKPOINT

1. Watch commercial TV for at least four commercial breaks, making no notes.
2. How many of the ads can you remember?
3. What was the key message of each?

However, expenditure on TV continues to grow quickly for both media and production. Table 10.4 shows its progress between 1985 and 2005.

Radio

The BBC monopoly on broadcasting made commercial radio a relative latecomer in the UK. Although Radio Luxembourg and the offshore 'pirate' stations pioneered the way in the 1960s, it was not until 1973 that the first commercial stations broadcast from the UK mainland. In other

TABLE 10.4 *UK advertising expenditure on television*

	£m			PERCENTAGE OF TOTAL
	1985	**1995**	**2005**	**2005**
TRANSMISSION CHARGES	1,188	2,827	4,097	85
PRODUCTION COSTS	188	506	723	15
TOTAL	**1,376**	**3,333**	**4,356**	**100**

ADVERTISING STATISTICS YEARAGE BOOK, 1997; MARKETING POCKET BOOK 2007

countries, especially the USA, the explosion of popular music in the 1950s and 60s helped establish the radio as an effective advertising medium to the fast-growing youth market.

Today commercial radio broadcasts on a regional and local basis to an audience that has expanded to include motorists, stay-at-home parents, senior citizens, factory workers and other sub-groups. Independent radio stations now abound, with a reach of over half of the UK population. There are mainstream commercial radio stations such as Magic, which attracts around five million listeners. There are also specialist stations such as Premier Christian Radio and Swansea Sound, which focus on specific groups based on specialised interests and geography.

The advantages of radio as an advertising medium include:

■ *Low cost*: Radio advertising is still relatively cheap in terms of the costs per listener.

■ *Selectivity*: Radio can provide advertisers with access to specific groups at specific times, such as car owners whilst driving, stay-at-home parents whilst working in the home and teenagers whilst listening to music.

■ *Geographic segmentation*: Although radio can provide mass coverage, it can be restricted to a geographic area for local businesses.

Radio has disadvantages including:

■ *Single sense*: Because it works only through our hearing, radio's creative and impact possibilities are limited.

■ *Attention*: The radio is frequently played in the background with low attention given to content.

■ *Impermanence*: Like TV ads, we are only fleetingly exposed to a radio commercial, which has only a few seconds to make its impression or be forgotten.

Cinema

Although the popularity of television, videos and DVDs was initially expected to reduce cinema audiences, there has actually been an increase in the number of cinema-goers since the 1980s. In 1985, there were 70 million admissions to cinemas; by 1996 this had grown to 123 million and to 165 million in 2005. The success of films made especially for the big screen, and improvements to cinema facilities and standards of comfort have made it more worthwhile to leave the convenience of home entertainment in favour of a visit to the cinema. Audiences are predominantly young, with 57 per cent aged between fifteen and thirty-four years old. Other advantages of cinema advertising include:

■ *Impact*: The size, colour, movement and stereophonic sound from the big screen combine to make its potential impact second to none.

- *Control*: Unlike TV, the advertiser has the controls over such variables as sound volume and colour quality – and the viewer cannot turn off the ads.

Disadvantages include:

- *Audience size*: Whilst not quite the 'dying breed' they were once feared to be, cinema-goers are still limited in total numbers and regularity of visits.

- *Youth-bias*: On average only 30 per cent of cinema audiences are over thirty-five years old.

Outdoor

'Outdoor' is the term used to cover advertising on posters that may appear on sites such as hoardings, buses, trains, the underground, shelters and washrooms. Posters were used intensively by tobacco companies following their ban from advertising on television. Their relatively low cost and blanket coverage also makes them popular for advertising political parties.

FOR EXAMPLE

Posters were the chosen medium for one of the most famous advertising campaigns. In the 1930s, Guinness used simple statements of benefit – 'Guinness for strength' or 'Guinness is good for you' – accompanied by tongue-in-cheek illustrations such as a workman carrying a metal girder obviously too heavy for normal mortals. The campaign made an Irish stout into an everyday part of English life and gave Guinness an entrée into almost every pub in the land. These claims would not be allowed with the current codes of practice.

One of the early posters for Guinness

IMAGE COURTESY OF THE ADVERTISING ARCHIVES

Advantages of poster advertising include:

- *Repeat exposure*: As we are creatures of habit, we tend to pass the same hoardings more than once and see buses carrying poster advertising on the same routes. This means we are exposed to the same message several times.

- *Low cost*: Multiple poster sites spread across a town or city can be rented relatively inexpensively and production costs can be kept low with simple copy and graphics.

- *Low competition*: Sites are usually well separated from other poster sites so that there is little confusion of messages.

- *Supportive*: Poster advertising is often used to support other media, which takes the bulk of the spending. The government's offering of shares during the privatisation of industries such as gas and electricity was advertised in this way, with posters highlighting the theme of the main campaign on TV and in the press.

Disadvantages of poster advertising include:

- *Creative limitations*: Little detail is possible on posters, which minimises the creative opportunities.

- *Short viewing opportunity*: Posters are often on busy roads, offering drivers little chance to absorb the information because they are concentrating on driving conditions.

- *Unselective*: Posters tend to be seen by a wide variety of people and can often be differentiated only by geographic market segments.

- *Access*: The tobacco and drinks industries built up substantial portfolios of poster sites rented on a long-term basis, which compounded a general shortage of well-positioned sites. Other advertisers can have difficulties gaining access to good sites, although legislation to restrict tobacco advertising further will change this situation.

To address some of these problems, there has been a growth in washroom posters, predominantly in motorway service stations. Research suggests that the average male spends 55 seconds reading a washroom poster and the average female spends 105 seconds. The position of the posters commands more undivided attention than the average poster site; they are situated above hand basins, hand driers and urinals, and on the back of toilet stall doors. The location in service stations can help in more precise targeting.

FOR EXAMPLE

Vauxhall wanted to promote their Vectra model to company drivers with a male bias. They ran a male washroom poster campaign, supplemented by standard six-sheet posters across all national motorway services in the UK. Awareness research of the washroom campaign showed that over 80 per cent of people interviewed remembered the Vauxhall Vectra as the model being advertised in the service area. In addition, interviewees who were aware of the washroom advertising were five times more likely to consider the Vectra as an option for a company car than the unaware group. This campaign gained awareness amongst a key target market, but also moved them towards interest and possibly desire.

Lucozade also used a washroom campaign to promote its Soltis sub-brand. Soltis is a stimulation drink, designed to increase awareness. The brand targeted weary drivers to make them aware of the benefits of a drink designed to keep them awake with the taglines of 'Fight Your Eyelids' and 'Alertness Fast'. The four-week campaign ran in male and female washrooms across all 131 motorway service stations. It resulted in a sales increase of 563 per cent for Lucozade Soltis. In addition, the increase in footfall created by posters to the cold drinks section lifted sales across all Lucozade brands, with a 34 per cent sales increase for Lucozade Sport and 75 per cent sales increase for Lucozade Lemon Crush 345 ml. Over the four weeks, the posters achieved an estimated twenty-five million impacts, equating to over eight million individuals.

Direct mail

Direct mail is basically advertising by post. It became increasingly popular with advertisers in the 1970s and had grown to over a billion items mailed by the 1980s. Computerisation has helped the direct mail industry to develop even more strongly since then. It has increased expenditure

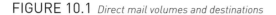

FIGURE 10.1 *Direct mail volumes and destinations*

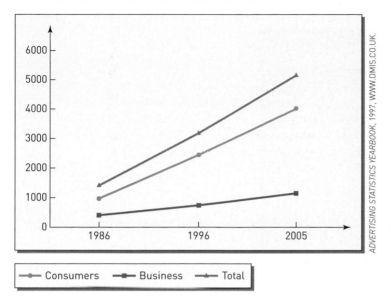

ADVERTISING STATISTICS YEARBOOK, 1997, WWW.DMIS.CO.UK.

by 118 per cent and volume by 87 per cent over the last ten years. Total expenditure now exceeds £2.3 billion on over five billion items mailed. Its growth has been accelerated by both technology and the effectiveness of the medium. It is estimated that for every £1 spend on direct mail £14 of revenue is generated. Consumers buy mostly clothes, books and electrical goods.

The volume is divided between consumer and business mailing, as shown in Figure 10.1.

As Figure 10.1 clearly shows, consumer direct mail is more common, accounting for over three-quarters of the mailings. But both segments are in strong growth. The average UK household received 13.2 items of direct mail every four weeks, but this varies according to socio economic group, with AB households receiving an average of 28.5 in the same time period. Business managers get even more mail than AB consumers. They average as much direct mail in a week as most households do in a month (13 items).

Response rates differ as well. Consumers open 67 per cent, open and read 42 per cent, and respond to 32 per cent. Managers by contrast have 15 per cent of their mail filtered out by an information gatekeeper. They open 70 per cent, redirect 9 per cent to a colleague and file or respond to 20 per cent.

Whilst mail shots often provide information and aim to generate awareness and interest, they very often include a call for action. This is often making a donation or purchase. Table 10.5 shows the most common reactions to a direct mailing.

Since in 2005 £2.4 billion was spent on direct mail (41 per cent on postage and the remainder on production), it is important to maximise the chances of success.

Research suggests that the following factors are important in encouraging consumer response. They are more likely to respond if they:

■ Are already a customer/have dealt with the company

■ Feel it is relevant

■ Have heard of the brand name

■ Are already interested in/considering this type of product or service

TABLE 10.5 *Actions taken as a result of mailshot: surveys of business users of direct mail in 2006*

ACTION	%
USED A VOUCHER OR COUPON	48
BOUGHT SOMETHING IN THE SHOPS	44
VISITED A STORE	41
LOOKED FOR INFORMATION ON THE INTERNET	34
ORDERED SOMETHING BY PHONE	28
KEPT IT FOR INFORMATION	28
ORDERED SOMETHING BY POST	27
MADE AN ENQUIRY BY PHONE	27
TRIED OUT A NEW PRODUCT OR SERVICE	26
ORDERED SOMETHING ON THE INTERNET	24

WWW.DMIS.CO.UK.

NOTE

Numbers do not add up to 100 per cent because more than one action can be taken by each correspondent.

In addition, potential customers are more likely to respond if the mailshot:

■ Is correctly addressed

■ Looks like it contains a free sample

■ Has the name of the company on the envelope

The ability of direct mail to target buyers more precisely than other media make it a particularly appropriate selling aid in business markets where careful use of the direct mail 'rifle' beats a more random 'shotgun' approach. Salespeople use direct mail to introduce themselves to potential customers that they have identified, or as a follow-up to demonstrations they have made. However, the largest growth has been in the area of consumer rather than business mailings. The private sector has realised the value of advertising services such as insurance and DIY through direct mail, and the lessons from the success of companies like Readers Digest, who have long been experts at selling through the post, have been learnt by others. But it is non-profit organisations that have lead the way in an increasingly sophisticated use of direct mail.

FOR EXAMPLE

Charities are one of the biggest users of direct mail, representing about 10 per cent of consumer mailings. Oxfam first wrote to its supporters asking for money in the 1950s, and appeals by post are now an integral part of charitable fundraising. Direct mail can be targeted at known supporters, and it produces immediate returns in the form of donations without the need for further follow-up. It is also an 'invisible' form of marketing with a cost-effective image, important to charitable organisations which do not wish to be seen spending funds on more ostentatious promotions. As the volume of mail arriving in our homes has increased, charities have become more creative in commanding our attention. Mail shots regularly inform donors about how their money is being spent. Recognising the benefits that information technology offers to direct mail marketing, charities such as Oxfam have developed profiles of supporters on their lists so that they can appeal to their specific interests. The immediacy of direct mail allows charities to reach their supporters within days of disasters or emergencies for which special appeals are required.

ADVERTISEMENT REPRODUCED COURTESY OF THE SAMARITANS

Effective and affecting mailing from the Samaritans

The Samaritans ran a campaign under the theme 'Life Goes On' which celebrated the lives of people who had contacted them and went on to die in old age. This emphasised the work that they did in preventing suicide in younger people and was very effective in encouraging donations.

Other advantages of direct mail include:

- ■ *Measurable*: The results from direct mail are measurable directly because the receiver is invariably asked to respond in some way. The cost per response can be calculated to judge the campaign's cost-effectiveness.

FOR EXAMPLE

....

The costs of a particular mail shot including postage were £500 per thousand mailed. For every thousand sent, fifty replies were received, a response rate of 2.5 per cent. The cost of each reply was therefore £10 (£500 divided by 50). The sender of the mail shot could now estimate if it was worth spending £10 for each response.

- ■ *Testable*: Mailings, particularly larger ones, can be tested before the complete list is mailed. A sample is mailed and evaluated to arrive at a cost per response before the mail shot is 'rolled out' to the full list, or aborted.

- ■ *Targeted*: The list to which a mail shot is sent is crucial to its success; an out-of-date or inappropriate list can ruin the effectiveness of the best-designed mail shot. If an organisation does not possess an adequate list from its own records, these can be purchased from mailing houses, who offer ranges of specialised lists from the names of process engineers to purchasers of gardening tools.

Disadvantages of direct mail include:

- *Image*: The image of 'junk mail' is not helped by the quantity of unsolicited material received by the modern household and office. This has swollen by the door-to-door delivery of leaflets, samples and coupons in order to reduce mailing costs.

- *Waste*: A high proportion of mail shots are not read or acted on.

- *List quality*: Lists rapidly become out of date as people move or change jobs and keeping them up to date is a constant and costly operation. Organisations can damage their image by sending several copies of the same mail shot to one address, but duplications of names are notoriously difficult to eradicate.

CHECKPOINT

Think of a time when you were contacted directly to buy something or to make a sales appointment. How effective do think this approach was compared to less direct ways of buying the same service or product (e.g. retail)?

The internet

The Internet has become an important advertising medium, generating much activity in recent years as organisations have competed for attention on the World Wide Web. The Internet offers a number of new ways of promoting products and services:

- *Websites*: Websites are the key to advertising on the Internet and most established businesses now have their own site carrying information about their products and services. A website is a specific location on the World Wide Web managed by an individual or an organisation, usually consisting of several web pages, introduced by a homepage of contents. Website files are housed and maintained by 'hosts' or 'servers'. Internet hosts have grown dramatically from an estimated 230 in 1981 to 100 million by 200 and over 400 million in 2007 (Internet Systems Consortium, www.isc.org). Websites carry marketing communications about the host organisation for potential customers, employees, investors and other stakeholders including product information, news and events, and job vacancies. They are also a source of market information because they can be programmed to identify the number and geographic origin of site visitors. 'Cookies', or small files inserted by website servers into visitors' computers, provide more detailed information on visitors' behaviour (e.g. which web pages were opened, time spent on the site, number of repeat visits, and purchases made). This data can then be used to personalise messages and information for visitors when they revisit a site. For example, visitors to the Tesco Direct website can review their previous purchases or favourite items placed in their electronic 'shopping carts'.

- *Portals*: Portals are websites that form gateways into the Internet by offering the user a starting point from which to navigate around the complex myriad of sites and services on the World Wide Web. Some (such as Google and Yahoo!) are essentially 'search engines' which help to locate any type of information on the Web. Others are more specialised and targeted at particular interest groups (e.g. Business Answers UK at www.businessanswers.co.uk is a portal for business-related issues). If successful, such portals attract many visitors so that they can sell advertising on their sites.

- *Banner advertising*: 'Ad banners' are the most common form of advertising on the Web, so-called because they form a banner across the top of a web page, carrying promotional messages and links to the advertiser's website. The success rate of the advertisement is measured by the number of 'click-throughs' to the advertiser. They may be paid for like more traditional forms of advertising (from small sums for relatively unknown sites, up to £10,000 per month for popular sites). Banners are also exchanged through reciprocal arrangements under which two or more organisations agree to link their sites to increase traffic to each other.

- *Pop-ups*: Marketing communications may also appear in smaller windows once a site is opened. These 'pop-ups' are often used to advertise specific promotional offers such as free software downloads or competitions. They often contain cookies to gain information about the user. However, many people who use the Internet set their browsers to block pop-ups, so they are never seen.

- *Rich media advertisements*: Advertising on the Internet can attract attention through interactivity, animation and sound. For example, a building society's site can ask potential customers to type in the amount and term of the mortgage they want and give an immediate quotation. Many websites offer downloads containing 'rich media' software of high specification graphics and sound, that makes possible highly creative and interesting communications. However, many web users do not have sufficient computer software, memory or connection speed to access these rich media sites or become frustrated because of the long download times.

Advertising on the Internet has several advantages:

- It can be relatively inexpensive to set up
- Visitors to websites can be tracked to provide market information
- It has the potential to reach audiences world-wide immediately
- It can be very creative and interactive

The significant disadvantage is that it is very difficult for an advertiser to be noticed by their target market in a relatively disorganised, unstructured system of millions of websites. 'Visibility' of a website is as least as important as its design. For this reason search engines, such as Google and Yahoo, have become very important. These search the text of web pages on the instructions of a user who asks for sites containing certain keywords or phrases. As search engines rank the sites found according to their relevance to the user's search, advertisers need to ensure their site is ranked as near to the top as possible because users rarely bother to look beyond the first ten names. This entails constant vigilance and management to ensure that websites are configured to the search engines' criteria for listing results ('hits') of keyword searches. As each engine uses different criteria to search millions of web pages, managing the visibility of a website has become a skilled job.

Organisations now use a variety of offline promotional methods to increase traffic to websites because of the difficulties in raising and maintaining visibility online. These include main media advertising through television, radio and direct mail, as well as general publicity by including website addresses on letterheads and marketing literature.

All of these factors mean that advertising on the Internet may not be as cost-effective as it may at first appear. Whilst sites can be designed and hosted relatively cheaply, maintaining sites and promoting their visibility can become more expensive.

MARKETING MISTAKES

Norwich Union is an Aviva company, a large insurance group, with 35 million customers worldwide, and the biggest in the UK. It is a leading provider of life and pension products in Europe and has substantial businesses elsewhere around the world. Its main activities are long-term savings, fund management and general insurance. But even it can make mistakes.

Norwich Union had to axe its strap line of 'Quote me happy' in the UK in 2007, after complaints that it was failing to give consumers the most competitive quote. Developed in 2003, the strapline was followed by 'Make you happy' and 'Keep you happy'. Although their motor insurance rates increased, they failed to change the message. The moral of the story is that advertising only works if the message it is communicating is true. Consumers are cynical and cannot be fooled for extended periods.

Advertising on the Internet is now growing very fast. In 2006 it reached £2 billion in the UK, an increase of over 40 per cent over the previous year, to take an 11 per cent share of the total UK advertising market. It is now ahead of the newspaper advertising but still half that spent on TV (Internet Advertising Bureau, www.iabuk.net).

10.1.5 Evaluating the results

The evaluation of an advertising campaign involves measuring how well it communicated its message, and what effect it had on sales or other tangible objectives of the organisation.

Effectiveness of communication

Advertisers want to know how well their campaign communicates a message to its target audience. This can be done by:

- ■ *Pre-testing*: Before an ad is launched it can be tested by showing it to a selected audience

- ■ *Post-campaign recall*: Research is carried out to determine which advertisements the target audience saw. This research uses *spontaneous* recall (e.g. 'Thinking back over the past week, which commercials can you remember seeing or hearing?'). It also uses *prompted* recall (e.g. 'Which of the following advertisements do you remember seeing or hearing recently?') in order to judge the attention achieved by an advertisement.

- ■ *Tracking*: In order to fully test the effectiveness of promotions, some organisations set up customer panels to permanently track their awareness and attitudes to products.

Effect on organisational objectives

The ultimate justification for advertising is not just that it communicates well but that it helps an organisation meet its objectives. For example, tracking research may indicate that brand awareness has been improved through advertising, that the communication objectives were met. But how does this translate into sales? Unfortunately this is never easy to answer because it is difficult to isolate advertising as a single variable. A straightforward comparison of sales or income

FIGURE 10.2 *Planning and implementing an advertising campaign*

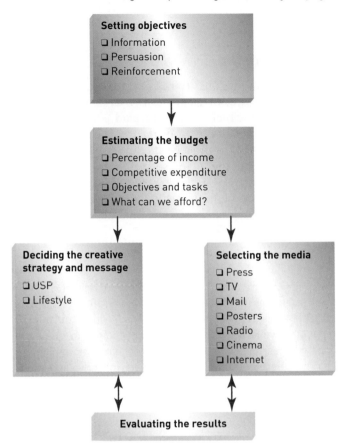

generated with advertising expenditure does not take account of other factors such as competitive activity or economic trends. More thorough research can attempt to isolate other variables by comparing results in similar geographic areas with and without advertising. Evaluation of advertising remains an inexact science, justifying perhaps the complaint of one chief executive who said that 50 per cent of his company's advertising didn't work, but he didn't know which half!

The five aspects involved in planning and implementing an advertising campaign are summarised in Figure 10.2.

CHECKPOINT

Consider an advertising campaign you have seen recently on TV or in the press.

1. Do you think the objectives are to inform, persuade, or reinforce, or a combination of these? Why do you think these objectives were chosen?

2. What is the creative strategy and message – USP, lifestyle or a different strategy?

3. Why do you suppose the chosen media was selected?

10.2 SALES PROMOTIONS: PUSHING AND PULLING BELOW THE LINE

10.2.1 'Above and below the line' advertising

Sales promotions are sometimes referred to as 'below the line' (BTL) advertising, compared to advertising, which is 'above the line' (ATL). The 'line' was originally drawn by advertising agencies to distinguish between advertising activities for which they were paid a commission on media purchased ('above'), and other activities for which their involvement was charged directly to the client as no commission was applicable ('below'). In practice the line is blurred as many sales promotion activities rely on advertising to promote them, and special offers and incentives are an integral part of many promotional campaigns. Also, as e-marketing has grown, the distinction has become even less clear. Many agencies use multiple media in integrated marketing communications campaign so the old ATL/BTL distinction has become outdated.

FOR EXAMPLE

Both British Airways and Virgin have used sales promotions as part of their overall advertising strategy to woo the business traveller. British Airways' 'BA Miles' and Virgin's 'Flying Club' offer the possibility of free air travel to frequent travellers who collect enough points to qualify. Research has indicated that business and first-class passengers rate such schemes more highly than the cheapest available fare. Most airlines therefore offer a frequent flyer incentive scheme as an integral part of their marketing effort, and feature this in advertising and other sales efforts.

Sales promotions can be defined as inducements or incentives outside of the normal terms of trade to encourage sales within a specific time period. Their popularity has increased to the point where expenditure in the UK runs at over £3 billion a year.

Sales promotions are not just targeted at final consumers. They can be used to 'push' products through the distribution system by incentives to the trade or to salespeople, as well as to 'pull' products through to end users.

10.2.2 'Push' promotions

Trade promotions

Some promotions attempt to push more products through the distribution chain. These may offer distributors inducements to stock certain products or to display them in a certain way and include the following types of promotions:

- **Profit incentives**: Increased discounts for products purchased in a given period; bonuses or retrospective additional discounts for purchases above a certain level; one-off additional discounts for stocking a product range for the first time.

- **Credit incentives**: 'Sale or return' facilities, or extended credit for a limited period; delayed invoicing to dealers for certain products.

■ *Staff promotions*: Dealer staff training; a competition for dealer sales teams; participation in events such as golf tournaments.

■ *Joint promotions*: Free in-store display materials; exhibitions; shared mailings to customers; contributions to promotional expenses.

Many organisations operate a combination of promotions to ensure their products are well represented through the channels of distribution.

Salesforce incentives

Sales promotions to an organisation's salesforce reward particular achievements with prizes and awards. They can be used for several objectives, including:

■ Improving the overall sales performance of the organisation by offering prizes and special bonuses to those that sell most

■ Targeting the sales of specific products by making them the subject of special incentives on a short-term basis

■ Improving the teamwork and motivation of the salesforce by using incentives as the focus for regular news bulletins, meetings and other communications which keep salespeople informed about what is happening elsewhere

FOR EXAMPLE

One insurance company motivates its salesforce through a combination of annual and monthly competitions backed up by newsletters and meetings. There is a top annual prize of a £5,000 holiday and awards for the next best fifteen performers. Monthly incentives of vouchers to spend at Currys and Dixons are used to reward those who meet varying targets which are regularly changed – sales of a particular policy, or opening the most new accounts, for example. A newsletter announces winners and new incentives, wall charts display individual performances, and monthly meetings are held to review progress.

10.2.3 'Pull' promotions

As consumers we are offered an increasing variety of incentives to buy products. These include discounts, samples, coupons, competitions, sponsorship, multiple packs, point-of-sale displays and credit facilities. Both manufacturers and retailers use sales promotions.

Manufacturer promotions

Promotions by manufacturers include incentives to consumers that are 'redeemed' either directly or through the retailer.

FOR EXAMPLE

Coupons have become a popular promotional device, with over five billion circulated each year in the UK. These are often distributed through mailings or inserts in newspapers and offer the consumer free products or discounts on presentation of the coupon. This form of incentive has been boosted recently by the publication of several new 'free-standing inserts' (FSI). 'Shoppers' Friend' and 'Money Savers' are two such publications which follow the style of successful 'coupon magazines' in the USA. Packed with coupon offers ranging from money off toilet tissues to free admission to theme parks, they are distributed as an additional section in many newspapers.

Retail promotions

Retailers also run their own promotions with loyalty cards and special offers of their own. Supermarkets now offer a host of promotions including money off, holiday promotions, gifts, bulk purchase discounts and demonstrations. For example, in one year alone, Tesco gave 13,000 educational items to 8,000 schools in return for coupons collected by parents shopping in their stores.

10.2.4 Sales promotions on the line

Sales promotions have had a chequered history and are still regarded by some as the least acceptable form of advertising. Some incentives seem to encourage consumers to buy what they do not need and others are accompanied by high-pressure selling techniques. For example, criticisms have been made about the use of incentives to induce people to see 'hard sell' presentations of time-share holidays and other products. Even well-known brand names have received adverse publicity over the less ethical aspects of sales promotions.

FOR EXAMPLE

One promotion threatened to discredit the whole industry. In 1992, Hoover offered consumers two free return flights to Europe or America if they purchased any of its washing machines or household appliances worth more than £100. The company expected that its very generous promotion would attract buyers who would be put off taking up the offer by the small print which laid down strict conditions about how and when the flights could be taken. In the event, a large numbers of consumers bought cheap appliances at around £120 and claimed their air tickets worth £500, Hoover ran into difficulty honouring the offer, leading to scepticism over the value of such promotions.

CHECKPOINT

Evaluate a sales promotion campaign you have been exposed to as a consumer. What were its objectives and how effective do you think it was?

10.3 PUBLIC RELATIONS: PROMOTING AN ORGANISATION TO ITS PUBLICS

10.3.1 Who are the 'public' in public relations?

The Institute of Public Relations define PR as 'the deliberate, planned and sustained effort to establish and maintain mutual understanding between an organisation and its publics'.

An organisation's public relations activities attempt to maximise the benefits of favourable publicity and minimise the damage done by adverse communications. PR is used to present positive aspects of an organisation whilst attempting to exercise some influence over the less controllable communications which impact on an organisation's image.

FOR EXAMPLE

Virgin Airways and British Airways issued a series of press releases with their versions of events over the allegations of a 'dirty tricks' campaign. Amongst other claims, Virgin accused BA of planting 'hostile and discreditable stories' in the press, including an attempt to destabilise Virgin by falsely claiming that they were no longer able to get credit to pay for fuel. The public feuding was part of an attempt by both airlines to influence politicians and aviation authorities over access to flying routes and airports. Virgin were pressing for more competition on some of BA's most lucrative flying routes and wider access to take-off and landing slots at Heathrow airport.

This dispute illustrates the importance of 'publics' other than customers to an organisation. American and European aviation authorities, the Department of Transport and members of parliament were all involved in decisions that would have a significant impact on both Virgin and BA. In Chapter 2, we examined the environment of the marketing process, looking at the influence of internal forces (such as organisational objectives and priorities) and external constraints (such as the political and socio-economic factors). PR can attempt to influence all these environmental forces. Whereas other types of marketing communications are focused mainly on customers and consumers, PR is aimed at a wider range of targets.

The 'publics' important to an organisation might include:

- *The workforce*: The most important PR is often accomplished internally by involving employees in the goals and achievements of an organisation. A mutual understanding of what goes on and a sense of belonging can be encouraged by internal communications such as newsletters and activities from social outings to service awards. An active social involvement is often an indicator of a well-motivated workforce.

- *Suppliers and distributors*: Other organisations involved in the supply chain of the industry are also important contacts with whom to communicate on a regular basis. Suppliers and distributors benefit from information about organisations with whom they do business. Rumours among 'the trade' can have an important influence, for example on the credit-worthiness of a company. PR can help manage these informal communications amongst professional and industry contacts.

- *The local community*: Organisations, like private citizens, are members of a local community such as a town or a district. Good relations and understanding with that community and its representatives can benefit all parties. It may help resolve planning problems or issues over trading hours, for example. PR activities, such as sponsorship of local causes and participation in community events, can help integrate an organisation into its local community and foster a sense of mutual support.

- *The financial community*: The cash resources made available to an organisation are controlled by an internal and external financial community including boards of directors, public fundholders, banks, investing institutions, financial analysts and city commentators. PR can influence which way the funds flow. For example, publicly quoted companies try to build relationships with financial institutions, pension funds and other important investors to enhance their share price. Public services such as education and transport use PR to sell the value of their services to central and local government decision-makers in order to maximise their share of the allocation of tax receipts to the various public services.

■ *Policy-makers*: Many bodies, including the European and UK parliaments, local councils, trade associations and regulatory bodies, make policies, laws and regulations that have direct and indirect effects on the success of an organisation. Pressure groups and individual petitions, often supported by PR in the form of press releases and public statements, can influence the formulation of policy. We have already described how one influential pressure group, the breweries, persuaded the government to modify the original proposals by the Monopoly and Mergers Commission for the supply of beer to changes more acceptable to the industry (see Chapter 2, section 2.4.4, page 57). Many local issues involve the use of PR including proposals to build roads or to close schools.

■ *Customers and consumers*: Indirect marketing communications are an important input into the image of an organisation formed by customers and consumers. PR can attempt to influence these less controllable communications, such as stories in the press and word-of-mouth comments, by ensuring that the organisation's viewpoint is at least represented.

Organisations develop and maintain relationships with these and other stakeholders who are important to its long-term success. PR is often used to help mutual understanding and is particularly needed in times of change.

FOR EXAMPLE

A state secondary school was going to be run by a private company. Following declining pupil numbers and poor inspection reports, the education authority had decided to hand over the management of the school to a company who would change the school into a technology college, specialising in science and IT subjects. This move had been hotly debated among parents, staff and governors with accusations and counter-accusations between the supporters and opponents of the change. A new head teacher began a PR campaign to heal some of the wounds once the decision had been taken. This involved communicating with many groups with an interest in the future success of the school. Meetings with teachers and parents reassured them that the very survival of their school depended on making it more specialised and outlining the benefits to pupils of planned investment in new facilities. Information sheets explained the changes to pupils so that any feelings of insecurity about the future of the school were minimised. Governors met to discuss the implications and briefed members of the local community about the benefits. Meetings were held with representatives of the local education authority and the central department for education to work out arrangements for the transition. Relationships were developed with local suppliers, who were asked to quote for contracts for administrative services. At the end of a very hectic period the school emerged with an image enhanced not only by the extra resources under its direct control but also by the way in which it appeared to manage them. This positive image soon spread by word of mouth among parents and the school received more applications to take pupils as a result.

10.3.2 PR activities

A variety of methods are used to communicate with the various publics important to an organisation.

Media

Relationships with the press and other media are important means to the end of communicating with an organisation's publics. Larger organisations try to develop long-term relationships with key journalists so that when issues arise they can ensure that their viewpoint is heard. Smaller organisations may benefit from the free publicity that can be obtained from stories in the local or trade press.

Developing media relations is a key part of a PR strategy. It involves:

- *Setting PR objectives* that are consistent with the overall marketing strategy and can be integrated into the marketing mix. This implies considering what image an organisation wishes to project in line with its market position and the audiences it wishes to communicate with in line with its target market segments.

- *Identification of the relevant media*, that is, media that is directed at the pertinent audience and conveys the appropriate marketing message. 'Downmarket' publications cannot be used to project 'upmarket' images.

- *Preparation and development of newsworthy stories* – the press and TV are interested in news – good or bad – and not information which says nothing new, however interesting it may seem to the organisation publishing it. The media publish stories about the launch of new products but not about the benefits of existing ones. We read headlines such as 'school goes private' or 'local firm opens new factory', rather than 'school teaches eleven- to sixteen-year-olds' or 'firm continues to employ 200 people'. Organisations have limited windows of opportunity to ensure that their newsworthy stories are published; an active PR strategy seeks these out and communicates them to the media.

- *Media contact* – the standard means of communication is by a press release, sometimes supported by press conferences if the occasion is important enough. These can be supported by informal meetings and phone calls with journalists to develop an ongoing relationship.

Information

Organisations generate many types of information about themselves that form part of their corporate image. This information is not restricted to leaflets and promotional literature but includes statutory documents (such as annual reports and accounts), reference material (such as prospectuses and catalogues), and internal publications (such as company newsletters). Some organisations give out information through video films, training courses, visits to their premises and open days.

The design and delivery of all types of information, no matter how specialised, helps create impressions of an organisation which contribute to its corporate image. PR's role is to ensure that these impressions are consistent with each other and with the marketing strategy of the organisation.

Lobbying

If an organisation wishes to influence decisions that could affect its future, it needs to make its point of view known amongst decision-makers. The cultivation and lobbying of key decision-makers is part of the PR function. It can be done in a relatively formal way by membership of trade pressure groups or the employment of consultants specialising in political lobbying. It is also done informally by getting to know people in influential positions. At a local level this might include borough councillors, chambers of commerce members or leaders of amenity groups and residents' associations.

'Good causes'

Some organisations try to project an image of responsibility and care for their community and environment by linking their name to 'good causes'. This may involve sponsorship of charities, sporting events, fundraising activities or shows. Organisations that may be perceived as environmentally 'unfriendly' try to improve their image in this way; the tobacco companies were leading sponsors of professional sport (until prevented by legislation), and energy corporations sponsor many 'green' causes. Organisations can enhance their image with their local community by supporting shows and festivals.

Crisis management

When an organisation becomes embroiled in a crisis, PR can help manage the situation and limit the damage done to its image. British Airways have tried to minimise damage to its reputation over the Virgin Airways dirty tricks affair by differentiating carefully between the way the whole organisation is trained to treat passengers and the way a few individuals mistakenly tried to deal with competitors like Virgin. By developing clear viewpoints on controversial issues and making them known internally and externally, an organisation may hope to ride a particular storm. Avoidance of difficult issues is not always a guarantee that they will go away, however.

FOR EXAMPLE

British Petroleum (BP) decided on a low-key attitude in response to the huge oil spillage from the tanker Braer off the Shetland Islands. Although the incident highlighted the international problems of oil transportation and the potential harm to wildlife and the environment from spillage, the company's PR department decided that this was not a good time to be drawn into a public debate on tanker safety. Neither the tanker nor the oil belonged to BP and the company did not wish to be implicated in a disaster in which they had no direct involvement. The environmental pressure group Greenpeace had other ideas. Thanks to a leaked BP internal memo advising executives to 'keep their heads down on this one', Greenpeace drew public attention to what they considered to be the complacency of the major oil companies. Advertisements, headlined 'oil leak', quoted the memo in full and demanded more environmental action rather than fine-sounding rhetoric from the oil corporations. BP spends large sums of money in order to convince the public that it is a responsible, environmentally aware multinational. Ironically, its green record came under attack due to an incident outside of its direct control.

The BP example illustrates the need for sure-footed PR strategies to cope with the possibility of publicity – positive and negative – from any direction. In its early days as a profession, public relations may have been regarded as little more than a method to get free advertising. It has now become an integral part of marketing communications that organisations can rarely afford to overlook.

10.4 SPONSORSHIP

Sponsorship is a business relationship between an organisation and an individual, event or another organisation. The sponsoring organisation gets rights or associations that may be used for commercial advantage in return (normally) for giving money.

There is a broad range of opportunities for sponsorship, including low-key ones such as sponsoring a local school or village fête, or global opportunities such as the Olympics. Sponsorship has increased dramatically over the last decade, driven by six factors:

- Restrictive government policies on tobacco and alcohol advertising

- Escalating costs of media advertising

- Increased leisure activities and sporting events

- Proven track record of sponsorship

- Greater media coverage of sporting events

- Reduced efficiency of traditional media advertising (problems of clutter and zapping)

Sport sponsorship is by far the most popular sponsorship medium, worth £428 million in the UK alone in 2005 (Ipsos-MORI Sportscan). Sport offers many advantages to potential sponsors: high visibility through extensive media coverage; the ability to attract a cross-section of the population; the potential to service specific niches and the capacity to break down cultural barriers.

In order to benefit most from expenditure on sponsorship it is necessary to specify objectives, even though these may be relatively intangible. The most common objectives for sponsorship are to gain publicity, create entertainment opportunities, encourage favourable brand and company associations, improve community relations and create promotional opportunities. These are dealt with in turn below.

10.4.1 Publicity

Many sporting events have extensive media coverage, and companies can take advantage of sponsorship to gain publicity. Barclays, for example, currently sponsors the UK football premier league. Football is the most watched sport in the UK, capturing 42.3 per cent of the adult population. Viewers' commitment to the sport is underlined by the fact that 11.0 per cent pay to watch and 20.2 per cent read about it before and afterwards (TGI/BMRB). Football supporters cover the demographic spectrum, as do people who might need the financial services of sponsors such as Barclays.

10.4.2 Entertainment opportunities

Organisations use their sponsorship of events to create corporate hospitality opportunities. Barclays' sponsorship of the Premier League, for example, allows them to take major corporate clients to popular football matches. This in turn can increase business sales.

10.4.3 Favourable associations

Company sponsorship encourages favourable brand and company associations. Sponsorship of athletics events by GlaxoSmithKline, for example, reinforces the position of its Lucozade brand, and in particular its Lucozade Sports sub-brand.

10.4.4 Community relations

Sponsorship improves community relations, which can be particularly appropriate for SMEs. For example, a small company could sponsor the local junior hockey team or tabards for the local school's walking bus.

10.4.5 Promotional opportunities

■ Create promotional opportunities

Promotional opportunities can come as a result of sponsoring sporting, community, or other activities. For example, the Chartered Institute of Marketing sponsors the Academy of Marketing (academic) conference. In return they gain the goodwill of the academic community as well as their logo on the conference bags and promotional material placed in the bags.

FOR EXAMPLE

....

Manchester United is probably the most popular football club in the world, with an estimated 75 million fans around the world. Of these, fewer than 8 per cent have been to Old Trafford, their home football ground. So their fan base is mostly of virtual supporters who watch their team on TV. Its popularity allows it to attract a whole raft of sponsors.

■ AIG is the principal sponsor. It is a leading international insurance and financial services organisation that have made a four-year agreement with Manchester United costing £56.5 million. This is for the privilege of having their logo on the players' shirts, making it the biggest shirt sponsorship deal in English football.

■ Budweiser is the 'official beer' of Manchester United. Its sponsorship allows it exclusive lager pouring rights at Old Trafford.

Manchester United has many sponsors including AIG, the financial services group

- Nike is the 'official sportswear sponsor' of the club. It provides the team with 'Cool Motion' double-layer kit, similar to those worn by Brazil when it won the World Cup. Fans can buy replica kits, as well as training wear and other United merchandise. Many players also wear Nike boots.

- Audi UK is the 'official car supplier', in a two-season agreement. Approximately twenty Audi models are available for use as personal transport by senior team executives and high-profile players. Whilst the initial two-year deal is UK-centric, Audi is working on extending the relationship longer term for a global sponsorship agreement.

- Air Asia are the 'official low-fare airline' for the club. The airline is Asia's equivalent of easy Jet. The chief executive sees the benefits of sponsorship in the transference of some of the football club's brand image to their own: 'Manchester United stands for creativity, passion and the best of football. The partnership signifies our determination to be the best, and have the highest quality product.'

- Royal Resorts are the Official Leisure Property Development Partner for the club. The deal promotes residential projects, using the Club's global marketing platform. Royal Resorts have promotional areas at Old Trafford, as well as stadium advertising, web promotion and direct marketing aiming to build the brand.

- Tourism Malaysia is the 'official destination partner'. Its sponsorship objective is to promote Malaysia as an outstanding tourist destination, increasing the number and length of stay of visitors.

- Century FM is the 'official radio station'. It is a local radio station that transmits all games in stereo, whether home or away, to a population of 5.1 million people living in the north-west of the UK. They host The Legends Football Phone-In every weekday giving listeners the chance to talk to former players.

- BetFred is the 'official betting partner'. The deal allows the company to provide in-stadium betting at Old Trafford for fans on match days and their own online sports betting, poker, casino, games, arcade and lotto sites. Fred Stone, the founder of BetFred and a lifelong Manchester United fan, says of the partnership: 'This is a dream come true. I've been a season ticket holder at United for forty-five years and the opportunity to be an official partner was a deal I could not pass up. This deal is about associating ourselves with the world's best.'

CHECKPOINT

Can you name another current sponsor of major sporting events? How successful do you think the sponsorship has been?

10.5 DIRECT MARKETING

In concluding the two chapters on promotions (Chapters 9 and 10), we consider 'direct marketing', a popular modern concept that embraces many of the promotional tools we have discussed. Direct marketing was originally used to describe direct mail and mail order. The concept has now expanded to include all of the elements that facilitate direct contact between a targeted consumer and a supplier. It bypasses traditional marketing channels or distribution methods (see Chapter 11) and selects promotional methods that communicate directly with the target market. These include: telemarketing, direct response TV, the Internet, direct mail and personal selling. Originating in mail order businesses such as Grattan and Littlewoods, direct marketing is quoted as being the fastest growing element in the promotional mix.

CHECKPOINT

Think of a time when you were contacted directly to buy something, or make a sales appointment. How effective do think this approach was compared to less direct ways of buying the same service or product (e.g. retail)?

10.6 SUMMARY

- Advertising campaigns can be planned and implemented in five stages:
  - Setting objectives of informing, persuading and/or reinforcing
  - Estimating the budget by considering expenditure as a percentage of income, competitive expenditure, objectives and tasks, and/or what is affordable
  - Deciding the creative strategy and message, for example USP or lifestyle
  - Selecting the media from press, TV, radio, cinema, posters, direct mail and the Internet
  - Evaluating the results
- Sales promotions, or 'below the line' advertising, can be:
  - 'Push' promotions such as trade promotions or salesforce incentives
  - 'Pull' promotions to consumers such as discounts, samples, coupons, competitions, sponsorship, point-of-sale displays or credit facilities
- Public relations (PR) is defined as the efforts to establish and maintain understanding between an organisation and its publics.
- 'Publics' important to an organisation include the workforce, suppliers, intermediaries, customers, local community, financial community and policy makers.
- Methods used to communicate with publics include media relations, published information, lobbying, support for 'good causes' and crisis management.
- Sponsorship offers the sponsoring organisation the opportunity to improve its image with its target market by gaining positive associations. It can also allow companies to avoid legislation prohibiting advertising.
- Direct marketing is a fast-growing promotional element that bypasses normal distribution methods to communicate and deal directly with consumers. It uses many elements of the promotional mix such as telemarketing, the Internet and direct mail.

10.7 ACTIVITIES

CASE STUDY

EAU DEAR

Dasani was launched in the UK by the Coca-Cola company as a brand of bottled water, in 2004. This was a competitive reaction following the success of Aquafina, produced by their arch rival Pepsi Co. It was one of many brands of Coca-Cola water products sold around the world which differed in composition between its different markets. For example, in the United States Coca-Cola used water from local municipal water supplies, filtered it using the process of reverse osmosis, and added trace amounts of minerals, including salt. US consumers were unconcerned about the process; as far as they were concerned 'water was water'.

The climate in the UK was very different. European consumers have grown up with European brands such as Evian, Malvern and Buxton Spring Water which make much of their natural sources. Only two months after launch, it became public that tap water from the UK national supply was being treated, bottled and sold under the Dasani brand name. Although Coca-Cola never implied that the water was being sourced from a spring or other natural source, they marketed it as being especially 'pure'. Hence, the public revelation of it being simply treated tap water caused a media stir.

The media made mocking parallels with a popular episode of the well-known BBC situation comedy *Only Fools and Horses*, in which the protagonist Del Boy attempts to pass off tap water as spring water. In the TV programme, the scheme fails when the local reservoir becomes polluted (also because of Del), causing the bottled water to glow yellow. The episode contributed to the severe negative reaction to Dasani by the press and public. Clips from this episode were shown in news reports and other programmes relating to the Dasani flop.

But this was not the end of Dasani's problems as the following article in the *Guardian* illustrates with reality following fiction:

theguardian

Things get worse with Coke

Bottled tap water withdrawn after cancer scare
Felicity Lawrence, consumer affairs correspondent, Saturday March 20, 2004.

First, Coca-Cola's new brand of 'pure' bottled water, Dasani, was revealed earlier this month to be tap water taken from the mains. Then it emerged that what the firm described as its 'highly sophisticated purification process', based on Nasa spacecraft technology, was in fact reverse osmosis used in many modest domestic water purification units.

Yesterday, just when executives in charge of a £7m marketing push for the product must have felt it could get no worse, it did precisely that.

The entire UK supply of Dasani was pulled off the shelves because it has been contaminated with bromate, a cancer-causing chemical.

So now the full scale of Coke's PR disaster is clear. It goes something like this: take Thames Water from the tap in your factory in Sidcup, Kent; put it through a purification process, call it 'pure' and give it a mark-up from 0.03p to 95p per half litre; in the process, add a batch of calcium chloride, containing bromide, for 'taste profile'; then pump ozone through it, oxidising the bromide – which is not a problem – into bromate – which is. Finally, dispatch to the shops bottles of water containing up to twice the legal limit for bromate (10 micrograms per litre).

The Drinking Water Inspectorate confirmed yesterday it had checked the Thames water supplied to the factory and found it free of bromate. Because it is unsafe at high levels, standards for bromate in tap water are strictly monitored.

Bromide is a naturally occurring trace chemical which has a sedative effect. It is said to have been added by the British army to soldiers' tea during the Second World War to dampen down their lust. But when it is oxidized into bromate it becomes 'a pretty nasty carcinogen', according to David Drury, one of the principal inspectors for the DWI.

'I've checked Thames water's supply this morning and it is free of bromate,' he said. The legal limits are set to have a wide margin of safety, and the Food Standards Agency advice yesterday was that while Dasani contained illegal levels of bromate, it did not present an immediate risk to the public.

'Any increased cancer risk is likely to be small. However the levels are higher than legally permitted in the UK and present an unnecessary risk. Some consumers may chose not to drink any Dasani they purchased prior to its withdrawal given the levels of bromate in it,' the FSA said.

Coca-Cola said it was voluntarily withdrawing all Dasani 'to ensure that only products of the highest quality are provided to our consumers'.

Coca-Cola recalled half a million bottles and withdrew the Dasani brand from the UK market in March 2004. Ironically, the bromate was not present in the tap water before Coca-Cola's treatment process. Coca-Cola added calcium chloride to meet UK laws requiring calcium in all bottled waters. The company claims that the amount of bromide in the water led to the formation of unacceptable levels of bromate during the process used in purification.

The withdrawal of the product and the resulting PR disaster has been likened to the New Coke fiasco. Coca-Cola's plans to launch Dasani as natural spring water in France and Germany were shelved after the bad publicity in the UK.

QUESTIONS

1 Coca-Cola decided to withdraw Dasani. Do you think they had any choice? Explain your answer.

2 What research might Coca-Cola have carried out to prevent this disaster?

3 How would you recommend that Coca-Cola re-enter the bottled water market?

DEVELOPING A MARKETING PLAN

ADVERTISING, SALES PROMOTION, PR, SPONSORSHIP AND DIRECT MARKETING STRATEGIES

Complete your promotional plan by establishing advertising, sales promotion, PR strategies and optionally sponsorship and direct marketing strategies:

- What will be your objectives?
- How much do you plan to spend?
- What media will you use and what types of sales promotions will you consider?
- What will be the creative strategy?
- How will you evaluate the results?
- What PR activities do you intend?
- Will you use sponsorship?
- Will you employ direct marketing?

10.8 FURTHER READING AND REFERENCES

Marketing communications

Blythe, J. (2006), *Marketing Communications*, 3rd edition (Financial Times Press).

A number of practitioner journals contain examples and cases of promotional campaigns and topics, including:

Advertising Age
Campaign
Direct Response
Marketing Week
Marketing
Marketing Direct
PR Week
Revolution

Advertising

Advertising Works Series, WARC, Henley. The latest is *Advertising Works* 15 (2006).
Butterfield, L. (editor) (1999), *Excellence in Advertising* (Butterworth Heinemann).
Jay, R. (1998), *Profitable Direct Marketing* (Thomson Learning).
Ogilvy, D. (1995), *Ogilvy on Advertising* (Prion Books).

Internet advertising

Chaffey, D. (2006), *Internet Marketing: Strategy, Implementation and Practice*, 3rd edition (FT Press).

Sales promotions

Blythe, J. (2000), *Marketing Communications* (Financial Times/Prentice Hall), Chapter 10.
Davies, M. (1992), 'Sales Promotion as a Competitive Strategy', *Management Decision*, Vol. 30, No. 7, pages 5–10.

Public relations

Tench, R. and Yeomans, L. (2006), *Exploring Public Relations* (Prentice Hall).
Baines, P., Egan, J. and Jefkins, F. (2004), *Public Relations: Contemporary Issues and Techniques* (Elsevier).

Direct marketing

Thomas, B. and Housden, M. (2002), *Direct Marketing in Practice* (Butterworth Heinemann).
www.theidm.co.uk
www.dmis.co.uk

Chapter 11

PLACE: MARKETING CHANNELS

LEARNING OBJECTIVES

By the end of this chapter the reader will be able to:

- Understand the options to be considered in making goods and services available to customers
- Assess the variety of marketing channels that link suppliers and buyers
- Analyse the strategies available for selecting and managing marketing channels
- Appreciate the types and trends in modern retailing
- Assess the advantages and disadvantages of franchising

INTRODUCTION

This chapter looks at how products and services are 'placed' into the market through channels of distribution – a further important ingredient in the marketing mix. We examine the choices of marketing channels available and strategies for managing them. Marketing channels have changed significantly in recent years: the Internet has added a new dimension to distributing goods; retailing has become increasingly concentrated in the hands of a few large chains; and franchising has standardised the way we receive products and services on a global basis. These and other developments mean that marketing channels have become a very dynamic element in the marketing mix.

11.1 PLACING PRODUCTS: LOCATION, LOGISTICS AND CHANNELS

As one of the '4 Ps' in the marketing mix, 'place' refers to how goods and services are made available to customers in the marketplace. The concept of 'place' refers not only to the location in which products are offered, but also the channels of distribution through which products move

CASE STUDY

....

FABIO FABRIK – DISTRIBUTING VISION

Antonio Sollicor knew that he had a serious conflict of interest to resolve. His meetings with representatives from the ophthalmic trade had made it quite clear that selecting and managing channels of distribution in the UK for his company's products was not going to be an easy matter. He was the international marketing manager of Fabio Fabrik, Italian manufacturers of spectacle frames, lenses and ready-made reading glasses. Their range of upmarket 'designer' optical products were expensive, but many customers in Italy, France, Germany and other continental European countries were prepared to pay the price for good design and the desirable 'Luce' brand name on their spectacle frames. As he was responsible for all sales outside of Italy, Sollicor was particularly keen to make progress in the UK, a market in which his company sold comparatively little but which had been opened up by deregulation.

In the past, British customers were reluctant to buy anything other than utilitarian frames and few indulged in the continental habit of owning several sets of spectacles to suit the occasion or the outfit. The NHS scheme, which provided financial assistance to those who qualified, still accounted for over 40 per cent of dispensed spectacles and tended to depress the average price of a pair of glasses. (The average spend on a pair of NHS voucher spectacles was £60 compared to £90 for privately dispensed spectacles.) Luce frames alone without lenses were priced from £85 to £225, but they had begun to sell through a select number of opticians. The 1988 Health and Medicines Act deregulated the ophthalmic market, ending the registered opticians' monopoly position. It abolished free sight tests for all and encouraged more competition in the supply of optical products. The market has also been affected by a number of regulatory changes, including amendments to the 1989 Opticians Act, which allow supermarkets to sell contact lenses. Frame design began to gain a higher profile among customers, tentatively encouraged by a profession which began to realise the importance of offering higher quality branded products in a competitive marketplace. Consumers had begun to show an increasing interest in designer label frames and Sollicor was encouraged by research indicating more acceptability of wearing glasses as a fashion item.

Sollicor had found it difficult to establish effective distribution channels for Fabio Fabrik in a fragmented optical trade. Many of the 7,000 optical retailers were independents with an estimated 25 per cent share of the market. However, this had fallen substantially since deregulation as a number of major retail chains had expanded through organic growth and acquisition. Four market leaders, Specsavers, Boots, Dollond and Aitchison, and Vision Express, and a growing number of smaller chains had emerged since the legislative changes. The top four accounted for nearly three-quarters of the market. Specsavers had expanded rapidly by setting up joint venture franchises with professional opticians; it had over 380 outlets in the UK. Boots' 300 outlets were divided almost equally between free-standing and in-store outlets; it particularly concentrated on own-label and exclusive frames, which accounted for two-thirds of sales. Dollond and Aitchison was the oldest established chain with 380 branches in the UK; it had launched an innovative Internet service allowing customers to scan in a photograph of themselves for a 'virtual fitting' of different frames. Vision Express, part of Grand Vision, was Europe's largest optical retailer, with over 490 outlets across Europe. It was one of the trade's most prolific spenders on advertising. Total advertising expenditure by opticians had increased rapidly after deregulation.

Initially Luce branded products were available to any optical retailer who wished to stock them, but Sollicor was considering changing his strategy. He had been approached by Horatio's, an ambitious new group which operated on a franchise basis emphasising elegant style and design in their themed outlets. They were asking for more exclusive rights to the Luce range, which they claimed would give them the confidence to emphasise it in their promotional campaigns and would enhance the exclusive image of the products. 'Each of our retail outlets is owned by the franchisee manager,' Horatio's founder, Jenny Nelson, had told Sollicor, 'which gives them the motivation to increase the average value of each sale by explaining the benefits of high-quality, well-designed frames to customers.'

Sollicor also had to find effective distribution channels for his company's range of ready-made reading glasses. The 1988 Act made it possible to buy ready-mades over the counter from any shop without a sight test. This market, which did not exist before deregulation, grew rapidly to sales of over two million pairs of reading glasses in a few years. This was fuelled in part by the ageing profile of the UK. People over the age of forty-five – a group that has more need of sight correction – were increasing in number. Sollicor knew this was not only good news for the UK market but also for global demand, with nearly two-thirds of the world's population needing some form of sight correction. However, on average less than a quarter of people actually possessed corrective lenses. There were wide differences regionally: In North America, Japan, Australia and Western Europe those in need of corrected vision usually had access to it; but a high proportion of the population in Eastern Europe, Latin America and Asia were still in need of optical correction, with less access to optical services and lower incomes to pay for it.

Fabio Fabrik made an attractive range of ready-made glasses under the Luce label and although they would retail above the common price range of £15–£20 per pair, they would still be well below the £80 average price of glasses dispensed through an optician. However, Sollicor had spoken to opticians who were far from persuaded by arguments that ready-mades were targeted at consumers who did not need specialist advice in spectacle selection because their eyes were not defective, just weakened with age. Some of his customers told him of their outright opposition to the sale of ready-mades: 'Each person's eyes require individual treatment – sometimes they differ from each other so there is no guarantee that the purchaser will find the right lenses without expert help. And ready-mades mean fewer eye tests to spot more serious problems in good time.' He knew that other distribution channels were more enthusiastic because chemists, department stores and even garages sold ready-mades. Knowing the importance of understanding buyer behaviour, he had read research indicating that the majority of consumers thought that knowledgeable staff and a clean and friendly environment were important to them in choosing an optician. The research also confirmed that, although people thought that deals and lower prices were important, there was still a demand for the smaller local optician, and recommendation was a key factor in consumer choice.

Although ready-mades were still a small part of the total £3.18 billion UK market for ophthalmic goods and services, Sollicor acknowledged that his company could enter this fast-growing segment relatively easily because it already produced a suitable range. His problem was how to win support for Luce products from opticians, the key distributors of frames and lenses, whilst establishing effective distribution for ready-mades whose introduction had been opposed by the profession.

'If we see Luce ready-mades in all the chemists and garages of the land, it will undermine the value of the brand and not encourage us to recommend the same company for high-quality bespoke frames,' one of his biggest accounts had told him.

QUESTIONS

1 What different aspects of 'placing' his product in the marketplace does Sollicor need to consider? Which major decision areas does the place element of the marketing mix cover? *See section 11.1*

2 Consider the types of distribution channels that are illustrated in this case. What are the advantages and disadvantages of using these intermediaries for a company such as Fabio Fabrik? *See section 11.2*

3 Which distribution channels should Sollicor select for the different lines in the Luce range? How should he manage these? *See section 11.3*

4 What trends in the general distributive and retail sector are illustrated in this case? What future developments do you think could be particularly important for the distribution of optical products? *See sections 11.4 and 11.5*

from producer or supplier to the final user and the physical methods that are used to achieve this. The Internet has added further possibilities to how products and services are transferred to customers.

11.1.1 Location

Access to customers

Physical location is a key ingredient in the success of many types of business, particularly retail and business services that rely on customers visiting their premises. It has been said that the three most important factors in the success or failure of retail outlets and hotels are location, location and location. Retailers in sectors such as food, clothing and household goods need easy access to appropriately sized populations to survive as most people still do a majority of this type of shopping within a few miles of where they live. Customers choose hotels on the basis of where they are situated before considering other factors.

Location is also a major factor in the delivery of many public services in areas such as local government, education and healthcare. As public services have become more focused on service users, location has become an important issue. For some services it is a key influence, but outside of the direct control of local managers. For example, most parents choose to send their children to the primary school that is nearest to them, so that the viability of a school depends crucially on the size of the population in their immediate catchment area – a factor over which headteachers and governors have no control. For other public services, cost restrictions limit the choice of location. For example, local councils might prefer to locate their various services in decentralised sites near to centres of population, but normally they are forced to adopt the less expensive option of centralising all departments in one, less accessible building. The National Health Service has tended to concentrate its resources in large regional hospitals that are more efficient but often less convenient than smaller community units, which have been closed.

Access to resources

The location of some types of business is less dependent on proximity to a customer base. Manufacturers may produce for regional, national or international markets and so they do not need to be geographically near to customers. Developments in communications technology mean that many intangible products can be made available anywhere by telephone, email or the Internet.

FOR EXAMPLE

....

Banks and building societies originally evolved on a geographic basis because customers needed to visit their local branch to negotiate loans and mortgages or deposit and withdraw money. The names of many institutions reflect their geographic origins – for example the Midland Bank (now HSBC – formerly the Hong Kong and Shanghai Banking Corporation), the Bank of Scotland, the Halifax (now part of HBOS plc), Woolwich plc (now part of Barclays), Bradford and Bingley plc and Chelsea Building Society. Financial transactions can now take place remotely using the Internet, telephone or post. This has allowed direct banking to emerge, and brands such as Egg and First Direct have no physical branches. Traditional banks and societies have changed the way they operate substantially in order to compete in the new environment. Marketing strategies are now less reliant on location of branches and more dependent on the provision of a wider range of competitive services. A spate of mergers and takeovers has reduced the number of branch outlets in the High Street, as online and telephone banking services have become increasingly popular.

In these circumstances, location may still be an important consideration in the cost base and service levels provided by the company. Access to resources, such as appropriately skilled employees or suitable premises, is dependent on location. For a manufacturer, the location of suitable premises near to a skilled labour force may be crucial to their ability to deliver competitively priced products on time. The key resource for service industries such as banks and building societies is people. Customer services have been concentrated in call centres located in areas of relatively high unemployment and low labour costs to ensure access to a good supply of inexpensive employees. Poor reaction to the location of call centres in India has led at least one bank to advertise the fact that their call centres are UK-based.

11.1.2 Physical distribution or logistics

The methods by which goods and services are transferred from supplier to consumer require careful consideration. Sometimes referred to as 'logistics', physical distribution can represent a significant proportion of the final cost of a product. It includes order processing, warehousing, storage, transportation and handling, all of which can add considerably to the manufactured costs of a product. Modern developments have changed physical handling systems dramatically:

- ■ *Containerisation*, or putting goods into large containers or trailers, allows products to be moved easily between two or more different transportation methods. Containers can be transferred quickly and efficiently from ship to lorry, to rail or to plane, making it possible to select the most effective mode of transport for each leg of the journey.

- ■ *Computerisation* has improved many stock control and order processing systems, reducing costs to the organisation and achieving higher service levels to the customer – once the inevitable bugs are removed from the system. 'Just-in-time' (JIT) systems are designed to provide the customer with components for manufacturing as they are needed. This reduces the need to carry large stocks of items, and therefore reduces the cost of manufacturing.

FOR EXAMPLE

....

Michael Dell began to assemble and sell computers whilst still at university and went on to revolutionise computer making. His business model was relatively simple: he supplied computers direct to end-users according to their own specification. It meant that customers got the computer they wanted at lower prices. The model worked for the customers and it also worked for Dell Computers, which became the number-one PC supplier. A key factor in Dell's success was his ability to reduce component stocks to well below the industry norm. PCs are made mainly from standard parts. By delivering direct according to a customer's specification, Dell reduced the stocks he had to hold to a minimum. In practice, the number of options available to customise a computer is limited mainly to the speed of the processor and size of the memory. This made it possible for Dell to offer made-to-order PCs whilst keeping stock levels down. As computer technology changes so quickly, it is particularly important to avoid having obsolete stock. Lower stock levels than his competitors made Dell's company more profitable, with more money to invest in marketing to build an even larger share of the market.

■ *Online products* have eliminated the need for physical distribution altogether. Some product categories can be digitised and transferred from one computer to another over the Internet. This has the potential to completely change the way in which some sectors, such as the music, publishing and information industries, distribute their products.

FOR EXAMPLE

....

Music can be distributed directly over the Internet because musical content itself can be digitised and downloaded onto computers. However, it has proved difficult to turn this into a profitable business model. Napster developed a huge following by offering free downloads, but this violated copyright laws. David Bowie's *Hours* album was offered as a download-only version two weeks before it

Flow of content between client, server and customer

was released in hard-copy form through standard distribution channels. However, it made only 800 Internet sales at the cost of alienating traditional retailers. The Internet has become an important medium for promoting and ordering CDs and tapes and it is beginning to realise its potential for direct delivery of music. This is developing rapidly as the major companies are beginning to enter the field. For example, EMI now make albums available for digital download, and BMG has relaunched Napster as a legitimate paid-for service.

© S.I.N/ALAMY

David Bowie's Hours *album could be downloaded two weeks before its official release*

11.1.3 *Channels of distribution*

Most products move through various distribution channels such as agents, wholesalers or retailers, which act as intermediaries between producer and final customer. These intermediaries usually take title to the goods; that is, they buy them from the previous link in the chain before selling them onto the next.

FOR EXAMPLE

Producers of cola such as Coke and Pepsi sell their products through a variety of channels. One route is through franchised bottling companies around the world, who purchase syrup and the rights to sell on the final branded consumer product to wholesalers and retailers of soft drinks. The cola producers also sell their syrup direct to large retailers who bottle it under their own label. Agents buy cola syrup from the producers and sell it to restaurants and bars with the necessary equipment and supplies to provide the final product on tap. A drink purchased in a dispensing machine, shop or bar has passed through multiple channels of distribution before reaching the final consumer.

Decisions on marketing channels sometimes do not receive the same level of attention as other marketing decisions. Yet distribution channels crucially influence the other elements of the marketing mix:

- ■ *Products* are often developed or acquired because they complement existing distribution channels.

- ■ *Pricing* has to take account of the traditional margins that wholesalers and retailers expect in the particular trade or industry.

FOR EXAMPLE

A wine producer in France knows that a bottle of wine sold by their vineyard for one euro (or approximately £0.65) will retail in the UK for close to £4 once taxes are added, but also once the various intermediaries such as the importer, wholesalers and retailers have added their appropriate mark-ups. This is an important influence on his pricing decisions because the UK is a key export market.

MARKETING MISTAKES

YOUR TROUBLES ARE ROVER

Over-capacity amongst Europe's car producers has led to a number of takeovers and rationalisation of ranges. Some have proved more successful than others. In 1994 the German car manufacturer BMW acquired the Rover group from British Aerospace for £800 million. Rover's special relationship with the Japanese group Honda, which had given the British car company access to much-needed technical and production expertise, was broken by the deal. Rover's management remained convinced that they would benefit more as part of BMW because it gained them access to a distribution network that they claimed could give them an extra 100,000 car sales from day one. BMW's strong distribution networks, particularly in Germany and the USA, could boost sales of Land Rover and smaller cars like the Metro and the Mini which complemented BMW's executive range. In the event, the strategy worked for only part of the range. Land Rover and a new generation Mini proved complementary to the BMW ranges and benefited from new investment and strengthened distribution.

However, Rover continued to lose market share whilst BMW's own brands gained ground. In 2000, BMW sold this part of the business through a management buy-out because the ranges had proved too close to fully differentiate in an increasingly competitive market. The new Rover entity proved short lived, however, and finally went out of business in 2006. The partnership with BMW was meant to herald the renaissance of Rover. The Rover cars were technically strong – the Rover 75 won ten international motor industry awards. The range benefited from improved access to market channels through the addition of the BMW distribution system. What went wrong? The image of Rover was not right for the markets to which it now had access. It had become a symbol of the decline of the British motor industry, associated for too long with unreliability and labour disputes. Car expert Jeremy Clarkson dismissed the Rover brand as the 'least cool badge in the business. Rover, the name is a dog'.

© MOTORING PICTURE LIBRARY/ALAMY

Rover 75: just being a great car was not enough

■ *Promotions,* however persuasive, are not effective if the product is not readily available in the appropriate place in the market.

FOR EXAMPLE

Two entrepreneurs decide to launch a new magazine. The concept is tested and receives high praise from the intended market. The entrepreneurs therefore draw up plans for a launch campaign of promotional activities to the target customers. They put their plans on hold, however, when initial meetings with key wholesalers and retailers indicate they are not prepared to stock the product because they believe that sales would not justify the shelf space. The new company set up by the entrepreneurs does not have the credibility to overcome this barrier to entry to traditional channels to the market, so it needs to come up with an alternative distribution method for their publication.

CHECKPOINT

If you were one of the entrepreneurs that had been rejected by the wholesale/retail distributors for a new magazine, what would you do? What alternatives could you pursue? (See section 11.3.1 for what the entrepreneurs actually did.)

The types and roles of distribution channels are explored more fully in section 11.2.

11.2 MARKETING CHANNELS

11.2.1 Channel levels

A manufacturer is usually faced with the choice of selling products through a number of channel levels or distributing direct to the customer. Some of the choices available through traditional distribution channels are illustrated in Figure 11.1.

This shows different channel levels, or layers of intermediaries, that can become involved in the distribution process, each one adding to the length of the distribution chain. Although definitions vary from industry to industry, some commonly used terms are as follows:

- **Agents**: Independent intermediaries who represent producers or suppliers, often with particular responsibility for a geographic territory. For example, they may import a range of

FIGURE 11.1

Distribution channel levels

goods from one or more overseas manufacturers into their home country. In turn, they supply wholesalers, retailers or sell direct to end users.

- *Sales agents*: Intermediaries who represent producers and suppliers, but unlike agents they usually do not take title to the goods because they act in a marketing and sales administration capacity only. For example, smaller publishers of greetings cards often use independent sales agents or 'agents on commission' because they cannot individually justify the costs of personal selling to fragmented stationery and gift retailers. Brokers sell insurance direct to the final customer in return for a commission from the insurance company, who write the policy. Office equipment manufacturers appoint sales agents to distribute their products directly to organisations or through distributors and dealers.

- *Wholesalers*: Organisations that buy a range of stock from producers or their agents, which they then resell to the retail trade. A full-service wholesaler provides a range of facilities including selling, order processing and delivery. For example, newspaper and magazine wholesalers receive print runs in bulk from the publishers, which they break down into smaller quantities for onward transmission to the many retail outlets around the country.

- *Retailers*: Those who sell goods or services direct to the final consumer. Retailing outlets vary from hypermarkets to village stores and include an increasing variety of non-store methods such as mail-order catalogues, telemarketing and electronic shopping. The different types of retailer and trends in the sector are discussed in section 11.4.

- *Distributors and dealers*: Sell goods direct to the end user but in this case the customer is often a business or an organisation. For example, educational books and other teaching products are often sold to schools through independent distributors. Dealers sell office products such as furniture and stationery to small businesses. Distributors representing specialist manufacturers provide restaurant owners with the equipment they need. Even though a majority of their sales are business-to-business, some dealers also have a retail outlet open to all as the distinctions between wholesalers, distributors and retailers become increasingly blurred. For example, dealers originally set up to sell PCs and software to the local business community found their services increasingly required by individual customers as the computer revolution spread from the office to the home.

Producers employ the channel options that they consider appropriate to their organisation, its products and the market.

FOR EXAMPLE

Letraset, the manufacturer of stationery graphic transfer products, developed distribution networks around the world to suit the circumstances of the market and the resources of the company. In the UK, the 'instant lettering' product was sold to the graphic art user via retail outlets. Some very large, specialised accounts, such as government departments, were supplied direct. In each overseas market an exclusive agent was set up to manage the local distribution system. In large markets such as the USA these agents also sold through wholesalers to the smaller retailers. As Letraset grew, it began to establish its own subsidiary companies in major markets in Europe, North America and Australasia. These subsidiaries took on the role previously played by the importing agent. Letraset also sold a range of transfers for children, often offered as promotions for other products such as breakfast cereals. These sold through sales promotion agencies who were the specialised distributors for this type of product to organisations such as cereal producers. In international markets sales agents were appointed to co-ordinate the efforts of these distributors.

11.2.2 Advantages of intermediaries

As they usually do little to change the actual product, what roles do intermediaries play to justify their place in the chain to the ultimate consumer?

■ *Reduced investment*: By shifting the responsibility for stockholding further down the chain, a manufacturer can reduce the amount of their own funds tied up in stocks. They can also minimise their investment in premises, transport, systems and other aspects of the distribution infrastructure.

■ *Local knowledge*: An intermediary such as an agent or a wholesaler usually operates in a geographic area where they understand the business environment and have good local contacts. If an organisation wishes to expand into areas where they have little experience, they may need the knowledge and networks of a local intermediary, at least for a while.

FOR EXAMPLE

As we have described above, Letraset set up distribution agents in countries around the world. As their products were protected initially by patents, the company wanted to take full advantage of this limited window of opportunity. By penetrating international markets whilst competition was limited, they put themselves in a strong market position for the tougher times when the patents expired. They could only do this by using the resources and knowledge of national agents who were able to sell product quickly into their local distribution networks. Later, Letraset wished to profit more from its strong market position, using its increased resources to cut out some of the channel levels to keep a larger share of the financial pie in the company. Many agents were replaced by directly controlled subsidiaries that were able to build on the work of the agent by focusing solely on Letraset products.

■ *Economies of scale*: A distributor or retailer selling more than one manufacturer's products spreads the distribution costs, which should achieve some economies of scale.

■ *Transactional efficiency*: By consolidating a number of producers' products in one place, an intermediary cuts down the number of transactions required to give customers what they need.

FOR EXAMPLE

Robin Hood and his Merry Men were concerned at the increasing risks of buying their bows and arrows in Nottingham. Four of them took it in turn to visit local artisans who supplied bows, strings, arrow heads and shafts. This required sixteen transactions to secure what they needed, a time-consuming and risky process not only for the wanted men but also for the artisans if they were caught supplying the outlaws. Happily, a middleman set himself up in Nottingham market selling the goods of the four artisans, thereby halving to eight the number of the risky transactions needed to supply Hood and his men. Hood also decided to reduce their exposure by getting Friar Tuck to make the purchasers on behalf of himself, Little John and Will Scarlett, reducing the number of external transactions to only one.

Reducing the number of outside contacts through the use of a middleman could have increased security for Robin Hood and his Merry Men.

Intermediaries could have helped Robin Hood and his men conceal their identities.

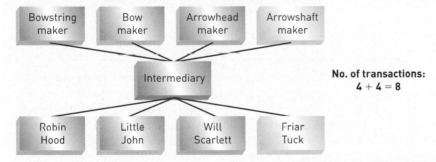

FIGURE 11.2

Transactional efficiency

A: Direct contacts

No. of transactions:
4 × 4 = 16

B: Transactions through an intermediary

No. of transactions:
4 + 4 = 8

■ *Breaking bulk*: Sometimes intermediaries take a large consignment of goods and break it down into more manageable units for the next distributor or customer in the chain. This process of 'breaking bulk' takes place, for example, when an economic shipment quantity, such as a full container of electronic goods, arrives at an importing wholesaler and is divided up into the smaller quantities required by retail outlets.

11.2.3 Disadvantages of intermediaries

Some manufacturers still opt to sell direct to the final consumer; so what are the disadvantages of using intermediaries?

■ *Loss of contact with the marketplace*: Organisations that rely on intermediaries for their distribution and selling are one or more steps removed from the consumers they are trying to serve. They can become reliant on intermediaries for information about developments in the marketplace, so that the distribution channels become more influential over product developments than the producers.

FOR EXAMPLE

The channels of distribution for food have become increasingly controlled by the large retailers. In the UK, three groups, Sainsbury, Tesco, and Asda, control 50 per cent of retail food sales. Farmers have become increasingly remote from the public they serve, powerless to influence the type of products that are made available to the consumer in these large retail outlets. One of the largest landowners in England is trying to change this trend by shortening the lines of communication between producer and user. Keen to make more organic food available from his estates in the Duchy of Cornwall, the Prince of Wales decided to launch his own branded food products. Using organic wheat and oats from 'The Home Farm' in Tetbury, Gloucestershire, and other Duchy of Cornwall farms, Prince Charles commissioned the design and manufacture of a range of biscuits branded as 'Duchy Originals'. Unlike most food products, where the origin of the ingredients remains relatively unknown to the consumer, these biscuits proclaim the name of the farm and its agricultural policies on the packaging in an effort to put the farmer back in touch with the consumers of their produce, with more say in what they eat.

■ *Less control over marketing methods and effort*: If intermediaries present the product to the final consumer, they have considerable influence not only over how it is marketed but also the amount of effort used to sell one product compared to its competitors.

FOR EXAMPLE

An electrical retailer provides in-store information and advice to consumers on a range of branded goods. Although the manufacturers have invested heavily in promotions in support of their brands, they rely on staff employed by the retailer to present the appropriate benefits of their products to customers. The retailer is also responsible for after-sales service and the administration of guarantees and warranties. These and other potentially major influences on customer perceptions of a branded product are in the hands of a third party. The retailer's management and staff also exercise choice over which products receive most effort in terms of display, promotional effort and selling time.

■ *Less revenue per item sold*: Intermediaries cost money as margin is taken at every level of the distribution channel. Although this is not a fixed amount but varies with the level of sales, the potential loss of revenue to a manufacturer can be substantial. Retailers commonly keep between one- and two-thirds of the final consumer price of most products. If agents' and wholesalers' margins are added, the producer can receive as little as 25 per cent of the final retail price.

FOR EXAMPLE

A jacket is for sale in an upmarket store for £150 excluding VAT (£176.25 inclusive of VAT). Because it is a fashion item that will date rapidly, the retailer needs a 60 per cent margin to justify the stock risk. This means that the retailer had bought the item for £60 from the wholesaler, who was making a 20 per cent margin on the garment, having purchased it from the importer for £48. The importer also made a 20 per cent margin, having paid the garment manufacturer just over £38 for the jacket, or 26 per cent of its final selling price (without VAT).

CHECKPOINT

You have developed a new ice cream, which you manufacture on a dairy farm (see page 366). What marketing channels would you consider?

11.3 CHANNEL STRATEGY: SELECTION AND MANAGEMENT

Strategic decisions on channels of distribution cover the *selection* of the appropriate distribution system and the *management* of that system so that it meets organisational goals. These two topics of channel selection and management are discussed in the following sections, followed by a summary of the influences that determine channel strategy.

11.3.1 *Channel selection*

The selection of distribution channels involves consideration of the existing market situation to decide on the *direction* of the channel in relation to competitive products and an assessment of the *intensity* of the distribution required.

Channel direction

In today's competitive markets, new products have to earn their place in a distribution system. Limited shelf space in retailing outlets is hard fought over as the numbers of products have proliferated. Electronic point-of-sale devices (EPOS) monitor the movement of goods from retailers shelves so that poor performing products can be quickly replaced or repositioned in the store. Faced with the need to compete for exposure to customers in the marketplace, producers can select from two basic alternatives:

- *A frontal strategy* of using the same channels as existing products. This may be appropriate if:
  — The new product has clear advantages over competitive products

— There is evidence of consumer demand because the product appeals to a new market segment or it has a track record of success through other channels

— The distribution channels are likely to favour the new product because it offers them better profits or because of their past relationship with the producer

■ *A bypass strategy* of going around the competition by using alternative arrangements. When the distribution channels are full or hostile to new additions this may be the only alternative. The Internet has opened up opportunities to bypass existing channels and sell direct to consumers, and reduce costs at the same time. For example, the travel industry is becoming less reliant on travel agents as a method of distribution as most operators offer online booking services. Some now encourage customers to book on the Internet by offering discounts. Potential distribution bottlenecks in other markets can also be side-stepped.

FOR EXAMPLE

The two entrepreneurs whose plans to launch a new magazine (see page 366) were blocked after exploratory talks with the major wholesalers and retailers decided that the only option was to distribute direct to the reader. The powerful wholesaling and retailing operations of WH Smith and John Menzies accounted for over two-thirds of the market and their co-operation was vital to the success of any new publication sold through newsagents. As these distributors were not convinced of the viability of the publication, the entrepreneurs redesigned the product and sold it as a newsletter-style magazine on an annual subscription basis downloaded over the Internet or by direct mail. They sold the new publication to businesses for redistribution to their employees. This minimised their transaction costs as they were selling multiple subscriptions to one customer, albeit at a much reduced price.

This approach proved successful and the publication achieved a good following. It allowed the entrepreneurs to return at a later date to the distributive trade and negotiate with them on favourable terms to give the necessary space in the major retailers to the publication.

Distribution intensity

The number of customers reached by a distribution strategy is a function of how intensively the potential channels are used. Where wide coverage is required an intensive strategy sells products through as many outlets as possible. Narrower market penetration indicates the need for more selective distribution. Distribution intensity can be typified as a continuum, as shown in Figure 11.3 below.

■ *Exclusive distribution* implies that the producer wishes to maintain high service levels to a select number of customers. A small number of intermediaries distribute the product because the producer wants to keep control of the channels or has limited production capacity.

FIGURE 11.3 *The continuum of distribution intensity*

FOR EXAMPLE

....

Duchy Originals Oaten Biscuits (see page 370) are available in a limited number of outlets. They are available in some wholefood shops and upmarket stores such as Fortnum and Mason. This is in line with the exclusive image of the product as well as its limited production capacity.

■ *Selective distribution* covers the principal areas for a product without extending beyond its main target markets.

FOR EXAMPLE

....

Letraset's early distribution strategy was to cover international markets as rapidly as possible, as we have described. However, within each geographic market, the distribution was restricted to graphic art dealers with sufficient resources to offer rapid service to their customers from a well-stocked range. In this way Letraset hoped to make their product readily available to their prime target customers without over-extending themselves in the marketplace.

■ *Intensive distribution* seeks to provide as many customer purchase points as possible. It is the norm for impulse consumer products, particularly those in the mature phase of their product life cycle, which need as much exposure as possible to maximise sales.

FOR EXAMPLE

....

Cola drinks are distributed intensively and are to be found in a wide variety of sales outlets including supermarkets, small corner shops, garages, newsagents, restaurants, bars, hotels, trains, planes, motorway cafes and dispensing machines in public places. Geographically, the distribution of the leading brand Coca-Cola is so intensive that it covers almost every country on earth and has made 'Coke' a universally understood word.

ENTREPRENEURIAL MARKETING

....

When Fraser Doherty was fourteen, he began selling jam, using his grandmother's secret recipes. The first success was his granny's marmalade, which Fraser sold door to door around the Edinburgh suburb where he lived. Within a year, his jams had proven so popular that he was cooking up to 1,000 jars a week from his parents' kitchen. He impressed local business agencies so much he was given an Enterprising Young Brit award from then-Chancellor Gordon Brown. Developed from his grandmother's original recipe, Fraser's jam included 'super foods' naturally rich in a range of nutrients that are claimed to have a beneficial effect on health. He also used grape juice to sweeten the fruit instead of refined sugar or artificial sweeteners.

From the original door-to-door selling he soon moved on to farmers' markets and supplying delicatessens across Scotland. Fraser took his healthier fruit spreads to one of Waitrose's regular 'Meet the Buyer' events where the supermarket felt that his Super Jams had the potential for a larger market. At the age of eighteen, he is now one of the youngest people to supply a UK supermarket. He has secured a deal with Waitrose worth over £170,000, requiring him to supply 120,000 jars of his super jams for their supermarkets.

As a result Fraser has taken production out of his parents' kitchen and moved it to a large jam factory in Herefordshire. His target is to secure 5 per cent of the £90-million-a-year jam market within the next five years, netting around £4.5 million in retail sales.

© LLOYD SMITH

Jammy teenager gets big distribution deal

CHECKPOINT

What are the potential risks and advantages in accepting the Waitrose contract?
How would you advise Fraser on this deal?

11.3.2 Channel management

Distribution channels made up of largely independent operators sometimes work efficiently and co-operatively, but often they do not. To resolve some of the conflicts that arise, members attempt to manage the channel through co-operation and coercion.

Channel conflict

There are many opportunities for the participants in a particular distribution channel to come into conflict with the other members.

■ *Horizontal conflict* arises when distributors on the same channel level disagree. For example, one dealer may complain that another is 'poaching' their business, or neighbouring retailers start a price war by discounting the same product. This may happen when there is unclear specification on the rights and responsibilities between channel members.

■ *Vertical conflict* arises between different levels of the channel. Producers may come into conflict with the retail or wholesale sector over trading terms and pricing policies. Conflicts of interest arise as channel members seek to enlarge their share of the same cake by changing discount structures, improving payment terms or reducing their stock-holding requirements at the expense of the next member of the distribution chain.

FOR EXAMPLE

....

Nashua, an American office equipment supplier, established a subsidiary in the UK to distribute their range of office copiers. To maximise sales whilst keeping the investment and risk at reasonable levels, the UK manager set up offices with a direct salesforce in Greater London, Birmingham and Manchester only and sold through a network of distributors and dealers in the rest of the country. Problems were not long in surfacing. The first issue was how to deal with large multi-site customers. Should they be serviced by Nashua's salesforce or the dealer in whose territory the central buying office was located? What would happen if machines were then sent from the central buying office to locations in other agent's territories? Complaints from dealers who discovered that equipment had been sold into their territory without their participation and disputes over 'customer ownership' became common. The next issue was over profit margins. Some dealers were single line – that is, they stocked only Nashua's products. They demanded higher discounts as reward for their loyalty which, they claimed, resulted in higher sales penetration than that achieved by the multi-line dealers who could pick and chose over which supplier to recommend.

Conventional distribution systems such as the one described in the example above can become inefficient and problematic as independent members try to meet their own objectives without regard for the health of the system as a whole.

11.3.3 Vertical marketing systems

Vertical marketing systems (VMS) have developed as a way of managing and controlling distribution channels to resolve some of these issues. In a VMS, the channel members – producers, wholesalers, retailers or dealers – operate as a unified system. This is achieved by combinations of coercion and co-operation. Some channels are controlled effectively by one very powerful member. Others are either owned by one organisation or bound by strong contractual links between all the parties.

Corporate vertical marketing systems

A corporate VMS unifies successive stages of manufacture and distribution under a single owner. A producer may decide to achieve control of the distribution channels by *forward integration*, that is buying into or setting up their own wholesaling and retailing operations. Or retailers may decide to own their own suppliers by a process of *backward integration*.

FOR EXAMPLE

....

In the UK, the major footwear manufacturers are also the largest retailers. The British Shoe Corporation was the market leader with 20 per cent of the market both as a producer and retailer of shoes, until its demise in the 1990s. This large conglomerate of over 2,000 outlets trading as Freeman Hardy and Willis, Saxone, Dolcis, Trueform, Shoe City, Curtess, and Cable and Manfield, was broken up into smaller groups. The largest of these is Stylo Barratt, which owns Barratt shoes and Saxone. The largest UK footwear group is now C&J Clark, a family-owned manufacturer and retailer trading through 600 outlets as Clarks Shoes, Peter Lord, Ravel and K shoes.

Although a corporate VMS exercises a great degree of control through ownership, there are disadvantages:

■ *Resource intensive*: Owning and managing a complete distribution chain absorbs such large amounts of financial and management resources that it may lead to neglect of other areas, such as product development and customer service.

■ *Expertise*: It is arguable whether one organisation can excel at both manufacturing and retailing. Retailers such as Marks and Spencer have deliberately avoided ownership of production and concentrated on retailing, their traditional area of expertise. The Burton Group moved away from their manufacturing base in the 1970s in order to concentrate on a targeted retailing approach.

■ *Conflict*: Vertical integration does not eliminate the possibility of conflict. In some cases it exacerbates it.

FOR EXAMPLE

Letraset developed their distribution internationally first through agents and then subsidiary companies distributing through the local dealer network (see page 367). As the market for 'instant lettering' matured, the company embarked on a strategy of forward integration to secure growth by taking a share of the dealers' business. Retail operations were bought or set up in Canada and Australia in order to test the concept. The reaction from the independent dealers was universally hostile. They felt threatened by a major supplier operating on the same channel level as themselves and many looked for alternative sources of supply for the first time. The company was still dependent on the dealer network for a large percentage of sales and when their own retailing operations did not match their profit expectations they abandoned the strategy.

Contractual vertical marketing systems

A contractual VMS co-ordinates the distribution system not by ownership but by contracts between the participants. These contractual arrangements include:

■ *Co-operatives* between producers, wholesalers or retailers who agree to join together to gain economies of scale or increase their purchasing power.

FOR EXAMPLE

Smaller vineyard owners set up co-operatives to wholesale their wines and undertake production activities such as bottling to spread the fixed costs and minimise individual investment. In the UK, several wholesale buying groups have emerged in the food sector to service independent retailers under pressure from the power of the grocery multiples. So-called 'symbol group convenience stores' such as Spar, Londis, VG and Mace are independently owned outlets that compete not only by offering late-night shopping but also low prices through the buying power of their symbol group.

■ *Franchises* legally define the rights and responsibilities of the parties involved in a distribution system. Franchising is a business arrangement in which one party (the franchisor) allows others (the franchisees) to use a business name, or sell products in such a way that the franchisee can still operate as a legally separate business. It can mean as little as an agreement to sell a company's products in a specific territory or as much as a complete business package specified by the franchisors. It is this latter type of so called 'business format franchising' which has today become common in some industries such as fast food (Kentucky Fried Chicken, Burger King, Pizza Hut, McDonald's) and instant print (KallKwik, Prontaprint). Although franchising does not eliminate conflict, it does result in a set of mutually dependent operators whose interests all lie in making the system work. As it has become such an important force in distribution networks, franchising is considered in more detail in section 11.5.

An administered vertical marketing system

An administered VMS is one in which the buying or supplying power of one the members ensures the co-operation of the rest of the channel. The concentration of retail outlets in some sectors has given the multiple chains such buying power that they can effectively tell the manufacturers what to do.

FOR EXAMPLE

....

The UK clothing industry has been increasingly dominated by large multiple retailers. The largest groups, including the Arcadia Group (Burtons), Sears (Fosters, Hornes, Miss Selfridge), Marks and Spencer, Next, Matalan, GPS (Gap), Debenhams and BHS control over half of the sales of clothing and footwear in the UK, giving them enormous buying power over producers. They have added to their buying muscle by their marketing strategy of selling mainly their own brands, which gives them complete control over product specification and quality standards.

In other industries, the power of the producer unifies the distribution channel.

FOR EXAMPLE

....

Letraset's share of the graphic art lettering market was so high in the UK that it became the generic term for rub-down lettering. Sales of Letraset became a significant proportion of the total business of many of the dealers, some of whom were either ex-Letraset employees or trained and advised by the company in how to make a graphic art dealership work. Regular seminars and sales conferences promoted the unity of the dealer network, which Letraset dominated until their product was made obsolete by the introduction of computer graphics.

The types of vertical marketing systems are summarised in Figure 11.4.

11.3.4 Horizontal marketing systems

Horizontal marketing systems involve two or more organisations on the same channel level who co-operate to pursue a marketing opportunity.

FIGURE 11.4 *Vertical marketing systems (VMS)*

Vertical marketing system

Corporate VMS — Single ownership of: Production → Distribution channels

Contractual VMS — Contractual relationship e.g. co-operative or franchise between: Producer → Wholesaler → Retailer

Administered VMS — Channel controller uses power to unify independent: Producer → Wholesaler → Retailer

Customers: organisations or individuals

FOR EXAMPLE

Two car producers, Honda and Austin Rover, co-operated to help each other in their respective areas of strength. The arrangements through which Rover gained access to Honda engineering expertise and Honda gained penetration of European markets through Rover's existing networks, ended when the German car maker BMW acquired Rover from its parent company British Aerospace. This did not produce the expected synergy, and in 2000 BMW sold most of the Rover business back to a management consortium.

FOR EXAMPLE

Food retailers sought to increase their turnover by widening their distribution horizontally. Out-of-town superstores added petrol filling stations on some of their sites to service the car-borne shopper. Tesco, Asda and Sainsbury became major petrol retailers with filling stations at their superstores. They also expanded their in-store facilities, including in-store pharmacies throughout the UK, run by independent pharmacists dispensing NHS prescriptions. Other facilities include post offices, banks, photo processing and dry cleaning.

11.3.5 Influences on channel strategies

Channel strategies – the selection and management of distribution channels – are influenced by a number of factors, as illustrated in Figure 11.5.

FIGURE 11.5

Influences on channel strategies

Market structure
❏ Number of customers
❏ Frequency of purchase
❏ Location
❏ Environmental constraints

Product characteristics
❏ Value
❏ Measurements
❏ Standardisation
❏ Durability

Channel strategy
❏ Selection
  • Direction
  • Intensity
❏ Management
  • Vertical
  • Horizontal

Channel structure
❏ Power of intermediaries
❏ Performance
❏ Margins

Organisational characteristics
❏ Objectives
❏ Resources
❏ Experience

Market structure

The numbers of customers, their frequency of purchase and location is a key influence on channel length and width. If a product has many potential customers who buy relatively often in geographically dispersed locations, it requires intensive distribution and greater numbers of channel levels to reach the market. For this reason, low-value consumer products such as confectionery items are sold through a variety of wholesale and retail outlets, whilst high-value industrial products such as aeroplanes have a selective distribution restricted to few or no intermediaries between producer and buyer.

Constraints in the business environment also shape the distribution system. The Monopolies and Mergers Commission report on the distribution of beer in the UK, which recommended the loosening of ties between licensed outlets and the big breweries, led to a shake-out in the number and type of public houses in the UK.

Channel structure

The power and performance of the existing channels of distribution are an important selection consideration. A well-organised distribution structure offering adequate margins is attractive to producers. A fragmented, disorganised system may influence them to look elsewhere or set up their own. Product innovations sometimes initiate fundamental changes to distribution systems because the full potential of the new product is not realisable through conventional channels.

FOR EXAMPLE

The inventors of the plain paper copier found the existing print trade too short-sighted and fragmented to seize the opportunity of their breakthrough. The Xerox Corporation decided to build their own marketing and distribution system in the USA by renting the new copying equipment direct to customers. Although they did not have the resources to expand internationally on their own, they still preferred to bypass existing channels when selling overseas. In the UK they set up Rank Xerox, a jointly owned company with the Rank Organisation, whose principal activities until then were in the entertainment industry.

Product characteristics

The characteristics of the product itself help determine how it is distributed. High value or complex products requiring personal selling and explanation (e.g. houses or pensions), tend to have shorter channels than low value, simple products (e.g. soft drinks or stationery products). Physical measurements such as weight and size constrain the types of outlets that can be used: car showrooms are restricted to sites away from town centres, whereas services such as banking and estate agency can be located anywhere, including virtual sites on the Internet. Custom-made products and services with little standardisation require producer and customer to communicate directly and therefore channels are short (e.g. picture framing, opticians and hairdressers). Long-life, durable products (e.g. furniture and tools) can survive in the warehouses of a lengthy distribution process, whereas perishable and fragile items (e.g. milk, bread, glass) need shorter, more immediate channels.

Organisational characteristics

The objectives, resources and experience of the organisations involved influence not only the channels used but also how they can be managed. A small business with the limited objective of making a comfortable living for its owner follows different distribution strategies to more ambitious organisations that are seeking to become market leaders. In many sectors there is a trade-off between the costs of distribution and the degree of control that can be exerted over the channel members. This is illustrated in Figure 11.6.

An organisation's distribution strategy often evolves in line with its resources and experience to take account of this trade-off.

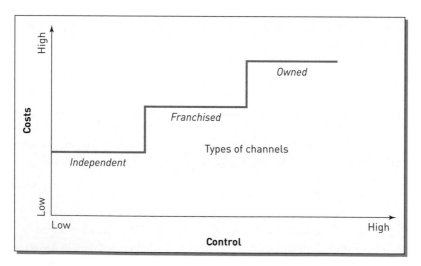

FIGURE 11.6

Costs versus control in channel options

FOR EXAMPLE

The Body Shop developed rapidly because it managed the relationship between distribution control and costs in various phases of growth. Anita Roddick was so encouraged by the success of her first Body Shop in Brighton in 1976 that after only six month's trading she decided to open another one in Chichester. The costs of this second outlet were high: to raise the necessary £4,000 finance, she sold half the shares of her fledgling company to an outside investor. However, the ownership of her own outlets helped her to develop an innovative range of body care products marketed in a radically different way to traditional cosmetics. Once they had proved that their ideas were commercially sound in their own shops, Anita and her husband Gordon Roddick realised that fast growth for the new concepts could not be achieved through company-owned outlets because of their very limited resources. The next phase of growth came from selling their body care products in the distinctive plastic bottles to other independent retailers. Initially, the Roddicks made only loose arrangements with the new group of Body Shops that emerged, reflecting their emphasis on growth at minimal cost during that time. This evolved later into a tightly controlled franchise operation as the resources and experience of the company grew. The Body Shop now carefully selects its franchisees and controls and monitors their activities on a regular basis.

CHECKPOINT

You have developed a new ice cream which you manufacture on a dairy farm (see pages 366 and 371). Which marketing channels would you select? What distribution problems would you foresee?

11.4 RETAILING: TYPES AND TRENDS

11.4.1 *Categories of retailer*

Retailing is sometimes thought of in the narrow sense of selling products in store and shops. In fact, *retailing is the general term for a wide variety of activities involved in the selling of goods or services directly to the end user for individual consumption.* It covers the marketing of goods through outlets of many sizes, from supermarkets to kiosks. It may include the consumption of goods or the provision of services on the premises as in hotels and restaurants, or it may not involve premises open to the customer at all, as in the case of mail order or online retailing.

Retailing can be grouped into various categories according to the emphasis given to such variables as the product line or the types of premise used, if at all. These categories are illustrated in Figure 11.7.

FIGURE 11.7

Categories of retailing

Depth and width of product lines

As customers we tend to think of retailers according to the products they sell, so that the depth and width of the product lines on offer is an important distinguishing feature.

- *Speciality outlets* carry a narrow product line in some depth. Most High Streets are dominated by these types of retailers, specialising in products and services from shoes (e.g. Clarks) and confectionery (e.g. Thorntons), to property and financial services (e.g. estate agents, banks and building societies).

- *Department stores* offer a wide range of products divided into various category areas, or departments, under one roof. Although many stores have had to carefully reposition themselves to survive the twin threat of supermarkets and speciality shops, they contain some of the flagship names in British retailing such as Harrods, Debenhams, House of Fraser and the John Lewis Partnership.

- *Variety chains* offer a limited number of product ranges in depth. Marks and Spencer specialises in clothes, footwear and food; WH Smith offers stationery, magazines, books and music. Other variety chains include Boots and Woolworths.

- *Supermarkets* carry a wide range of food and household products in large, self-service outlets at low prices. Their development in the UK was led by the grocery chains such as Sainsbury, Tesco and Asda but their success has encouraged other sectors from toys to car parts.

- *Superstores and hypermarkets* are giant supermarkets located in out-of-town centres. Whereas a typical supermarket might offer 10,000 product lines from 20,000 square feet of floor space, a superstore occupies at least 25,000 square feet and sells 20,000 items. Hypermarkets range from 50,000 to 150,000 square feet of selling area, displaying enormous volumes of products. The mix is moving away from food to non-food, with Tesco claiming that 50 per cent of their new space is devoted to non-food items.

Customer service levels

Levels of service in retailing vary according to the needs of the product and the emphasis placed on service in the marketing mix.

- *Personal service* has diminished as an essential part of retailing as goods have become standardised and pre-packaged. However it is still needed if products are tailor-made to customer requirements (e.g. picture framing) or for services such as travel agencies or insurance brokers. It is also featured by retailers who differentiate themselves from competitors by emphasising higher service levels, for example some department stores and restaurants.

- *Limited service* has become the norm in many speciality stores and variety chains. Goods can be self-selected but staff are available for help and advice.

- *Self-service* keeps contact with staff to a minimum, usually restricting it to paying at centralised cash points. It is now the familiar shopping experience, not only in supermarkets but also in other retail environments from online shopping and catalogue showrooms to banking and petrol stations.

Price position

Competitive prices are an important element in most retailers' marketing strategies. There is, however, a relationship between other factors, such as convenience and customer service levels, and price. Some retailers offer more service or convenience for higher prices: Department stores offer higher levels of personal attention, whilst convenience stores stay open for longer hours. Both tend to be more expensive as a result. Some retailers sacrifice service levels and concentrate on low prices.

- *Discount stores* have become familiar in the household goods sector including electrical specialists (e.g. Dixons, Currys and Comet), and furniture retailers (e.g. MFI).

- *Cash-and-carry or warehouse retailers* emphasise the price advantage for consumers to buy in bulk. For example, Majestic Wine Warehouses sell wine in no-frills outlets away from the High Street, offering more variety than supermarket wine departments and lower prices than off-licences and traditional wine merchants, although customers must buy at least one case (twelve bottles).

- *'Category Killers'* are so-called because they take the strategy of 'piling it high and selling it cheap' to such an extreme that other retailers find it hard to compete. They are superstores which specialise in a clearly defined product category at discount prices. Examples include the furniture retailer IKEA and Toys 'R Us, both currently expanding rapidly in Europe and the USA. This type of retail operation has succeeded by bringing economies of scale and buying power into sectors where the fragmentation of the existing retail structure made it relatively inefficient.

TABLE 11.1 *The concentration of UK grocery retailing*

	NO. OF STORES	TURNOVER £m
TOTAL GROCERY MULTIPLES	6,487	79,287
TOTAL IMPULSE	76,438	33,006
CO-OP GROCERS	3,184	6,374
MULTIPLE FORECOURTS	4,030	2,040
MULTIPLE OFF-LICENCES	3,541	2,018
SYMBOL GROUPS	6,875	4,905
INDEPENDENTS	54,933	12,615
OTHER IMPULSE	3,875	5,054
TOTAL	**82,925**	**112,293**

ACNIELSEN, 2005.

Ownership

Mirroring the trends in North America and Western Europe, the UK retail trade is becoming more concentrated in terms of ownership and sales through the larger groups.

■ *Small retail businesses* are defined as independents with one outlet and smaller multiples with a turnover below £4.5 million. These are still the most numerous category of retailer, but their numbers are falling and they take a diminishing percentage of total retail sales. In 1997, the sales of these outlets represented only 23.9 per cent of total UK retail sales of £178.2 billion (see Table 11.1).

■ *Large retail businesses* outperform other retailers in key measures such as turnover per outlet and stock turnover, and these efficiency advantages have helped them take an increasing share of retail business. They now account for over three-quarters of the UK retail trade through less than 20 per cent of the total number of outlets. Although their prices are generally lower, they operate on similar gross margins to independents and small multiples because of their buying power and other economies generated from their higher turnovers.

Table 11.1 shows the breakdown of retail business in the grocery trade, illustrating the divide between the big firms and the small. Whilst the large grocery multiples account for only 8 per cent of stores, they enjoy 71 per cent of sales. The independents have by contrast 66 per cent of outlets but only generate 11 per cent of revenue. (This is a good example of why it is important to understand market shares in terms of both volume and value.)

■ *Co-operatives* began as self-help movements in the eighteenth and nineteenth centuries and continue in the retailing sector today as co-operative societies such as the Co-operative Wholesale Society (CWS), which operates department stores, supermarkets and convenience stores. Although they have had mixed fortunes over recent years, the Co-operative Group accounted for nearly £4 billion of retail sales in 2006, benefiting form an expansion into financial services and pharmacies. Their 'green' credentials have also helped sales due to their positioning as an ethical retailer.

- *Franchises* have become the fastest growing form of contractual VMS. They attempt to gain the efficiencies of a well-organised, controlled marketing channel whilst retaining the independence of individual members. (Franchising is described more fully in section 11.5.)

Location

Location is a key factor – in some cases *the* key factor – that distinguishes one retailer from another.

- *High Street* locations have the highest costs but customer traffic still attracts speciality retailers, variety chains and department stores.

- *Out-of-town* shopping has grown substantially. Led by furniture and DIY multiples such as MFI, B&Q, Homebase and Do It All, out-of-town superstores took advantage of increased car ownership by developing in more spacious, lower cost retail parks away from congested high streets. The leading food groups such as Tesco, Sainsbury and Marks and Spencer soon followed, although on the whole they have preferred to develop on sites devoted solely to their use.

- *Neighbourhood or convenience stores* have stepped into some of the gaps left by the withdrawal of major chains from town centres. Food retailers, confectioners and newsagents sell a limited range of goods priced above superstores in recognition of their longer opening hours and ease of access by local populations. Most are independent, although a majority operate within a 'symbol' or buying group, such as Spar. Others are owned by convenience store companies, and an increasing number are oil-company owned due to their popularity with customers in petrol station forecourts.

- *Shopping centres* have become another feature of modern retailing. These are large-scale developments, usually over 100,000 square feet, which provide a cluster of retail outlets under one roof. Many are in town centres, such as the large (350,000 square feet) Charles Darwin Centre in Shrewsbury. Regional shopping centres, including Brent Cross in north-west London and the MetroCentre in Gateshead, are even bigger, servicing large population groups from lower cost, out-of-town sites on good access routes.

- *Internationalisation* is on the increase. Early attempts by Sainsbury and Marks and Spencer to enter overseas markets ended in failure. Other companies have learnt from their mistakes and are now actively pursuing territories outside the UK. This has been encouraged by the challenging domestic environment and the opening up of some of the world's potentially lucrative markets, including India, China and Russia. Retailing success stories tend to have the following factors in common: they use local labour, including senior management teams, and source products locally. Joint ventures, where the incomer teams up with established local players, are also often successful because they enable retailers to better understand the markets they enter and to provide a tailored approach for each region.

FOR EXAMPLE

Tesco is now active in thirteen countries, including the US, and is doing battle with the world's leading food retailers, including Wal-Mart and the French hypermarket chain Carrefour. The joint venture approach is being used by Dixons in Russia, where it has teamed up with the leading electrical retailer Eldorado. The DIY chain B&Q now commands 50 per cent of the market in Shanghai, China's biggest city, with a population of 17.4 million. This will make it difficult for any new rival to enter this key Chinese market.

Non-store retailing

Non-store retailing has had considerable publicity in recent years with the development of the Internet and online shopping. In fact 'home shopping' has a long history and takes a variety of forms.

- *Mail order*: Traditionally, orders taken and delivered by post from the large catalogues distributed by companies such as Littlewoods and Grattans. Although full-range catalogues still exist, technology and targeting have changed the industry. Today most orders are taken by phone or online and paid for by credit card. Smaller catalogues target specific market segments with tailored products. The Pro Idee catalogue offers products with a high-tech image, whilst Readers Digest targets consumers with information on specific subjects ranging from astronomy to gardening.

- *Direct mail*: Even more targeted than mail order, with offers from bank loans to bedspreads sent to selected mailing lists.

- *Teleshopping*: Used increasingly to achieve the same ends as mail order – direct contact with a customer, who is offered the possibility of buying without leaving home. Although some companies sell direct over the telephone only, most offer the alternative of ordering online.

- *Online shopping*: A relatively recent phenomenon. There were earlier attempts to introduce forms of electronic retailing (or e-tailing). As with Internet shopping, customers could use computer terminals at home to search for the product they wanted, enquire about features, pricing and delivery terms, place orders and arrange payment. Although services were tried in the USA and Europe, they failed to develop because too few customers subscribed to the system and invested in the necessary special equipment. The growth of the Internet made special systems and equipment unnecessary, and online shopping is now developing quickly.

- Although over half of shoppers have now purchased online, the value of consumer purchasers was estimated at £19.2 billion in the UK in 2005, or around 10 per cent of total retail purchases (IMRG). This does not include eBay, which is classified as an auction site. Penetration is higher in some categories, such as books, music, software, videos, consumer electronics and clothes. The most popular UK online retailer is Amazon, which had a reach of 26.3 per cent in 2006. ('Reach' is the number of visits to a site expressed as a percentage of the total Internet population.) Established airlines (e.g. British Airways) and travel companies (e.g. Eurotunnel) now offer tickets online. Existing food retailers have extended their services by offering home deliveries ordered over the Internet (e.g. Tesco.com).

- *Network or multilevel marketing* is the latest in many forms of door-to-door selling which have emerged over the years. A network of sales agents promotes a manufacturer's products not just to consumers but also to other agents. As agents receive commission on everything that is sold either by themselves or the other agents they have introduced or 'sponsored', they can earn a substantial income, although most people in a network are part-timers supplementing their income. Some American organisations (e.g. Amway and National Safety Associates, NSA) have developed extensive networks of self-employed agents using these systems selling household cleaners and personal care and diet items.

Whilst the industry still makes exaggerated claims about the earning capacity of its agents, it has moved on from the discredited days of 'pyramid selling'. Regulations now exist in Europe and North America to prevent some of the unscrupulous operations which have developed. In these pyramid schemes, distributors paid an entrance fee and bought stocks of product, which they then attempted to sell on at a profit to other agents or consumers. There were no fixed prices and stocks were often passed on to agents at prices above their real consumer value. UK regulations now limit the entry fee into a network and insist on formal contracts between the supplying company and the independent distributor. Above all, schemes have to demonstrate that their products have genuine end users.

'Party plans' are another style of network in which agents organise household gatherings to demonstrate products including plastic containers (e.g. Tupperware), cosmetics (e.g. Avon) and lingerie (e.g. Ann Summers).

11.4.2 The new channel 'captains'

Channel 'captains' or 'controllers' use their influence to resolve issues such as the levels of service given to customers, the financial deal available at each channel level and demarcation disputes between members. As the examples given in section 11.3 have shown, channel captains can be an independent producer (e.g. Letraset), wholesaler (e.g. Spar), or retailer (e.g. Marks and Spencer); they can be franchisors (e.g. Body Shop) or vertically integrated corporations (e.g. Clarks). Modern trends in consumer marketing have shifted control from the producers of branded goods to the large retailers. The development of branded products earlier this century gave their producers considerable muscle in the marketplace. Brand leaders such as Kellogg, Mars, Heinz and Kodak could dictate terms to the wholesalers and retailers who had to stock their products or lose sales. The producers effectively controlled how their goods were marketed, from setting the recommended retail price to determining how they should be displayed and promoted in store. Today, the development of retailing giants in key sectors such as food and clothing has shifted the balance of power further down the distribution channel, because the retailer can call the marketing tune and sets quality and service standards.

FOR EXAMPLE

....

Sainsbury challenged the world's leading brand Coca-Cola in what were called the 'the cola wars'. Sainsbury replaced its own-label brand of cola, which accounted for about 24 per cent of its sales, with 'Classic Cola', an exclusive Sainsbury product purchased from a Canadian supplier. Coca-Cola, which made up 62 per cent of Sainsbury's cola sales prior to the launch, threatened legal action on the grounds that the new product closely resembled the name and packaging of its own famous brand. Their protests were intensified by initial reports that sales of the new 'Classic' made up 70 per cent of Sainsbury's sales in the first few weeks whilst 'the real thing' fell to 27 per cent of purchases within the supermarket's outlets.

More recently there have been moves back towards the development of working partnerships. The major retailers seek out preferred suppliers, choosing one supplier in each category and working with them to develop sales in that area together.

Own-branding

The launch of an exclusive branded cola product by Sainsbury is a recent development in a longer term move towards 'own branding' by the major multiples. Some retailers only sell their own branded products (e.g. Mothercare, Primark). Others sell a high percentage of own-branded products, or 'retailer brands' as they are often called (41 per cent of grocery sales by value in 2005). Many are still keen to sell manufacturers' branded products, knowing that a large investment has been made to build the brand reputation. For example, DIY retailers still sell a high percentage of branded products (23 per cent own brand by value in 2005, leaving 77 per cent to manufacturer brands). However the growth of own brands to over £69 billion in the UK has shifted the balance of power towards the large retailer and put a question mark against the long-term value of manufacturers' branded products.

CHECKPOINT

Create a retail 'map' of an area you know well and use personally.

1. Draw an outline street map and place the principal types of retailers on it. Categorise them by ownership types (e.g. large multiples, franchises, independents) and other important classifications.

2. Describe the main changes you have witnessed in the area. If possible, talk to someone from an older generation to obtain a longer-term perspective. What developments do you foresee in the future?

3. Consider which shops you use and the patterns of shopping within your family and amongst your friends. How have these changed in recent years?

11.5 FRANCHISING

Franchising was defined (in section 11.3) as an arrangement in which one party (the franchisor) allows others (the franchisees) to use a business name or sell products in such as way that the franchisees can operate their own legally separate business.

Today there is a major distinction between two forms of franchising: product or trademark franchising and business format franchising.

11.5.1 Product and trademark agreements

By making agreements to distribute their products through licensed dealers, manufacturers created an early form of franchising. Breweries were probably the first franchisors when they introduced a system that 'tied' otherwise independent publicans to one producer of beer. Car manufacturers and oil companies developed the distribution of their products through various licensing arrangements under which a local dealer or distributor took responsibility for sales in a certain territory in return for some element of profit. The producers developed their products and the goodwill associated with the trademarks; the local distributor contributed local knowledge, contacts, effort and usually some investment. Such distribution arrangements are still common, for example, in the soft drinks industry.

Manufacturing processes are also distributed in this way. If the inventor of a patented process wishes to exploit their innovation on a wider basis than their resources allow, they may permit other manufacturers to use the process under licence in return for a royalty.

FOR EXAMPLE

Alastair Pilkington's invention of 'float glass' enabled his company to manufacture a distortion-free glass at low cost to replace cheap but optically imperfect 'sheet' glass or expensive, hand-polished 'plate' glass. The size and fragility of the product favour local manufacture, and as Pilkington did not wish to set up manufacturing plants all around the world, he 'distributed' the concept by licensing other manufacturers to use the new system.

Intangible assets such as well-known names and celebrities are also franchised to reach a wider public. Products are endorsed by fictional characters or real people under licensing agreements specifying how the name or image may be used and what royalties are payable for the privilege.

11.5.2 Business format franchising

Franchisor and franchisee may enter a more comprehensive relationship than a simple trademark or licensing arrangement. *Business format franchising* goes beyond the supply of products and trade names to cover many more aspects of how a business is run. Franchisors offer a complete package, allowing the franchisee to use a format which has been developed and proven commercially whilst retaining legal independence. The business format offered by the franchisor may cover many aspects including:

■ Trade name, business style, logo, house colours

■ Detailed product or service specification

■ Training and help to set up and ongoing advice on running the business

■ National and local marketing

■ Centralised purchasing or supply of products

■ Management control and operating systems

■ Research and development of new products and processes

In return the franchisee pays the franchisor agreed sums of money which usually include:

■ An initial franchise fee as a one-off payment to the franchisor to cover the goodwill of the name and training. This can vary from £1,000, rising to £25,000 for the more expensive franchises (e.g. McDonald's).

■ The costs of setting up and running the business as specified by the franchisor. These include the costs of buying equipment, fitting out premises, stock, promotional literature and stationery. The minimum start-up investment for franchises varies enormously depending on the value of the name and the nature of the business (e.g. £4,500 for Unigate Dairies and £700,000 for Burger King).

■ Annual charges or fees. An ongoing service fee is charged, often as a percentage of sales (typically 5 to 15 per cent of invoiced sales value). Other levies on the franchisee include contributions to national advertising and training for staff.

A franchise agreement sets out the obligations of both parties, including how the franchisee is to run the business, what payments they make and what the franchisor will provide in return.

The franchising market

Franchising has developed strongly in the USA, where it now accounts for over one-third of all retail sales. Entrepreneurs such as Colonel Sanders and Ray Kroc pioneered the concepts from the 1950s. Sanders travelled around America persuading people to cook chicken his way as Kentucky Fried Chicken (now KFC) franchisees. Ray Kroc modelled his franchise on the standardised burger production techniques of the McDonald brothers. Today US franchisors have spread their concepts internationally with globally recognised brands such as Domino's Pizza and Burger King.

FOR EXAMPLE

When the McDonald brothers, Dick and Mac opened their first restaurant in 1940 in San Bernardino, California, they could never have imagined the phenomenal growth that their company would enjoy. From extremely modest beginnings, they hit on a winning formula, selling a high-quality product cheaply and quickly. However, it was not until Ray Kroc, a Chicago-based salesman with a flair for marketing, became involved that the business really started to grow. He realised that the same successful McDonald's formula could be exploited throughout the United States and beyond.

There are now more than 30,000 McDonald's restaurants in over 119 countries. In 2002, they served over sixteen billion customers, equivalent to a lunch and dinner for every man, woman and child in the world. McDonald's global sales were over $41 billion, making it by far the largest food service company in the world.

In 1955, Ray Kroc realised that the key to success was rapid expansion. The best way to achieve this was through offering franchises. Today, over 70 per cent of McDonald's restaurants are run on this basis. In the UK,

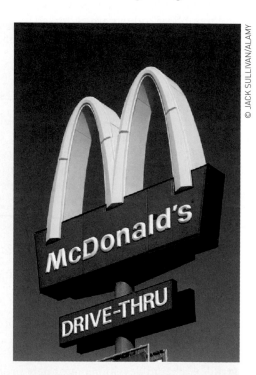

Drive Thru was a concept suggested by a franchisee

the first franchised restaurant opened in 1986 – there are now over 1,200 restaurants, employing more than 70,000 people, of which 36 per cent are operated by franchisees.

As a classic example of business format franchising, McDonald's (the franchisor) grants the right to sell McDonald's branded goods to a third party (the franchisee) wishing to set up his or her own business. The licence agreement allows McDonald's to insist on manufacturing or operating methods and the quality of the product.

Under a McDonald's franchise, McDonald's owns or leases the site and the restaurant building. The franchisee buys the fittings, the equipment and the right to operate the franchise for twenty years. To ensure uniformity throughout the world, all franchisees must use standardised McDonald's branding, menus, design layouts and administration systems. Whilst the franchisees have to agree to operate their restaurants in the McDonald's way, there still remains some scope for innovation. Many ideas for new items on the menu come from the franchisees responding to customer demand. Developing new products is crucial to any business, even one which has successfully relied on a limited menu for many years. Consumer tastes change over time and a company needs to respond to these changes. Innovation injects dynamism and allows the firm to exploit markets previously overlooked or ignored. The introduction of the Egg McMuffin in 1971, for example, enabled McDonald's to cater initially for the breakfast trade. Filet-o-Fish, Drive-thrus and Playlands were all products or concepts developed by franchisees.

In the UK, franchising is less significant than in the US but it is a fast-growing sector. It accounts for over 5 per cent of total retail sales, with an estimated turnover of £10.3 billion in the the UK in 2005, an increase of 13.2 per cent on the previous year. The market is generally split into dairy franchises and non-dairy franchises. The total number of non-dairy franchises is estimated to stand at around 29,100, while dairy franchises total fewer than 2,000.

Table 11.2 shows how UK franchised outlets are divided by market sector. Although fast-food outlets are the most visible franchises in the High Street, business services have grown rapidly to become the most numerous sector.

TABLE 11.2 *UK franchised outlets by sector*

SECTOR	PERCENTAGE OF TOTAL FRANCHISED UNITS	EXAMPLES
HOTELS AND CATERING	22	Perfect Pizza, KFC, Wimpy
PROPERTY SERVICES	22	Drain Doctor, Stainbusters
BUSINESS AND COMMUNICATION SERVICES	17	Kall Kwik, Interlink Express
STORE RETAILING	16	Costcutter, Birthdays
PERSONAL SERVICES	15	Stagecoach Theatre, Toni and Guy
TRANSPORT SERVICES	8	Avis Rent-a-Car, Kwik Fit

11.5.3 The advantages and disadvantages to franchisors

Factors which attract organisations to franchising as a distribution method include:

■ The ability to extend the distribution of products or concepts quickly. As expansion is funded mainly by the franchisees, less capital is required from the franchisor.

- The recruitment and retention of committed managers who as franchisees have the additional motivation of business ownership.

- More control over outlets than totally independent distribution channels.

However, disadvantages for franchisors include:

- Less control over franchisees than fully owned outlets.

- The continued obligations of the franchise agreement to provide central support services, even if the franchisor wishes to exit from the business.

CHECKPOINT

Investigate franchises that may be on offer to you. (You can do this through the Internet or a variety of publications, e.g. *The Franchise Magazine*). Select one that attracts you and summarise the advantages and disadvantages of this business opportunity.

11.6 SUMMARY

- The place element of the marketing mix involves decisions about the location in which goods and services can be purchased, the distribution channels through which they pass from producer to final user and the physical distribution methods used.

- The Internet represents both a threat and an opportunity to distribution methods because it can both replace and complement existing channels.

- Intermediaries between producers and consumers operate on a number of different channel levels. They include agents, wholesalers, distributors, dealers and retailers.

- Advantages of intermediaries include reduced investment, local knowledge, economies of scale, transactional efficiency and breaking bulk.

- Disadvantages of intermediaries include less control over marketing methods and effort and less revenue per item sold.

- Channel strategies cover the selection and management of distribution systems:
  — *Selection* involves decisions on the direction and intensity of distribution
  — *Channel management* decisions attempt to overcome conflict and create efficiencies through vertical or horizontal marketing systems

- Vertical marketing systems (VMS) can be corporate, contractual or administered.

- Horizontal marketing systems operate on the same channel level.

- Factors that influence channel strategies include market structure, channel structure, product characteristics and organisational characteristics.

- Retailing can be categorised and evaluated by trends in the depth and width of product lines offered, customer service levels, price position, ownership, location and non-store retailing such as online shopping. The large multiples have become channel 'captains' in some sectors because of the concentration of retail sales in their outlets.

- Franchising is a fast-developing channel system which can be subdivided into trademark and licensing agreements, and business format franchising.

11.7 ACTIVITIES

ON THE CARPET

'You have 12 months to improve sales or we will have to consider closing down the UK operation.' Christopher Davidson repeated the words of his managing director over to himself as he drove away from the company headquarters in Rotterdam. It had been not been an easy meeting. The UK subsidiary that he managed was performing well below other European markets and the patience of the directors of Novalis, the Anglo-Dutch holding company, was running out. Novalis International was one of the leading manufacturers of artificial playing surfaces, selling their branded 'Noval-Sport' synthetic grass carpets and other sports surfaces around the world. In the UK, as in most European markets, a fully owned subsidiary was responsible for the local marketing of the product range. Davidson had only just taken over as general manager in the UK and now he knew why his predecessor had departed in some haste. Sales had stagnated over the last three years, at a time when they showed substantial growth in all other European markets. 'The marketing in the UK is all wrong. I know you can't change it overnight but unless we see an improvement soon, we have to consider reverting to agents rather than continuing the expense of our own subsidiary.' The meaning of the managing director's words could not have been clearer. Davidson had to act quickly to save his own job.

Background Participation levels in sport and leisure activities had been expanding considerably for several years. Adults had become more aware of the need to keep healthy and fit, whilst having more free time in which to do so. The demands of academic subjects may have kept down the time devoted to sport in schools, but there was increasing recognition of the importance healthy exercise played in the development of younger people. In the UK, home of many traditional sports such as football, rugby, bowls, cricket and tennis, newer activities such as ice hockey, basketball, rollerblading and ten-pin bowling had been imported on an increasing scale, partly stimulated by the interest of younger generations demanding more variety in their diet of sporting activities.

Facilities for most sports had improved considerably in the last decade, but the authorities responsible had found it difficult to keep pace with the demand for the specialised provision of many different types. A noticeable trend had been the concentration of sports facilities in one area of intensive use. The acres of grassed playing fields and open-air facilities, which can only be used in good weather and daylight, were giving way to sports halls, leisure centres and artificial grass pitches, used intensively from early morning to late at night irrespective of the weather conditions.

The development of artificial surfaces for sports from tennis and hockey to bowling and baseball had been part of this trend. From the original, abrasive nylon, artificial turf pitches, these had developed into more user friendly, all-weather playing surfaces. Overhead floodlighting, multi-use pitch marking and easily movable equipment meant that a range of sports could be played intensively on one surface, rather than needing large areas of land dedicated to one type of sport.

The product The surface of an all-weather pitch was usually constructed of a porous, polypropylene carpet in-filled with either sand or water. This provided a true and durable surface that could be used in most weather conditions for many types of sport. Noval-Sport, a leading brand of these polypropylene sports carpets, was manufactured in rolls and then laid and joined *in situ* on a specially prepared surface. It came in four qualities depending on the depth of pile and playing characteristics required. Novalis's confidence in its quality was shown by the minimum ten-year guarantee offered with each surface laid by an approved subcontractor, an unusually long warranty in the industry.

Davidson knew, however, that the carpet was only the tip of the iceberg as far as an artificial pitch was concerned. Underneath, several other layers were all crucial to the durability and life of the pitch. Immediately underneath the carpet was a shock-pad, usually made of rubber, which provided cushioning to the hard play surface. The specification of the shockpad had to be carefully matched to the requirements of the pitch because it affected the bounce of balls on the playing surface. Beneath the shockpad was a base made of various levels of foundation material such as stone and macadam. The composition of this base, and the accuracy with which it is laid, was crucial to the trueness and longevity of the pitch. Foundations susceptible to frost, for example, could cause damage to the pitch through the expansion of frozen water in the base.

A key part of Davidson's job and those of the small team of sales engineers that worked for him was to make sure that the construction of the whole pitch, and not just the surface carpet, was correctly specified and built.

The distribution   Davidson's predecessor had appointed a small number of approved agents – building companies whose expertise in design and quality in construction could be totally relied on. The problem was that they were very few in number: one in England, one in Scotland, and one in Northern Ireland. Only by contracting with these agents did the Novalis-Sport long-life guarantee apply.

All-weather pitches were sold and laid by construction companies who bought the artificial carpet and shockpad from companies such as Novalis. In the UK, only a small number of contractors specialised in building artificial pitches with the expertise to take a wide range of customer requirements through the various stages of design to the final, completed pitch. Davidson needed to be sure an approved agent not only understood construction matters but also the specific technology of artificial pitches, not to mention the extras that often go with them, such as fencing and floodlighting. A larger number of contractors offered a less complete service. Some builders could handle only smaller contracts such as tennis courts. Others offered a design consultancy or a project management service. All were potential customers for Novalis, as integral parts of the decision-making process which could specify a Noval-Sport, or a competitive, product. Inevitably, Davidson and his team were often

called in to advise at various stages of this process, particularly the design and tendering stage.

The market   The market for artificial play surfaces had taken off over the last two decades. The pressure on the use of open spaces combined with the advantages of synthetic surfaces in terms of durability, trueness of surface, and usage in all weathers and at all hours, made them increasingly popular for many sports including football, tennis, bowling, hockey and golf driving ranges. Hockey in particular was now played on this type of surface for all serious competitions because the trueness of the surface allowed for more precise ball control. The extra wear characteristics made it a popular alternative for tennis because it was more like grass than standard asphalt pitches. Evening training under floodlights for football and other sports was also popular on these surfaces. Densely populated areas of Europe in Holland, Belgium and Germany were the frontrunners in the laying of artificial pitches. In the UK, their installation was given a real boost by the availability of lottery money, through the Sports Council, for the improvement of sports facilities.

Customer segmentation   The buying of artificial pitches was a complex process, often involving many organisations in the installation of one pitch. Davidson segmented the market into a number of different types, involving substantial and smaller buyers and private and public sectors. Private clubs, part of large private sector businesses, were involved in the provision of leisure facilities such as indoor tennis courts, which use artificial carpets. Some were commercial operations in their own right; others were provided by large companies for the benefit of their employees. Contracts for this business, often multi-million pound sales, were fiercely contested by the trade. In the public sector, local councils, still a major provider of sports facilities, were often involved in large projects, sometimes in partnership with private companies. Education establishments, from schools to universities, represented another segment involving public sector finance. The remainder of the market tended to be very fragmented, made up of a variety of smaller clubs, some with charitable status, a few privately owned. Customer requirements ranged from a small artificial green for the local bowls club to the provision of multiple tennis courts and hockey/football pitches for a regional sports centre.

The decision-making unit One of Davidson's key problems was to find out who made the decision to specify the surface. Usually a number of people and organisations had an input. These included:

1 The end users, often represented by a committee of a sports club or representatives of a board of governors of a school or university. Sales presentations to the end users were sometimes made by Novalis, sometimes by a contractor making a bid for the business, or both.

2 The fund providers, such as the Sports Council, the Department for Education, the local authority or a private company. These organisations were increasingly acting jointly to provide money for a specific project. For example, lottery money was normally allocated on the basis of a percentage of the total costs, with the rest coming from other sponsors.

3 The advisers involved in the design and management of the project – architects, surveyors, project managers, consulting engineers, sports consultants or a combination of these.

4 Building and construction companies bidding for part, or all, of a project involving artificial surfaces. These ranged from specialised sports surface companies to more general contractors.

Pricing Often, contractors were appointed to projects by a tendering system in which they specified the type and price of surface they recommended. A typical price for one football-sized pitch, or three tennis courts, including the preparation of the site, laying of the base, shockpad and carpet and the provision of fencing and floodlights was £250,000 to £500,000 plus VAT. The price of the Noval-Sport carpet and shockpad was a relatively small part of the total cost, representing 15–25 per cent of the price of the contract. The building industry was generally price sensitive, with competitive quotations obtained for projects of this size.

The replacement costs for just the artificial carpet, which had a lifespan of seven to twenty years depending on use and quality, was up to £100,000. Noval-Sport had two main qualities, which were reflected in their prices. The lower quality was priced favourably compared to the competition, but Novalis sales advisers tried to always recommend the higher quality carpet. Although this was priced some 20 per cent above competitors, it had a guaranteed life of ten years and normally lasted twenty years or more, which made it less expensive in the long run.

The marketing problem The turnover of Novalis UK had stagnated at a time when the market was growing strongly. Although it was still regarded by many in the trade as the best quality, Noval-Sport carpets had lost its position as market leader, overtaken by more aggressive manufacturers who had invested heavily in sales and promotion campaigns. A French company, 'Surface Sportive', were particularly active in hospitality and publicity campaigns surrounding contracts at high-profile venues such as the All England Lawn Tennis Club.

Davidson had two main marketing problems. Although his brand was well known, his small sales support team of three people including himself, were so busy following up enquiries and troubleshooting that they had little time to develop new contacts in a very fragmented marketplace. For new business they relied heavily on the approved agents, who were proving a bottleneck because of capacity problems.

'You have to give me time to sort out our sales strategy', Davidson had argued at the meeting with the Novalis directors. 'We haven't seen the full benefit of the lottery money now being invested in pitches because our agents are working to capacity and turning down work. If I allow others to lay our carpets, quality becomes an issue as some of them are definitely not up to our standards. Do you want me to make sales at the cost of potential problems in a few years time when surfaces laid by inexperienced contractors start to deteriorate?'

A second problem was that their products were perceived as more expensive.

'I know it lasts longer, and we guarantee that, but often our contractors are bidding mainly on price because that's how they are trained. The users may find we are cheaper in the long run, and the funding bodies are also interested in the longer term. But the building trade still likes to compete on price because they believe that the lowest bidder usually wins. Its hard to sell on the basis of savings in ten years time or more.'

Davidson had promised to return to the following Novalis board meeting with a presentation of his marketing strategy and plans for the future. He knew that this was something he could not sweep under the carpet.

QUESTIONS

1 What are the alternative marketing channels open to Davison? List the advantages and disadvantages of the options.

2 Recommend a marketing channel strategy for Davison. How would you manage the channels?

3 What will the impact of your strategy be on other elements of the marketing mix, especially pricing?

DEVELOPING A MARKETING PLAN

THE DISTRIBUTION STRATEGY

How will you place your product or service into the market? Consider issues of location and marketing channels. Define your channel strategy in terms of:

■ Selection (direction and intensity)
■ Management (creating efficiencies and overcoming conflict)

11.8 FURTHER READING AND REFERENCES

Channel management

Christopher, M. (2005), *Logistics and Supply Chain Management: Creating Value-adding Networks*, 3rd edition (Financial Times/Prentice Hall).

Retailing

Berman, B. and Evans, J. (2004), *Retail Management*, 9th edition (Prentice Hall).
Euromonitor (2006), *Retailing – United Kingdom*.
McGoldrick, P. J. (2002), *Retail Marketing*, 2nd edition (McGraw Hill).

E-commerce

Hanson, W. and Kalyanam, K. (2007), *Internet Marketing and e-Commerce*, 2nd edition (South Western).

Franchising

Keynote Report (2006), *Franchising Market Report*.
www.lloydstsb.com/business

Chapter **12**

MARKETING DECISIONS AND PLANNING

LEARNING OBJECTIVES

By the end of this chapter the reader will be able to:

- Understand the need to take account of contextual differences before taking marketing decisions
- Appreciate these differences particularly in relation to SMEs, non-profit organisations, services, business-to-business and international markets
- Assess differences between traditional and entrepreneurial marketing
- Develop an appropriate structure for a marketing plan
- Complete the marketing process by developing a marketing plan for a particular product or service

INTRODUCTION

This chapter summarises how marketing plans and decisions are made in different contexts. Modern marketing concepts are applied in a wide variety of circumstances and business environments – from large to small businesses, private and public sectors, and organisational and consumer markets with local and global reach. A premise of this book is that basic marketing principles can apply in all of these situations, but strategies and tactics have to adapt to the context. The practical examples used in the text have been drawn deliberately from a wide range of contexts to emphasise this assumption. This chapter draws together some of these variations in the application of marketing. It examines how internal and external considerations shape the application of marketing strategies and tactics. Many of these circumstances are discussed elsewhere in the text but are summarised here for further discussion and ease of reference.

This chapter also looks at the formal and informal processes involved in planning a marketing campaign. It examines how marketing plans are produced, identifying the four stages of analysis, objectives, methods and evaluation, reviewing each stage in some detail. It outlines the benefits of planning, stressing the need for integrated, specific plans which look behind the current situation to assess opportunities and threats in the marketplace.

CASE STUDY

···

LinkLine ELECTRONICS

Hayden Blane founded LinkLine Electronics in the late 1990s, when governments around the globe were looking to entrepreneurs to create new economic growth. Although he had no formal management training or qualifications, Blane found it relatively easy to obtain the £150,000 required for working capital, equipment and machinery. In return for the loan, the bank manager did ask for a business plan, which was duly written by a firm of accountants and gathered dust in Blane's filing cabinet thereafter. 'I don't have time to write or read plans. I'm too busy putting them into practice', he argued.

His energetic selling and opportunistic approach to the market paid off. Although the pattern of trading was typical of a new start-up with first-year losses, LinkLine was making profits by its second year and achieved a turnover of £500,000 by year three. Sales continued to climb and exceeded £600,000 in 2001 (year four) when LinkLine recorded profits of £60,000.

Blane had carved out a viable niche in a very competitive market by designing electronic circuits for specialised applications, tailor-made to individual customer needs. His customers were other larger electronic companies who had a problem: they were developing products that could not use conventional circuits because they were unsuited to the environment in which they would be operating.

'Some of my early customers wanted ultra-lightweight circuits for space probes', Blane explained. 'Others needed electronics that were unaffected by temperature extremes, for example, in ignition modules for engines that had to start even whilst very cold but continue to run when the engine had become much hotter. I had the technology to cope with many of these specialised applications, but I had to adapt to suit each customer. It was not something you could easily predict or write up as a standard marketing approach or sales plan.'

Then came problems. Sales fell in 2004 for the first time and the trend continued the following year when turnover was only two-thirds of the peak a couple of years earlier. Many of LinkLine's customers were in the military, space or automotive sectors – markets that had been hit by both falling prices and external events. Blane responded in typical entrepreneurial style by redoubling his selling efforts and looking for new markets.

'I went to companies making spare parts for cars, for instance', Blane explained. 'I figured that if people were not buying new cars, they would need more repairs which, in turn, meant more spare parts. So I found a new market – designing and producing replacement ignition modules. And I can now sell the same product globally, as cars are the same all over the world.'

This not only gave Blane a new market, but also a different business environment. He was now selling a finished product direct to major retailers and distributors in international markets, rather than making a component to be sold to another UK manufacturer that would sell on through the marketing channel.

Unfortunately, this did not immediately help LinkLine's profits. Blane had to cut his prices because of the competitive market and long distribution chains of the new business, and his profit margins fell. Nevertheless he survived when many other small businesses did not.

The bank had become increasingly nervous about LinkLine's finances, and when a major customer went bankrupt leaving Blair with a large unpaid debt, they threatened to call in their overdraft which had grown to £100,000. Blane was furious, claiming his business had now turned the corner as his recent trading record, as shown in Table 12.1, proved.

Reluctantly, Blane agreed to the bank's proposal that an adviser should help him draft a marketing plan.

'I suggest you focus your marketing plan on providing sales leads, new ways in to potential customers', he suggested to the adviser. 'If I don't sell more, I don't survive so my number one priority is sales and promotions. And as I am the one who does most of the marketing, I don't have time to write up elaborate plans which no-one else but me would need to read.'

TABLE 12.1 *LinkLine trading record*

(£ 000s)	2001	2003	2004	2005	2006
SALES	610	920	790	620	680
GROSS PROFIT	300	440	400	250	270
OVERHEADS	240	350	360	310	260
NET PROFIT	60	90	40	(60)	10

QUESTIONS

1 LinkLine is a small, entrepreneurial business. How might this influence the marketing activities available to the company? *See section 12.1*

2 LinkLine sells to other businesses rather than to the end user. How will this influence the marketing activities that the company is likely to undertake? *See section 12.4*

3 LinkLine has become involved in international markets. What new considerations will Blane have to take into account? *See section 12.5*

4 What would you include as the main stages in a marketing plan for LinkLine? *See section 12.6*

5 If you were the marketing adviser to LinkLine, what further information would you require to complete the plan? Group the information into the stages you identified above. *See sections 12.7 to 12.10*

12.1 ENTREPRENEURIAL MARKETING

12.1.1 Small and medium-sized enterprises (SMEs)

In earlier chapters, it was emphasised that the mix of activities to implement marketing strategies needs to be tailored to the internal and external circumstances of the business. A key influence is the size of the enterprise, which may constrain the resources available for marketing activities or influence the culture of the organisation. This has become an increasingly important factor as small businesses have become more numerous and economically significant in western economies. In the UK, the great majority of businesses are small- and medium-sized enterprises (SMEs): 99 per cent of all businesses employ less than 50 people, and 95 per cent employ less than 10 (see Chapter 2, section 2.2.3).

A feature of SMEs is that they tend to be managed by one or two key individuals that own and run the business. These individual entrepreneurs tend not only to develop the strategy, but also to implement the marketing activities. Because they are such a dominant influence, their own personal experience, skills and attitudes become a major factor in the selection of the marketing mix.

'Entrepreneurial marketing' describes marketing as practised in entrepreneurial contexts, recognising that marketing as practised by entrepreneurs is different. Research indicates that entrepreneurs tend to act in an informal, unplanned way, relying on individual intuition and energy to make things happen. A typical marketing manager, on the other hand, takes action based on a deliberate, planned process involving a careful identification of customer needs and manipulation of the marketing mix through formal market research. These contrasting behavioural patterns of the archetypal entrepreneur and marketer make it easier to understand why small business owners (who are especially, but not exclusively, associated with entrepreneurship) should have particular problems with marketing according to the textbook.

Entrepreneurs' attitudes to marketing

Entrepreneurs tend to have a limited view of marketing. They tend to define marketing in terms of selling and promotions to attract new business, whilst ignoring other aspects such as product development, pricing and distribution. However, this does not necessarily mean that they overlook these other areas of marketing, only that they are unaware of the terminology. Indeed, business owners' narrow view of marketing is not always borne out by what they actually do. For example, entrepreneurs rate recommendations from customers as the number one way of attracting new customers. However, this does not mean that they put little effort into marketing; such recommendations are often hard won. To an outside observer, it is all too easy to accept a business owner's comment that they 'do not have the time or resources for marketing', when those same owners devote many hours building relationships with satisfied customers who then recommend the business to others.

This environment tends to give marketing in the small firm a distinctive style of informality with few formalised plans and restricted expenditure. Marketing practices in new ventures tend to evolve with the business. An initial phase of proactive marketing activity when the business is first set up may be superseded by a more reactive approach in which marketing efforts respond to customer enquiries or competitive threats. More positive marketing approaches may be adopted as the firm grows, leading to the planned, integrated campaigns of larger companies.

These factors mean that small business marketing does differ in practice from that of larger organisations.

12.1.2 Impact on the marketing mix

Product innovation considerations highlight the entrepreneur's dilemma. Without new products, small companies do not last long in competitive markets, yet the costs and risks of new product development can stretch their limited resources to unacceptable levels. Many small companies become too dependent on a narrow product line as a result.

Despite these constraints, small businesses can be more innovative compared to larger counterparts because of their entrepreneurial management style and shorter internal lines of communication. At times, entrepreneurs may seem at odds with the marketing concept of identifying a need in the marketplace and then trying to find a way of fulfilling that need. They often start with the idea for a new product or service, and then try to find a market for it. Opportunities are often created from intuitive feelings about a market derived from personal experiences, rather than more rigorous, objective research. SME innovation tends to come from inventions that find a home in the marketplace, rather than careful research into customer needs that is then translated into new products. Although they risk misunderstanding market needs, entrepreneurs have the advantage that they can act quickly and opportunistically because they rely only on their own judgement. (See Chapter 1, section 1.5.2.)

Pricing often represents a small firm's competitive advantage. In some markets this is a sustainable competitive advantage. For example, personalised services are not usually susceptible to economies of scale, so that the lower overheads of smaller businesses allow them to provide good quality services at lower prices. However, larger firms in industries that offer more standardised products and services can use their buying power or production economies to undercut smaller operators who have to seek competitive advantages elsewhere or go out of business. This has been the trend, for example, in many retail markets in which the small shop can compete on the basis of convenience and personal service, but not on price. There is evidence that small business-owners do tend to under-price their products and services through over-reliance on price as a competitive weapon. It is common practice to use cost-plus pricing methods and to neglect other factors such as what the customer is prepared to pay. Often they neglect to include their own time as a cost.

Place in terms of physical distribution is a restricted element in most small firms' marketing mix. Although some distribute products nationally, most small businesses do not make use of extensive distribution systems. With over 90 per cent in the service sector, small firms are restricted mainly to serving their local market. Distribution in international markets is particularly uncommon because most small firms do not export, although the Internet has made global markets more accessible to them.

Promotional methods in small firms tend to rely on interactive marketing communications, especially word-of-mouth recommendations and personal selling, rather than advertising and sales promotions. The role of word-of-mouth marketing is considered in more detail in section 12.1.4.

12.1.3 Entrepreneurial marketing communications

Interactive marketing

Entrepreneurs usually spend a considerable part of their working day in contact with customers, practising forms of interactive marketing. This involves a high level of interactions with their customer base that managers in larger firms struggle to match, even with the latest technological advances. Entrepreneurs specialise in interactions with their target markets because they have strong preferences for personal contact with customers rather than impersonal marketing through mass promotions. They seek conversational relationships in which they can listen to, and respond to, the voice of the customer, rather than undertake formal market research to understand the marketplace. In many smaller firms, the ability of the owner-manager to have meaningful dialogues with customers is often the unique selling point of the business. Interactive marketing for small firms implies responsiveness – the ability to communicate and respond rapidly to individual customers. Entrepreneurs interact with individual customers through personal selling and relationship-building approaches, which not only secure orders but generate recommendations to potential customers as well.

12.1.4 The influence of word-of-mouth communications

Entrepreneurial marketing relies heavily on word-of-mouth marketing to develop the customer base through recommendations. Research studies inevitably cite recommendations as the number one source of new customers for small firms. Such recommendations may come from customers, suppliers or other referral groups.

For smaller firms with limited resources, reliance on recommendations has advantages:

■ Referrals incur few, if any, additional direct costs

■ Most owner-managers prefer the slow build up of new business which word-of-mouth marketing brings because they would be unable to cope with large increases in demand for their services

Word-of-mouth marketing has disadvantages:

■ It is self-limiting: Reliance on networks of informal communications restricts organisational growth to the limits of those networks. If a small business is dependent on recommendations for new customers, its growth is limited to those market areas in which its sources of recommendations operate.

■ It is non-controllable: Owners cannot control word-of-mouth communications about their firms. As a result, some perceive there to be few opportunities to influence recommendations other than providing the best possible service.

In practice, successful entrepreneurs find ways of encouraging referrals by more proactive methods. Direct incentives can help but often it is the customers' feeling of involvement or participation with a small business that is most linked to their recommending behaviour. Parents who become more involved with their children's school, through helping in class or fund-raising activities, are more likely to become strong advocates of the school. Similarly in the private sector, successful owners encourage involvement of some sort with the business, so that customers feel an added sense of commitment to it, and in turn this improves word-of-mouth communications.

FOR EXAMPLE

....

An entrepreneur buys a health and fitness club where sales had been stagnant for many years. He soon finds out why. The membership is dominated by body-builders primarily interested in increasing muscle bulk through demanding routines of lifting heavy weights. These members represent a small section of the total health market, and are resistant to recommending the club to new members who are primarily interested in general fitness rather than body-building. In order to enlarge this limited network for recommendations, the owner encourages fitness instructors to use his gym for aerobic and other classes. Only then is he able to introduce a new type of member more interested in fitness and health than perfect pectorals. This type of member gradually increases in numbers through word-of-mouth communications. He stimulates these recommendations by offering a different class of 'premier membership' to those who introduced a new member. This operates like a 'club within the club', encouraging greater involvement of members by more frequent access to facilities and incentives such as free holidays.

12.1.5 Networking

Formal market research plays an important part in each stage of the traditional marketing process. Market orientation relies on research to determine customer needs. Strategic segmentation and targeting is determined by market research. The success of adjustments to the marketing mix is tracked by consumer research. Successful entrepreneurs shy away from such formal research methods. They prefer more informal methods of gathering market information, usually through networks of contacts involved in the industry or trade. Successful entrepreneurs maintain an external focus to their activities, which alerts them to opportunities and threats in their environment. Their informal information-gathering techniques allow them to monitor their own performance in relation to competitors and react to competitive threats. They are also open to new ideas and opportunities through a network of personal and interorganisational contacts. This process restarts the marketing cycle by forming the basis for further innovative adjustments to the activities of the enterprise.

12.1.6 Entrepreneurial marketing practice

This description of marketing as practised by successful entrepreneurs compared to more traditional marketing methods suggests the need for an overview of entrepreneurial marketing that identifies the differences. Successful entrepreneurial marketing consists of a circular process: innovative developments and adjustments to products and services are targeted at identified customer groups. These are contacted through interactive marketing methods, with a particular emphasis on word-of-mouth marketing. Informal information-gathering through networks monitors the marketplace and evaluates new opportunities, which may, in turn, lead to further innovations.

This can be conceptualised as a circular process of the '4Is' of innovation, identification of target markets, interactive marketing methods and informal networking, as illustrated in Figure 12.1.

CHECKPOINT

Consider a small business where you are a customer – this might be in catering, hairdressing, household services or retailing, for example. How did this business attract your custom? What marketing do they do to keep you as a customer? What marketing improvements could they make?

FIGURE 12.1 *Entrepreneurial marketing – the 4Is*

12.2 NON-PROFIT SECTOR AND SOCIAL ENTERPRISES

12.2.1 Types of non-profit organisations

Public services, social enterprises and charities that do not operate for profit have become increasingly involved in marketing decisions, as the examples given in other parts of this book illustrate. Although the sector does not have a tradition of overt marketing practices, non-profit organisations have shifted towards customer-orientated strategies because of changes in the methods of funding and increased competition. This general trend has taken on several specific forms. At one extreme, some organisations have joined the private sector and adopted profit objectives. At the other extreme, functional departments have become cost centres responsible for providing specific services to internal purchasers.

Several public sector organisations have moved totally or partially into the private sector. In the UK, the privatisation of public utilities such as gas, electricity and water exposed major organisations to competitive forces for the first time. Public corporations in telecommunications, airports, air travel and steel production are now answerable to shareholders rather than taxpayers.

Public services in education, health and local government have been divided into more autonomous units responsible for providing a specific service for an allocated budget. As the budget allocation depends in many cases on the number of 'customers' served, individual units have an incentive to compete between themselves to maximise their income. For example, the money given to a school depends mainly on the number of pupils in attendance, which encourages each school to market its services to attract the maximum possible number of students.

Non-profit institutions such as theatres, orchestras, museums and research bodies now compete more openly for public and private funds. Cutbacks to the amounts of public funds made available have forced them to market themselves more aggressively, not only to those who pay money to benefit from their service (e.g. visitors to a museum), but also to the private sector for sponsorship and to government agencies for allocations of public funds.

Charities and social enterprises such as Oxfam, the National Trust, RSPCA and Greenpeace use marketing strategies in two separate directions. First, they need to persuade people to give them money because they rely on donations and grants from individuals and corporations and other fundraising activities. Second, they use a variety of marketing activities from personal selling to PR in their roles as pressure groups in support of chosen causes. Funding in particular has become more competitive as the number of social causes has increased faster than the levels of charitable giving and grants available.

Numerous other non-profit organisations, from political parties and religious movements to sports and social clubs, are dependent on the support of their membership. Many use marketing campaigns to increase membership or promote their beliefs.

12.2.2 The non-profit marketing environment

Although many non-profit organisations have adopted marketing strategies, their specific environment does influence their ability to fully adopt marketing concepts, (see also Chapter 2, section 2.2.1). For example, there are many influences that potentially inhibit public services from becoming fully customer-orientated:

■ *Restricted markets*: Public services exist in markets subject to ongoing regulation and direction from one or more sources. Their ability to compete directly may therefore be limited.

■ *Confusion over who is the customer*: More than one group of people can lay claim to being the 'customer' of public services because of the separation between those that pay for the service, those that choose it, and those that use it. In education there is a clear split between those that ultimately pay for the service (taxpayers), agencies that control the purse-strings (education authorities), people who decide what is on offer (inspectors, teachers and governors), those who decide which particular institution to attend (parents and pupils) and those that directly receive the service (pupils). The users of a service may not be the most obvious target of marketing campaigns. It may be a misnomer to consider some users as 'customers' at all (e.g. inmates in prison), or inappropriate to consider their demands on a par with other stakeholders (e.g. the desire of pupils for longer playtime and no homework).

■ *Open access*: Most public services are available to all and have to take account of the needs of a very diverse range of people. The opportunities to target services on segments of users with similar needs may be limited: health authorities have a responsibility to provide services ranging from emergency admissions to maternity care; the police and fire services have a duty to protect all citizens irrespective of location and socio-economic group. Evidence of the deliberate targeting of a public service through rationing of some groups for the benefit of others has been greeted with public outcry and political intervention.

■ *Public service ethos*: The need for public services has been explained in terms of the need to atone for the failure of market forces to safeguard the public good by providing welfare to those disadvantaged by the interactions of the marketplace. This notion that a benevolent public realm is needed to compensate for the excesses of the marketplace does not sit easily with the encouragement of private sector practices within the public sector. Some public sector managers have resisted business approaches on the basis that they represent concepts that are alien to the ethos of their service. To some, the very language of commerce represents a threat, so that the culture of marketing is seen to be unacceptable.

■ *Public accountability and scrutiny*: Because they are intended for the general good, public services are accountable to a wide audience. All activities can be scrutinised by the public or their political representatives in a way that does not exist in the commercial world, especially for small enterprises such as private family businesses. An important factor in the management environment of schools is the legal requirement to appoint at least eight governors, in contrast to equivalent-sized private sector enterprises, which are controlled typically by one owner-manager. Ultimate responsibility for public services rests with politicians, who may be more cautious because of their exposure to public criticism than innovative entrepreneurs answerable only to themselves.

■ *Objectives may be multiple and contradictory*: Unlike the private sector where the profit objective tends to be the rule, public sector organisations have multiple and often contradictory objectives. The requirement on many public services to cut costs and improve services simultaneously may not be realistic unless they restrict public access to their services. For example, health services may face the choice of providing a higher standard of care for a selective group of patients or offering a lower-quality service available to everyone.

FOR EXAMPLE

FareShare is the national charity working to relieve food poverty by providing quality surplus food from the food industry and food-related services to organisations supporting homeless and other vulnerable people in the community. Surplus food is food that doesn't have a commercial outlet anymore but is still in life and fit for purpose. Due to various reasons such as stringent company policies and legislation food manufacturers, wholesalers and retailers are throwing away huge amounts of good-quality food for many reasons (e.g. packaging is damaged or promotional offers on packaging have ended). At the same time, many people cannot afford a regular supply of high-quality fresh food and have no daily intake of fresh fruit and vegetables. This lack of a healthy diet, combined with the other hardships such as homelessness impairs the immune system and leaves people vulnerable to ill health: the homeless have an average lifespan of just forty-two years compared to the national average of seventy-four years.

FareShare receives surpluses from food companies and redistributes them to organisations that support disadvantaged people in the community. It therefore has two sets of primary 'customers': food companies such as Sainsbury's, Nestlé and Prêt a Manger; and local projects and charities such as hostels, breakfast clubs and women's refuges that care for the homeless and disadvantaged. It also has end users that partake of the estimated 3.3 million meals a year that it provides. As it is funded by grants and donations, a fourth target market is the funding bodies such as the National Lottery and government grant holders. It relies heavily on volunteers who help sort the food and drive the vans that deliver it, so recruitment of volunteers is a further marketing activity. It also lobbies the government to get recognition and support so that 'No Good Food Should Be Wasted', – the message of their campaign.

The marketing of FareShare must appeal to all six groups: it markets environmental, corporate and social responsibility to food companies; appropriate food supplies to charities and social enterprises; a healthy diet to the needy and homeless; the benefits of recycling food including minimising land-fill waste, and the benefit of providing quality food towards a nutritious diet and food-related training for vulnerable people, to funding stakeholders; it appeals to volunteers to give up their time in a good cause; finally, it communicates to the government the issues on food poverty and food waste. Each group requires a different marketing mix. FareShare's website (www.fareshare.org.uk) illustrates this diversity of markets with multiple messages and appeals.

FareShare has multiple shareholders and needs to use different messages for its targets

12.2.3 Impact on the marketing mix

Non-profit objectives influence the application of the marketing mix in several ways. Product or service strategies typically take most emphasis. In the education and health services, for

MARKETING MISTAKES

A key public service is the provision of electrical power. This was considered so vital to the national well-being that the generation and distribution of electricity was originally owned by the state. The UK commissioned Windscale as one of the first nuclear reactors as part of its energy policy in the post-Second World War era. Initially this was also linked to the decision to maintain an independent nuclear capability for defence purposes. There were many safety problems, including the release of radioactive materials into the atmosphere following a fire, and the discharge of radioactive waste into the Irish Sea in the haste to develop the British bomb. In reaction to the protest and the bad press that these incidents generated, the government decided to change the name from Windscale to Sellafield. Unfortunately the unsafe practices and pollution did not stop and few were fooled into thinking the product had changed with the name. The protests continued for several decades after the name change – for example there was a 'Stop Sellafield' concert in 1992 head-lined by U2. Tinkering with the promotional element of the marketing mix does not work if the underlying problem with the product is not addressed.

Changing name did not improve the image of the Sellafield nuclear facility on the Cumbrian coast

example, the delivery of the curriculum or healthcare 'product' takes precedence over other marketing issues such as advertising or pricing.

Price issues often translate into the more general aims of providing 'value for money' services or the maximisation of revenues rather than the pricing of specific items practised in the private sector.

Promotional campaigns need to be carefully justified as a correct use of scarce resources. Many non-profit organisations rely on word-of-mouth communications to promote their cause. Others use direct marketing campaigns where there is a direct link between costs and results, such as raising funds for a charity.

Place is often an issue of location. For some public services it is an important marketing influence, but outside of direct management control. For example, the recruitment of pupils to a school depends crucially on one factor over which headteachers and governors have no control – where it is located. Where there is some choice, location is often determined by historic factors and cost considerations rather than customer convenience.

CHECKPOINT

You have been asked to prepare a marketing action plan for Greenpeace. Which target markets will you have to consider in your plans?

12.3 SERVICES MARKETING

12.3.1 Characteristics of services

Services have become an increasingly important part of developed economies as the manufacturing sector has declined. Although marketing principles were originally devised for tangible consumer goods, they are increasingly applied in a service context. Services have the following characteristics, which distinguish them from more tangible products (see also Chapter 7, section 7.1):

- *Intangibility*: We cannot normally touch, hold, see or even smell a service. This intangibility makes them difficult to demonstrate or sample, so that the reputation of the provider of a service becomes a crucial ingredient in the buying decision.

- *Inseparability*: Services are difficult to separate from those that provide them. People can personify the service and become an important ingredient in the brand (e.g. the leader of a political party).

- *Perishability*: Services cannot be stored. They cannot be produced in advance and held in stock until required. An empty seat on a train or an aeroplane is a lost sale for ever.

- *Heterogeneity*: Services are difficult to standardise as they are usually tailor-made for the customer in some way. Personal contact between the supplier of a service and the customer is therefore common.

- *Ownership*: Although purchased, services may not be 'owned' in the conventional sense. Services are sold on the basis of access to facilities, information and expertise (e.g. hotels, libraries and legal advice) or the use or rental of items (e.g. passenger transport by train, video hire, and bank loans).

12.3.2 Impact on the marketing mix

The marketing mix for services is often increased to seven by the addition of three more 'Ps' to take account of these characteristics:

- *Physical evidence*: A tangible aspect of a service that can provide some evidence to the potential buyer about the service on offer (e.g. the lobby of a hotel, the colour of a credit card).

- *People*: Often the crucial element in the perception of a service. Recruitment, retention and motivation of staff are therefore significant ingredients in the marketing mix.

- *Process*: An integral part of a service at which customers are often present (e.g. in a restaurant) or an integral part of it. As customers visit the premises of service deliverers such as hairdressers, dentists, teachers and restaurant owners, the process itself takes on a marketing significance. A happy experience matters as much as the quality of the service in forming the perceptions and future choices of the customer. The way the service is delivered can become as important as the end result. Mistakes and conflicts are difficult to conceal and relationships with a customer may never recover from just one processing error. This is not the case with tangible products because the manufacturing process is usually hidden from the eye of the consumer. We do not form impressions of a tin of beans from an involvement in the production process or knowledge of the number of rejects in the system (or if we do it often has lasting effects). Visibility of the process can be used as a positive marketing tool.

FOR EXAMPLE

Fast food and other restaurants often deliberately make the food production area visible to customers to add to the image of efficiency and hygiene which they wish to portray. Some restaurants are themed around the concept of involving customers in the cooking of ingredients selected by them. Automation and standardisation of some services can become important marketing tools to overcome the problems of variability of service provision. Automatic cash dispensing machines have improved banking services. Hotel groups and car rental companies have built worldwide chains based on the standardisation of services so that the customer knows what to expect no matter the geographic location.

CHECKPOINT

You have been asked to develop a marketing action plan for a local window cleaning service that has just been launched. How will it overcome the lack of existing customers for recommendations and referrals?

12.4 BUSINESS-TO-BUSINESS (B2B) AND BUSINESS-TO-CONSUMER (B2C) MARKETING

Business-to-business marketing has been developed as a specialised subject area because of generalised differences that exist between B2B and B2C markets. These differences are discussed in Chapter 3, section 3.6.2.

12.4.1 Characteristics of organisational or B2B markets

Products used by manufacturers, business and public services are often more complex than those sold in consumer markets. These products can be classified as:

- Installations, capital and accessory equipment, such as factory buildings, trucks, machinery, scientific equipment and computers
- Raw materials and component parts, such as iron ore, cloth, wire, yarn, circuit boards and buttons
- Supplies and services, such as lubricants, computer disks, cleaning and accounting

Demand in B2B markets is derived from other customers in the chain and ultimately the end user. Changes in consumption patterns further down the chain eventually affect those higher up.

Purchasing patterns are usually different. Industrial customers tend to be relatively small in number, purchasing in larger amounts, sometimes on an infrequent or contractual basis. Consumers tend to buy a large number of relatively small value products on a frequent basis. Consumer markets therefore tend to be made up of large numbers of customers spending small amounts reasonably often.

The decision-making process is often different. Customers in consumer markets tend to make individual decisions with only the most important purchases referred to more than one person (e.g. buying a house). Organisations frequently involve more than one person in a buying decision of any importance. A decision-making unit (DMU), consisting of a number of individuals who influence the buying process can be involved, particularly in 'new task' purchasing decisions. (See Chapter 4, section 4.5.)

There are exceptions to these generalisations. Some consumer markets involve infrequent purchases of complex, high-value products by a few customers (e.g. luxury cars, second homes). There are over four million businesses in the UK alone so products which are used by most of them (e.g. stationery, office furniture) are sold into relatively large markets. Most decisions made in many small businesses involve only one person – the owner-manager.

12.4.2 Impact on the marketing mix

In B2B markets these generalised differences have an impact on each element of the marketing mix:

- **Products** tend to be more customised and less standardised. Some industrial products are completely made to order (e.g. an electronic circuit for a mobile telephone, designed and manufactured by a subcontractor). Others are partly standardised with options available depending on the customer's specification (e.g. a fleet of passenger aircraft ordered by an airline).

- **Prices** tend to be quoted for individual orders and are therefore less uniform. Customised products need separate prices, and an organisation's purchasing power for more standardised products influences pricing levels.

- **Promotions** rely more on personal contact and less on advertising. In general, personal methods of promoting such as personal selling and exhibitions are more suited to communicating in industrial markets. Conversely, impersonal methods of communicating such as advertising are more appropriate to promoting to the large number of relatively small buyers typical of consumer markets. (See also Chapter 9, section 9.3.2.)

  The order of preference of promotional methods changes therefore between industrial and consumer markets:

  — In B2B markets, personal marketing communications such as direct selling are often the most used method, supported by an informative website.

  — In consumer markets, non-personal marketing communications such as advertising, sales promotions and public relations are commonly the most used methods, supported by direct marketing and personal selling.

- **Placing** products into industrial markets is more likely to involve a shorter chain of intermediaries or no intermediaries at all. A producer needs to keep direct control of marketing channels if customised products are personally sold and individually priced. Where the elements of the marketing mix can be more standardised, distributors and dealers are used (e.g. in the distribution of office equipment such as copiers and furniture). In these circumstances, producers have to consider a 'pull', as well as a 'push', strategy to ensure the flow of products into the next link in the chain.

FOR EXAMPLE

For some scientific applications, microscopes need a powerful light source to develop images of faintly visible specimens. CIL, an electronics manufacturing company, has developed an innovative product that uses light-emitting diodes (LEDs) to provide this light source. The new product was branded 'PrecisExcite' to emphasise its advantages of precision and reliability over traditional mercury bulb systems.

Prior to launching the new product, CIL had produced products for other companies that then carried out the marketing and distribution. For example, one customer designed and distributed marine safety equipment, but it subcontracted the manufacturing of the specialist electronic parts to CIL. As a subcontract manufacturer, CIL had a sales team that sold directly to other manufacturers but not further along the value chain. Therefore the marketing of PrecisExcite demanded new skills in developing a more complete distribution system and selling direct to end users.

In order to test the market, it was decided to find a group of users who could validate the benefits of the new technology and identify specific applications for scientific research. Thus the first stage was to find potential users in the marketplace and offer them demonstrations and trials of the equipment. Once this had proven satisfactory, the new product was offered to other users, but more importantly for long-term success, to the distribution channels that serviced the industry. This was achieved through sales calls and demonstrations, exhibiting at relevant exhibitions, emails to the target market and an informative website (www.coolled.com).

An image viewed with the help of PreciseExcite

CHECKPOINT

You are a self-employed business consultant serving clients in business-to-business markets. How would you go about marketing your services to obtain new business? What would be the important features of your marketing mix?

12.5 INTERNATIONAL MARKETING

12.5.1 Global or local?

International marketing – or marketing across national boundaries – has increased dramatically in recent decades. Developments such as the enlargement of the European Community, and the high growth rate of Asian economies such as China and India, indicate that it will become an even more significant factor in the future, spurred on by advances in communications, transfers of finance and transportation.

However, the size of many businesses restricts their trading to regional or national boundaries because they do not have the appropriate products, resources or motivation to expand internationally. Organisations involved in international marketing tend to be either global organisations or smaller organisations.

Global corporations such as Shell, Ford and Microsoft regard the world as one market and carry out manufacturing, research and development, finance, marketing and other activities in the most suitable place irrespective of national boundaries.

FOR EXAMPLE

Halliburton, a giant oil services company, was based in the USA. But it decided to follow the advice of its former chief executive (and US vice-president) Dick Cheney 'to go where the oil is'. It decided in 2007 to move it headquarters to Dubai, as the company believed the centre of gravity in global energy had shifted eastwards. There are also tax savings to be made by basing a global business in Dubai because the ruling Maktoum family have made it financially attractive to relocate there.

Such international organisations now tend to call themselves 'global', rather than 'multinational', corporations because the latter term has become associated with concern over the potential abuse of the substantial power and resources which these large corporations command with little accountability to the societies in which they operate.

Smaller organisations may have to consider international markets because of the restricted scope or competitive pressure of the home market. This might apply particularly to companies involved in specialised technologies and products, such as scientific instruments and computer software, which readily cross national borders.

12.5.2 Impact on marketing activities

The problems of marketing in countries with differing cultural, political and economic structures and conditions are considerable and have defeated many organisations that have attempted it. Marketing techniques and approaches have to take account of local requirements.

Research is obviously essential to understand the conditions, regulations and peculiarities of national markets. Although there are many sources of information, difficulties may exist in the interpretation and comparability of data.

Products can be sold internationally in three basic ways:

- *Standardisation*: The same product is sold in all countries through a strategy of market extension. This is appropriate in some industries (e.g. soft drinks and clothes) but not in others (e.g. magazines and newspapers).

- *Adaptation*: A product is modified and adapted to local conditions (e.g. right-hand drive cars in the UK).

- *New product*: A new product is developed in response to the unmet needs of individual nations (e.g. training courses for managers with limited experience of trading with western economies).

Pricing has to take account of new influences such as tariffs, local taxes, exchange rates and potentially higher distribution costs. The use of barter or 'countertrade' in which payment is made in goods rather than money can also become a factor.

Promotions are most likely to require local adaptation if only because of language differences. The high creative cost of television advertising has pushed many global corporations towards using 'umbrella' campaigns in which the visual and music content of an advertisement are standardised whilst the verbal message is localised.

Place considerations depend on the initial approach to international markets. Options include:

- Exporting or producing goods in one country and sending them to another

- Licensing, in which a local operator is given the right to produce or sell within a given market

- Joint venture between a foreign company and a national organisation who come together to form a new business

- Direct ownership of a foreign subsidiary to manufacture or sell products in their local market

12.5.3 *International marketing strategies*

These choices, which face organisations considering marketing on an international scale, can be categorised into different strategic approaches:

- *Globalisation*, which standardises products to generate the maximum economies of scale on the assumption that they are meeting universal needs that exist regardless of national differences.

- *Localisation*, which treats every national market as different, tailoring all aspects of the marketing mix to local conditions because of significant variations between countries.

- *'Glocalisation'*, which is a mixture of the first two approaches in that products and marketing activities are standardised wherever possible, but adapted where necessary within a uniform format to take account of significant local needs.

FOR EXAMPLE

The microscope industry is dominated by four key manufacturers: Olympus and Nikon from Japan, Zeiss in Germany, and Leica in the USA. All four companies have their own salesforce and distribution channels for their own products. They also sell add-on products made by other companies where these offer additional functionality at an acceptable quality standard. PrecisExcite, a new product that illuminates samples using high-powered LEDs (see page 411), was developed by a relatively small company in the UK. To maximise its potential, PrecisExcite is sold as a uniform product but distributed through various distribution channels that take account of local circumstances. It is sold through the main manufacturers that chose to recommend it; it is sold through agents on a country-wide basis in countries such as Australia; it is sold through more local dealers in markets such as the UK where the company had established their own presence. All of these distribution options are kept under review as the business develops and the local business environments change.

12.5.4 Impact of the Internet

The Internet has the capability to create marketplaces without boundaries. Bill Gates and others have presented visions of how information technology would transform global commerce following the widespread adoption of the Internet from the mid-1990s. However, despite its mass-market potential, the Internet has not transformed markets for all consumers. There are still constraints imposed by the technical, financial and cultural development of particular regions. Most Internet communications and transactions are business-to-business, rather than business-to-consumer. 'E-business' is transforming the ways in which global trade is conducted because of three principal benefits:

■ *Improved communications between customers and suppliers.* The Internet facilitates fast, cost-effective and convenient communications internationally. It is inexpensive to use and overcomes some of the problems of operating across different time zones. Quotes, product information, documentation and reports can be circulated faster and more easily at any time of day, to any country of the world.

■ *Lower costs of international transactions.* The Internet is becoming a universal middleman in global transactions. Unlike the human middleman, the Internet does not expect a cut of the proceeds. Transaction costs are becoming lower as buyers and suppliers make direct contact for the first time. This is sometimes in conjunction with other companies through a 'virtual marketplace' such as the WorldWide Retail Exchange, or 'reverse auctions' in which buyers communicate their purchase requirements and suppliers bid for the order, successively lowering the price. More commonly, it is the individual, direct contact between a buyer seeking goods and services finding an international supplier through the Internet.

■ *Easier access to relevant information.* Finding out about market conditions such as customer preferences and competitive activity is always more difficult at a distance. Networks and databases accessible via the Internet helped to provide appropriate information quickly and cheaply. It is now possible to research important information for entry into an overseas market such as potential distributors and competitors' products, pricing and advertising without leaving the office.

CHECKPOINT

You are the marketing director of a large international charity, raising funds across Europe and providing resources for your cause in many countries of the world. List the main marketing activities you would expect to be involved in 1) to raise funds and 2) to increase awareness of your cause.

12.6 THE PROCESS FOR MAKING MARKETING DECISIONS

12.6.1 The marketing process

Whatever the context, a process is required that identifies or anticipates customer needs and fulfils them in a way that meets organisational needs for profit or other objectives, if the marketing concept is to be implemented. This is a circular process of several stages (see Chapter 1):

■ Identification of customer needs

■ Identification of the strengths and needs of the supplying organisation

■ Organisation of resources to satisfy customer needs in line with organisational objectives

■ Monitoring and evaluation of the results of these activities

■ Identification of new or modified customer needs

■ Implementation of new or modified ways of meeting customer needs

Some organisations follow this pattern formally. Others use more informal planning methods.

FOR EXAMPLE

Alan Sugar founded Amstrad to capitalise on the demand for the new electrical audio goods such as transistor radios, tape recorders, amplifiers, tuners, turntables and car radios that boomed in the mid-1960s. Initially he did not develop any products himself; he identified the need for a more efficient distribution of the new products from the manufacturers or importers to the retailers and consumers and organised resources to do it. In doing so he was able to monitor the marketplace and found some consumer needs that were not being met by the existing manufacturers. At the time the clear plastic dust covers and plinths for record players were very expensive because of the high costs of the raw materials. Sugar decided to develop his own product using a lower cost injection moulding process provided by a subcontractor. He was soon selling dust covers at a fraction of the previous price, the success of which gave him the resources to look for more new products in the electrical and electronic markets. Like many successful entrepreneurs, Sugar did not go through the stages of the marketing process in a formalised, planned way. He nevertheless followed the process of identifying and satisfying a need, evaluating the results, modifying his approach, observing the results and beginning the process all over again as new opportunities came along.

Other organisations operate a more formal system to achieve the same end. This is particularly necessary as organisations grow in size and the variables affecting the matching process between supplier and consumer become more numerous and complex.

FOR EXAMPLE

The Royal Dutch Shell Group operates in several major industrial sectors, including energy, chemicals, metals and forestry, in more than a hundred countries. Identification and satisfaction of customer needs cannot be left to chance in this complex environment. The management structure is decentralised through a series of operating companies, each of which produce an annual business plan covering the next five years. An integral part of these plans is a statement of marketing strategy and details of marketing activities that are developed through a process of marketing planning.

12.6.2 The marketing planning process

Marketing planning is a structured way of looking at the match between what an organisation has to offer and what the market needs. It can be used to investigate the marketing options of an

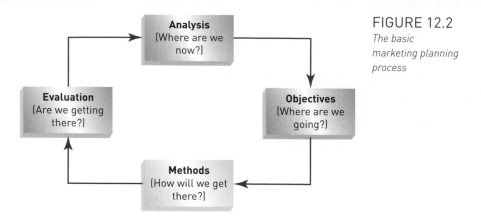

FIGURE 12.2
The basic marketing planning process

entire organisation with multiple products, or it can be used to plan the marketing of a single product or service, or a group of products. It provides an overall structure in which marketing decisions can be made.

The process has four basic stages which are similar to other planning models in that they ask the following questions in sequence:

■ *Where are we now?* This can only be answered by an *analysis* of the existing position both inside and outside of the organisation.

■ *Where are we going?* This requires an examination of where we are currently headed and where we should be headed through the setting of some precise *objectives.*

■ *How do we get there?* Detailed activity plans and marketing programmes are needed next, to establish the marketing *methods* that will be used to meet the objectives.

■ *Are we getting there?* We will need ways of measuring the impact of our activities through some system of *evaluation* so that we know at any time how we are doing.

It is a circular process in that it begins by an analysis of the existing situation and includes an evaluation of the new activities that have taken place. In turn this evaluation will become part of the analysis of the situation in the future so that the planning cycle can begin again. This basic process is illustrated in Figure 12.2.

Each of these four basic stages can be further subdivided, as we will discuss below.

CHECKPOINT

You have decided to sell one of your significant possessions (such as a car, computer or music system). How would you go about this? Describe the stages you would go through to make key decisions such as identifying the right price, selecting advertising methods and negotiating a final deal.

12.7 ANALYSIS (WHERE ARE WE NOW?)

The analysis stage includes finding out all the information that currently exists about the internal and external environments of the project and filling any obvious gaps through research. Some of the categories that are considered in the analysis stage are illustrated in Figure 12.3.

FIGURE 12.3
The analysis stage

12.7.1 *Organisational objectives*

The marketing plan is central to the planning and development of any organisation. It will have a significant influence on a whole range of issues from the cash flow to the scheduling of production or service delivery. It cannot, therefore, be developed in isolation from the corporate planning process. In particular, a marketing plan will take as its starting point the objectives of the business or enterprise.

FOR EXAMPLE

Suppose you have been asked to put together a marketing plan for a company called Kitchen Care, which is launching a new service that provides the detailed design and fitting of commercial kitchens from factory canteens to upmarket restaurants. Before considering anything else, you need to know how this new service fits into Kitchen Care's overall plans and priorities. You need to know what constraints may apply to its launch and how easily it fits with their existing operations. In short, you need to know their corporate objectives.

Some organisations formalise their corporate goals into a 'mission statement'. Others have definite objectives which are only communicated informally, and some have no clear objectives at all. A necessary prerequisite for marketing planning, however, is a statement of objectives in answer to the question 'What business are we in?' The answer given should reflect the 'over-arching goals' of an organisation – goals that reflect its core purpose, its reason for existing in the first place and its vision for the future. Its relevance lies in establishing a concise summary of the task to be done, not a recital of well-intentioned aims.

Corporate or organisational objectives are stated in many different ways. However, for marketing planning to proceed it is desirable to understand the following general points about the goals of an organisation:

■ *What business are we in? (Mission)*: What needs will be satisfied, or benefits provided, by the organisation's existence? In other words, how will its existence be justified in relation to its customers or those it seeks to serve? How will the organisation be different from others – what will distinguish it from others attempting to satisfy the same needs? In summary, how does the organisation define:

— Customer groups to be served (*who*)?

— Customer needs to be filled (*what?*)?

— Expertise/technologies to be utilised (*how?*)?

■ *What are the parameters? (Beliefs and values)*: What is the scope of the organisation's activities? What are the boundaries that it does not wish to cross, or potential expansion areas that it wishes to avoid? In particular how does the organisation see itself in terms of:

— Scope of activities

— Values of the organisation

— Legal and other constraints

FOR EXAMPLE

A marketing team at a well-known national charity produced a publicity plan using case histories of clients helped by the organisation. Unfortunately this overlooked a corporate policy that demanded complete confidentiality for clients and the publicity programme was scrapped.

■ *What are the priorities? (Specific objectives)*: What does the organisation want to achieve this year, and over the next three to five years? What are the top priorities in the short term and the longer term? If priorities are not made explicit, they can become contradictory.

FOR EXAMPLE

Whilst the sales department of an electronics manufacturer were planning on a large increase in units sold, the engineering department were planning on cost savings which would have made it impossible for them to provide the necessary technical support for a big jump in sales.

Organisations differ widely in how they specify their objectives. Many small firms, for example, have no written objectives at all but still have very clear aims and goals, usually inside the head of one or two key people. Other organisations have written mission statements, and some document not only their strategy but specific objectives as well.

FOR EXAMPLE

Some mission statements are more wordy than others. For example the Body Shop's mission, shown below, is very comprehensive and, consistent with their positioning in the marketplace, almost evangelical.

The Body Shop Mission Statement
Our Reason for Being:
To dedicate our business to the pursuit of social and environmental change.
To creatively balance the financial and human needs of our stakeholders: employees, customers, franchisees, suppliers and shareholders.

WWW.THEBODYSHOP.COM/ABOUTUS

To courageously ensure that our business is ecologically sustainable, meeting the needs of the present without compromising the future.

To meaningfully contribute to local, national and international communities in which we trade, by adopting a code of conduct which ensures care, honesty, fairness and respect.

To passionately campaign for the protection of the environment and human and civil rights, and against animal testing within the cosmetics and toiletries industry.

To tirelessly work to narrow the gap between principle and practice, while making fun, passion and care part of our daily lives.

THEBODYSHOP.COM.

Whilst this extended mission statement is very worthy, perhaps the Body Shop's mission is better summarised by the statements to the right.

At the end of the day the mission statement should be one that all the employers can remember.

Shorter examples are given below.

FOR EXAMPLE

GSK's mission is to improve the quality of human life by enabling people to do more, feel better and live longer.

GlaxoSmithKline (GSK) is a world leading research-based pharmaceutical company with a powerful combination of skills and resources that provides a platform for delivering strong growth in today's rapidly changing healthcare environment.

FOR EXAMPLE

Mission:

'To spread the spirit of rock'n'roll by spreading authentic experiences that rock'

Mottos:

Love All – Serve All
Save the Planet
Take Time to be Kind

FOR EXAMPLE

....

'PizzaExpress consistently produces delicious foods and drink at value prices served by friendly staff in stylish surroundings.'

FOR EXAMPLE

....

In the case of Kitchen Care (see page 417), there are no written statements of mission or corporate objectives like the examples above. However, you know there are clear views on where the company is going and what its market strategy should be, so you decide to interview the managing director and other key executives to try and establish the parameters within which you will have to work.

CHECKPOINT

1. Compare the mission statements above. What are the advantages and disadvantages of each?
2. Does the organisation for whom you work, or the institution where you study, have a mission statement? If it does, do you think it is an appropriate and meaningful statement of objectives? Is it sufficiently publicised? If there are no published objectives, draw up what you would consider to be an appropriate statement of mission and corporate objectives.

12.7.2 The marketing audit

When applied to business management, the term 'audit' means a review and appraisal of a specific function or activity. It is most commonly applied to the financial function involving an investigation into the accuracy and adequacy of accounting records over a period of time. When applied to marketing, it has a similar meaning except that it has a more strategic and forward-looking dimension as well. A marketing audit examines and evaluates the marketing operations of an organisation, but it also includes two other important aspects:

■ A marketing audit does not examine just the activities associated with marketing but also the underlying philosophy and concepts on which the activities were based. In other words, it evaluates whether an organisation is following the marketing concept, as outlined in Chapter 1, or whether it is operating under a different set of principles and policies.

■ A marketing audit looks at what has happened to date *plus* potential new areas and possibilities. It summarises the marketing environment, highlighting past successes and problems in order to evaluate future opportunities. It evaluates current information but also suggests further research requirements.

FOR EXAMPLE

Your audit of the marketing of Kitchen Care might reveal that the company had hitherto adopted a rather sales-oriented approach with most of its efforts going into selling its existing product range, irrespective of customer types and product applications. Sales staff had been encouraged to sell kitchen equipment and cleaning materials to whomever they could, with little after-sales follow-up or advice. Research into restaurant owners, however, revealed a lack of knowledge of new hygiene regulations in commercial kitchens and an opportunity to offer a more tailor-made service involving an advisory sales approach.

A marketing audit is concerned with establishing the environmental factors facing the organisation which have marketing implications now and in the future. Such an analysis will need to look internally and externally.

The internal audit

The internal audit examines the marketing areas over which the organisation has control and summarises the choices that have been made to date, including such information as:

- Past marketing objectives and success rates
- Sales or revenue – analysed by sector, for example geographic region, customer type, products
- Market shares and trends – are shares increasing or decreasing?
- Profit margins and pricing strategy
- Product range, perceived quality and historic developments
- Promotional methods used and success rates
- Distribution channels used
- Marketing resources available and past allocations – personnel, organisation and budgets
- Market research available.

The external audit

The external audit examines factors external to the organisation which can influence the planning and execution of marketing activities. These include the business and economic environments, marketing environment and competitive environment, as detailed below.

- *Business and economic environments*: This is often considered through a 'STEP' analysis, which reviews factors under the headings of:
  — Social and cultural
  — Technological
  — Economic
  — Political

FOR EXAMPLE

Exclaimer Ltd is a small business that offers a software utilities package allowing companies to control the look, content and processing of emails throughout an organisation. This year they benefited from a change in legislation. Since 1985, the Companies Act has required private companies to show the company's information clearly in all of its business letters, cheques and other documents. This includes:

- Full corporate name
- Company's place of registration
- Registered number
- Registered office address

On 1 January 2007 a new EU directive extended this legislation to cover electronic communication. It insisted that a company's name should also appear clearly on all websites and electronic communications, including faxes, emails and text messages if sent in a business context. The penalty for failure to comply with the new regulations is a fine of up to £1,000. This meant that Exclaimer's product moved from being optional to mandatory overnight. Every private company in the EU has to use Exclaimer's Mail Utilities product or its equivalent. In the first month after the legislation came into force, the company's turnover doubled, with customers actively seeking the company out rather than them having to pursue the customers.

- *Market environment*: This examines trends in the total market such as:
  - Its size, growth and trends in volume and value
  - Benefits sought and offered
  - Standard terms and conditions of sale
  - Principal distribution methods
  - Purchasing patterns (e.g. seasonality, prices paid)
  - Usual communication methods (e.g. salesforce, direct mail)
  - Trade associations and their influence

- *Competitive environment*: This examines the competitive forces at play within the market or industry. As well as reviewing the competitive standing of the traditional rivals, competitive forces include other factors:
  - Potential new entrants
  - Barriers to market entry
  - Potential substitute products or services
  - Relative power of buyers
  - Relative power of suppliers
  - Existing organisations, their reputation and likely activities.

A summary of information which might be contained in such an analysis is shown in Figure 12.4.

FIGURE 12.4

Checklist for marketing audits

1 INTERNAL AUDIT

❏ Historic marketing – objectives, methods and success
❏ Sales or revenue – types and sources
❏ Existing customers – groups, perceptions, behaviour
❏ Product/service range – perceived quality, developments
❏ Profit margins and pricing
❏ Research – available information and gaps
❏ Resources available – people, budgets
Strengths and weaknesses in relation to the external environment
Assumptions on which information is based

2 EXTERNAL AUDIT

Environmental factors:
❏ Social and cultural
❏ Technological
❏ Economic
❏ Political
Market information:
❏ Size and growth
❏ Trends
❏ Potential new customers
❏ Benefits sought and offered
❏ Purchasing patterns
❏ Communication methods
Competitive forces:
❏ Existing competitors
❏ Potential new entrants
❏ Barriers to market entry
❏ Substitute products or services
❏ Power of buyers
❏ Power of suppliers
Opportunities and threats revealed by the external audit
Assumptions on which information is based

12.7.3 SWOT analysis

A useful way of summarising the internal and external marketing audit is by a SWOT analysis, which focuses on:

Strengths

Weaknesses

> These tend to relate to the internal audit

Opportunities

Threats

> These tend to relate to the external audit

A SWOT analysis is normally a short summary of the key issues to emerge from the marketing audit. It represents a useful tool for relating the needs of the marketplace to what an organisation believes it is good at. A SWOT analysis helps to show where there is a good fit between an organisation's strengths and market opportunities and where there are threats which may expose areas of weakness.

FOR EXAMPLE

....

A SWOT analysis of Kitchen Care included the following observations:

■ **Strengths**: Established product range; large database of customers; trained salesforce

■ **Weaknesses**: Low value per sale (most of their products cost relatively little); many small accounts (customers bought relatively small amounts from them); low sales revenue per salesperson (because of the first two weaknesses)

■ **Opportunities**: New European hygiene and healthcare regulations; trend to subcontract to outside firms many health and safety aspects of commercial kitchens, such as cleaning and pest control

■ **Threats**: Competitors offering complete 'hygiene service' including cleaning; many small commercial caterers ceasing to trade because of need to conform to new regulations

Kitchen Care decided to combine their strengths with the opportunities in the market and offer a complete kitchen design and maintenance service. This would also have the benefit of increasing the value of each account (addressing a weakness) and counter competitive threats. However, the audit also revealed that the company had little formal information on customer attitudes to existing and potential new services, so a need for further research was highlighted.

12.7.4 Assumptions

The marketing audit makes certain assumptions over which the organisation has little or no control, particularly when it looks ahead to potential opportunities and threats. These may be about the national economy (e.g. the rate of inflation, rates of exchange), or about competitive activity (e.g. resources available to competitors, strategies adopted by them). Whatever they concern, it is important that these assumptions are made clear in the marketing plan. They can be used in several ways, including:

■ Evaluation of the plan once activities have begun. It is important to identify correct and incorrect assumptions in any assessment of the outcomes of the plan.

■ Assessment of the risks involved in adopting the plan. If some assumptions are crucial to the success of the plan, these need to be identified and questions asked such as:

— What is the likelihood of this not being so?

— What are the consequences of this not being so?

12.8 OBJECTIVES (WHERE ARE WE GOING?)

....

Once a thorough analysis of the existing and potential marketing environment has been made, the next step is to establish some objectives.

The focal point around which a marketing plan revolves is the setting of marketing objectives. These are quite simply the results wanted from the planned marketing activities. However, they should not be so general that they are confused with the overall objectives of the business of

FIGURE 12.5

Marketing objectives

which they are a part. Nor should they be too specific about individual aspects (of, for example, pricing or distribution targets), which are part of the methods used to achieve the marketing objectives. They represent *what* is to be achieved in measurable terms, but not *how*.

Guidelines for setting marketing objectives involve relating products or services to markets with measurable results.

12.8.1 Products and markets

Marketing objectives are primarily concerned with *products or services* and *markets*. Setting marketing objectives involves matching products and services to their markets. However, we have already stressed that planning is not just about what already exists but also what may potentially exist. Marketing objectives therefore look at *new* as well as *existing products* and *new* as well as *existing markets* (see Chapter 7, section 7.6.4).

FOR EXAMPLE

A restaurant chain had the stated marketing objective of 'matching their menu and services to customer requirements'. Unfortunately, this was not helpful to the managers as it did not go on to specify which customers were to be targeted nor what their requirements were. Different groups require different menus and service. Was this restaurant aiming to provide a relaxed atmosphere that would appeal to those who wished to linger over their meal? Or was it trying to serve those who needed more functional fast food? Marketing activities that arise from very general objectives can easily become misdirected and confused.

FOR EXAMPLE

Managers at a hospital developed a marketing plan which included the intention of 'informing patients better'. While this may seem a commendable objective, it is not specific enough on its own to represent any real progress. A marketing plan would need to detail which patients were to be informed about what, by whom and how.

12.8.2 Measurable results

Marketing objectives are *measurable* and *time specific*. In order to know when an objective has been achieved it has to be measurable. A key question to ask about objectives, therefore, is 'how will we know if we have been successful in reaching our objectives?'.

FOR EXAMPLE

The objectives specified in Kitchen Care's marketing plan were:
'To increase market share and profitability by launching a new commercial kitchen design and maintenance service.'
This could be criticised on several counts:

■ There are no objectives which can be specifically measured. What level of increase in market share or profits makes a satisfactory result?

■ There is no time period specified. How soon do we expect results – this year, next year?

■ The market is not specified. To which market are we launching this new service? In which market are we expecting to increase our share?

To overcome such criticisms, more measurable objectives were agreed as follows:

To launch a kitchen design and maintenance service, targeted at owner-managed restaurants, testing the concept in the first year in Lancashire, Yorkshire and Derbyshire with a sales budget of £500,000, and launching the service nationally with sales in excess of £2 million by year 3.

Quantifiable objectives that can be used to measure progress in specified time periods are essential for meaningful feedback and monitoring of the plan. In summary, marketing objectives are concerned with what products or services are to be sold in which markets, in what quantities or values, and when.

CHECKPOINT

You are the owner of a fast-food restaurant with a limited and rather dated menu of grilled burgers and fried chicken appealing mainly to customers in the 15–24 year-old range. In order to improve sales you wish to look at either new products or new markets or a combination of the two. Suggest some possible marketing objectives in these categories.

12.9 MARKETING METHODS (HOW WILL WE GET THERE?)

Marketing methods specify *how* marketing objectives are to be achieved in the context of the organisation's environment. Once marketing objectives have been set, the next stage of the planning process is to work out and specify the strategies and activities that help the organisation meet those objectives.

12.9.1 The marketing mix

The decisions about which product to sell at what price, in what place, supported by what promotions are the key elements in most marketing strategies. This area is likely to be a large part of the plan as it will include activities that have been discussed in Chapters 7–11.

FIGURE 12.6

Marketing methods

12.9.2 *Marketing programmes*

Detailed action plans or marketing programmes can be specified from the overall strategies for each of the variables in the marketing mix. At this stage the resource implications of the programmes can be calculated and budgets drawn up.

FOR EXAMPLE

Kitchen Care decided on the product specification of their proposed new service, drew up a pricing schedule, and decided on the place (in this case the geographic area) where it would be sold. A promotional programme was scheduled, involving a mailing to prospective customers, training in the new service for the sales team, and an action plan of selling activity. These activities were costed and the resource implications quantified into a budget for the product launch.

12.10 EVALUATION (ARE WE GETTING THERE?)

Evaluation of the progress of a marketing plan requires that control mechanisms and methods for feedback are established at the outset.

12.10.1 *Controls*

Once the marketing plan is being implemented, how can its progress be monitored and controlled? This calls for standards against which results can be measured, and contingency plans for modifying marketing programmes if results do not match expectations.

■ *Standards* of performance stem from the objectives set for the marketing plan. This is why it is important to make these objectives as specific as possible, stating both quantities and timescale.

FOR EXAMPLE

Kitchen Care's objective was to achieve sales of their new service of £500,000 in the first year. This provided an obvious standard against which the progress of the plan could be judged.

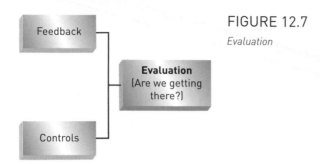

FIGURE 12.7

Evaluation

- *Measurement* of results may not be as simple as this, however. What if our marketing objective is to take a 10 per cent market share in the first year? We will need to set up a method to measure market share during the year. This involves making assumptions about the size of the total market and its likely growth rate during the period of the plan so that we can estimate our share of the whole.

- *Contingency plans* are needed to cope with significant variances from the plan. If results are a long way short of the standards anticipated, how long do we wait before making changes and what kind of changes are envisaged?

FOR EXAMPLE

Kitchen Care's plan involved testing the market by limiting its launch in the first year to Lancashire, Yorkshire and Derbyshire. If sales were insufficient to avoid losing money in the first year (which was calculated at 80 per cent of the first year's sales target, or £400,000), then the new service would not be offered to other geographic areas at that stage, but would be modified and re-tested for a further year.

12.10.2 Feedback

Although it is important to look at quantifiable results to control the implementation of a marketing plan, it is also necessary to look behind the figures to find out why results are what they are. How are customers reacting to our plan? Is their perception of what we are offering, and how we are offering it, as we expected? There are many sources for the feedback necessary to answer such questions including internal sources of information and external sources of feedback.

- *Internal sources* of information includes anyone within an organisation who has contact with the marketplace and receives feedback from customers and potential customers.

FOR EXAMPLE

Kitchen Care held weekly meetings with their sales people to specifically ask for feedback on the launch of the new service. Others in the company were also able to contribute to feedback from the telephonist who received inquiries to the maintenance engineers and cleaners who carried out the service.

■ *External sources* of feedback include formal and informal ways of obtaining feedback outside of an organisation. One important indicator will be any new activity of competitors in reaction to a marketing programme. Formal market research may also be necessary to test customer reaction to part of a marketing plan.

FOR EXAMPLE

Promotions can be followed up in this way with surveys carried out to probe peoples' reaction to advertising approaches. Kitchen Care tested their mail shot to potential customers by interviewing a sample of those who had received the mailing and asking for their reactions to it.

12.11 THE COMPLETED PLANNING PROCESS

The evaluation stage is not only the final stage of a marketing planning cycle. It is also the beginning of the next. Information provided by the evaluation of one plan provides further data for the analysis stage of another plan or an update of the original plan. Figure 12.8 shows the completed process.

FIGURE 12.8 *The completed marketing planning process*

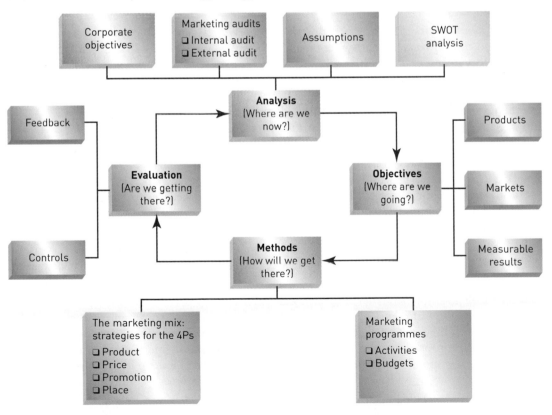

CHECKPOINT

You have decided to get a new job or apply for a course of study, and wish to market yourself to prospective employers or education establishments. You decide to do this in a structured way by drawing up a marketing plan for yourself. Use the headings of analysis, objectives, methods and evaluation to write a plan to market yourself. As a minimum, produce a personal SWOT analysis and specific objectives with outline methods to achieve them.

12.12 SUMMARY

Although marketing principles can be applied in many different circumstances, decisions concerning marketing strategies and the mix of activities to be used will vary according to the context.

■ *Small enterprises* often follow the marketing concept of orienting their organisation around customer needs but may not have the resources, skills or motivation to use extensive marketing campaigns. Marketing strategies tend to be informal, restricted in scope, simplistic and evolutionary. Although small firms can be very innovative, many rely on narrow product ranges. Pricing is a key competitive weapon where economies of scale are not available, although many small firms under-price their products and services. Distribution is often restricted to localised markets. Promotions rely on word-of-mouth and personal selling.

■ *Entrepreneurial marketing*, or marketing in entrepreneurial contexts, can be as successful as more traditional marketing, however. It tends to rely on interactive marketing methods with more direct customer contact. It makes use of proactive word-of-mouth strategies that attempt to stimulate recommendations, and the use of networks to provide market intelligence and business opportunities. Entrepreneurial marketing can be summarised as a sequence of: innovative products/services, identification of target markets, interactive marketing methods and informal networking for information ('4Is').

■ *The non-profit sector* includes public corporations, public services, institutions, charities and social enterprises. There are potential inhibitors on marketing activities because of restricted markets, confusion over who is the customer, multiple objectives, open access to all, public scrutiny and a public sector ethos. These often focus the marketing mix on product considerations and limit promotional activities.

■ *Services* are characterised by intangibility, inseparability, perishability, heterogeneity and ownership. This adds a possible further '3Ps' to the marketing mix because of the increased importance of the *physical evidence* of a service, and the *people* and *processes* that deliver it.

■ In *business-to-business (B2B) markets*, products tend to be more complex and demand is derived from customers further down the chain. Purchasing patterns normally involve less frequent purchases of relatively expensive products compared to consumer markets, and the buying process may involve a decision-making unit (DMU). These differences influence the marketing mix: products and prices tend to be more customised and less standardised; promotions rely more on personal methods such as selling and less on impersonal activities such as advertising and PR; distribution channels are often shorter than in consumer markets.

■ *International marketing* is marketing across national boundaries. Research into the cultural, political, economic and other local conditions is essential. Products can be sold into international markets in unmodified form to benefit from scale economies, modified to take account of local conditions, or developed as new to meet unfulfilled local needs. Approaches to international markets include exporting, licensing, joint ventures and direct ownership. The options for marketing strategies are globalisation, localisation or 'glocalisation'. The Internet is having a particular impact on international marketing as it provides opportunities for better worldwide communications, lower transaction and distribution costs, and rapid access to market intelligence in other countries.

■ The marketing concept is implemented through a process which is either followed informally or planned in a more structured way.

■ A structured marketing planning process asks the following questions representing stages in the process:

— *Where are we now?* The analysis stage, which looks at corporate goals, conducts internal and external marketing audits, makes assumptions and summarises with a SWOT analysis.

— *Where are we going?* Setting objectives in relation to products and markets by establishing measurable results.

— *How do we get there?* Deciding marketing methods, which include strategies for the marketing mix, activity programmes and budgets summarising the resource implications

— *Are we getting there?* Evaluation of the results through controls and feedback.

12.13 ACTIVITIES

BACK TO SCHOOL

Introduction 'Marketing may seem an alien concept in education, but we have no choice but to use it more, if we wish to keep our school open.' Sue Lin, the headteacher of Abbotsfield Primary School, looked at the solemn faces of the seven teachers facing her as she spoke. She knew that one of them would have to lose their job at the end of term, and others the following term, unless recruitment of pupils into their school improved. Numbers at the inner-city school for five- to eleven-year-olds had been falling for some time and the budget could no longer sustain the present staffing levels. 'We need to market our school, but in a different way to the methods we have already tried, and I need your ideas', she said, hoping that her staff could come up with something she had so far failed to find – a successful way of marketing their primary school.

The situation Her predecessor as headteacher had described the area around the school as 'a leafy ghetto' when Sue Lin first arrived two years ago. Across the road from Abbotsfield were tree-lined roads of relatively affluent housing, but behind the school was a 1960s tower block estate – 'the result of a social experiment which went wrong', the retiring headteacher had described it. The children at Abbotsfield school came mainly from that estate. A geodemographic analysis of the school's parents profiled them as predominantly 'multicultural, low income and single parents, with high levels of unemployment and crime'. The surrounding area was densely populated, served by several other primary schools. Two were within easy walking distance and parents from the Victorian and Edwardian houses across the road, mainly from B, C1 and C2 socio-economic groups, sent their children to these middle-class schools.

Changes in the policies of the local council meant that the numbers of children living in the

Marketing applies in many contexts, including schools

tower blocks were gradually falling, and Abbotsfield's traditional catchment area was drying up. The school had a physical capacity to take 245 children in its seven classrooms, with a further forty-five part-time places at the attached nursery school. Although the nursery school was full, 30 per cent of places in the main school were empty, with one classroom unused. The numbers of pupils recruited for each of the last four years had shown a decrease.

Abbotsfield school was part of Lampdale Education Authority, which was responsible for a total of nineteen primary schools in an inner-city area. These schools together had a total of 5,300 places, but with 4,350 pupils attending them, there was surplus capacity and the Authority was anxious to save money by closing one or two of their less popular schools.

Market forces Changes to the way schools are managed had introduced market forces into primary and secondary education from the late twentieth century. Legislation had forced schools to become more competitive towards each other. Each school's budget was now largely determined by how many pupils attended there – the more pupils a school attracted, the more money it was allocated. At the same time, parents now had an open choice of which school to send their children, providing it had spare places. In those schools that were full, places were allocated primarily on the basis of who lived nearest. Less popular schools could be caught in a downward spiral: as many costs were relatively fixed, less money meant that there was less to spend per pupil, which in turn affected education standards and facilities. This negatively influenced parents against sending their child to the school, so there was even less money to spend, and so on until the school became unviable and was forced to close.

The consumer Abbotsfield was caught in just this downward spiral. (Appendix 1 summarises its financial resources.) Sue Lin recognised the problem when she became headteacher, but she assumed that she could turn the school around by improving its reputation amongst local parents. She knew that parents selected primary schools mainly on the basis of two factors – location and reputation. Location was a key factor not only because of the convenience of closeness to home but also for social and security reasons, such as the attendance of friends and the safety of the journey to school. Although this was largely an uncontrollable factor as far as Abbotsfield was concerned, the school was in a densely populated area, with plenty of school-aged children in close proximity to the school.

'This means that if we can improve the reputation of our school, we will attract more parents,' Sue had explained to one of the early Governing Body meetings at which she outlined her first plans. 'A recent report on school choice emphasises that parents choose on the basis of reputation if location factors are equal.' She had gone on to explain how she intended to improve their reputation. 'What influences parents to believe a school has a "good" reputation is not totally clear. They rely heavily on word-of-mouth recommendations from other parents and friends in forming their impressions of a school. But we do know what they mean by a "bad" reputation. It means poor discipline, badly behaved pupils and a poor academic record. This is what we need to improve if we are to change our reputation from bad to good.'

Standards of education The new headteacher had zealously set about implementing her plans to improve the school when she arrived. First, she tackled the question of discipline by agreeing expected codes of behaviour with staff and enforcing them. A strict school uniform policy was introduced to symbolise the new order and, after a few teething problems and misunderstandings, the school became a well-ordered and disciplined place.

Academic standards were also improved. Abbotsfield was helped by one of the few advantages of unpopular schools: At a time when crowded primary school classrooms of thirty-five children or more had become a major political issue, it always had relatively small classes of fewer than thirty pupils. Several members of staff left when they realised that the new head expected them to work well beyond normal school hours to prepare classes for the next day. The new staff were hand-picked by Sue Lin to ensure they could deliver the highest possible standards. And they did. By the end of the second year, a school inspection concluded that:

> The quality of education is good. Although standards of achievement are below those expected nationally by children of the same age, they are above those expected in relation to the children's baseline attainments on joining the school. The emphasis given by the school to the teaching of the basic skills is successful and children's competencies in literacy and numeracy are sound. Standards in all subjects of the national curriculum are sound or above. The standard of work in French is particularly good throughout the school. Technology, especially in the provision of computer equipment, and the teaching of physical education require improvement. (Inspection Report.)

Initial marketing activities Sue Lin saw the endorsement by the inspectors of the good educational standards as the right moment to try to change people's perceptions of the school. Her marketing activities concentrated initially on PR, advertising and sponsorship. An extensive PR campaign targeted the local press with news about the school. Their achievements in the teaching of French were used as one particular theme. For example, a school journey to Lampdale's twinned town in France attracted considerable attention, with several photographs of the children and their French counterparts in the local press. A sponsorship deal with a nearby McDonald's restaurant also created considerable publicity. The school brochure was upgraded from the original duplicated sheets to a glossy production including colour photographs of school life. It was circulated directly to prospective new parents who enquired at the school, and also, via estate agents, to families moving into the area. Open days for new parents were extensively advertised in the papers to try and improve attendance at the event itself and also raise awareness of the school.

Sue Lin was bitterly disappointed when all her efforts went unrewarded. For all the activity, recruitment to the school that year did not improve. Moreover, the marketing activities themselves were becoming more difficult to sustain. The local press was at first keen to print reports of school events but after the first year this tailed off and the conversion of press releases to printed stories became low. Potential new parents showed a lack of enthusiasm for looking around the school or attending open days. The new brochures stayed largely on the shelf.

Market research Bemused by the lack of response to her efforts, the headteacher decided to find out what people felt about the school. As she could not get access to sufficient numbers of prospective new parents, she decided to conduct research amongst existing parents and teachers to find out their perceptions about Abbotsfield. Students from a nearby business school designed and administered a questionnaire, sent to all parents, teachers and

governors. Over 55 per cent of parents responded, and some of the results are shown in Appendix 2. Sue Lin was particularly disturbed when she read the following analysis provided by the students:

> Many parents believe they are not involved in the life of the school. When asked to rate their overall involvement, 65 per cent said they felt 'not at all' or 'a little' involved. Only a small minority (7 per cent) felt 'involved a lot'. Parents are at odds with the views of the school inspectors as they feel the teaching of many of the core subjects is not good. Mathematics is perceived to be a particular problem with over half of parents rating it as poor or very poor. Even the teaching of French, which has a high profile at the school, is seen to be poor or worse by almost a third of parents. Other areas where the school has made deliberate efforts to improve performance such as discipline and communications are not rated highly by many parents.

These findings are consistently at odds with the views of teachers and governors who rate standards and achievements more highly, although they broadly agree that the levels of parental involvement at the school are low. (Market Research Report.)

Could do better? The headteacher realised that if she were to be awarded marks for her marketing efforts to date, they would be very low indeed. But, with the limited resources at her disposal, how could she do better?

APPENDIX 1 TO CASE-STUDY

Abbotsfield school – Financial Information

£000S	YEAR 1	YEAR 2
Income (including carry forward)	605	586
Lettings and money raised	2	3
Total income	**607**	**589**
Expenditure:		
Teaching and other staff	484	472
Educational resources	34	29
Premises costs	48	47
Other expenditure (incl. marketing)	37	38
Surplus/carry forward	**4**	**3**

APPENDIX 2 TO CASE-STUDY

Abbotsfield School – Market Research

Sample questions and results from the school survey of parents. (Results are shown as the percentage response for each case.)

1   Please rate your involvement in aspects of the school listed below on a scale of 1 to 4, where 1 is 'not at all involved', 2 is 'involved a little', 3 is 'involved occasionally' and 4 is 'involved a lot'.

	1%	2%	3%	4%
Helping in the classroom	39	34	20	7
Fund-raising events	15	36	29	20
School functions (e.g. Xmas play)	13	38	27	22
Parents' evenings	17	34	29	20
PTA social events	35	38	18	9
Marketing the school to other parents	37	36	21	6
Overall involvement in the life of the school	27	38	28	7

2   Please rate the teaching of the subjects listed below on a scale of 1 to 4, where 1 is 'very poor', 2 is 'poor', 3 is 'good', 4 is 'excellent'.

	1%	2%	3%	4%
Reading	9	34	38	19
Mathematics	8	43	29	20
Science	9	32	39	20
Art	0	4	63	33
French	6	26	52	14

3   Please rate the school's performance in the areas listed below on a scale of 1 to 4, where 1 is 'very poor', 2 is 'poor', 3 is 'good' and 4 is 'excellent'.

	1%	2%	3%	4%
Discipline in school	11	23	28	38
Keeping parents informed	19	23	42	16
Answering your queries in person	15	27	39	19
Answering your queries on the telephone	21	25	39	15

QUESTIONS

Write an outline marketing plan for the school that takes account of its particular context (e.g. a non-profit-making, small enterprise that provides a service). In particular:

1 Analyse the data given and conduct a marketing audit. What are the strengths, weaknesses, opportunities and threats of the school?

2 Set measurable objectives for the marketing plan.

3 Suggest the mix of marketing activities you would implement.

4 Give details of how would you control and evaluate the plan.

DEVELOPING A MARKETING PLAN

PLANNING FOR MARKETING

In the first activity, you chose the subject for a marketing plan, and you have collected information chapter by chapter. The final activity is to present this as a marketing plan.

- Decide the headings for your plan: are the headings discussed in this chapter appropriate or will you require some different ones?
- What analysis will you present to underpin your plan?
- What measurable objectives will you set?
- What will be the elements in the marketing mix?
- How will you control and evaluate the plan?

12.14 FURTHER READING AND REFERENCES

Marketing contexts

Kotler, P. and Levy, S. (1969), 'Broadening the Concept of Marketing', *Journal of Marketing*, Vol. 33, January.

Services marketing

Bateson, J.E.G. (1999), *Managing Services Marketing:Text and Readings*, 4th edition (South Western).
Gronroos, C. (1994), 'From Marketing Mix to Relationship Marketing: Towards a Paradigm Shift in Marketing', *Management Decision*, Vol. 32, No. 2, pages 4–20.
Gummesson, E. (1987), 'The New Marketing – Developing Long Term Interactive Relationships', *Long Range Planning*, Vol. 20, No. 4, pages 10–20.

Industrial/business-to-business marketing

Brennan R., Canning, L. and McDowell, R. (2007), *Business-to-Business Marketing* (Sage).
Fill, C. and Fill, E.K. (2005), *Business to Business Marketing: Relationships, Systems and Communications* (Prentice-Hall).

Small enterprise and entrepreneurial marketing

Carter, S. and Jones-Evans, D. (2006), *Enterprise and Small Business: Principles, Practice and Policy*, 2nd edition (Prentice Hall).
Stokes, D.R. and Wilson, N.J. (2006), *Small Business Management*, 5th edition (Thomson Learning).

International marketing

Levitt, T. (1983), 'The Globalisation of Markets', *Harvard Business Review*, May–June, pages 92–102.
Muhlbacher, H., Dahringer, L. and Leihs, H. (2006), *International Marketing: A Global Perspective*, 3rd edition (Thomson Learning).

Public sector marketing

Adler, S.M. (2006), *Results-Oriented Cause Marketing* (SWEP).
Chapman, D. and Cowdell, T. (1998), *New Public Sector Marketing* (FT Prentice Hall).

Writing a marketing plan

McDonald, M. (2005), *How Come Your Marketing Plans Aren't Working?* (Kogan Page).
McDonald, M. (2002), *Marketing Plans: How to Prepare Them, How to Use Them*, 5th edition (Elsevier).

Internet marketing planning

Chaffey, D. (2006), *Internet Marketing: Strategy, Implemenation and Practice* (Pearson Education).

Index